THE BACKGROUND OF
CURRENT WORLD PROBLEMS

The Background of
Current World Problems

by

J. LEO CEFKIN

Professor of Political Science
Colorado State University

DAVID McKAY COMPANY, Inc.

New York

THE BACKGROUND OF CURRENT WORLD PROBLEMS

Library of Congress Catalog Card Number: 67-15042

MANUFACTURED IN THE UNITED STATES OF AMERICA

VAN REES PRESS • NEW YORK

To the memory of
My Mother and Father

PREFACE

THE INTERNATIONAL EDUCATION ACT of 1966 authorizes the Federal Government "to assist in the development of resources for international study . . ." By this Act Congress has recognized the need to improve and expand the study of international affairs in American colleges and universities so that the United States may better ". . . meet the requirements of world leadership."

This volume, while substantially completed prior to the adoption of the Act, was similarly motivated by a need for an introductory text explaining the essentials of international politics for the general student body. Its aim is to develop international understanding by learning basic concepts which serve to make current events more intelligible. Its ambition is to provide the student having but a single course in international relations with concepts and frames of reference which give meaning to the stream of contemporary history.

The first part of the text, consisting of four chapters, constitutes an introduction to the field of international politics. In enunciating ordering concepts the author has often sacrificed nuance to gain explicit expression. If the presentation exaggerates the rational and even simplistic character of international politics, this is done to counteract the general feeling that international affairs are a stream of unrelated events that just happen.

Chapters 5-13 focus attention on three long-term underlying tensions of international life found at the root of the international crises of our time: the cold war, the rise of nationalism in the underdeveloped lands and the quest for economic development.

College students today have not lived through the postwar years when the conflict between East and West began. In a time of attenuated cold war it is useful to analyze the cause for its rise, the reasons for cautiousness and hostility in East-West relations, and the difficult issues which remain and prevent final termination of the cold war. The study of nationalism in Asia, Africa, and Latin America serves to introduce the student to areas of the world still neglected by programs of study in institutions of higher learning. Economic development is dealt with most briefly in a single chapter. A concluding chapter deals with continuing problems of American foreign policy.

Various people have been most generous in assisting me with advice, with secretarial help and with library research. Most diligent and most invaluable has been the help given me by my wife who edited and monitored my prose until it became precise and clear. Whatever value this volume may have is in large part a result of her effort.

I am also indebted to the Faculty Improvement Committee of Colorado State University whose generous assistance with research funds literally enabled me to write this book. Last but certainly not least, I thank my students at Colorado State University who, over the years, have enrolled in my course in Current World Problems and who have cheerfully permitted me to try out my ideas and concepts on them and whose reactions have constituted so great an influence upon the final product. Let it be pointed out, lest there be any doubt on this score, that the shortcomings, awkwardnesses, and errors of data and judgment are wholly my own and the fault of nobody else.

April 1967   LEO J. CEFKIN

Table of Contents

ix

PART IV. CONCLUSION

PART I

The Behavior of States

CHAPTER 1

We Live in a World of States

THIS book is about international politics, one aspect of the broad study of international relations, which also includes cultural, economic, and social relations. The study of international politics is predominantly the study of political relations among states.

What happens in the political relations among states is not often a result of unexpected or accidental forces. Things happen because men who lead states want them to happen. In a sense one can say that the outcome of political relations among states is the result of forces, sometimes cooperative, sometimes antagonistic, between states acting in the world arena. However, the study of international politics is somewhat less than susceptible to scientific treatment. By this we mean that rules or laws governing the relations among states and the outcomes of these relations that would be valid, that is, those rules or laws that could be applied in a variety of situations, have not been discovered and are not likely to be discovered. There is much that we know, however, about the behavior of states that can be utilized as an analytical tool in our study of international politics. A number of results is always possible in the interaction of states. We may be unable to determine which particular result will occur but we can point out the variety of resolutions possible in interstate relations and the factors that tend toward each of these results.

Although we view the subject as something less than a science, this book will nevertheless approach the study of international politics as one that is susceptible to objective analysis and as one in which, under some circumstances, the behavior of states may be predictable. Even if the relations among states develop in a wide variety of ways, an understanding of why states act the way they do is entirely possible. As long as states behave rationally, the study of international politics can be made sensible, the actions of states more predictable, and the outcome of the interaction among states at least somewhat predictable.

The quest for a science of international politics is as important as it is elusive. The record of history is replete with misassessed opportunities, false estimates, and self-destructive policies. The best diplomats have been informed, resourceful, and imaginative, but they hardly qualify as "scientists" in the profession of international relations. Their established place in history results from the wise decisions that they made—their choice of the best decision among a range of possible decisions. In this way they most often exhibited the touch of the artist rather than the accuracy of the scientist. International politics is, above all else, "the art of the possible."

THE STATE: THE BASIC UNIT OF INTERNATIONAL POLITICS

The state is the most prominent actor on the international scene; however, in a sense states are inanimate and can have no relations like those between human beings. The state is an abstraction. It is a legal abstraction, and this means that the term "state" as it is used in international law describes an entity that has a recognized jurisdiction over a body of land and people living on it.

A *state* has four characteristics: first, it must have a body of land; second, this land must be populated; third, the land and the people must be ruled by a government; and, fourth, that government must be sovereign.

While the meanings of land, people, and government are clear, the term sovereignty requires some elaboration. We say a state is *sovereign* when there is no temporal authority over it. There can be no authority higher than sovereign authority. In this sense, sovereignty is virtually synonymous with the term independence. The idea of independence appears simple and self-evident. Either a state has it and by virtue of its independence is recognized as a state, or independence is absent and the territory is a colony or part of a larger state or something else, not a state. An independent state does as it wills. But the practices of international politics often defy precise definition. Like George Orwell's "equal" pigs, some states are, in fact, more independent than others. A good example of the problem raised by the concept of sovereignty involves the nature of the states of Eastern Europe commonly known as satellites. As a matter of international law and international comity, these states are recognized as sovereign. They have also been generally recognized as having, at best, a limited independence. All too often, at least until recently, they did as they were bidden by the rulers of the Soviet Union. In this sense, satellites were not truly independent. Yet, the world recognized them as sovereign. A legal fiction has been employed in this respect. Independence, and therefore sovereignty, is sufficiently demonstrated when the state acts for its people. Thus, for instance, in 1947 when the government of Czechoslovakia wanted to attend and participate in a conference for the distribution of Marshall Plan aid, the Soviet Union effectively forbade Czech participation in this meeting. Yet, because it was the government of Czechoslovakia that in the last analysis declined the invitation, even though it did so under pressure, the act of declining the invitation was recognized as the act of a sovereign state. Furthermore, the state is believed to be sovereign when a significant number of other states recognize it as sovereign and demonstrate this recognition by an exchange of diplomats.

The state thus defined is the actor on the international scene. But, as an inanimate abstraction, its relations must be carried out by its leaders. Thus, the United States cannot really have relations with the Soviet Union but an American president may talk with the Soviet leader. Their conversation is aimed at advancing the welfare of their countries. The country—the state—is conceived as an entity having interests that its leaders pursue.

Even individual citizens are not without importance in the political relations between states. Increasing tourism provides a definite, if immeasurable, influence on the feeling people have for one another, upon whether people of one state like or dislike people of another state. Individuals can influence the foreign policies of their lands. Organized groups of persons—pressure groups—also exert influence on foreign policies. Even more, it is common today for groups of individuals to be organized into bodies that are international in character. Such international organizations are called private international organizations and they—like all other pressure groups—have an influence on the foreign policies of states and the nature of relations among them. The United Nations accords some private organizations the status of consultative bodies and permits them to voice their views within its councils. However, the state is the chief participant in the political relations between states.

NATIONS

Many writers use another term, nation, as a synonym for state, yet the terms nation and state are not synonymous. In part, the confusion between the terms "nation" and "state" results from the lack of agreement on a definition for "nation." [1] Authorities see a variety of characteristics in the nation. Some allude to common territory, culture, language, social institutions, economic system, government, historical tradition, racial stock, beliefs and myths, and patriotic sentiments as the leaven that combines persons into a nationality.[2] Others single out only a few of these factors. One authority holds that "among the cultural characteristics of nationality, *language* is, and always has been, pre-eminent." [3]

Despite the disagreement on definition, there is a general agreement in the actual identification of existing nations. The Americans,

[1] The following books provide a variety of definitions of "nation," as well as offering a discussion of the subject:

Boyd C. Shafer, *Nationalism: Myth and Reality* (New York: Harcourt, Brace, 1955).

Carlton J. H. Hayes, *Essays on Nationalism* (New York: Macmillan, 1926).

Carlton J. H. Hayes, *Nationalism: A Religion* (New York: Macmillan, 1960), pp. vi–vii.

Carlton Clymer Rodee, Totten James Anderson, and Carl Quimby Christol, *Introduction to Political Science* (New York: McGraw Hill, 1957), pp. 25–26.

Ernest B. Schulz, *Essentials of Government* (Englewood Cliffs, N.J.: Prentice-Hall, 1958), Ch. 4.

Elie Kedourie, *Nationalism* (New York: Frederick A. Praeger, 1962).

Ernest Renan, *What Is a Nation?* Quoted in G. Schwartzenberger, *Power Politics* (London: Stevens and Sons, 1951), p. 55.

Joseph Stalin, *Marxism and the National Question* (New York: International Publishers, 1942), pp. 9–17.

Hans Kohn, *Nationalism, Its Meaning and History* (Princeton: Van Nostrand, 1955).

[2] Shafer, *op. cit.*
[3] Hayes, *Essays on Nationalism, op. cit.*

Canadians, Swiss, Germans, Chinese, Swedes, Poles, etc., are generally agreed to constitute a national group. The fact that the Germans have no common territory, the Canadians and Swiss no common language, and the Americans no common racial stock or religion is not considered sufficient to deny that each group is a nation. Not all characteristics listed hold for all nations.[4]

Carlton J. H. Hayes, in his book *Nationalism: A Religion,* in effect defines nation in terms of language and appears to deny the existence of a multilingual nation.[5] Renan, in limiting his definition of the nation to "a soul, a spiritual principle," [6] has suggested a criterion that is widely accepted. In addition, his identification of the "possession in common of a rich heritage of memories..." and the "actual agreement, desire to live together, and the will to continue to make the most of the joint inheritance..." [7] is universally applicable. All existing nations would conform to this definition.

In the last analysis a nation exists because a core of people consider themselves to be a unique collection of persons of one nationality and bear a powerful emotional sentiment of loyalty toward this nationality; this sentiment is called *nationalism.* When a people go through a period of common historical evolution, this makes them psychologically and culturally similar to one another and different from others whose historical experiences were quite different. The consciousness of their similarity to one another and their differentiation from all other such groups becomes the basis of nationality. Their belief that this is an important association leads to feelings of nationalism.

The unifying influence of language cannot be denied. Yet, it is not sufficient to create nations and does not necessarily reflect the existence of nationalities. Thus all English-speaking peoples do not feel a sense of national attachment with one another. Nor do the Spanish-speaking or German-speaking peoples desire an inclusive national identification. On the other hand, language differences notwithstanding, the typical German-speaking Frenchman from Lorraine is an ultranationalistic Frenchman. States such as Canada and Switzerland are multilingual but they are also national states. It

[4] Shafer, *op. cit.,* "To almost any generalization about nationalism... exceptions can be raised..."
[5] Hayes, *Nationalism: A Religion, op. cit.*
[6] Renan, *op. cit.*
[7] *Ibid.*

makes no difference whether a person is from French-speaking Quebec or English-speaking Winnipeg; in both instances the national identification is with Canada. The citizen of Switzerland, when asked his nationality, would answer Swiss, and he might give this answer in German, French, Romanche or Italian.

We are often not conscious of our psychological identity with others of the same nationality. It is the foreigner among us who more easily discerns the psychological characteristics common to us so that many foreigners visiting the United States, even briefly, feel they know what the American people are like. There is even a good likelihood that their characterization of the American people will not be far different from that of Count de Tocqueville in his description of the American character in his book *Democracy in America* [8] written in 1835. Similarly, when we go abroad we feel sure that we can make appropriate generalizations about what the French or Italians or Russian or Chinese people are like.

Invariably the unique characteristics of a nationality are expressed in its art. A skilled student of painting can identify, even without knowing the painter, his nationality. When the Bohemian composer Dvorak wanted to write a symphony about the new world that he had just visited, he used American folk songs for some of his thematic materials. But this fact notwithstanding, the skilled listener can identify the *New World Symphony* as music that must have been written by a Slav. Dvorak could not escape his national culture. A people develop national foods, national dress, national myths, and national styles in humor. The British may place special value on the age of things, the Germans on good order, and the Americans on the size and speed of things. Such values are manifestations of the uniqueness of each nation.

The existence of nations with the all-important manifestation of the spirit of nationalism is of great concern to the student of international politics. For most people today, the identification of the individual with his nation is one of the very strongest and most important identifications he makes. The nation is the object of primary loyalty and most men today are nationalists.

Our definitions of nation and state are significantly different. We have said that the individual gives his first loyalty to his nation.

[8] See Vol. II, Vintage edition, Third Book, Chapters I–V.

However, the practical distinction between nation and state is important in relatively few instances because today most nations are states and most states are nations. By this we mean that the boundaries of most states are coterminus with a national unit. National groups have established national states or, as they are often called, *nation-states*. To ask a citizen of the United States whether he owes his first loyalty to the state, called the United States, or the American nation is to ask a meaningless question because they are physically one and the same. It is only when boundaries of the nation and state are not one and the same that such a question has meaning and special problems occur.

Most states in the world today are nation-states, but there are some states that have within them many nations and a few that divide a nation. A state that contains many different nations is called a *multinational state*. The best example of a multinational state today is the Union of Soviet Socialist Republics. About two hundred different nationalities reside in this state. If one were to ask a person on the streets of Erivan what his nationality is, he would in all likelihood answer that he is Armenian; in Kiev the typical Soviet citizen is of the Ukrainian nationality; in Vilna, of the Lithuanian nationality. Yet all are citizens of the Soviet Union.

If we were to ask questions about nationality of a citizen of Leipzig, he would reply that he is "German." The same is true of a citizen of Munich and yet each of these Germans is a citizen of a different state. When the state divides a national group, as would be true in East and West Germany, North and South Korea, or North and South Vietnam, we call such a state a *subnational state*.

If our allegation is correct that the most significant loyalty of the individual is to his nation, then the multinational state quite typically faces the problems of finding ways of reconciling the national loyalty of the individual with loyalty to the state. It is not surprising that during the Second World War the troops in the Red Army that defected most frequently to the Germans were those of the nationalities other than Russian, such as soldiers from the Ukraine, Mongolia, or Soviet Central Asia. The government of the Soviet Union is conscious of the multinational character of its state and has tried to secure the loyalty of its non-Russian citizens by the use of force, making disloyalty a most serious crime, and by permitting the various national groups to enjoy their culture and thus feel that loyalty to their nation is not contradictory to the loyalty that the multinational state exacts.

A comparable situation exists in the subnational state. Because the individual's identification with his nation is so strong, the people of a subnational state typically seek as their major objective the reuniting within a single state of the entire nationality. Consequently, in Germany, Korea, and Vietnam, the most enduring problem faced by the people of these states is that of national unification.

The importance of national identification is also demonstrated by the existence of national minority groups within other states. These groups seek to retain their national culture, preserve their national symbols, and hold on to other identifying characteristics of their nationality. On occasion national groups also seek the establishment of their own state; this is called *national self-determination*. At the end of the First World War when democratic ideology championed the right of all national groups to establish states coterminus with their nation, in other words, national states, many such groups tried to establish national units that would obviously be weak in political and military strength, and less than viable as an economic unit. Therefore, democratic theory notwithstanding, a sizable number of such national minorities were not allowed to establish states. Instead, under the auspices of the Principal Allied and Associated Powers their national identity was protected by minority treaties.[9] These instruments gave to such minorities political, religious, and cultural rights designed to preserve their sense of nationality. The specter of a large number of small uneconomic national units raised the fear of "Balkanization." The term "Balkanization" derives from the existence of many small national groups in the mountainous Balkan peninsula. If the country of Yugoslavia had been subdivided into multiple national states according to the aspirations of the various national groups at the end of the First World War, instead of the state of Yugoslavia, we might have the states of Serbia, Croatia, Slovenia, Dalmatia, Bosnia, Montenegro, Herzegovina, Macedonia, etc. Few of them would be able to prosper as a political or economic unit.

A similar problem is faced in Africa today where a large number

[9] Clyde Eagleton, *International Government*, 3rd ed. (New York: Ronald Press, 1957), pp. 276–277.

of states have recently come into existence. Some of them are very small and poor and hence the fear arises among some African leaders that their continent is becoming "Balkanized." The resolution of this particular problem, the conflict between a "national" identity and the viability of the state as an economic and power unit, is far from finally resolved. For the time being those who do not object to the "Balkanization" of Africa because this provides African states with a large number of votes in what is for them the highly significant General Assembly of the United Nations seem to have won out, and more than thirty-five African nation-states have been established, some exceedingly small in area and population.

Still another manifestation of the strong identification of the individual with his nation is to be found in the phenomenon of *irredenta*. An area of irredenta is one in which a substantial portion of the people are nationals of an adjacent state and wish their area annexed to that state. In the area of Trentino-Alto-Adige there live side by side some people who claim Italian nationality, and others who claim Austrian nationality. The area had been a part of Austria until the end of the First World War. This area was then known as the area of Italian irredenta, and one of the goals of Italy in the First World War was the acquisition of this area from Austria. Today this area might well be described as an area of Austrian irredenta. It is the people claiming Austrian nationality who now wish to see Italy punished for her participation in the Second World War on the side of the Axis by the detachment of this area from Italy and its addition to Austria. Surely no solution is found by moving frontiers around to assuage the national sentiments of all peoples. To take territory from Italy to satisfy Austria, or vice versa, simply shifts the incidence of disaffection.

All of this emphasizes that in the eyes of most people the identification with the nation is a vital identification. While such identification creates no confusion between nation and state where, as is true in most cases, they are one and the same, it is in the cases of the multinational state, the subnational state, or the state with national minorities and areas of irredenta that tensions deriving from the absence of an embracing nationalism arise.

The rise of the national state cannot be precisely fixed in time. It evolved together with the industrial revolution and the growing popular spirit of democracy. In the nineteenth century it was a middle-class movement. The establishment of a national state was the desired goal as against the feudal division that preceded it. The division of a country into feudal duchies, manors, and small states poorly suited the needs of developing industries and businesses and acted as a fetter on the cultural and democratic political development of people. In a number of instances revolutions were necessary to form national states and end feudal separation.

During the nineteenth century Italy and Germany became nation-states. In each instance the intellectuals were an important element in the nationalist movement. They were not the only groups that sought the establishment of the nation, and indeed in both cases it was a king and his prime minister who successfully accomplished the integration of the Italian and German states into large national units. But it was the widespread feeling for nationhood, the sentiment of nationalism, that led to the creation of the nation-state in the nineteenth century.

In our own time the process has been turned on its head and now states create nations.

In the Middle East today a number of entities exist that consider themselves nation-states. The states existed as administrative entities for the convenience of the Turkish, British, or French rulers of the territory. Thus, for instance, the country of Lebanon did not exist until the French helped set it up. Their purpose was to piece out of what was generally considered Syria a small section along the Mediterranean coast where a sizable number of Christian Arabs lived. In creating a separate entity, Lebanon, a land with a near Christian majority, was thus established. Over a period of years within this land, at least among the Christian intellectuals, a feeling of nationalism developed toward Lebanon—Lebanese nationalism. Thus this state, which was brought into being by outside forces, eventually developed a nationalist sentiment among its residents.

Sub-Saharan Africa today provides another good example of states creating nations rather than, as was true in the nineteenth century, nations creating states with nationalism predating the establishment of the nation-state. When the European colonial powers divided up Africa in the last quarter of the nineteenth century they did not find anything resembling a national state. Africa was largely tribal and the spirit of nationalism was unknown. European states pieced out parts of Africa for their administrative convenience. In so doing they paid little consideration to existing tribal lands. Often they drew international boundaries right through tribal lands. Thus the French, Germans, and British cut up the lands of the Ewe people in the process of establishing their colonies of Dahomey, Togoland, and the Gold Coast. This type of tribal separation tended to destroy tribal unity and create conditions conducive to other kinds of unity.

Over a period of years attributes of nationality naturally developed among some of the people within these colonies. An increasing number of Africans were provided with opportunities to go to other places and to mingle with other tribes. Travel made possible wider contact among tribes and urban development facilitated the mixing of persons of different tribes in the growing African cities. Some Africans were given an opportunity to study abroad and to live in and to see the highly developed societies of Western Europe and North America. A process of detribalization was thus taking place and, at least for a small but significant educated elite, the life of the tribe lost much of its attraction. A need existed to substitute an entity for the tribe and it was quite natural, especially to the detribalized intellectual who had lived in Europe and North America, to want to build a nation-state within his own land. He could not go back to the tribal compound. He could no longer accept the backwardness and superstition of the tribe and he conveniently embraced nationalism. The nation-state was a successful and useful form of human organization. Today increasing numbers of Africans think of themselves as Nigerians, Ghanaians, Guineans, or Kenyans, rather than as Ibo, Ewe, Malinke, or Kikuyu. They have adopted their state as a basis for a new nationhood. In our time, therefore, it has been the state that has brought into being the nation.

But no matter how national states were created or when they were established, each is based upon a large measure of popular support that is best expressed as the feeling of nationalism. The people consider the interests of their nation as their own. No argument is more convincing to people than that the policy proposed would serve the national interest and would help achieve the goals of the national state. All people want to see their nation, and through their nation themselves, prosper and secure a "place in the sun."

THE GOALS OF STATES

We may speak of states pursuing objectives or goals that serve their advantage and that help articulate their destiny. Goals may be universal—that is, pursued by all states—or particular—that is, pursued by some states. Goals may be constant—that is, pursued all the time—or they may be variable—that is, pursued some of the time.

There are three universal goals that are constant. The most important of these is security. By *security*, in this respect, we mean that a state seeks to hold its territory without diminution, that it seeks to maintain its own political system and have no foreign rule imposed on it, and that it seeks to preserve its culture free from foreign impositions. A second universal and constant goal is *prosperity*. A third such goal is *prestige*. All states want wealth and want to be recognized by others as entities of significance if not of great importance. There are many variable goals. Some states pursue the international *status quo* while others want to revise that *status quo* in their favor. *Status quo* and revisionist goals are variable. At any time in history only a minority of states are likely to pursue revisionist goals. Most are satisfied with the *status quo*. Some states seek the spread of an ideology or a religious faith. Others may seek an ingathering of their nationals within the state. All such goals are particular to just a few states (we shall discuss the *status quo* and the revisionist goals when we deal with variety among states on pp. 21–24).

The Future of States

Some believe nation-states are an outdated anachronism in the age of space exploration and nuclear power. National states came into existence at a particular period in history; the world was not always a world of national states. The nation-state system came after the feudal period and it developed parallel with the evolution of modern communications and transportation, hand in hand with the industrial revolution. One might well suspect that the national state will not be the final form of organization used by man for the purpose of governing himself. Although most of the people of the world today are nationalist, there is evidence that nationalism, and the national state with it, will also evolve out of existence.

The best evidence that some people are ready to accept a *super-national state* is found in the development of the European Community and its trade organization, the Common Market. The Common Market is largely concerned with economic cooperation among its six member states.[10] Its primary purpose is the creation of an economic unit with the capacity for creating a prosperous economy for its members. The Common Market countries have also moved in the direction of political integration, the logical conclusion of which would be the creation of a single state for all of the Common Market countries.

The main appeal of such European unity lies in its economic advantages. Over and above these advantages are important political considerations that make such a larger state attractive to peoples in the countries involved.

One might say that the people of Western Europe have had their "binge" with nationalism; they no longer become excited when the flag is unfurled. They are increasingly conscious of the fact that a world divided among sovereign nation-states pursuing antagonistic goals allows conditions under which devastating war is always possible. Furthermore, several of the states that make up the European Common Market, and others as well, have already played a role as a dominant power in the world. These countries no longer bestride the world as the super-powers of our time, and people realize that the basis for a great power status for France, Western Germany, Italy, or even for Great Britain is lacking and hardly likely to arise again. It is only with the creation of this larger Western European state that Frenchmen and Germans and the other countries that make up the European Community [11] can realistically hope to be citizens of a super-power in our time. The concomitants of power and prosperity are available within the Community. A

[10] France, Italy, Western Germany, Belgium, Netherlands, and Luxembourg.

[11] The European Community is a widely used term for three interrelated agencies of the "Six": the European Coal and Steel Community, set up in 1952 for the purpose of eliminating national restrictions on all operations in the coal and steel industries; the Common Market, whose official name is the European Economic Community (E.E.C.), which came into being January 1, 1958, with the purpose of unifying the economies and abolishing all trade barriers over a twelve- to fifteen-year period; and Euratom, set up at the same time as the Common Market for a cooperatively developed atomic energy industry limited to peaceful uses.

Common Market state would have a population about equal to the United States. The addition of Great Britain to the Community would give it a gross national product approaching that of the United States. The Community has significant natural resources and formidable human resources. It is also the world's most important export market. The union of the Common Market states would surely make it an entity of great power. To the degree that the economic programs of the Common Market succeed, the economy grows, and the *per-capita* income increases, people will be ready to forget their nationalist sentiments for the practical consideration and benefits of a greater Common Market state. The first years of operation by the Community produced economic growth and rising standards of living beyond expectation.

Similar integrative movements are taking place in other parts of the world. The Arab states are being pressed to give up their more local nationalism in favor of the larger Arab unity (see Chapter 9). The case for the integration of Britain's West Indian islands into a West Indian federation is being vigorously argued in that part of the world, and at the moment of the creation of a number of new African states the movement for pan-Africanism has widespread support both among intellectuals and among some of the most powerful heads of state of that continent. Indeed, the debate among the African states today is not one of whether the more local nationalism ought to be encouraged or discouraged, but rather the means and the timing for pan-African federation. Local nationalism exists and the best way to achieve unity and create powerful and more viable states is through the integration of economic enterprise and through economic cooperation. There is some expectation that eventually states of East Africa or West Africa, perhaps even of all tropical Africa, will become one.

There is, therefore, enough evidence to predict that the national state will give way to a unit of government that will be able to better provide the security, peace, prosperity, and prestige that people want from the nation-state, and that these goals often cannot be achieved by national states. One might hazard the guess that the danger of thermonuclear war would create a powerful impetus for bringing nationalism and the nation-state to an end. Eventually, some wider unity, perhaps even the creation of a world government, appears highly possible. This look into the future notwithstanding, it must be emphasized that in our own time man is still largely nationalist, and, for reasons that may have very little to do with logic, prefers to remain a citizen of a national state.

VARIETY AMONG STATES

We begin our study of international politics with the premise that states, most of them nation-states, are pursuing their interests. Goals are adopted by states in terms of interest but also in terms of capability, that is, what can be achieved. It is part of the reality of contemporary life that states are also interdependent and must choose to do only that which is possible in relation to the conflicting, competing, or cooperating interest of other states.

There are many states in the world today, adding up to a hundred and twenty or more. They vary in many ways—in size, population, economic development, objectives, etc. Some, like the Vatican City with an area of one hundred and nine acres, are very small; others, like the Soviet Union, covering one-sixth of the earth, are large; some states, like China with a population of about 700,-000,000, are highly populous; others, like Gambia with 284,000, have a very small population; some states, like the United States having a *per-capita* gross national product of $2,974,[12] are prosperous; others, like India with a *per-capita* gross national product of $81,[13] are very poor; some are highly developed, others are underdeveloped to the point of being primitive. Our study of world affairs must take note of those elements of variety among states that affect international politics. The varying power of states is a fact of great significance in the study of international politics, and this we shall examine in the next chapter. The fact that some states are highly developed, others underdeveloped, and still others in the process of developing has a singular effect upon the goals that states pursue. The size, the resource position, the population, and the military strength of states all vary, and these differences have a bearing on the nature of their political relations.

The economic and political structures of countries differ. No two states have exactly the same economic or political system. We cate-

[12] Source: Statistics and Reports Division, U.S. Agency for International Development, May, 1964. These figures are for 1962.
[13] *Ibid.*

gorize political systems as democratic or dictatorial and economic systems as capitalist or socialist. These terms can provide a useful shorthand for identifying the essential character of a political and an economic system. But these are also emotionally charged terms, which hide more than they reveal. Some precision through definition is helpful for effective communication.

Economic Systems

Economic systems under which states operate are more often than not mixed in character. The description of an economic system as capitalist or socialist is likely to mean that a state has either more capitalist or more socialist elements in it. There are no purely capitalist or purely socialist states in existence. A *capitalist* state is a state in which commerce, agriculture, and industry are by and large privately owned and conducted for the purposes of making a profit for the owner. A *socialist* state is a state in which commerce, agriculture, and industry are publicly owned either by the state or people organized in cooperatives. The purpose of socialist production is the welfare of the people rather than personal profit. The capitalist economy promotes the popular weal through profit. Profit, in theory, is gained by those who serve the public need best. A socialist economy need not pursue profit as a goal. Most states have both public and private sectors in their economy and their economies are mixed. Yet this fact does not deny that there are a number of states whose economic systems are preponderantly capitalist and others which are overwhelmingly socialist.

Economic systems should be judged by the abundance they help produce and the material well-being of the people which they serve. Even though capitalism and socialism have become articles of faith —theories that men believe in—in the last analysis the choice between them will ultimately be decided on the basis of which economy brings the greatest prosperity to the greatest number of people. The nature of the economic system used by states is rarely the subject of dispute between them. Differing economies may produce conditions that lead to clashes of interest between states but not markedly more so than the conflicts that develop between states with similar economic systems. The "cold-war" conflict is not a clash of economic systems. It is mainly a clash of political interests in which different economies contribute to this conflict only in minor ways. Coexistence between states with differing economic systems presents no insuperable obstacles.

POLITICAL SYSTEMS

Socialism and capitalism denote economic systems. They are not at all synonymous with the terms democracy and dictatorship, which denote political systems. Democracies may have either a socialist or a capitalist economy, and dictatorships can also be socialist or capitalist. Sweden, Denmark, and Israel are socialist democracies. The Soviet Union, Bulgaria, and Yugoslavia are socialist dictatorships. The United States and Japan are capitalist democracies, whereas Portugal and Spain are capitalist dictatorships.

There are two major political systems in use today, democracy and dictatorship. *Democracy* is a system of government in which the majority rules but the minority has defined rights. By majority rule we mean that the majority decides in essence two things—who shall rule and toward what ends they should rule. Thus it is presumed that when Americans vote for a president or the British or French vote for their parliament, they do so on the basis of the quality of the candidate but also with reference to the program that he proposes to implement. Minority rights are in essence the right of the minority to become a majority by convincing an adequate number of people that the minority position is the correct one.[14] Usually minority rights must include the right to speak, the right to publish, freedom of religion—indeed, the freedoms that are typical in any of the bills of rights in modern constitutional systems.

A *dictatorship* is a system of government in which one or a few make decisions without consultation or reference to the will of the people. There is neither majority rule nor minority rights. Modern dictatorships justify their own existence by claiming a monopoly of wisdom and virtue; what the dictator says is right and good because the people are not able to decide for themselves what is their true interest.

There are two kinds of dictatorships. One is *authoritarian* and is interested primarily in the political arena. The authoritarian dictator wants a monopoly of political decision-making and wants to be secure in his rule against oppositions. He is not concerned with

[14] Minority rights in quite another sense refer to civil rights, that is, equal status for persons without regard to race, nationality, or religion.

nonpolitical matters—art, science, or even literature when the subject of the literary output has no political overtones. The authoritarian dictatorship is negative in that it forbids certain types of expression. Salazar's Portugal and Franco's Spain are examples of authoritarian dictatorships.

A second kind of dictatorship is *totalitarian* and seeks to control the totality of human life and human relationships. The Italian Fascists enunciated the essence of the totalitarian ideal in their slogan, "all in the state, nothing outside the state, nothing against the state." The totalitarian dictatorship is therefore concerned not only with a monopolistic control over political movements, political ideas, and political speech, but also, at least in theory, with all areas of human association. The idea of the totalitarian dictatorship is one all-encompassing and undeviating loyalty directed toward the dictatorial authority. In Italy the Fascist state was to be the all-comprehending object of totalitarian loyalty. In Nazi Germany it was Adolf Hitler himself who was to be the recipient of total loyalty. In Russia it has been the top leadership of the Communist Party that has been the fount of all wisdom and the object of total loyalty.

The totalitarian dictatorship is positive as well as negative. Not only is a wide range of expression proscribed but a large area of expression is also prescribed. People must vote, speakers must say certain things, and writers must attest to the grandeur of the dictator; silence is not enough.

The totalitarian state is concerned with all areas of human activity. Thus, the novel *Dr. Zhivago* received the attention of the highest levels of Soviet leadership and led to the official censure of its author, Nobel Prize winner Pasternak. The Soviet composers Shostakovitch, Prokofiev, and Khachaturian have been frequently castigated by the Communist Party for composing music that is ideologically harmful—for writing *"bourgeois"* music. Artists, authors, architects, writers, scientists, etc., have been called upon to apologize and criticize their work for harmful tendencies in their artistic and scientific production. The Communist Party in the Soviet Union thus becomes the enunciator of all wisdom. Art, philosophy, and science must conform to the design demanded of them by the totalitarian dictator.

Totalitarian dictatorship can be best perceived in contrast to the pluralism that is inevitable in any modern democratic system. By *pluralism* we mean that the citizen of the democratic society is permitted, even encouraged, to enjoy multiple loyalties. One has a loyalty to his family, to his church, to his school, to his lodge, as well as to the state. Indeed, the rationale of the pluralist outlook is that to the degree that the citizen may enjoy a variety of other loyalties he will give his loyalty willingly to the state as well.

The totalitarian dictator demands a singleminded and undeviating loyalty. Only the lack of feasibility has reduced the all-comprehending conformity ideally sought. Church and family have held out against such an all-embracing loyalty. The Chinese Communist communes were directed against the family unit as a unit of competing association. On occasion members of a family are expected to denounce one another in the service of the dictatorship. The Slansky purge trials in Czechoslovakia in 1952, based on trumped-up charges, featured a wife's denunciation of her husband. Madame Lisa Londonova supported the conviction of her husband as an "imperialist spy" with assurances that her two older children "promised to remain good Communists all their lives." She wanted no mercy shown her husband, only a "just verdict against" him.[15] The totalitarian state compels loyalty while the pluralist state wins it.

STATUS QUO AND REVISIONIST STATES

States differ significantly in the goals they seek to achieve. For the purposes of our study of international politics perhaps the most important contrast in this respect is that between states pursuing *status-quo* goals and those pursuing revisionist ones.

By a *status-quo* state we mean a state that is satisfied with the world as it is and seeks no change or, alternatively, a state that refrains from the use of force in the bringing about of the changes it desires. In other words, a state that considers the maintenance of peace more important than change is by our definition a *status-quo* state. States that consider things as they are so objectionable that change must be brought about, and consider the means for achieving this change entirely secondary, are called *revisionist* because they must alter the *status quo*. Force is used whenever it can

15 *New York Times,* November 24, 1952.

be used successfully to achieve the goal. The distinction therefore rests on the means that states use to secure change. Only a revisionist state uses force to achieve the change it wishes to bring about.

The revisionist state is also referred to as an expansionist or an aggressive power. The term revisionist is used because it is largely devoid of emotional content. Our purpose is not to divide states into good and bad states but to provide an objective identification of goals determining a state's foreign policy. Not all revisionist states pursue malevolent objectives. A state that wants to free people from oppression may be serving a most laudable aim, and the use of force in this regard may be moral. Nevertheless, such a state would be pursuing a revisionist policy. Would not a state be justified in using force to revise power relations in its favor against a neighbor that itself harbored aggressive aims toward it? If democracies were to wage aggressive war against backward and reactionary monarchies or dictatorships to bring about a better order, would not such a revisionist policy be morally justifiable?

In our own time and in the recent past there have been a few states that have been aggressors and have pursued revisionist goals. Most states have been *status-quo* powers. Because *status-quo* powers outnumber revisionist powers their combination for mutual security appears as the logical response to expansionist policies. A revisionist state seeks to strengthen itself *vis-à-vis* other states so that it can achieve its revisionist goals. When one-sided concessions are made to a revisionist power it uses these concessions as an advantage to make new and bolder demands. The revisionist state often makes demands not to satisfy its grievances but to gain in power. Power leads to new demands, the purpose of which is additional power. One-sided concessions made to a revisionist state are called *appeasement*. Appeasement has meaning only in relation to a revisionist state. Unilateral concessions resolve nothing and serve to endanger both peace and security. A *status-quo* state may present grievances and make demands upon its neighbors but, once the grievance has been satisfied, not only is the problem settled but the disturbing element in the relations between these states is also eliminated. Here concession may very well lead to lasting settlements.

The Munich Agreement of 1938 is the oft-cited tragic illustration of the principle that appeasement does not work. Not only was the morality of that pact questionable in that the British and

French agreed with Hitler and Mussolini to the cession of territory to Germany that belonged to Czechoslovakia, but it was also short-sighted and perhaps even stupid in that it did not preserve peace. Chamberlain acclaimed its purpose as "peace in our time" but instead it guaranteed that war would come under worse terms than ever because in the process Hitler would have become stronger.

Seemingly, all Hitler wanted was the Sudetenland area of Czechoslovakia. It was an area peopled by Germans, and the Nazi Party under the leadership of Konrad Henlein was very strong there. Hitler solemnly promised that the demand for the Sudetenland was the "last demand" he would make on Europe and if given the Sudetenland he would refrain from waging war. The concession made at Munich bore predictable results. Six months later Czechoslovakia was occupied by Germany and its independent existence was ended. Poland became the next country on the agenda of expansion. A halt to German aggression could no longer be postponed and there remained no alternative to war. In that war the Czechoslovaks' military strength, the defensive positions of the Sudetenland, and the Skoda Works armaments were no longer available to Great Britain and France.

Identification of a state as a revisionist or *status-quo* power is one of the most important as well as one of the truly difficult problems faced by the diplomat. This determination more than anything else should define the way in which the states respond to demands made on them by other states. Mutual concessions between revisionist and *status-quo* powers are permissible as long as the revisionist state does not gain *vis-à-vis* the *status-quo* state from such concessions. When neither side is weakened in such an exchange and tensions are moderated as a result, mutual concessions are actually advantageous to the *status-quo* state. *Status-quo* states must prevent the growth of dominating power on the part of the revisionist states. The exchange of land for a promise, for example, the Sudetenland for the promise to keep the peace in Europe, is a dangerous exchange. The security of *status-quo* states is predicated on their capability of containing the revisionist power. Therefore, *status-quo* states must retain their capacity to deter aggression. If the dynamism exhibited by the Soviet Union since 1944 has led United States policy makers to the decision that the Soviet Union is a revisionist power, then those policy makers must maintain, at the very least, a balance of armed strength. An overbalance of armed strength in favor of the Soviet Union or a breakthrough in the technology of thermonuclear war on her part endangers peace and security. It was no more than prudent that, when the testing of nuclear devices in 1962 by the Soviet Union registered important advances in "the state of the art" for her, the United States undertook its testing program to prevent falling behind.

SUMMARY

We have seen that ours is a world of sovereign states. Most of them are national states whereas some are multinational or subnational. Each of these states pursues interests as is its sovereign right. International politics is largely a study of the way in which conflicting and competing as well as cooperating interests of the several states of the world are resolved as they seek the satisfaction of the goals they pursue. The outcome of competing relations among states responds to a number of factors that influence the determination of these conflicts. In the last analysis one element more than any other explains best the outcome of relations among competing states, namely, their relative power.

CHAPTER 2

The Power of States:
Why Some States Are Strong

SOME states enjoy a great deal of worldwide influence, but most states have relatively little influence. Why are some states more influential than others? Two possible answers would appear plausible. First, the intrinsic wisdom of what is said or proposed by a government has its own influence. In other words, a moral and rational position has persuasive influence on the behavior of all states, and their action derives largely from a desire to act in accordance with commonly agreed upon standards of what is right and good. All too often such an outlook tends to view relations between states as something of a high school debate in which the debater with the best argument wins. It is all a matter of right and wrong rather than a conflict of interests that is at stake. It would be a mistake to view the relations between the United States and the Soviet Union, or between the East and the West, in such terms.

A second explanation for the outcome of conflicting positions holds that who does the talking is more significant than what is said, that the state with the greatest power is most influential in achieving its purposes. Khrushchev may have behaved badly at a meeting of the General Assembly, and boorishly taken his shoe off and banged it on the table, yet people listened to him, and what he said was persuasive, not necessarily because of the moral stature of his ideas or the logic of his position, but because he spoke for the Soviet Union, a very powerful country.

Power is the ability of states to influence the behavior of other states. The ability to influence stems largely from the strength of the state. It has been pointed out that the "reality of power" is distinctly different from the "belief in power." Many times the power of states has been erroneously evaluated but, as long as a false assessment of power is accepted and used as a basis for action, the actual strength of the state is irrelevant. Power has often been poorly estimated. One can point to a number of examples where a state's power was underestimated and as a consequence decisions to use force were adopted with disastrous results. Israel in 1948 and again in 1956, and the Soviet Union and the United States in 1941, proved to be far more powerful than was generally believed. Before both the First and Second World Wars the power of Italy was overestimated and consequently in the early months of the First World War and again in the period between the wars a great deal of political maneuvering took place and concessions in her favor were offered by states seeking to win Italian support. Italy proved to be far less powerful than was generally thought. States sometimes pretend to be stronger than they really are. The use of bluff in international relations is a well-established technique which on occasion pays off. These considerations notwithstanding, techniques for scientifically judging the power of the state are now well advanced. Rational and accurate estimates can be made. We will, therefore, not distinguish between the actuality of the power and the belief in power. We shall assume that statesmen estimate the power of their own state as well as other states with adequate accuracy and that their actions are largely guided by correct evaluations.

A number of factors constitute the bases upon which the power of a state rests. Among them are factors that provide some quantifiable data that enable one to measure and relate the components of power. Such factors are called *tangible* factors of power. These include geography, natural resources, population, education, science and technology, industrialization, and military power-in-being. Each of these factors provides figures that can be calculated—square miles, temperature, humidity, production statistics, children in school, men under arms—and upon which assessments may be made. Other factors that bear on the power of states, such as leadership, morale, national character, and forms of government, cannot be quantitatively evaluated. These we call *intangible* factors.

TANGIBLE FACTORS OF POWER

GEOGRAPHY

Few today would agree with the French diplomat Jules Cambon who wrote that "the geographical position of a nation, indeed, is the principal factor conditioning its foreign policy—the principal reason why it must have a foreign policy at all." [1] While currently authorities disagree as to just how important a role geography plays in the power of a state, geographic determinists, that is, those who hold that geography is not only the most important power factor, but also perhaps the only factor in that determination, are today very few in number. There was a time when geography did in fact play a much more important role than it does today, and in those days geographers and military men put great stress on the relation between geography and power.

Geography, as we define the term here, consists of five subfactors: *size, climate, shape, location,* and *topography.* An earlier view gave all of these subfactors a role of importance in the estimate of power. However, today geography is a factor of little importance. Of the subfactors listed above, only size is significant. It is significant because a country that is large may contain a large population, and a sizable population, as we shall see later, is a weighty factor in the evaluation of power. There is also the greater likelihood that a vast country will have a variety of resources, and resources have an important relationship to the power position of a state. Finally, in warfare the ability of the state to defend itself in depth adds to its military strength. Certainly the Soviet Union would have been defeated had it been a country about the size of European Russia, most of which was conquered by the Nazis in the Second World War. It is only because it had the vast hinterland to fall back on, and could organize its defenses in depth and relocate industry in the East that the Soviet Union was able to survive the early years of German attack. States large in area may disperse their strategically important military and industrial assets, making these more difficult to destroy.

It was generally agreed, not too long ago, that climate was a decisive factor for the power potential of a state. According to some

[1] *Foreign Affairs,* Vol. VIII, No. 2, 1930, p. 173.

authorities it is not possible "to say that man has emancipated himself from his 'climate' influence by means of sheer technical advances..." or, again, "one may conclude that technological improvements are not likely to have any perceptible effect in softening or lessening the fundamental force of the great climatic agencies." [2]

Seemingly, states located in tropical and frigid climates could never become powerful. In tropical areas two conditions placed unconquerable limitations on power potential. First, the tropical climate was enervating and people were sapped of energy and vitality. Second, the tropical climate produced a variety of vectors that made it unhealthy and almost impossible for man, or at least for a white man, to live a life free from debilitating diseases.

The development of modern technology and especially the development of medical technology has altered both of the above limitations on the power potential of tropical countries. The eradication of tropical diseases moves forward apace, and these diseases will surely become less troublesome as further developments in medical science take place and newer techniques of sanitation are learned by the masses. Air-conditioned offices, factories, and businesses are within the grasp of tropical states. Methods of producing a more abundant agriculture await only the application of human intelligence and resources to overcome the deleterious effects of tropical climates. Nigeria and India with their large populations, abundant resources, and talented leadership may yet become great world powers, the limitations of climate notwithstanding.

It has also been said that a central location in the Northern Hemisphere is essential to a status of great power. Countries such as Australia, New Zealand, Argentina, and Indonesia could never become great powers because they were located in a peripheral part of the world. At a time when communication is instantaneous, when man can travel anywhere within hours, and at a time when international television has become a reality, there is no location that is too peripheral to disqualify a state from becoming a great power. If Australia or Argentina do not achieve such a position it will be due to other circumstances. The factor of location itself does not impose limitations that cannot be overcome for a state seeking to become a great power.

[2] Walter R. Sharp and Grayson Kirk, *Contemporary International Politics* (New York: Farrar and Rinehart, 1941), p. 48.

A state's topography was considered to be a vital element of its defense capability and the facility with which it could maintain contact with other states. Tall mountains, broad oceans, and deserts were considered barriers that made easy contact between states difficult. Isolated states did not play an influential role in world politics but, on the other hand, barriers denying easy access made such a state more defensible. One need only reflect on the development of modern transportation and communications to conclude that topographic barriers are effectively overcome. Airplanes, missiles, telegraph, and radio have reduced the significance of topography.

Geographic Determinism. In the earlier decades of this century some geographers took the position that geography was the most important determinant of potential international strength. Some even seemed to be saying that it was the only important determinant of power. Two outlooks largely based on geographic factors illustrate well both the insights and the limitations that geographic determinism provides in an analysis of the power of states.

The earlier of these two theories was formulated by the American Admiral Alfred Thayer Mahan (1840–1914). From Mahan's standpoint the power of states rested mainly on their use of the seas. He called attention to a most important truth, that seas and oceans were not simply barriers dividing states but highways bringing them together. The utilization of such highways by states enjoying ready access to oceans and seas molded world history. He reasoned further that insular states such as Great Britain in his time, and the United States in the future, could develop their merchant fleets and naval strength and rapidly transport men and materials to the most remote parts of the world. Naval strength was the key to world power. Navies protected sea lanes and blockaded enemies. Countries that took advantage of their insular position by building a large merchant marine, protected by strong navies, could become great and unchallengeable world powers. The key to world power lay, therefore, in control of oceans and seas.

Almost as a rejoinder to Mahan's "sea-power" theory, the British geographer Sir Halford Mackinder (1861–1947) called attention to the role of land masses in the determination of power. Beginning with an exposition of the view that much, if not most, of history must be explained in terms of underlying geographic factors—a theory called geopolitics—Mackinder pointed to the existence of a "pivot area" that was "inaccessible to ships." [3] This "pivot area" Mackinder later renamed the "Heartland." The key to world power rested in control of the Heartland, an interior area of the Eurasian continents, bounded by the Volga basin in the west, the Siberian maritime provinces in the east, the frozen seas of the north, and the high Asian mountains of the south. After the First World War Mackinder expressed the opinion that the Heartland could fall to the control of a single power that would use its Heartland base to establish "a single world empire." [4] Development of such an empire was to come through the conquest of the continents of Europe, Asia, and Africa, which would inevitably follow the conquest of the Heartland. The control of these continents, which Mackinder labels the "World Island," would enable the conqueror to then lay hold of the remainder of the world. In *Democratic Ideals and Reality,* Mackinder interpreted history as a continuing struggle between land power and sea power. Because the Heartland was impervious to attack from the sea, a state that controlled it could not be defeated by a naval power. Eastern Europe, with its tremendous human and natural resources, provided a key to the control of the Heartland. Mackinder summed up his geopolitical strategic view, which he hoped would guide the statesmen of victorious powers devising the peace settlements after World War I, by writing, "A victorious Roman general, when he entered the city, amid the head-turning splendor of a 'Triumph,' had behind him on the chariot a slave who whispered in his ear that he was mortal. When our statesmen are in conversation with the defeated enemy, some airy cherub should whisper to them from time to time this saying:

> Who rules East Europe commands the Heartland:
> Who rules the Heartland commands the World Island:
> Who rules the World Island commands the World.[5]

Accepted literally, the Heartland concept must lead one to believe that Russia, in control of the Heartland, must conquer the World

[3] Paper read before the Royal Geographical Society on January 25, 1904, entitled "The Geographical Pivot of History." Reprinted in Andreas Dorpalen, *The World of General Haushofer* (New York: Farrar and Rinehart, 1942).

[4] Sir Halford J. Mackinder, *Democratic Ideals and Reality* (New York: Holt, 1942), p. 2.

[5] *Ibid.,* p. 50.

Island. The logic of Mackinder's theory leads mechanistically to a presumption that Moscow's world domination is already determined.

Both the sea-power theory of Mahan and the geopolitical concept of Mackinder have become untenable with the development of air power. It is obvious today that no area is invulnerable to attack, if not by sea, then by air. Indeed, the Polaris-firing atomic submarine, which can surface in a frozen sea, probably invalidates the concept that any area exists that is invulnerable to attack from the sea. The concept of the superior position of the Heartland also rested upon the assumption that the development of railways and roads provided an advantage to military forces operating on interior lines. This view has not gone unchallenged. The American geographer Nicholas J. Spykman, of Yale, argued that a major naval state, such as the United States, with its efficient techniques of transportation and communication, could control the seas as well as the marginal areas between the Heartland and the seas, which he called the "rimlands." [6] The ability to better transport men and materials looms as more important to the state's power than any geographically determined military posture of operating on interior or exterior lines.

One must reject geographic determinism. The power of a country and what it may do on the international scene is not determined by its geography. Geography may place limits on the actions of states but these limits are, at best, flexible. Geography may provide advantages to states, but none that cannot be overcome by such non-geographic factors as economic development, military strength, and leadership. Any estimate of the power of a state that is based upon geography has poor foundation indeed.

NATURAL RESOURCES

To say that natural resources are an important power factor is to say the obvious. Certainly any state that contends for status of great power must have an adequate supply of a broad spectrum of natural resources. However, to say that resources are important is not the same as saying that these resources must be available within the confines of the state. The availability of resources is quite a differ-

[6] *The Geography of Peace* (New York: Harcourt, Brace, 1944), p. 43. "... who controls the Rimland rules Eurasia: who rules Eurasia controls the destinies of the world."

ent thing from their presence within the state. One need only reflect on Great Britain's position as a great power. The British never were richly endowed with natural resources. They had adequate supplies of coal and food at the time that industrialization began there. These two resources supported Britain's industrial revolution, which was carried out before that of any other country. With manufactures available for trade the British had no difficulty in securing the resources they needed. Even if resources could not be obtained through trade, the strong military machine created with industrial support allowed Britain to acquire by conquest territory that contained useful resources. In the nineteenth century its power was based upon its industrial preeminence. It is this that enabled Britain to secure in full measure raw materials.

It is a fact that states which deal in manufactures are in a superior trading position to those which offer crops or mined resources. Manufactures are more stable in price. Manufactures are more highly prized in the world economy and are in greater demand. Countries which have industrial equipment and manufactured commodities to sell have no difficulty in securing raw materials. Indeed it may be argued that a state having natural resources but no other elements of power is actually weakened by the presence of these resources because it then becomes an attractive target for conquest.

Autarchy. The casual observer may feel that the absence of resources lays a state open to mortal danger in that its imported resources are subject to interdiction during times of war. This circumstance led some states to attempt a policy of autarchy. *Autarchy* is a policy of living within one's means of resources. The United States could theoretically pursue a policy of autarchy, if Americans were willing to give up televisions, radios, telephones, automobiles, and indeed all modern conveniences that depend on imported resources, and return to a standard of living of one hundred and fifty years ago. During the 1930's, Germany and Italy, states poorly endowed with resources, pursued such a policy. By exploiting domestic resources, even those of poor quality and high cost, by appealing to their citizens in the name of patriotism to work harder and consume less, by encouraging the use of substitute materials— aluminum for copper, margarine for butter, shale oil, cheaper flours in bread—by rationing consumption, autarchic self-sufficiency was approximated. Dictatorships can control consumption and thereby effectively reduce standards of living. As a long-range policy autarchy needs a dictatorship because people prefer a higher standard of living to doing without imports; and consequently they must be forced to accept an autarchic policy.[7]

Security in Resource Position. Since the Second World War all states have rejected autarchy. Virtually every country is dependent to some degree on imported resources. But this does not mean that resources imported from abroad are subject to the vagaries of interdiction. In assessing the resource position of a state, its boundaries give a false impression. The state itself is not a resource unit. The fact that the United States has no nickel is of little significance when its neighbor to the north has abundant supplies which are easily purchased. To all intents and purposes the United States and Canada, and perhaps Mexico as well, become a single resource area. There is no significant difficulty on the part of any of the Common Market countries in securing resources available in any of the other Common Market countries. One must look beyond the confines of the state in estimating the resource position of a country. States have learned to stockpile scarce resources to make them available even during times of war.

Modern technology has developed a variety of synthetic substitutes for certain natural resources. Synthetic substitutes are growing in number and they significantly reduce the importance of shortages in a large number of natural resources.

The Changing Importance of Particular Resources. One final aspect in relating resources to power deserves attention. The importance of particular resources changes over the years. Before the Second World War coal and iron were considered the most important of all resources. In our own time oil is replacing coal as a source of energy and one can already look forward to the time when oil for the purpose of producing energy will be replaced by atomic power. One book, published in 1939 and listing the resources of greatest importance, did not even include uranium.[8] The advent of the atomic age has changed the importance of that resource. In recent years new minerals, such as beryllium (which is used in the

[7] Sharp and Kirk, *op. cit.,* pp. 380–386.
[8] Frank H. Simonds and Brooks Emery, *The Great Powers in World Politics* (New York: American Book, 1939), pp. 80–81.

hardening of the nose cones of missiles), have become important strategic resources. Resources once important may lose their importance. New resources that seemed of no significance or were even unknown can become critically important. Any evaluation of the relation between resources and power must take into consideration the changing character of technology, which may upgrade or denigrate the importance of any resource.

POPULATION

"It is no mere coincidence that every great power in the world today has a population of at least forty-five million, while the two most powerful nations are both far larger." [9] Although no authorities believe that any one factor determines power, they agree that a large population is an important element of power. A powerful state must be able to function in many areas. It must be able to produce; it must have significant military forces; it must have a variety of talents and skills within its population, and all of this can be found only within a populous state. Population is therefore closely related to the power of the state. Americans sensed this shortly after the Civil War when some of the tasks that had to be done for the development of industry and transportation could not be done unless our population increased. Those were the years of easy immigration into the United States, when Chinese were encouraged to come and help build railroads. Underpopulation must be overcome before a state can fulfill its power potential. Underpopulation must be understood not only in terms of numbers of people but also in terms of necessary skills. The state that lacks engineers or scientists or teachers, all essential to the modern industrial economy, is underpopulated in essential skills.

The term *demography* is often used inaccurately as a synonym for population. It is a more encompassing term. It means not merely the numbers of people but includes such vital statistics as age groups, birth rates, and the number of men and women. In relating demography to power, age groups become a matter of great significance. The very young and the very old contribute little to the power of the state and indeed become a power liability because the

[9] Katherine Organski and A. F. K. Organski, *Population and World Power* (New York: Alfred A. Knopf, 1961), p. 3.

state must use its wealth to maintain them. The productive years are most important in a power equation. Furthermore, as we shall see, power is related to military force, and here an even more restricted age group is significant for mainly males between the ages of sixteen and thirty-five are used in military service.

Young people attending school, being cared for by their parents through the first eighteen or twenty-two years of their lives, add nothing immediately to the power of the state. We know that as a result of their education they will eventually contribute more to the wealth and power of the state than was invested in them. In this sense schooling and upbringing are investments in the future power of the state. This is true only if the young people live a reasonably long and useful life. This insight, when applied to states where life expectancy is low, leads to the conclusion that even a meager investment in the young is hardly more than repaid when by the age of thirty or thirty-five average life ends.

To say that a large population is an essential concomitant of power is not to say that the larger the population the greater the power. There is no direct and simple relationship between numbers of people and the power of the state.

Population and Power. Certainly a ranking of states in order of population would be a poor guide to their relative strength.[10] A state may be overpopulated, and overpopulation detracts from its power. Overpopulation is an elusive term. It cannot be equated with population density. The most densely populated states are not necessarily overpopulated. An industrial economy can support a much larger population than an agricultural economy. New York City and London, Belgium, and England are all densely populated but none is overpopulated. A large population is essential for commerce and industry. Overpopulation should be defined in terms of a relationship between population growth and economic growth rate. When we say that a state such as India is overpopulated what we mean is that each new baby born adds to the strain of maintaining what is already an inadequate living standard. The significant question that must be asked with respect to population growth is how it affects the rate of economic growth. Overpopulation exists whenever

[10] The first ten in order would be China, India, USSR, United States, Indonesia, Pakistan, Japan, Brazil, West Germany, Great Britain.

each unit of population increase reduces the rate of growth of the economy. Alternatively, population balance exists whenever an increasing population adds to the growth rate of the economy.

The problems of economic development will be discussed elsewhere (see Chapter 13). Here we simply note that after the Second World War peoples living in underdeveloped countries appeared to have lost the illusion that poverty and injustice was to be their lot forever. There began what has elsewhere been referred to as "the revolution in the rising tide of expectations." People wanted a better life. They wanted a share in the wealth that their resources and a modern technology make possible. Overpopulation deterred investment in industrialization, which provided the key to the satisfaction of these expectations and was thus a major cause for continued poverty and economic stagnation. Overpopulated states have become increasingly conscious of the need to reduce population growth as an essential aspect of their desire to avoid upheaval.

When population growth took place in the industrializing countries during the nineteenth and earlier twentieth centuries that growth was relatively moderate and could hardly be called a population explosion. The growth in population derived from the more rapid decline of the death rate than the birth rate. Prior to the nineteenth century the high birth rate was balanced by an equally high death rate. With nineteenth-century industrialization and the progress of modern medicine and of modern methods of sanitation, the death rate declined and the birth rate continued relatively high. But as people congregated in urban communities the birth rate declined until population growth leveled off on the basis of a low death rate and low birth rate. Slow growth in population or no growth in population and, in some countries, even some reduction of population was the result. Because the growth in population during the earlier period of industrializing was more gradual and because the masses had little expectation of a high level of prosperity, population increase did not have an unstabilizing influence on those states that were experiencing rapid growth.

The situation today is markedly different. Medical technology has developed rapidly. Death rates are spectacularly reduced while birth rates remain at their previous high level. This takes place whether a country is industrializing or not because the benefits of modern medicine are made available before the processes of industrialization and urbanization have occurred, and, as a result, we have population explosions with serious consequences for the underdeveloped country.

States understand this and seek population balance. Since the end of the Second World War a number of ambitious programs have been undertaken to achieve population balance where overpopulation exists. The earlier solution of siphoning off excess population through immigration is now of little avail. Attractive areas open to immigrants are virtually nonexistent.

By and large three approaches have been devised to relieve overpopulation—agricultural improvement, birth control, and industrialization. States such as Japan have achieved much in this respect. By reorganizing their land-tenure system, by reclaiming land that had not been used, by improving their farming techniques, and by utilizing new fertilizers and better seeds, the Japanese have been able to make their agriculture far more abundant than it had ever been before. Some states have tried to add new high-protein food products to their diets. Thailand, for instance, expanded her fisheries industry with the help of the Food and Agricultural Organization of the United Nations.

A number of states are promoting birth control as a means of curbing overpopulation—the more extreme attempts at birth control have permitted abortion of unwanted pregnancies. A more typical attempt to reduce the number of births has been through promoting the use of contraceptives. For an underdeveloped land difficulties stand in the way of birth control through contraception. It is difficult to develop contraceptives simple enough for an illiterate population to readily understand and apply, and it is essential that a very cheap contraceptive be employed, like a pill that can be distributed free. India has invested a part of its budget to support pharmaceutical research seeking the invention of a safe pill inexpensive to produce and capable of effectively inducing temporary sterility. The Japanese, who have an aggressive program of birth control, have made abortion easy and provide widespread birth-control information. In recent years the Chinese have sought to deal with their problem of population growth by discouraging early marriage.

Industrialization, which all overpopulated states want to achieve, is a third method of dealing with the problem. We have already pointed out that a commercial and industrial economy can support a much larger population. Industrialization means urbanization. Urbanization naturally reduces birth rate. Consequently, industrialization has the dual advantage of providing an economy that can support a larger population and at the same time create social conditions that lead to the reduction in birth rate. It is little wonder, therefore, that states seek industrialization to overcome overpopulation.

Japan has demonstrated by the use of all three of these approaches that the problem can be brought under control. They have made their agriculture more abundant than it has ever been. There has been a great development of industrialization, and their birth control policy has produced tangible results. Growth in Japanese population has significantly declined as birth rates have plunged from 33.7 per thousand in 1948 to 18 per thousand in 1958, significantly below the birth rate of the United States in that year.[11] Japan is no longer an overpopulated country. Population balance has been achieved.

On occasion misguided people urge their government to refrain from making available the advances in medicine that would result in declining death rates for countries suffering from overpopulation. Not only is this stand lacking in humanity, and thus must be rejected on those grounds, but it is also an impractical proposal. Parents are the same the world over; they want their babies to live, and their children to enjoy good health. If the United States or the countries of Western Europe were to refrain from assisting in the reduction of death rates of the newly born, other states would be found who would fill the void to the lasting shame of the former.

In the power equation numbers of population in and of itself is not very significant and needs considerable refinement if it is to be usefully applied. In 1956 little Israel, with a population of about two million, inflicted defeat upon Egypt, with a population of at least twelve times that number. This fact illustrates in a most pointed manner the lack of correspondence between numbers of population and the power of a state. Varying factors benefited the Israelis in their attack on Egypt in the Sinai Peninsula. Among them was the

[11] Organski and Organski, *op. cit.*, p. 212.

good health of the Israeli relative to that of the Egyptian soldier. Egyptians living along the Nile River, bathing in the waters of the Nile, are likely to have bilharzia, a debilitating disease that reduces the energy and efficiency of those afflicted. In addition, the Egyptian population is disadvantaged in having fewer physicians in proportion to its population than the Israelis. Egypt had a population-physician ratio of 2600 to one, while Israel enjoyed a ratio of 410 to one.[12] Egyptian illiteracy is high while illiteracy in Israel's male population is virtually nonexistent. The Jewish culture dictates that all Jewish boys must be literate so that they may read the Bible. In addition, because the Israeli population has within it a large infusion of European Jews who are familiar with modern contrivances, they have been able to master more easily and more effectively the use of modern machinery and automatic weapons.

In the evaluation of power one man does not equal one man. The man who is literate, skilled, healthy, and imbued with good morale contributes far more to his state's power position than does one who is illiterate, unskilled, sick, and demoralized. Even such vital statistics as the size of military forces can be misleading. The soldier using automatic weapons produces a far greater fire power than a soldier using a bolt-action rifle. During the Second World War American soldiers were advantaged by use of the Garrand rifle which was semiautomatic and enabled them to shoot eight shots to one of the German or Japanese soldiers using a bolt-action rifle. This is, of course, not to say that one American soldier was comparable to eight German or Japanese soldiers, but this condition enabled the American soldier to produce more fire power faster than his opponent.

EDUCATION

Most states, both highly developed and underdeveloped, seek expansion and improvement in their educational institutions. Education is not only necessary for the individual who seeks a full life, but it is also a pillar upon which the power of a state rests.

Educational systems of developed lands which contribute best to the power of the state have both a vertical and horizontal dimension. The vertical dimension is made up of a school system having uni-

12 *World Health,* Vol. XV, No. 3, May–June, 1962, pp. 18–19.

versal primary education which provides a literate population; upon this base higher levels of education are given to fewer but still significant numbers of persons. A literate population is essential for carrying out the tasks of an automated society and providing the society with a large corps of effective participants in economic activity. Technically skilled people require more than just basic literacy, and consequently many people with a secondary education are also necessary. The need for higher skills and professionals necessitates numerous college graduates. Increasingly, postgraduate collegiate education is essential if a state is to have the inventions, scientific breakthroughs, good teachers, and great ideas essential to a status of great power. Doctors, graduate engineers, and the Ph.D.'s are absolutely necessary for super-powers. The vertical development of education must therefore provide education from the kindergarten through the most highly sophisticated postgraduate study at the doctoral level.

In addition there is a need for a horizontal development of education in which persons trained in varied skills are made available. Mechanics, clerks, secretaries, truck drivers, and a diversified service personnel are absolutely essential.

The power of a state is enhanced by the skills and training education provides. Power and its effective use come from imaginative applications of great ideas which are contributed by men of learning who have ample opportunities for intellectual exchange. Their ideas can be utilized only by the educated who perceive their value. Small wonder that governments are ready to invest large sums in public education of all types and at all levels.

SCIENCE AND TECHNOLOGY

Science seeks the understanding and mastery of the world around us. The utilization of scientific knowledge provides an advanced technology, an abundant economy, and an effective defense. In other words, science contributes in an essential way to the security, prosperity, and prestige of the state.

Abba Eban, for many years Israel's Ambassador to the United Nations, once said that "No modern statesman can afford to be scientifically illiterate." In the decade of automation, the exploration of outer space, the study of the smallest particles, antibiotics, and supersonic vehicles, even the layman can no longer afford to be scientifically illiterate. An effectively operating democracy requires that each citizen understand what science is and the condition essential to its effective operation. Public issues, such as the safe use of insecticides, test-ban treaties, fluoridation of water, control over agricultural production, and birth-control information, cannot be approached intelligently without some understanding of their scientific aspects. The people must also be able to express themselves wisely about the large sums expended by all levels of government in support of scientific enterprise.

A scientific establishment rests upon a scientifically literate population. President Eisenhower's Commission on National Goals urged,

> ... that every young person with the desire and the capacity to become a scientist ... (be given) access to the best science education our leading scholars can devise. Given the availability of such education, science will find its fair share of the pool of talent. But this pool of talent must itself be enlarged to the maximum, by seeing to it that those who have the capacity for the rigorous and academic discipline required for all the professions start their course of study early, are offered opportunities to develop their talents, and are urged to continue to do so.[13]

For science to prosper and to contribute in full measure to the power of a state, it must have material and personnel resources. Scientific advances require laboratories, equipment, and scientists. The long-term development of science needs investment in and attention to basic rather than just applied research.

Scientific knowledge provides a basis for technology. In this sense technology may be thought of as "the development of a better way of doing a known job or the discovery of how to do a previously impossible one."[14] Technology enhances, as does science, national power. Its advancement requires technicians, engineers, and other kinds of professional personnel. Its products result from research and invention. The allegation that the Soviet Union was producing twice the number of scientists and engineers as the United States has created concern that in the future the Soviet Union will have more new patents, inventions, and ideas than the United States and will thereby gain great advantage.

[13] *Goals for Americans* (Englewood Cliffs, N.J.: Prentice-Hall, 1960), p. 8.
[14] *Ibid.*, p. 193.

INDUSTRIALIZATION

The most important factor in the determination of national power today is industrialization. All economic development is of moment in assessing power, but industry must be emphasized for it contributes most to the power of a state.

If one agrees that the United States and the Soviet Union are the strongest powers in the world today, and this is certainly a valid allegation, then only industrialization can explain the development of American power and the more recent spectacular evolution of Soviet might. If Western Germany, Japan, and even Communist China have recently risen as states of growing strength, this can also be best explained by the growth of their industries.

It is not only a matter of casual observation that the most powerful states are also the most highly industrialized, but the relationship between industry and power is more than accidental. Military power, an important element of power, is based upon a highly developed industry and an advanced technology. Automated weapons, missiles, and nuclear weapons can be produced only by industrialized economies.

Industrial states enjoy trade advantages by producing the most widely sought after and most profitably sold merchandise. These trade advantages bring prosperity and power. The industrial state is also in the best position to offer assistance to underdeveloped states, which becomes an asset to the power position of the giver. An industrialized state can institute a high standard of living resulting in good morale of its population. A state enjoying a high living standard can develop useful branches of knowledge and skills. It can afford to educate its population. In hundreds of ways the industrialized state is advantaged and can by virtue of its industrialization exert its influence on other states.

Quantifying Industrial Might. Industrialization can be quantified. (By this we mean that the counting of relevant units is possible.) Before the Second World War figures for steel production were frequently used as a guide to the level of industrial development. Steel production figures may be highly instructive, and we would certainly find a high degree of correlation between steel production and industrialization. In some respects steel statistics are misleading as correlates of power. Steel production for the United States is not the same as steel capacity. The United States has, in the last decade, never produced its full capacity of steel; therefore, although in 1961 the Soviet Union produced about seventy million tons of steel [15] and the United States about ninety-nine million tons,[16] this statistic lacks an important element of information. The United States production of steel was about two-thirds of its capacity while Soviet production was close to 100 percent. Another objection to relying on steel production figures is the failure to take into account the utilization of other metals in place of steel.

A more comprehensive and reliable index for industrialization is the gross national product, which is generally used today. The *gross national product* of a state is the sum of goods and services produced by that state within the course of one year and may be expressed in dollar figures. We will find that the more highly industrialized the state, the higher its gross national product. This statistic also has certain limitations. Gross national product tells us what a country produces rather than its capacity to produce. The gross national product of the United States represents industry going at a level below its capacity; it could, with the proper decisions by government and industry, be increased if necessary. Also, the gross national product as a statistic needs refinement in that much of the goods and services are irrelevant to the power of the state. Putting gadgets on automobiles increases the cost and comes out as a contribution to a higher gross national product yet does nothing whatsoever to increase the power of the United States. If we compare the gross national product of the United States with that of the Soviet Union, we find it is more than twice as great (see Table I, p. 374); however, if we look at the data for that portion of the gross national product invested in national defense and in capital development within the United States and compare these figures with those for the Soviet Union, we would find that the United States and the Soviet Union invest close to the same sums. It is in consumer industries that contribute less to power that the comparative figures for the gross national product become highly favorable to the United States.

The study on "Worldwide and Domestic Economic Problems and

[15] *The World Almanac*, 1963 (New York: New York World-Telegram), p. 38.

[16] *Ibid.*, p. 698.

Their Impact on the Foreign Policy of the United States" [17] puts this matter in proper perspective.

> ... changes in the gross national product, and gross national product comparisons among countries, while useful, do not adequately measure the power position of the countries compared. This position is best gaged by the industrial base of a nation, for this is an important backstop for the military establishment and for a country's international trading position.

a. Soviet industrial production has been increasing approximately 8 percent per year since 1950, twice the U.S. growth rate of nearly 4 percent per pear.

   1. The U.S. economy has displayed consumption with moderate growth and Western Europe has in the fifties achieved growth with consumption. The Soviets' greater growth rate is due to their production for industry, in order to obtain still greater expansion of production.

   2. About one-half of Soviet investment goes into industry, and about 85 percent of this into the capital goods sector of industry to the neglect of consumer industries and consumer living standards.

   3. The emphasis on industrial expansion and the military establishment is seen in the fact that only 27 percent of Soviet industrial output is devoted to consumer goods. Some 30 years ago 60 percent of output was in the form of consumption goods.

   4. In 1956 Soviet production of industrial equipment equaled 65 percent of such production in the United States. Total industrial capacity came to 40 percent of the U.S. total; 30 years ago it was only 8 percent.

b. Projecting recent rates of industrial growth, Soviet industrial output is likely to grow 9 percent per annum, and by 1970 will approximate the present (1959) volume of U.S. industrial output. It is likely to equal 60 percent of the 1970 industrial output of the United States.

c. The Soviet industrial sector is thus growing at approximately twice the annual rate of the United States, and the projected expansions show nearly the same difference in growth rates.

   1. The basic reason for the past and projected difference in growth rates is the Soviet concentration of new capital investment in industry, particularly in the capital goods sector, i.e., an investment for industrial expansion, and little for consumption.

   2. In terms of productivity changes over time, the Soviet experience seems to approximate U.S. productivity growth rates.

[17] United States Senate, Committee on Foreign Relations, *United States Foreign Policy* (Washington, D.C.: The Government Printing Office, 1959), pp. 13–14.

3. But comparing present industrial labor productivity output per manhour in Soviet industry is considerably less than half that of the United States.

d. By 1970 the Soviet is likely to be a formidable industrial nation, relatively stronger than at present, and, in certain sectors, larger than the United States.

1. By U.S. standards—based on production for the consumer—their industrial sector will be unbalanced, but this is in accordance with Soviet plans.

2. Given their emphasis on the capital goods sector, it is probable that Soviet exports will grow substantially as well as their need for imports.

3. Soviet military capability will be greatly enhanced by the projected expansion of their industrial base.

In other words, Americans drive more cars, eat more, go on longer and better vacations, and live in greater comfort; but, all this is less than crucial to the power of the state.

MILITARY POWER-IN-BEING

When the Second World War began in September of 1939 the United States was very weakly armed. It had a little more than two years' grace before becoming involved as a combatant, and in that two-year period it was able to develop a formidable, indeed the most powerful, military machine in the history of mankind. Given time to prepare, with its industrial might, it was able to erect with relative speed overwhelming military force. Several decades ago industrial might loomed even larger as an element of power than it does today. A revolution has taken place in military technology that has made power-in-being a factor of great importance. Today military power must exist rather than be potential. Military power as a factor must be rated second to industrialization but only a highly industrialized technology can provide the basis for an effective mid-twentieth century military machine.

Just as in other fields of technology, there has been a revolution in military technology, which has been marked by two major advances. The first was the development of nuclear weapons, represented by A-bombs and H-bombs, providing a yield of destruction of such dimension that its destructive force is qualitatively different from all explosives used prior to the atomic age. The second was the development of missiles capable of flying at speeds of 18,000 miles per hour and covering a distance of 8,000 miles or more and sufficiently accurate, given nuclear explosives in their warheads, to destroy the targets at which they are aimed. This revolution in military technology has many far-reaching effects, among the most important being that, once war breaks out, time to prepare is no longer available. States must be constantly prepared to defend themselves, and that is why we are concerned with military *power-in-being*.

The defense of North America rests in part on a DEW line along the Arctic Circle from western Alaska eastward to Greenland. This DEW line provides the continent with some fifteen or thirty minutes of preparation time if the military is able to detect launching missiles at their sites in the Soviet Union.

The new military technology has created constitutional problems for the United States. Under its Constitution only Congress can declare war. Missiles directed at the United States would effectively bring it into war and make action by Congress irrelevant. Congress probably could not meet, let alone carry on deliberations about a declaration of war. Therefore, constitutional adaptation had perforce to be utilized if the country was to remain safe. With the attack of the Japanese on Pearl Harbor the role of Congress in declaring war had already become meaningless. On December 8, 1941, Congress did declare war, retroactively one day, but they had no choice as there was nothing else that they could do. In the Korean and Vietnamese fighting, war was not declared. The President, as Commander-in-Chief, simply ordered American military forces to carry out a police action. As Commander-in-Chief his right to do so was hardly brought into question. President Eisenhower announced two doctrines, one for the Middle East and the other for the Far East, in which he threatened to use military force as Commander-in-Chief without going to Congress for a declaration of war, and thus warned the Communist powers that response to Communist aggression would be immediate.

Military Power and Nuclear Capability. The constant and immediate availability of military power is a critical element in the edifice of national power. Great powers must have the capacity to wage three types of warfare—nuclear, conventional, and guerrilla.

The ability to wage nuclear war rests on the availability of atom and hydrogen bombs and a mixture of fast long-range bombers and missiles seated in dispersed bases for the delivery of these bombs.

A-bombs are fission bombs and have a yield measured in kilotons—
that is, thousand-ton units of TNT. The A-bomb that was used on
Hiroshima was a twenty-kiloton bomb. Atom bombs today range
from a much higher kiloton yield to a fractional part of the Hiroshima bomb yield. H-bombs, or hydrogen bombs, are fusion bombs
whose yield is measured in megatons—million-ton units of TNT.
The upward yield limit of H-bombs is probably unknown. It may
be unlimited. The largest H-bomb ever exploded, by the Soviet
Union in its 1961 tests, was in the magnitude of seventy megatons.
The significance of atomic weapons, especially of hydrogen bombs,
is such that for the first time in history man is now capable of completely destroying any and all areas of the world. One "small" hydrogen bomb produces more explosive power than all of the explosives used in all wars up to the present time. This means it is now
possible to estimate the number of H-bombs that would be necessary
to completely destroy all life in the United States, the Soviet Union,
or any other country. Given the correct placing of H-bombs, in
adequate number, a country could literally be completely annihilated. The crucial problem then becomes one of delivery.

Delivery of nuclear bombs is assigned to missiles or long-range
bombers of high speed. With respect to the latter, it is possible to
design aircraft that could travel 10,000 miles or more without stop
at the rate of three times the speed of sound. Missiles are even faster.
The advantage of long-range, high-altitude Mach-three bombers is
that they provide greater accuracy than do missiles. The advantage of
missiles is that they are largely invulnerable to defensive action. As
far as we know now there is no defense against missiles. The range
of missiles is grouped into four categories: Ground to air short-range
anti-aircraft missiles; MRBM (Medium Range Ballistic Missiles),
whose range is about 1,000 miles; IRBM (Intermediate Range
Ballistic Missiles), which can travel up to 2,500 miles; ICBM
(Inter-Continental Ballistic Missiles), with a range of 5,000 miles or
more. Although missiles are not as accurate as bombers, given an
atom or hydrogen bomb in the nose cone of the missile the yield of
these bombs is such that perfect accuracy is not essential. The area
of destruction can be reasonably estimated in a number of miles from
point of impact, and everything in the area other than hardened
bases would be destroyed by the force of the explosions.

Because there is no present defense against missiles, inhibition of nuclear attack rests entirely on the capacity to retaliate. The ability to retaliate, or, as it is sometimes called, second-strike capability, rests in turn on the availability of missiles and bombers to reach targets of the attacking state. The situation where states have the certain and invulnerable capacity to destroy one another has produced a military stalemate often referred to as a "balance of terror." Because ability to retaliate is the only known basis of "defense" against nuclear attack, during 1960 fear arose that a missile gap in favor of the Soviet Union was rapidly developing and that between 1962 and 1964 the Soviet Union might well be in a position to exploit her advantage by striking first against the United States and her allies and by "one press of the button" destroy their capacity to retaliate. The temptation of destroying American power for all time seemed ominous, and many believed that a Russian leader would surely avail himself of this opportunity. Temporary invulnerability was gained through the use of "fillers." The United States put into commission nuclear-powered submarines carrying the Polaris IRBM's. The Polaris submarine moving about the oceans could not be pinpointed and caught by a first strike and would thus be in a position to retaliate. A second type of "filler" temporarily available was the Minuteman ICBM missile mounted on the railroad train. Its mobility made it a land-based Polaris. It was also proposed that a portion of the Strategic Air Command bombers be continuously in the air, so as not to be caught on the ground in a first-strike attack. Since the 1960 scare the United States rapidly developed an invulnerable nuclear response to first-strike attack. A nuclear stalemate exists between the United States and the Soviet Union. Each power can visit unacceptable losses upon the other. As a consequence, as long as the stalemate continues, a rational policy of nuclear aggression is excluded.

The capacity to fight a nuclear war involves an adequate stockpile of atomic and hydrogen bombs of varying yields. The size of the stockpile required can be determined and provision made for the destruction of every conceivable target.[18] There is no point in stockpiling an infinite number of nuclear devices. An excessive number of nuclear bombs—"overkill"—adds nothing to the power of the state because once targets are destroyed additional bombs become use-

[18] It is presumed that there is now no shortage of bombs although the means of delivery may still be in short supply.

less. Therefore, in comparing the nuclear strength of the Soviet Union with that of the United States, the sheer number of bombs available to each power is a poor guide.

Invulnerable nuclear strength requires hardened bases that cannot be destroyed by anything other than a direct hit. No state has the capability of pinpointing and assuredly hitting such an installation. In addition to hardened bases, nuclear capability is based upon an adequate number of missiles. It is presumed that missiles emplaced in soft bases that can be readily knocked out would not survive a first attack. Their second-strike usefulness can only be averred if there is a likelihood that the attacking power does not itself have adequate numbers of missiles to knock out all of the widely dispersed missiles, both hard and soft, located around the world. Those remaining after a first strike could therefore retaliate.

Missiles are powered by two types of fuel, liquid and solid. Liquid fuel, although it has the capability of powering a missile at great speed over long distances, has the unhappy faculty of requiring time to complete its arming. The fuel itself is so highly volatile that it cannot be kept in the missile for any length of time. The injection of fuel into the missile takes enough time so that such missiles cannot be immediately ready. The Atlas missile is a liquid-fuel ICBM. Solid fuels can be permanently stored within the missile and, consequently, more rapidly fired. The Titan and the Minuteman are solid-fuel ICBM's.

Besides bombs, planes, various types of missiles, and hardened bases, civil defense is also a part of the nuclear capability of the state. Defense against thermonuclear devices is genuinely improved with the use of shelters for fall-out protection. It is possible to construct bomb shelters that are blastproof but these are judged impractical. Practicable civil defense rests upon fall-out shelters that are designed to protect a population against contamination and no more. This they can do, and in the event of a nuclear attack it would still be possible for large numbers of persons to find their way to fall-out shelters and remain there until the dangers of radiation sickness produced by fall-out are over. The relation of civil defense to nuclear capability is simply this: without civil defense the population of the state becomes a hostage to the attacker who is in a position to figuratively say, "We have our nuclears zeroed in on New York, London, Paris, Manila, and Istanbul. Are you ready to accept a nuclear exchange with the destruction of those populations?" The availability of fall-out shelters could provide a measure of protection and as such would serve to reduce the temptation to make use of nuclear blackmail. It has been suggested that the presence of fall-out shelters would also serve to inform other states that military policy is not based upon the expectation of striking first. If the United States did not have fall-out shelters for its people, the Soviet Union might well draw the conclusion that it is not bothering about fall-out shelters because it is its intention to strike first to wipe out the Soviet Union's capacity to retaliate. To the degree that it is important that the Soviet Union know that the strategy of the United States is a second-strike strategy only and that it harbors no intentions of preventive war, the existence of fall-out shelters may be reassuring of second-strike intentions. It reduces the likelihood that the Russians would feel a need to preempt an attack.

States ought to be adequately informed about one another's intentions and capabilities to wage war so that wars resulting from false estimates may be avoided. Countries harboring aggressive intentions must be advised that nuclear blackmail cannot work, and this can be made clear only by an invulnerable capacity to retaliate and the will to use it. By the same token potential aggressors ought to be informed that use of nuclear weapons is limited to retaliation against aggression. Otherwise they would be tempted, even if only out of desperation, to strike first.

Capacity to fight a nuclear war carries with it the obligation to remain abreast of developments in the technology of nuclear warfare. Among the most ominous or hopeful developments, depending on how one looks at it, is the improvement of an anti-missile missile. Should a state produce an effective missile-destroying missile and become invulnerable to nuclear attack, it would have a decisive advantage over states not having this weapon. The Soviet Union with an anti-missile missile could surely pursue revisionist plans. The United States enjoying a unilateral monopoly of such a weapon would have great diplomatic advantage although as a *status-quo* power it would not use this advantage to the point of initiating war. The renewal of nuclear testing by Moscow in September, 1961, followed shortly thereafter by the United States in 1962—this coming after a three-year moratorium—was occasioned by the desire to keep up or get ahead in the race for nuclear supremacy. The purpose of testing according to President Kennedy was threefold. First, and possibly least important, was improving the weight-yield ratio of nuclear weapons, packing a large explosive into a smaller package so that a missile of smaller thrust could be used. Second was to ascertain whether the implements that had been developed since the tests of 1958 actually worked—proof tests. Third, and possibly most important, was the perfection of an anti-missile missile and other technological break-throughs with the hopeful objective of providing the United States with a measure of invulnerability against nuclear attack. Russia's test series in the summer of 1962 did not lead to further testing by the United States. The purpose of testing is not to equal the number of tests of the adversary. At least from the point of view of the United States there appeared to be no intention to match the Soviet Union test for test. The goal of tests was to ensure that the country did not fall behind in its nuclear capability. Tests mounted for nonmilitary political purposes are unjustified.

Conventional Military Power. Under the umbrella of nuclear stalemate, localized wars and limited acts of aggression can still occur. These cannot be prevented or contained by a nuclear arsenal. Countries possessing nuclear weapons but lacking adequate conventional military power will be unable to deal with brushfire wars and armed attacks in areas of peripheral importance to the great powers. To protect their interests around the world great powers must be able to fight conventional wars anywhere.

Conventional military strength today emphasizes mobility, gadgetry, and fire power. Motorized and airborne fighting men using automatic weapons, radio communication, electronic "ears" and "eyes," and computer-informed intelligence characterize the military forces for limited warfare.

Military Power and Insurgency. Finally, military power-in-being involves the capacity to fight guerrilla warfare (counter insurgency). Guerrilla (insurgency) warfare gives the aggressor an advantage of ambiguity. There is no outright, fully stated attack based upon a declaration of war. Presumably the guerrillas are simply "disaffected revolutionaries" who are trying to overthrow a "reactionary" regime. To retaliate massively against such attack is inappropriate and may not even end the guerrilla action. Guerrilla warfare is ambiguous in that the real sponsorship of the attack is hidden. To strike at the Soviet Union or Communist China in retaliation for Communist guerrilla action in Laos or Vietnam is a ludicrous expansion of a localized conflict. Guerrilla attack should be defeated through the training of nationals subjected to this style of warfare—meeting insurgency with counter insurgency. Popular support for the government against the aims of the guerrillas is the basis for such a defense. This does not preclude utilization of automatic weapons and radio communications. What is necessary is mobility and self-reliant fighting units who are not dependent upon long lines of supply and who can improvise tactics to suit each situation.

INTANGIBLE FACTORS OF POWER

A number of influences that have great importance in an evaluation of power are difficult to calculate with precision. Evaluation of a state's power must take these factors into consideration. At least four such factors need to be studied: *leadership,* the *morale* of the people, the *character* of the people, and the *form of government* of the state.

LEADERSHIP

There is a temptation to argue that leadership is all important. A state with all of the tangible assets of power that does not use its power potential effectively because its leaders do not take full advantage of its power is possessed of power that counts for naught. History is replete with cases of great leaders who have succeeded in maximizing the country's power and weakening its adversaries. A study of the record might reveal an even greater number of leaders who failed to utilize the power potential of their state and brought their country to disaster through the pursuit of maladroit policies. Good leaders strengthen the state. Good leaders put forward beneficial and attainable goals. Good leaders use the state's power wisely and effectively to achieve their goals.

Leadership cannot be analyzed by set criteria or by known rules of behavior. In character, personality, and style leaders differ widely. Some are flamboyant while others are austere. Joan of Arc may have been inspired; Bismarck was calculating; Napoleon and Churchill, Roosevelt and Stalin, and Gandhi and Adenauer were different in their personalities and temperaments—yet all were great leaders. Style of leadership may vary; nevertheless a number of essential qualities can be identified. Leaders must be well informed. Essential knowledge includes the capabilities of one's own state and those of other states, both friends and foes. The leader must also understand the country's aims and those of other states whose actions bear upon their achievement. Accurate and wide-ranging intelligence data must inform the decision-making process. Another characteristic of effective leadership is flexibility. Once goals are determined, the means of achieving these goals can and indeed should change as conditions change. Finally, in our own time when the masses are an important element in the power of the state, effective leaders must be understood and followed by the people. Their appeal must be popular, and popular appeal is ultimately based upon tangible evidence of success rather than flamboyance and demagoguery.

On occasion a leader exhibits charismatic qualities. A charismatic leader is treated by his people as though he were endowed with divine talents. His leadership is blindly followed. Hitler, Gandhi, Nkrumah, and Napoleon were charismatic leaders. In those states where the populace remains largely unconcerned with the policies of their state, leadership may be limited to elite groups. Leadership in Africa and the Middle East is largely in the hands of traditional authorities, educated elites, or propertied classes.

Effective leadership must be decisive. This is not to say that leaders must on all occasions act; temporizing may be wise. But whenever an advantageous action is indicated the leader must act with resolution, make firm decisions, and carry them out. Perhaps no more terrible decision has ever faced leaders of great powers than to take steps that could lead to war. The era of nuclear warfare is also an era of nuclear blackmail. A decision not to give in could result in thermonuclear war. Leaders must be willing to accept great destruction and be prepared to destroy the enemy in defense of vital interests. Assurance of the will to fight for crucial points—West Berlin, the Turkish Straits, Malaysia, or South Vietnam—is the only way in which the leaders of *status-quo* states can maintain the *status quo* against the onslaught of revisionist powers. Leaders paralyzed by fear will fail.

Leadership is preeminently a position of moral responsibility. No people want leaders who do not command their respect and the respect of the peoples and leaders of other states. Respected leaders must enjoy moral stature beyond question. It is not only what they say that is of significance but also what they do. When Winston Churchill said during Britain's darkest hour that the British would fight in the streets and on the beaches and would never give up, the British people were ready to do just that because they knew that Churchill would be there with them. If Churchill had beamed that speech to Great Britain from the safety of Washington, D.C., the effect could have been far different.

NATIONAL CHARACTER

We have already made the point that the peoples of a nation-state have a unique national character. (See Chapter 1.) Germans have been characterized as militaristic, Indians as peace loving, Americans as pragmatic and individualistic, and Russians as persistent. These generalizations are or have at least at one time been valid generalizations of national character. What is the relationship between these characteristics and the power of the state? A people that accept militarism as a way of life will intensify the military strength of the state. German militarism in the nineteenth and earlier twentieth centuries meant that not only did Germans accept the discipline of military life whenever they were members of the armed forces, but also that the military enjoyed a venerated place in the minds and the hearts of the German people. German militarism was an aspect of an orderly and directed life. It meant that rules were obeyed and that soldiers excelled in carrying out orders. The individualism of the American, on the other hand, meant that he was a much harder person to direct. Both in civilian and military life the self-reliance and motivation to do that which he believes ought to be done rather than carry out the leader's decision plays a definitive role. One aspect of this national characteristic is that the American soldier, especially in combat, tended to be undisciplined but highly self-reliant. The American soldier operating without his officer still operated with great effectiveness.

The Indian national character places great value upon the peaceful settlement of conflicts. In this respect the Hindu tradition stands in contrast to the Judaic-Christian-Moslem faiths, which put greater emphasis on just solutions than peaceful solutions.

National character does influence the power of a state. Some characteristics—individualism, self-reliance, and militarism—are advantageous to power; others, like the love of peace, unhappily, are not. If

Britain's battles were really won on the playing fields at Eton, then America's battles were won on the baseball, basketball, and football fields in every community of the United States. The athletic training of the American male that provides him with experience in cooperation, in carrying out assigned tasks, in making rapid decisions, and in developing physical coordination, has been an asset to the power of the United States.

The character of a people is not a permanently fixed condition. It may undergo change. In the seventeenth century the Swedes were looked upon as an aggressive people. Today we think of the Swedes as peace loving, and indeed they have been a peace-loving people for a century or more. There are grounds for suspecting that events of a traumatic nature in the life of a people serve to change their character. Perhaps it was the defeat of Sweden at the hands of Peter the Great in the battle of Poltava that was the traumatic experience that changed the Swedish character. Is there not reason to believe that militaristic Germany and militaristic Japan have both undergone a change and that neither of these nationalities is militaristic today? The traumatic experience of the war's great destruction ending in total defeat has impressed itself in the popular attitudes that earnestly seek the preservation of peace. Certainly the popularity of pacifist movements in these states and the difficulty that Japanese leaders are having in trying to reconstruct their military defense might provide some evidence that the Germans and the Japanese have undergone a change of national character. Are the Chinese still a peace-loving people? Has not a decade or more of experience with Communist regimentation changed them from a peace-loving people into a highly disciplined group ready to pursue goals through war?

NATIONAL MORALE

The importance of good morale to power is obvious. When morale is high a people will work hard, fight hard, and cooperate with their fellow nationals to achieve the aims of their land. Low morale produces internal dissension and lack of dedication to common purposes.

The question that must be answered with respect to morale is what makes for good morale and what destroys it. Morale is often unpredictable. When the Japanese struck at Pearl Harbor they may have expected a successful strike there to produce collapse in the morale of the American people. After all, the people of the United States were already divided about Roosevelt's policy of assistance to the democracies fighting the Axis states. The House of Representatives in 1941 approved by the margin of only a single vote the extension of the draft law for the duration of the war emergency. There was much evidence that the American people were already divided and their morale low. Today we know that the attack on Pearl Harbor united the American people and extirpated overnight their isolationist outlook. But this result might well have been unexpected.

The morale of a people is high when they feel that they have stakes in the success of their state. Africans serving in the armies of the Republic of South Africa would have poor morale because the success of the Republic of South Africa would not advantage them at all. If it were possible to contemplate Jewish soldiers in the army of Nazi Germany certainly their morale would have been less than dependable because the Jews had no advantage in the victory of Nazi Germany. Minority groups are often the target of propaganda by an enemy seeking to undermine morale but the success of such appeals is unpredictable.

One possibly could have expected that Japanese-Americans serving in the army during the Second World War might have proved to be unreliable. After all, all persons of Japanese ancestry living in California were removed from that state, forced into relocation centers, and treated as potentially disloyal persons. What expectations might the United States Army have had for the performance of a military unit made up of Japanese-Americans fighting in Europe? Yet the 442nd Regimental Combat Team made up of Japanese-American soldiers was one of the finest fighting units in all of the armies of the United States. They served well, and they served well in large part because their morale was high. If morale is a key to the success of the state, it is also a factor that is most elusive to predict.

Morale is unpredictable because it is unstable. Good morale can become bad overnight or *vice versa*. The exposé of a revered and trusted leader as a charlatan, thief, or a liar could provide a shattering effect on the morale of a people. A people that have come through great trials successfully may find that as a result of these trials they gain confidence in themselves and their morale becomes high.

FORMS OF GOVERNMENT AS A FACTOR OF POWER

The relationship between the two forms of government, dictatorships and democracies, and the power of the state cannot be precisely detailed. Some dictatorships work effectively while others do not. Some democracies are highly efficient and well-ordered power units while others are just the opposite.

A dictatorship may be effective because it is able to mobilize human and material resources with efficiency and can command and direct these resources to achieve desired ends. The power advantage of the dictatorship is greater when the dictator has popular support, and such support is likely when the dictator has been successful. Triumphs lead people to consider their leader to be infallible—a charismatic figure. The power advantage of dictatorship also derives from the elimination of divided counsel. Dictators brook no opposition and consequently there are no conflicting views.

If dictatorship has certain power advantages it also offers serious disadvantages as well. A dictatorship is no more effective than the talents of its dictator and those whom he consults. Mediocre dictators collect mediocre advisers. A dictator making unpopular decisions induces disaffection within the population. This leads to the diversion of the state's power to sustain internal security. The unpopular dictator is vulnerable to subversion. Even in these times, when the techniques of suppressing opposition have become highly developed, dictators are nevertheless overthrown. Latin-American states provide ample illustration of this point. From the point of view of the international community dictatorships tend to be unpopular. Dictatorships often are revisionist, and the combination of internal oppression and external expansionism gives birth to opposition on a world scale.

The ultimate weakness of the dictatorship is that it denies the individual his self-esteem. Democrats believe there inheres in every individual a sense of his own dignity and each person naturally feels outraged at being ordered about, officiously policed, and "pushed around." Dictatorial states are police states little concerned with human feeling. Stalin is reputed to have advised that the way to govern is to "beat, beat, beat." However, human dignity ultimately leads men to demand the right to be the master of their fate by choosing their leaders and voicing their opinions.

The power of the democratic state profits from the willing rather than the coerced support of the people. To the degree that the democracy can create a sense of popular participation in the decision-making process of the state, the people feel that the success of the state is their success and the decisions of the state derive from their wisdom. The democratic state needs not fear the function of opposition. Opposition serves to refine and perfect through its criticism official conduct and policy. Democratic principles create a general attitude that the goal of government is the well-being of the people.

The power disadvantages of democracy come from failures of leadership or divisions in leadership. Under these circumstances indecision is possible. If the effectiveness of the dictatorial state is no greater than the effectiveness of the dictator, the effectiveness of democracy is based on the wisdom of the people expressed in their choices of leadership and policy. A democracy by definition permits opposition to exist. This may make it a target for subversive elements. The preservation of democratic qualities is considered more important than the suppression of the small number of subversives. Extreme cases of subversion need not be tolerated. Germany's Weimar Republic erred in permitting both the Nazis and the Communists to maintain paramilitary formations. These bodies challenged the authority of the state. Their existence had little to do with the rights of men to speak their minds, and German democracy would have been stronger rather than weaker by the suppression of strong-arm units. Between the suppression of movements seeking violent overthrow and the preservation of the right of heresy, there exists a broad range of freedom of expression without compromising security.

LIMITATIONS IN THE ASSESSMENT OF NATIONAL POWER

The factors analyzed in this chapter provide us with the basis for an objective analysis of the power of a state. One would have good reason to expect that by taking into consideration all of the factors dealt with above the misassessment in the power positions of Italy before the First World War and during the interwar period or of Russian and American power by the Germans in 1941 might have been avoided.

However, the estimate of national power if not entirely impressionistic is still far from scientifically accurate. Even after one avoids an estimate of power based on a single factor, even after one takes into consideration the process of continuous change and, as a consequence, reevaluates power in the light of changing circumstances, and even when we judge the power of the state in relation to other states, especially adversary states, rather than as an absolute, we are not able to accurately determine the relative power of states. Perhaps the development of better computers and programming techniques will refine the accuracy of power evaluation, but as yet one cannot feed into computers data provided in analysis of the several factors dealt with above and come out with an accurate rating of power among the states of the world.

The imponderable factors facing the policy makers in their assessment of power are such that a precise estimate may never be possible. Among these imponderables is the fact that not each element of power is equally important. One factor cannot be equated with another. The relative importance to be given to each factor is disputed by experts and weighting them is an art rather than a science. Some experts may consider military power-in-being the most important factor, others have reckoned population the weightiest factor, and still others have considered industrialization and leadership most vital. There is no way of determining how much weight should be put upon each of the factors in an overall evaluation.

Another difficulty encountered in the evaluation of power is that some factors are impossible to quantify in a meaningful way. How does one rate the relative advantages of morale, national character, or leadership (both civilian and military) on the part of rival states?

Having recognized that factors of power are constantly changing we must also recognize that often change is unpredictable. Today both the United States and the Soviet Union are trying to perfect an anti-missile missile. The date of the breakthrough in this effort, if it ever comes, is still unknown, but should a state make a breakthrough with this weapon it would enjoy an immediate power advantage. Leaders die, catastrophes take place, scandals are discovered, and new inventions are patented. The changes that result from each such twist of fate, from each accident in history, may be as far reaching as they are unpredictable.

SUMMARY

Human intelligence has learned some of the most important answers to the question of why some states are strong and others weak. This knowledge enables man to maximize strength and minimize weaknesses. The all-important guesses that are made about the relative strength of states are more informed and probably more accurate than they ever have been but they are not beyond error.

Power is a result of a number of factors. Among the most important are industrialization, military power-in-being, leadership, and morale. Industrialization may be assessed through the gross national product of the state. Military power-in-being rests on the capability of fighting nuclear, conventional, and counter-insurgency war. Leadership and morale are not tangible and are largely evaluated by impressions. Yet they play a crucial role in the power of a country.

Other factors have less of an influence but may not be disregarded. A large population provides power advantages if it does not constitute overpopulation. Natural resources are more a question of availability than indigenous supply. Education, science, and technology are essential bases for power. Geography, on the other hand, has marginal significance in an era of automation, missiles, nuclear weapons, and advanced industrial and medical technology.

Our evaluation of national power should lead us to conclude that the United States is the most powerful state in the world today because it has by far the highest gross national product, formidable and well-rounded military power, a large and talented population, and adequate resources available to it. By and large Americans have reason to feel that their morale is good, their leadership superior, their national character an asset, and their democratic government advantageous to the power position of the state.

CHAPTER 3

International Relations

THE FIRST two chapters of this book looked at the world in terms of *independent* states. Each state had goals and the accomplishment of them constituted the basic impulse of its foreign policy. However, this is only half the picture of the world in which we live. Ours is also a world of *interdependent* states. For many reasons—political, economic, social, and technological—no state can go it alone. One must say with John Donne that no *state* is "an island unto itself." The interdependence of states makes relations among them a necessity.

The quest for peace is one of the most pressing reasons for international relations. Maxim Litvinov's slogan that "peace is indivisible" was probably true in the 1930's when he said it. It certainly is true today. In this century two of the wars that have been fought have been world wars. There is simply too great a danger that even a local war may develop into a most destructive world war. Peace requires international cooperation for the banishment of war.

As states seek prosperity, they increasingly turn toward mutually advantageous economic relationships. International trade brings states together. Attractive living standards dictate exchange in a large number of commodities and natural resources. Prosperity and depressions in any of the major countries have worldwide repercussions. Expectations for higher standards of living in underdeveloped areas have made economic development an international concern. The economic necessity for cooperation has become self-evident. Autarchy, in the sense that a state seeks to cut itself off from the economic problems of other countries, is no longer a possibility for states pursuing a higher standard of living for their people. To the contrary, bilateral and multilateral trade agreements and regional and international trade organizations have become the style of the day. Most-favored-nation treatment—the quest for trade advantages equal with the most favorable trading rights given to any state—has become every state's goal.

The development of modern transportation and communication has encouraged the spread of international relations of a "people-to-people" character. More people travel abroad today. Young men and women have foreign "pen pals." The rapidity and ease of telephonic, telegraphic, radio, and even television communications via Telestar is a growing reality for increasing numbers of people. Consequently, attention is devoted to the end that these contacts will support, rather than disturb, friendly international relations.

Man has widened his horizon to encompass the globe; therefore, there is a concomitant development of international institutions of an economic, social, and technical character. Thirteen specialized agencies,[1] and a number of international commodity agreements among producers and consumers of particular products (such as wheat, cotton, tin, rubber, and sugar) are in existence. The number of private international organizations grows year by year.

Literally countless developments are taking place to make this a shrinking world in which states and their people are becoming ever more interdependent. States depend upon one another for the maintenance of international peace. They depend upon one another for commodities and resources necessary for a modern economy. They work with one another for their mutual prosperity. They cooperate with one another to limit the spread of epidemics and to seek solutions for the hazards to health. They help one another develop their economies, their educational systems, and their technical skills. Such is the world in which we live.

The study of international politics lends itself to analysis in terms of three types of international relationships. In one of these the nature of the contact with other states is limited and, in particular, alliances are avoided. The dangers of war are minimized, so it is

[1] The International Atomic Energy Agency has the attributes of a specialized agency but is not officially considered to be one. See Leland M. Goodrich, *The United Nations* (New York: Thomas Y. Crowell, 1959), p. 276. For a list of the agencies see Chapter 4, p. 91.

believed, by limiting the character of foreign association. Another relationship is motivated by the belief that in this anarchic world of sovereign entities there is need for law, order, and authority. Some countries, therefore, promote rules to govern the behavior of states. They want to establish international standards of a legal, moral, and ethical character and thereby institute norms of international behavior. A third relationship arises when states faced with international anarchy seek their own safety through combination, through a system of alliances. The need to become involved in international relations leads states to pursue one or more of these policies in their relations with other states.

LIMITING CONTACTS WITH OTHER STATES

In an earlier time, states could literally isolate themselves from contact with other states. Both the Chinese and Japanese in the eighteenth and early nineteenth centuries approached total isolation. The United States practiced a policy of limited isolation in that it abjured alliances with European states, but even this limited policy of isolation was a failure when applied to the conditions which existed in the twentieth century.

In our own time, very few states can isolate themselves from contacts with other states. This may be possible for a small state in the Himalayan Mountains or a diminutive state that is not traversed by the highways of international contact, but isolationism is neither possible nor desirable any longer. Remote Nepal and Sikkim have been drawn into the vortex of international affairs by the conflicts of their neighbors.

NEUTRALISM

At the present time the most significant attempt to inhibit certain kinds of contacts among states takes the form of neutralism. By neutralism we mean a policy of abstention from cold-war alliances. There may be varying nuances in the policies neutralist states pursue; they may be friendly, or lean to the "East" or the "West," but so long as a state is not a member of a cold-war alliance it is considered to be neutralist. Despite bias in favor of East or West, most neutralist powers examine each question on its merits and take their positions accordingly.

Neutralism does not preclude the seeking of other areas of contact. Indeed, neutralist states seek all the economic, cultural, and technical contacts available.

Neutralist policies are justified in terms of one or more of the following reasons.

First, neutralist states wish to avoid a shooting war. Neutralism here appears as a policy of safety, of getting out of the line of fire should shooting begin. Countries in the Southern Hemisphere may well believe that war in the Northern Hemisphere could be escaped.

Second, some states have held that their military position is too weak to make any significant contribution to the power configuration of a cold-war alliance. Thus, Tunisia, which pursues a neutralist policy but which is on the whole more friendly to the West than to the East, appears to consider her contribution to the power position of the West so minimal as to be almost irrelevant to the military power of the West.

Third, most neutralist states hold that affiliation with one of the blocs in the cold war imposes onerous military obligations. Such obligations are incompatible with the development goals of the state. It is often averred that as states divert their human and material resources to military preparedness they create deleterious economic conditions that work to the advantage of revolutionary and Communist movements and this in fact weakens the anti-Communist world. A better defense against a Communist take-over can be made through the pursuit of economic welfare and economic development, thus undercutting the appeals of Communist propaganda.

Fourth, a sizable number of neutralist states hold that the issues in the cold war are irrelevant to them. It makes no difference to them whether East or West wins in the cold war. Such states do not accept the concepts of *status-quo* and revisionist states. They perceive no special danger from either side in the cold war.

Fifth, another consideration is the ability to benefit from trade with and economic assistance from both East and West, which neutralist powers may obtain. A number of neutralists have been able to trade with and win aid from both sides in the cold war.

Finally, neutralist states often believe that as long as they maintain their neutralism they are in a position to mediate issues in the cold war. Their hope is that they will be called upon to act the role of the "good broker" and be expected to come forward with disinterested and fair proposals of settlement when the danger of war between the great powers becomes acute. To date there has, however, been no significant mediation of cold-war issues by neutralist powers.

Neutralist policy is sometimes supported by legal instruments known as nonaggression pacts. These are promises of signatory parties to refrain from acts of aggression against one another. In the 1950's Communist China signed such pacts with Burma, India, Indonesia, and other states. The inherent weakness of these agreements was underlined when Peking attacked India in 1962. Nonaggression pacts are not self-enforcing. They are based merely on a promise. The sanction available whenever the pact has been violated has been nothing more than the castigation of the violator as a liar and a breaker of promises before the court of world opinion. Since the end of the Second World War some countries have refused to participate in nonaggression pacts on the ground that they are not worth the paper they are written on because they are not enforced. Indeed, they may very well be deceptive when states labor under an illusion of safety from aggression while in fact no such safety exists. The Soviet Union, a supporter of nonaggression pacts, had such pacts with Japan, Finland, Poland, Rumania, and the Baltic states. In each instance the pact did not prevent the Soviet Union from using force, even aggression (though they did not call it that), when it suited its purpose.

ESCAPING INTERNATIONAL ANARCHY THROUGH THE DEVELOPMENT OF NORMS OF BEHAVIOR FOR STATES

States are sovereign and their behavior can only be self-regulated. A state may curb its actions for fear of untoward consequences but it recognizes no higher authority. Despite every state's assertion of sovereignty, which implies no limits upon its desired behavior, a large number of them have sought peace and their own security by promoting a process of self-regulation. They believe that all states should accept international law and international standards of moral and ethical behavior as well as a mutually advantageous disarmament plan to make life on earth less dangerous and more felicitous.

INTERNATIONAL LAW

The best-developed and on the whole the most promising attack on international anarchy comes from the attempt to develop the rule of international law. Effective world law must be based upon an acceptable code of law that states are pledged to respect and also upon institutions with authority to act.

International law is primitive in the sense that there is no comprehensive body of law acceptable to most of the states. The United Nations through its General Assembly has undertaken, as one of its most important functions, a program of codifying international law. The purpose of a code is to establish laws that will provide legal criteria for judging the behavior of states and to set up standards of justice to which all members of the UN would subscribe. Not only is international law incomplete in that many areas of contact among states are not regulated by law, but also the content of the law is itself in dispute. Some states accept international laws quite different from those followed by other states. Thus, the United States recognizes that the jurisdiction of states out into the open seas extends for three miles. The Swedes hold to a four-mile limit, the Mexicans to a nine-mile limit, and the Costa Ricans claim a two-hundred-mile limit. The Soviet Union claims a twelve-mile limit, while several states refuse to commit themselves to any limit.[2] How far out into the sea does the jurisdiction of a state extend? Agreement is lacking.

The General Assembly exercises its responsibility for the codification of international law through an International Law Commission, made up of twenty-five members, each from a different state and each an expert in international law.[3] The purpose of the Commission is the promotion and "the progressive development of international law and its codification."[4] The Commission tries to work out conventions that, when they are accepted by the General As-

[2] *International Conciliation No. 520,* Max Sorenson, "Law of the Sea," November, 1958, Carnegie Endowment for International Peace, p. 244.
[3] United Nations Office of Public Information, *Everyman's United Nations,* 7th ed. (New York: 1964), p. 423.
[4] *Ibid.*

sembly and ratified by states, are generally accepted as international law. This is no mere job of research and drafting. The Commission must hammer out agreement on international law where it is in dispute. The Commission has chipped away at the differing positions taken by members of the United Nations on the question of the extent of jurisdiction over and the use of territorial waters. This is a typical example of its work. The question is still open and far from resolved, but states have been brought closer together and codification of the laws of the sea has been significantly advanced.

International law is an existing reality, but it is not made by an international legislative body, enforced by an international executive, or tried in an international court. It is, on the contrary, made in the legislatures and enforced by executives and adjudicated by the courts of each country according to their own light. In addition to needing development and codification, international law, if it is to become a normative regulation of behavior, also needs centralization of the law-making, law-executing, and the law-adjudicating processes. The United Nations General Assembly provides in an incipient sense an international legislative body. It is true that a decision of the General Assembly, except in special circumstances, is considered a recommendation. As such, it is not true law. Sanctions are not automatically provided against those who refuse to be bound by such "legislation." Ernest Gross has stated the situation felicitously when he wrote, "Advanced systems of order punish all acts which the group treats as crimes. Rudimentary systems—such as the United Nations—treat as crimes only those acts which the group is prepared to punish." [5]

The Secretary-General enforces decisions made by the other organs of the United Nations. As such, in an incipient sense, an international executive appears to be in the making. The most advanced of the international institutions of law is the adjudicatory agency, the International Court of Justice, one of the six principal organs of the UN.

The International Court of Justice is available to all members of the United Nations and to other states that are given specific permission to use it by the General Assembly. Switzerland falls into this second category. The Court hears cases submitted to it when

[5] *The United Nations: Structure for Peace* (New York: Harper and Brothers, 1962), p. 5.

two important conditions are met: first, all the parties to the litigation agree to the Court's jurisdiction in the case, and, second, the litigants agree to carry out the Court's decision. These provisions in the Statute of the Court duplicate those of its predecessor, the Permanent Court of International Justice associated with the League of Nations, and, over the period covered by the existence of both these courts, their success in getting states to carry out judgments has been exceptionally high. Only one state, Albania, in the Corfu Channel Case, has failed to abide by the Court's decision. The great need is to get states to agree to submit their disputes to the Court. Once submission is made states are, by and large, ready to accept an adverse judgment of the Court if that be their fate.

The Court is constructed in such a way that voluntary submission of litigation is made easier because all areas of the world and the various legal systems are represented by the elected justices of this body. In addition, the Statute of the Court provides, in Article 31, that all litigants are entitled to have a national of their own country or a country of their choosing placed on the Court as an additional justice with full powers.

The most serious weakness of the World Court is its largely voluntary jurisdiction. In order to enhance the jurisdiction of the Court, the Statute, in Article 36, Paragraph 2, provides some compulsory jurisdiction. This section is called the *optional clause* and allows a state to accept the automatic jurisdiction of the Court in cases where the other party or parties to the litigation have also accepted the optional clause. The Court is thereby given compulsory jurisdiction whenever the criterion of reciprocity is present. The optional clause is brought into play only to the extent that states have accepted the Court's jurisdiction. The United States, as well as most of the other states which have agreed to the optional clause, have done so with certain reservations. For instance, the United States has reserved to itself the right to renounce the jurisdiction of the Court under this clause five years after its initial acceptance (in 1946) by giving an advance notice of six months. The United States has also reserved to itself the right to refuse the Court jurisdiction of all questions that it itself considers domestic. Therefore, any litigant facing the United States before the Court under the optional clause also may refuse the Court jurisdiction if, in its opinion, this encroaches upon its domestic area.

The optional clause gives the Court jurisdiction over litigant states that have accepted the clause in four areas of competence: [6]

In 1963 thirty-six states had accepted the Court's jurisdiction under the optional clause.[7] This means that, whenever these states have a dispute in the four areas cited above, the Court has the authority to settle the dispute by rendering judgment.

The optional clause is one method by which the Court is given a wider and more effective function without violation of the principle of sovereignty, which states are so reluctant to give up. By accepting the optional clause, a state, by its sovereign action, agrees to be bound in specific areas and under well-understood conditions by decisions of the Court.

INTERNATIONAL STANDARDS OF MORAL AND ETHICAL BEHAVIOR

Less well developed than international law has been the development of an international moral consensus as a limitation on a state's behavior. For example, in the nineteenth century a moral consensus on the question of slavery inhibited the transportation of slaves from Africa to other parts of the world. The moral outrage of the destruction of Jews and other groups during the Second World War, particularly by the Nazis, led the General Assembly of the United Nations to adopt a convention on genocide that made acts of genocide morally reprehensible and outside the acceptable behavior of states. The control of narcotics trade and the attempt to promote human rights all bespeak the evolution of moral standards. These are moral norms that states observe. If the General Assembly should secure agreement to its conventions on human rights and the states ratify these conventions, then human rights would not only be part of recognized international morality but also an element of international law. Moral standards make the world a more peaceful and humane arena for international relations.

An international moral consensus is conceived as a function of the

[6] Statute of the Court, Article 36, Paragraph 2.
  (A) all questions that involve the interpretation of a treaty;
  (B) disputes concerning international law;
  (C) the determination of a fact which when established would prove the violation of a treaty;
  (D) the fixing of reparations upon a state that has violated a treaty under point "C" above.

[7] *Everyman's United Nations, op. cit.,* p. 21.

international community. Morals are the community's standards of behavior. The violation of moral standards makes the violator an outcast of the community. Limited as the international moral consensus might be, it does serve to inhibit immoral behavior. No state wishes to appear as the "moral leper" among the states of the world. Transgression against moral standards is cause for popular revulsion. This is the cause of South Africa's difficulty; apartheid violates an international sense of moral behavior.

Over a period of time states have accepted high-minded principles to guide their own behavior. There are certain things that states no longer do because of their ethical standards. The use of bribery of high officials is rarely attempted in international politics. Ambassadors do not travel to their assigned lands with personal cooks and tasters for fear that they might be poisoned. Yet these techniques —bribery, brigandage, assassination—were not uncommon in the past. States accept limitations inherent in a "national sense of conscience," dictating right from wrong behavior, that inhibits some of the more reprehensible tactics, which might conceivably be otherwise tried.

DISARMAMENT

Another approach to the preservation of peace and security is to be found in the quest for disarmament. In most minds disarmament has become virtually synonymous with peace. Disarmament serves to make wars less lethal so that, should states resort to war, at least the destruction can be circumscribed and the conflict limited. Disarmament has popular appeal because it reduces the economic burden of expensive military hardware which is notoriously short-lived. Indeed, the crushing burdens of expensive weaponry have become a primary reason for seeking disarmament. Disarmament is an attractive goal in that agreements to disarm are tension-reducing instruments, which create an atmosphere wherein other issues in conflict can be more easily negotiated. A disarmament agreement would be likely to include international enforcement machinery, which would extend order and regulation and, consequently, reduce the scope of world anarchy.

Successful disarmament negotiations have taken place. The Rush-Bagot agreement of 1817 on naval limitations in the Great Lakes was concluded and implemented. The Washington treaties of 1922–23 on naval limitations did take effect. But the overall record in securing disarmament agreement has been discouraging. Contemporary problems of disarmament will be dealt with elsewhere (see Chapter 14); here we are concerned with the relationship between disarmament and world order.

Disarmament agreements have usually failed because states approach such agreements with the aim of securing national advantage. States have proposed disarmament agreements that would weaken their potential enemies and, because this purpose is transparent, these maneuvers have failed.

In the 1920's Britain urged France to reduce her army reserves as a first step for disarmament. The French at the same time proposed a reduction of British naval reserves as a better contribution to disarmament. The United States at the same time favored the reduction of military reserves, in which it was rather low, but objected to any reduction of military budgets.[8] In a similar vein, after the Second World War, when the United States was the sole possessor of the A-bomb, the Soviet Union instigated the "Stockholm Peace Pledge" calling for the elimination of atomic weapons from the arsenals of "all states."

Disarmament plans have failed to gain acceptance for other reasons as well. Sincerely motivated negotiations on disarmament have been shipwrecked on the rocky shoals of the conundrum: Does disarmament create security or is security a precondition for disarmament? Since 1919 advocates for both points of view have been unable to agree as to what comes first. In the 1920's and 1930's France counseled security first. Since the end of the Second World War the Western democracies have insisted on security against aggression before they disarm. States insisting on security as a precondition for disarmament propose arms control schemes based upon inspection, verification, and safeguards against surprise attack. Other powers, such as Russia, say that disarmament itself is synonymous with security.

Disarmament agreements involve technical as well as political problems. Even when states negotiating disarmament sincerely seek

[8] Geneva Institute of International Relations, *Problems of the Peace,* 3rd ed. (London: Oxford University Press, 1929), pp. 59–60.

to reduce and control arms, the tasks of securing solid evidence that the treaties are being kept are so complex that agreement on the technical particulars of enforcing an armament agreement presents a major, although not an insurmountable, difficulty.

States will not agree to disarm unilaterally. Disarmament must be universal. Leaders assume that just as arms races may provide breakthroughs that could unbalance a military standoff, so could unwise disarmament that is not phased and verified result in one side gaining and exploiting an advantage.

Disarmament requires agreement on ends and the means to achieve them. There is substantial doubt that general and complete disarmament is an attainable goal. In a sense we have "bitten of the apple." Were it possible to agree on and verify the total elimination of arms, armies, and military budgets, the knowledge of how to manufacture arms would remain. For this reason Kennedy's disarmament plan called for an international police force that could negate the effectiveness of a secretly created military force. Police power would necessarily become the monopoly of an international agency.[9]

In the 1960's the arms race continued. It must be stopped and the trend reversed. This calls for agreements on force levels (number of men under arms) and limitations on arms production and military expenditures. New technological breakthroughs must be eschewed by agreement to end the testing of nuclear devices underground. An understanding to prevent addition of new states to the "nuclear club" is probably essential. For all of this, unverified promises are insufficient to induce agreement. A system is needed for the control of arms that would allow a balanced reduction of arms, verify performance on agreements, and provide continuing control over the agreements in force. Until disarmament is effected, states need protection against surprise attack. This demands a method of surveillance over the movements of forces.

The catalogue of the above requirements shows that agreement

[9] In a lecture delivered at the Geneva Institute of International Relations in August, 1928, Salvador de Madariaga, former Chief of the Disarmament Section of the League of Nations Secretariat, made the insightful observation "that *in the absence of an organized world-community all disarmament conferences are armament conferences...*" (de Madariaga's italics), *ibid.*, p. 58.

on disarmament is one of the most difficult goals to attain. The terrors of nuclear war may provide an impetus equal to the difficulty, and states may yet achieve the agreements so avidly sought. At any rate, few states have been willing to give up this quest.

PEACEFUL CHANGE

Status-quo states are far more ready to accept normative regulation of their actions than are revisionist states. Norms operate in favor of maintaining the *status quo*. Because things change, situations may arise that prove unjust to some states. International peace requires some method for peaceful change of the *status quo*. Colonies seek their independence. States becoming industrialized seek new economic opportunity. States growing in power wish to have their power recognized in the councils of the world, especially in the elected councils of the United Nations. If states cannot peacefully secure redress of their grievances, the temptation to use force increases. Peaceful change cannot simply be left to common sense or goodwill. The United Nations is the logical body to decide upon alteration of the *status quo* based upon criteria of what is right and just.[10]

SECURITY THROUGH ASSOCIATION

Most states have rejected as neither possible nor desirable the policy of "going it alone." States have recognized that international normative limitations are inadequately developed and provide poor assurances for their security. As a result, they often combine with other states for their mutual advantage. Alliances are ancient devices of diplomacy. Two types of alliances have been utilized: the balance-of-power alliance and the mutual-assistance (or mutual-security) alliance. After the First World War a new associational technique for the preservation of peace and security was devised, that is, collective security.

[10] The League's Assembly was given the authority to "advise the reconsideration by Members of the League of treaties which have become inapplicable..." in Article 19 of the Covenant. The General Assembly is given similar authority in Article 14 of the Charter. It "may recommend measures for the peaceful adjustment of any situation, regardless of origin, which is deemed likely to impair the general welfare or friendly relations among nations..."

THE BALANCE-OF-POWER ALLIANCE [11]

The balance-of-power alliance comes into being when countries believe that they are endangered by the rise of any state to a position of preponderant power. In this view the world is seen not as a world of "good" states and "bad" states, *status quo* or revisionist, but a world in which all states will seek their advantage through expansion and aggression if this is possible. The danger to international peace and to their own security stems from the growth in power of any state. If state A grows strong then states B, C, D, and E are all threatened by this strength. Under these circumstances it seems no more than logical that states B, C, D, and E combine into an alliance to equal the strength of state A. Over a period of years another state, perhaps one in the alliance, say state B, will grow in power and its increasing strength is deemed to be a danger to the security not only of state A but even to its allies. Under these circumstances, state E may rationally detach itself from the alliance with B, C, and D and join with state A, creating a new international equilibrium, E plus A against B, C, and D. The existence of an equilibrium produces a situation in which no state can be sure that it may use force successfully; therefore, it does not threaten the existence or the territorial integrity of anyone.

During the eighteenth and nineteenth centuries the balance of power was believed to be the mechanism that prevented major wars in Europe. Napoleonic France disturbed the balance and touched off a series of wars. With the Congress of Vienna in 1815 the balance-of-power system was reestablished; and this mechanism, it is generally agreed, prevented large-scale war until 1914. In the nine-

[11] Despite the ambiguities that generally abound in the use of this term, and despite a serious question about its applicability, statesmen claim to have pursued a balance-of-power policy. The term is used here to mean equilibrium. To the degree that this term explains what statesmen believe the situation to have been or to the extent that this concept explains what statesmen believe they were doing, balance of power is a useful concept that needs to be explained. An extensive discussion of the meanings and validity of this concept is to be found in an article by Ernest B. Haas, "The Balance of Power: Prescription, Concept or Propaganda?" *World Politics,* July, 1953, Vol. 5, pp. 442–477, and more recently in Inis L. Claude, Jr., *Power and International Relations* (New York: Random House, 1962), Chs. 2 and 3.

teenth century Britain became the protagonist for peace through the balance of power. Great Britain's security was tied to preventing the rise of a dominating power on the continent of Europe, and Britain took responsibility for the maintenance of the balance of power to guarantee her own security as well as the security of other states. To this end Britain played the role of "holder of the balance." Britain did not ask who were the good states or who were the bad states. She simply asked, Given the existence of competing alliances on the European Continent, which is the weaker? She then joined the weaker side.[12]

Balance-of-power alliances make sense only if two underlying assumptions are accepted as valid. First, a state will not wage war if it is not reasonably sure of winning. Consequently, a rational state will not wage war against too formidable a counter alliance. Second, excessive power in the hands of any state is a danger to all other states. The latter assumption is questionable. It is belied by the conditions of our own time. At the end of the Second World War the United States was by far the most powerful country in the world. Its power was sufficient to spread its domain all over the world. It did not choose to do so. The United States has for a hundred years been able to dominate, far more than it has ever tried, the countries of Latin America. It has been satisfied with a position of leadership rather than outright possession of the Western Hemisphere as a matter of choice and not out of fear of any counterforce against it. Great powers may be satisfied with the *status quo* and pursue policies of peace even where they could use force successfully in quest of greater empire. Countervailing balance alliances against them are superfluous.

[12] Memorandum by Sir Eyre Crowe on the present state of British relations with France and Germany, January 1, 1907, *British Documents on the Origins of the War 1898–1914,* ed. by G. P. Gooch and H. Temperley (London: Coven His Majesty's Stationery Office, 1928), Vol. III, pp. 402–407, 414–420. Crowe says in part, "it has become an almost historical truism to identify England's secular policy with the maintenance of this balance by throwing her weight now in this scale and now in that, but ever on the side opposed to the political dictatorship of the strongest single State or group at a given time." See also Winston Churchill's address to the Conservative Members Committee on Foreign Affairs in March, 1936, quoted in his volume, *The Second World War: The Gathering Storm* (Boston: Houghton Mifflin, 1948), pp. 207–208.

THE MUTUAL-ASSISTANCE ALLIANCE

The mutual-assistance alliance is an agreement for common defense against an identifiable aggressor, not some vague, impersonal aggressor that might arise in the future. NATO, SEATO, and CENTO are mutual-assistance alliances of *status-quo* states. They are directed against the Communist powers, which are presumed to be expansionist and revisionist. These alliances are based upon the principle that all members must come to the defense of any of their number that have been attacked. The purpose of establishing NATO, CENTO, and SEATO has been the defense of the member states of these alliances against *Communist* aggression.

Mutual-assistance alliances are also possible among revisionist powers. The Axis coalition in the Second World War was such an alliance. Axis states did assist one another in their programs of aggression. Parts of the world were divided among them as areas for their exclusive exploitation.

When a mutual-security alliance is established by revisionist states for the purposes of furthering their expansionist aims, the quest for power is unlimited. The more power, the better their goals can be achieved. An alliance of *status-quo* states does observe a measure of economy in the development of their power. They appear to seek little more than a modest preponderance of power. They need only power sufficient to prevent aggression from the revisionist source. Additional power, the accumulation of power in a military sense, without reference to the amount necessary to cope with the threat they face would be useless and a waste of resources. Because they are *status-quo* states they would not use their margin of preponderance for aggression and therefore have no need for it. In this sense the mutual-security alliance of *status-quo* states seeks a margin of safety rather than either a balance of power or unlimited power.

COLLECTIVE SECURITY

At the end of the First World War the existence of competing alliances was believed to be one of the causes for war. Woodrow Wilson, a most important architect of the postwar peace, wanted no more alliances, especially those designed to maintain a balance of power. In place of alliances and the competition among alliances, Wilson proposed peace based upon collective security. By collective security he meant that all states should unite against any aggressor; all for one and one for all. As an ideal system collective security would take place when all states would come to the defense of the victim of aggression. The identity of the aggressor and aggressed was to be secondary and even immaterial. One need only establish that state A had committed aggression against state B and all states would then come to the defense of state B against state A.

Collective security was never conceived of as a self-operating system. It could only be made to work through an international institution like the League of Nations or the United Nations.

The League of Nations was the first collective-security organization. The heart of its collective-security action was to be found in Article 16 of the Covenant, which provided for economic and financial sanctions against any aggressor nation. In theory the effectiveness of economic and financial sanctions seemed incontrovertible. The trouble was that these sanctions were never effectively applied. When the United States failed to join the League of Nations, the British began to have second thoughts about the League as a collective-security agency. They were instrumental in watering down what appeared as a clear requirement of Article 16, that sanctions against an aggressor nation be automatically applied. Article 16 was reinterpreted so that sanctions were limited and qualified instead. Then, when the League had to act against aggression, it did so haltingly and with no effect, for example, as in the case of Manchuria and North China. In the war between Italy and Ethiopia, it finally did agree to impose some economic sanctions upon Italy, but these were inadequate and were not continued long enough to make them effective.

The United Nations was also to be a collective-security organization and was to undertake collective-security action against any aggressor. It was expected that, by and large, member states would obey their pledge to the Charter to "refrain in their international relations from the threat of use of force . . ." [13] Consequently, it was originally presumed that collective-security action would most likely be used against the former Axis states outside of the UN.

In theory, the United Nations was to defend against aggression undertaken by any state. And again, in theory, collective security was to be the last recourse of the Security Council for maintaining

[13] United Nations Charter, Article 2, Paragraph 4.

peace and security. It would not matter which state was the aggressor or which state was aggressed. If, for instance, Bulgaria attacked Greece, all states, including Bulgaria's ally the Soviet Union, would come to Greece's defense. Alternatively, should Greek aggression against Bulgaria be the occasion for collective-security action, all of the members of NATO would line up in support of Bulgaria against Greek aggression.

Some have argued that collective security seen in these terms neither exists nor possibly could exist. However, one could imagine a situation where a large number of those states that are not already allied with one another would come to the defense of any victim of aggression. Such an action would not be that of a mutual-assistance alliance and would be an act of collective security. When most states join against aggressors the purposes of collective security are adequately fulfilled. Collective security serves its purpose when it brings into being so formidable a coalition of states that no aggressor can successfully withstand this aggregate of power, and the aggressor state, having foreknowledge that it faces the retribution of the collective-security coalition, refrains from its course of action.

Collective security as well as the broader peace-serving function of the UN will be dealt with below (see Chapter 4).

THE METHODS OF INTERNATIONAL RELATIONS

States employ a number of methods in the conduct of their relations with other states. Diplomatic and consular relations account for most of the official contact between powers. War is also a means by which foreign-policy goals are attained. Over the centuries a variety of techniques have been developed for the peaceful resolution of disputes. An understanding of the purposes and uses of these methods will serve to make international diplomacy more intelligible.

DIPLOMACY AND CONSULAR REPRESENTATION

The chief means by which states conduct official relations with one another is through diplomacy; this includes official representation of states, negotiation, explanation and interpretation of policies, and the gathering of information. The diplomats who carry out these tasks may be regularly accredited from one state to another or they may be specially appointed for a single mission (plen-ipotentiary). In recent years the United States has used a roving ambassador. As official representatives all diplomats are authorized to speak for and otherwise represent their country, and are a normal channel for transmitting official messages from the host country to their state.

Most but not all negotiation is done by diplomats accredited to foreign states. Contemporary diplomacy makes use of negotiations at the level of foreign ministers and heads of state. In areas demanding special technical competence, such as in economic, cultural, or scientific matters, negotiation may be handled by specially qualified experts. Modern means of communication enable foreign ministries to instruct their diplomats continuously and in detail. Nevertheless, skill in negotiation is an important asset for a diplomat.

The style and the work of diplomats has undergone great change since the end of the First World War. That war served to discredit the virtue and the moral stature of the older style in diplomacy which was marked by quiet, behind-the-scenes negotiation and by responsibility only to the chief of state. That diplomacy was a continuation of the diplomatic tradition of aristocratic times. Even though we no longer condemn, out of hand, as venal and evil the diplomatic style of the eighteenth and nineteenth centuries, it seemed in 1918 that traditional diplomatic methods were themselves a contributing factor to the outbreak of war. Whether or not that style of diplomacy was to any extent responsible for war in 1914, the older diplomatic method became an anachronism with the development of democratic politics and with public opinion a factor in governmental decisions. It is a fact that *the people* are a force of considerable weight in the adoption of foreign-policy positions. Consequently, the contemporary diplomatic style is marked by popular limits placed upon the decision that leaders may take. Even dictatorships, which manipulate rather than consult the people, are confined to foreign policies that do not outrage the popular will. From the point of view of the foreign diplomat, this means that he must be an effective spokesman for his land and the policies his country pursues. He must promote friendship for his country and its people, and he does this by reaching the broadest masses of the population as well as the significant elite groups of the host land. The effective diplomat seeks to make a good impression for his country and promote sympathy or at least neutralize antipathy for the policies of his state.

Successful foreign policy demands accurate estimates of the effect upon other powers of a state's moves on the "international checker-board." The reaction of the leaders of the host state to foreign-policy initiatives by the home state may, in the extreme, be the difference between peace or war. Consequently, a major function of today's diplomat must be a continuing interpretation of the attitudes and interests in the host state. The need for a scientific estimate of the strengths and weaknesses of other states leads to an impressive amount of information-gathering and data-evaluation. But among the most important items in such an evaluation should be the opinion of the accredited representatives.

Consular services are closely related to diplomatic function. The use of consuls actually predates the exchange of diplomats.[14] Precise division of activity distinguishing diplomats from consuls cannot be drawn. Nevertheless, the province of consular activity pertains to business interests of the home state and also the protection of its nationals. Consuls collect information useful for businessmen back home and advise on matters related to the conduct of business in the area in which they are located. An important function of the consul is that of assistance to his nationals. Consuls are expected to help their nationals secure proper treatment and justice in foreign courts. Consuls grant visas, verify legal documents, care for property of deceased nationals, and may assist in the enforcement of their country's customs regulations. Many states separate their diplomatic from their consular services. Some, like the United States and Great Britain, have integrated their diplomatic and consular services. Under such circumstances consuls often move up into diplomatic posts.

States often exchange several consuls with one another. Larger cities may have a consul-general in residence whereas smaller cities will have offices directed by consuls or, in some instances, vice-consuls. On occasion, where a number of consulates are established within a state, a supervisory and coordinating post of consul-general-at-large is set up.[15]

---

[14] Elmer Plischke, *Conduct of American Diplomacy*, 2nd ed. (Princeton, N.J.: Van Nostrand, 1961), p. 11.
[15] M. Margaret Ball and Hugh B. Killough, *International Relations* (New York: Ronald Press, 1956), pp. 140–148.

WAR

The desire for peace and the widely held view that war today is suicidal is no adequate assurance that peace will be preserved. War may break out. The threat of war is not simply a threat that some accident may lead to war. Clausewitz's well-known aphorism, "War is nothing but the continuation of political relations by other means," [16] points up the conscious use of war as a device for achieving foreign-policy goals. Clausewitz no more than pointed out the record of history, that is, statesmen may seek to attain goals through persuasion, through the offer of rewards, through threats, and even occasionally through the use of bribes, but when other techniques fail they may decide to use force. War may rationally be considered as a means of fulfilling ends. This has been the practice. At best, one may hope that statesmen will make war only when these goals are vitally important and only when force is the only means that can succeed. Nevertheless, the vague hope that, because hostilities have within them the potentialities of becoming a thermonuclear war, states will refrain from fighting is belied by even the most recent history. Force has been used in the past and one can expect that, unless means are found to curb its use, it will continue to be used in the future. As recently as October, 1962, the United State was at the brink of war, and would have used force if necessary to achieve its goal of eliminating Soviet missiles from Cuba.

Since the end of the Second World War, several wars have taken place and they were not accidental. They were consciously initiated as a means of achieving aims. Happily, these wars have been of a limited character. There is no reason to believe that the use of limited war will soon end. Even in the case of thermonuclear war, Clausewitz's aphorism is still appropriate. If war should only be rationally used for important purposes, then thermonuclear war may also be justified to preserve the existence of the state. Despite those who believe "better red than dead," no people are willing to accept extinction of their country through foreign conquest. States will fight a thermonuclear war for their self-preservation. Atomic warfare may also be used by a revisionist power in pursuit of its goals when it feels that it does not face unacceptable losses through re-

[16] Carl von Clausewitz, *On War* (Washington, D.C.: Combat Forces Press, 1943), p. 16. (Published in 1831.)

taliation. A prudent view would hold that the revisionist power would strike if it had the necessary superiority in nuclear weapons. The temptation to literally, "by one press of the button," end for all time the power of the United States is a temptation the Soviet Union might not forego should such an opportunity present itself. An aggressive nuclear attack should be rated as likely should the deterrent position of the *status-quo* power lose its credibility. The horror of thermonuclear war is insufficient to exclude its use if great gain may thereby be won.

From time to time, since the end of the Second World War, the suggestion has been made that the West wage preventive war against the Communists. If preventive war was ever considered necessary or morally justifiable in the past, today it is rejected on the ground that it would lead to nuclear retaliation. Preemptive war is another strategy which has been put forward. Preemptive war assumes knowledge, beyond reasonable doubt, that a state is about to be attacked, and under these circumstances that state decides to strike first, to preempt the onset of the war.[17] The trouble with the doctrine of preemptive war is that there is no assurance that the so-called signs of attack are beyond doubt. Because nothing short of an actual attack provides adequate assurance that a decision to wage war has been made, the preemptive war, in effect, becomes a preventive war. With hardened bases there is no longer the need to preempt the action or undertake instantaneous retaliation. It is for these reasons that preemptive war has been rejected by *status-quo* states.

TECHNIQUES OF PEACEFUL SETTLEMENT OF DISPUTE

Experience has resulted in the invention of useful techniques for the pacific resolution of conflicts. These techniques are political—negotiation, good offices, mediation, enquiry, and conciliation—and legal—arbitration and adjudication.

NEGOTIATION

The simplest and most commonly used method of peaceful settlement of disputes is negotiation. Negotiation involves the use of per-

---

[17] Preemptive war differs in concept from preemptive attack. Preemptive attack assumes that once a war has begun, as a conventional or limited war, the defender may yet initiate (preempt) an attack with nuclear weapons.

suasion and bargaining to achieve desired aims. In this sense, negotiation is not coercive. Discussion held at gun point cannot be
termed negotiation without violating the commonly understood
sense of the word. Negotiation and coercion are different devices
utilized in international politics. It is also useful to distinguish between *negotiation* and *debate*. Negotiation aims at persuading the
other party to follow a given course of action as each side seeks to
influence the other. Negotiation may seek a mutually satisfactory
bargain. Debate, on the other hand, is aimed much more at the
persuasion of third parties. Debaters seek to influence public opinion, or the General Assembly, or the uncommitted states, rather
than one another. Summit conferences have been more in the nature
of debates than negotiations by heads of states. Debate is a useful
means for winning support, especially for weaker states which are
unable to use coercive means as an alternative to negotiation.[18]

Most negotiations are bilateral—between two parties. However,
in recent years multilateral negotiations, among many parties, have
become increasingly common.

Until the end of the First World War negotiations were invariably held in secret. Even the bargains reached often remained secret. When it seemed that secretiveness itself was a cause of war,
Woodrow Wilson demanded "open covenants openly arrived at," in
the optimistic belief that the spotlight of public view would keep
things honest and force negotiators to deal on the level of the people's interests and high moral principles. More recently it has been
learned that there is no special virtue in open negotiations. Indeed,
experience indicates that there is likelihood that open negotiations
will fail because they invariably become debates. Open negotiations
tend to lose their bargaining function. The public attention focused
upon the negotiator requires that he adopt high moral positions.
Compromises, therefore, appear to be unprincipled and immoral.
It is difficult for democracies to accommodate "amoral" positions
and consequently they avoid open bargaining. They can do little
more than state their position in open negotiations. If there is no
room for mutual compromise negotiations will rarely succeed. Concessions serve to make negotiators appear as winners or losers, and
no leader wants to face an electorate charged with being a loser.
With this experience in view, since a return to an older diplomacy

[18] Ernest A. Gross, *The United Nations: Structure for Peace* (New York:
Harper, 1962), pp. 65–68.

is inappropriate for popular democracy, diplomats have sought their "open covenants" through private, if not wholly secret, negotiation. An agreement that settles an issue without force is usually defensible even when it results from a number of bargains arranged in private.

GOOD OFFICES

Disputes may occasionally result in a rupture in relations between the disputing states, which makes it very difficult to get face-to-face negotiations. The device of peaceful settlement known as good offices has proved useful in such situations. Good offices allows a third party to act as a friendly "go-between." Theodore Roosevelt offered warring Japan and Russia facilities in Portsmouth, New Hampshire, in June, 1905, for the settlement of their war. The United Nations provided good offices in 1947 to bring the Indonesian nationalists in revolt and the Dutch together for negotiations. In the strict sense of the word, the concept of good offices is limited to the provision of facilities by the third party to bring disputants together.

MEDIATION

Good offices is frequently combined with mediation. Mediation is a friendly offer by a third party of proposals upon which a dispute may be settled. The offer of mediation is therefore never considered to be an attempt to give advantage to either side. The mediator sets terms that he believes to be sufficiently attractive to all sides to settle the issue in question.

ENQUIRY

Some disputes arise from disagreement over facts. In these circumstances an elucidation of the true facts could serve as a basis for ending the dispute. The Bryan treaties in 1913 provided for enquiry and investigation of disputes and for a year's "cooling-off" period.[19] Implicit in the "cooling-off" approach is the hope that after consideration without resort to hostilities some accommodation between the parties would be found, especially when all the facts are known. Even if no solutions are found, it was assumed that the people

[19] Samuel Flagg Bemis, *A Short History of American Foreign Policy and Diplomacy* (New York: Henry Holt, 1959), pp. 258–259.

would by that time become too bored with the dispute to take an interest in fighting it out.

CONCILIATION

Conciliation combines with enquiry the positive obligation of proposing terms of settlement to disputing parties. As a technique, conciliation is similar to mediation in that terms of settlement are proposed. It differs from mediation in the use of a commission of conciliation rather than a single mediator. It also differs in that enquiry is an integral part of the conciliation process. A conciliation commission is expected to promote agreement actively through urging compromise and concession and through making positive proposals of its own.

Negotiation, good offices, mediation, enquiry, and conciliation are political devices for peaceful settlement of disputes. The primary purpose is to secure settlement of the dispute. There is no requirement that any standards of justice or law be observed. As long as the necessary accommodation preventing the use of force has taken place and the dispute has been settled, then the method adopted may be deemed to have served its purpose. Arbitration and adjudication, on the other hand, are legal methods of peaceful settlement. Settlements reached through these techniques are based upon legal criteria and only agreements or decisions that are in accord with international law are intended.

ARBITRATION

During the nineteenth century a number of disputes were settled through an arbitral process.[20] Arbitration requires prior agreement on three matters before the process may begin. First is a panel of arbitrators. Generally an odd number of arbitrators—three or five are most common—are selected. To facilitate a choice of arbitrators, the First Hague Conference of 1899 established the Permanent Court of Arbitration. This Court is simply a panel of arbitrators compiled by having each member of the Court submit four names, two of whom are their nationals. These persons are then available

[20] Norman D. Palmer and Howard C. Perkins, *International Relations, The World Community in Transition,* 2nd ed. (Boston: Houghton Mifflin, 1957), pp. 291–293.

for arbitration duties whenever disputing states want to use the arbitral process. Second, states seeking arbitration must also agree on the terms of the dispute to be submitted to arbitration. Third, the laws that are to be applied in the arbitration must also be accepted beforehand. Hence arbitration requires prior agreement on a panel of arbitrators, the matter to be arbitrated, and the laws to be applied. Arbitration lacks the consistency that is built up by courts of law in adjudication. It is circumscribed by allowing the use of only such rules and laws as have been agreed to. Should an arbitral tribunal go beyond its terms of reference its award may then be refused.[21]

ADJUDICATION

The ordinary use of law through trial in court is called adjudication. Here judges make decisions based on the law they hold to be applicable. Decisions tend to establish precedents that are subsequently applied and make for continuity in decisions reached. The establishment of the Permanent Court of International Justice in 1922 led to a decreasing use of arbitration and an increasing use of adjudication. (The nature of the International Court of Justice of the United Nations will be discussed in Chapter 4.)[22] Not only does the International Court of Justice have the choice of law to apply in each case, but it also may reach decisions on the basis of *ex aequo et bono*—what is equitable and just—if the parties before it are willing.

THE INSTRUMENTS OF INTERNATIONAL RELATIONS

A variety of terms have been used to denote types of international agreements. The use of these terms is often imprecise, but an attempt should be made to explain them. The most commonly used term for an international agreement is *treaty*. The term treaty has two meanings. In the generic sense it means any international agreement. It may also refer to a specific type of instrument signed and ratified

---

[21] J. L. Brierly, *The Law of Nations*, 5th ed. (London: Oxford at Clarendon Press, 1955), pp. 274–292.

[22] For the role of the Court in relation to international law see pp. 67–69 above.

by two or more states. In the latter case, it implies important subject matter and spells out an agreement of high policy. Closely related in meaning to treaty is the international *convention*. Conventions differ from treaties in that they are always multilateral while treaties may be bilateral or multilateral, and conventions tend to treat non-political matters while treaties are more often political. Specialized agencies establish standards through the use of conventions. In the case of the International Labor Organization, its member states are required to consider, for the purposes of ratification, all conventions adopted by that body.[23] The World Health Organization is authorized, under its constitution, to adopt conventions that its member states are obligated to accept unless the state furnishes a statement declaring its nonacceptance and giving the reasons for its negative action.[24]

Conventions are typical instruments of international organizations. Other devices commonly used by international bodies are *recommendations* and *resolutions*. A recommendation is similar to a convention in subject matter. It is distinguished from the convention only in that it is considered to carry less weight. Thus the UNESCO Constitution requires a two-thirds majority for the adoption of conventions while recommendations may be approved by a simple majority.[25] The International Labor Organization distinguishes between conventions and recommendations by requiring that all members must consider for ratification only conventions adopted by the organization. However, member states may, but are not obligated to, consider recommendations of the organization.[26] Resolutions are devices for recording views, intentions, or desired action on the part of an international body. They usually follow the form of a statement giving the reasons for the view, intention, or the action proposed (the "whereas") and then a statement setting out the action proposed (the "therefore be it resolved").

Other instruments commonly used in international relations are pacts, acts, declarations, agreements, protocols, notes, memoranda, *proces verbal,* summary reports, and *modus vivendi*. A *pact* is synonymous with a treaty. NATO's constitutional document has been

[23] Constitution, Article 19, Paragraph 5.
[24] Constitution, Article 20.
[25] Constitution, Article 4, Paragraph B, 4.
[26] I.L.O. Constitution, Article 19, Paragraphs 5 and 6.

called both the North Atlantic Pact and the North Atlantic Treaty. An *act* is more often looked upon as an instrument of a law-creating nature.[27] *Declarations* are usually statements of agreement by conferring parties with regard to the policy they propose to pursue, or the conduct they intend to follow, or of an understanding that they have reached. An *agreement* is an instrument that may be used to denote any type of concurrence of policy or understanding between the signatory parties. *Protocols* have occasionally been meant as synonyms for minutes of a meeting. More often they are defined as "a somewhat informal record of an agreement between the High Contracting Parties."[28] However, the phrase "diplomatic protocol" is used to mean diplomatic etiquette. Diplomatic communications are called *notes*. A statement of views on a matter by a state is usually given as a *memorandum*. Longer statements comprehensively covering the development of relations between two states but issued by one of them as an explanation and exposition of its policy are denoted as *papers*. Papers are named according to color, most often white, and contain documents relevant to the relations discussed, that is, the "White Paper" on the *United States Relations with China*.

International meetings make use of *proces verbal* and summary reports. In United Nations' usage *proces verbal* are detailed, usually verbatim, minutes of meetings. *Summary reports* consist of records of the significant business of the meetings. *Modus vivendi* are preliminary arrangements agreed to for dealing with a dispute.

The complexity and imprecision of terminology related to international instruments must be borne in mind. The context in which the term is used is often essential to an understanding of the meaning intended. That a distinction between these various instruments is intended is beyond dispute. Thus the final act of the First Hague Conference of 1899 included three conventions, three declarations, one resolution, and six *voeux* (wishes). Other conferences have also issued a variety of treaties, resolutions, recommendations, agreements, declarations, and acts.[29] Such distinctions of the instruments that have been utilized would not have been made if they had not been intended.

[27] Plischke, *op. cit.,* p. 375.
[28] Sir Ernest Satow, *Guide to Diplomatic Practice,* Vol. II (London: Longmans, Green & Co., 1917), p. 174.
[29] Norman L. Hill, *The Public International Conference. Its Function, Organization and Procedure* (Palo Alto, Calif.: Stanford University Press, 1929), pp. 77–84.

SUMMARY

We have seen that the contemporary world is marked by an interdependence of states. Because no state can "go it alone" it enters into relations with other states. In doing so states pursue one or more of the following aims.

(1) They may try to avoid the major confrontation between East and West and, when they do, they adopt neutralism as a definitive characteristic of their foreign policy.

(2) They may promote the normative regulation of the behavior of states and seek an end to international anarchy. In respect to this interest states will further the work of the General Assembly's International Law Commission and support the function of the International Court of Justice. These states are likely to accept the optional clause. They are also likely to advocate peaceful change of existing treaties that have become unfair. Other areas of normative regulation, the development of international morals and ethical standards, will also win their support. Many states are interested in disarmament as a means of preserving peace. States occasionally are tempted to use disarmament as a means of gaining military advantage. Few disarmament agreements have been approved. An important reason for the lack of progress in this field is that most states want assurances of security before they disarm.

(3) States may seek their safety through alliances. During some periods of history balance-of-power alliances were created to produce an equilibrium of power. Since the Second World War the West has organized mutual-security alliances aimed at curbing the Soviet Union.

(4) States may try collective security as a means for ensuring peace through preponderant strength against aggression. The United Nations was designed to deal with aggression by collective security.

(5) The universal desire for peace does not preclude the possibility that states may go to war. Throughout history war has been a device for achieving goals. It may be used by a revisionist state that believes that its own losses in a conflict would be within acceptable proportions.

The development of international relations has called forth an articulation of means for settling disputes in a peaceful manner. It has also brought about a measure of consensus on legal instruments which facilitate the conduct of relations among states.

CHAPTER 4

Institutionalizing International Relations—
The United Nations and the
Specialized Agencies

MAN's desire for peace, security, prosperity, and friendly relations
has led to proposals for international organization. Over the centuries plans for peace and security through international organization were put forward by thinkers such as Emmanuel Kant, William
Penn, Emeric Cruce, and the Duc de Sully. However, it was only in
1919 with the creation of the League of Nations that an international
organization for comprehensive purposes was established. The United
Nations is the successor to the League. It has been set up to help
states cooperate on many things but especially for the preservation
of international peace and security.

The United Nations came into being on October 24, 1945. On
that day the requisite number of ratifications of the Charter were
deposited.[1] It now has its main headquarters in New York City. The
name United Nations was first used, however, for an alliance of
twenty-six states fighting the Axis powers in the Second World War.
This alliance was formally established on January 1, 1942, in Washington, D.C. There the participating states pledged (1) to make no
separate peace with the Axis powers and (2) to accept the Atlantic
Charter, written by Churchill and Roosevelt in August, 1941, as a
statement of their war aims.

United Nations is, therefore, a name given to two different agencies, the present United Nations Organization and the wartime alli-

[1] See the United Nations Charter, Article 110.

ance. Sometimes the term United Nations is given a broader connotation and is meant to denote a *system* of cooperating international organizations pursuing complementary purposes, each composed of member states. As such the system brings together the
United Nations Organization and thirteen specialized agencies.[2]

Each specialized agency is a separate international organization.
It has its own constitution, budget, and a membership that is not
identical with any of the others or with that of the United Nations.
Ireland is not a member of UNESCO; Monaco is a member of
UNESCO and the Universal Postal Union but not a member of the
UN; the USSR has not joined the International Bank for Recon-
struction and Development or the International Monetary Fund.
Each agency has its own headquarters: UNESCO is located in Paris;
The Food and Agricultural Organization in Rome; the International
Civil Aviation Organization is headquartered in Montreal; the
World Health Organization is located in Geneva, etc. The purposes
served by the specialized agencies are functional and technical. The
ILO is interested in the problems of labor; the World Health Or-
ganization, the problems of health; the Universal Postal Union, in
the transportation of postal items across national boundaries.

One of the reasons for the separation of specialized agencies from
the United Nations was to give undivided attention to the functional
area of concern. In addition, some believed that because the specialized agencies were technical and nonpolitical the representatives of
states working in these agencies would be technical experts rather
than political leaders. The fact that these experts talk the same
language would lead to easier cooperation, seldom present in the
political arena.

Because specialized agencies had as their primary purpose functional improvements their worth was to be measured in terms of the
advances made in their areas of interest. International peace was at
best to be a by-product of the work of the agencies. Many thought

[2] The agencies are the following: International Labor Organization;
Food and Agricultural Organization; United Nations Educational, Scientific and Cultural Organization; World Health Organization; International Monetary Fund; International Bank for Reconstruction and
Development; International Finance Corporation; International Development Association; International Civil Aviation Organization; Universal
Postal Union; International Telecommunication Union; World Meteorological Organization; Intergovernmental Maritime Consultative Organization.

that if states could learn to cooperate on technical matters—on health, on food, or on maritime problems—they would through this process also learn to cooperate in their political relations. That the activities of the specialized agencies did not enhance cooperation in the United Nations is already evident. The political disputes of the United Nations have affected negatively the dialogue within the agencies, also making them arenas for acrimonious debate.

The United Nations Organization rather than the United Nations system is the primary concern of this chapter.

PURPOSES OF THE UNITED NATIONS

The success of the United Nations Organization is entirely based on its success in maintaining peace and security although the organization has entered into other kinds of activities. Even if the UN should through its Trusteeship Council provide for the rapid and orderly independence of all of the trust territories, even if the organization should through its Economic and Social Council upgrade the standards of women and make easier the development of underdeveloped economies, the organization will have failed if large-scale war erupts. Alternatively, if the organization can maintain peace and security, failures in economic, social, humanitarian, or decolonizing activity will not have seriously reduced the value of the organization.

Economic, social, and colonial functions for the organization came rather late in the planning of the UN. The creation of a Trusteeship Council and the granting to the General Assembly of a competence in dealing with territories that were not self-governing was not written into the original proposals of the Charter submitted at San Francisco. The purposes of the UN Charter worked out at Dumbarton Oaks by the United States, Britain, and the USSR in 1944 called for the creation of an organization limited in its function primarily to the insurance of peace and security. The later additions to the Charter of economic, social, and colonial obligations was predicated on a presumed relationship between such subject matter and the maintenance of peace. In this view a stable peace depended on states enjoying a healthy economy and good social relationships both internally and with other states. The Atlantic Charter stated that economic inequities were a primary cause of war. It was also generally held that hostility between states based upon religious, national, and racial differences was a potential cause of war. Consequently, economic and social activities were considered a necessary contribution to international peace because they would eliminate causes of war. Alternatively, eliminating such causes of war and exploiting potentialities for cooperation in these areas would serve to make this a better world, in which peace is assured.

The interest of the organization in colonial matters may also be explained in terms of its peace and security purposes. The existence of colonies provides a twofold cause for international conflict. First, colonies may lead to competition among imperialist powers. Imperialist war, war for the redivision of colonies among imperialist powers, is a danger to world peace; consequently, the UN must deal with this matter and have the competence to inhibit imperialist war. Second, the general expectation that peoples living in colonies want independence leads to the fear of revolutionary war. Wars of national liberation can have international ramifications. They may lead to a wider involvement, that is, to world wars. The United Nations, therefore, must provide a process by which colonies can achieve their independence without recourse to war.

The UN was thus established primarily for peace and security purposes, but with economic, social, humanitarian, and colonial functions conceived as contributory to the main purposes of the organization.

UNITED NATIONS STRUCTURE

The United Nations operates through six principal organs: the General Assembly, the Security Council, the International Court of Justice, the Economic and Social Council, the Trusteeship Council, and the Secretariat. Each organ has an assigned role to play in the overall design; each of these organs has its own structure and methods of operation.

THE GENERAL ASSEMBLY

The General Assembly is the only organ of the UN in which the entire membership is represented. This alone gives it great importance and makes the General Assembly the proper body to elect non-permanent members of the Security and Trusteeship Councils, to

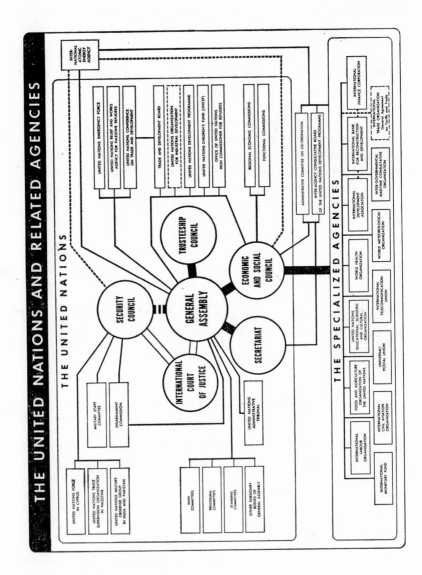

THE UNITED NATIONS AND RELATED AGENCIES

THE UNITED NATIONS

INTER-NATIONAL ATOMIC ENERGY AGENCY

UNITED NATIONS EMERGENCY FORCE
UNITED NATIONS RELIEF AND WORKS AGENCY FOR PALESTINE REFUGEES
UNITED NATIONS CONFERENCE ON TRADE AND DEVELOPMENT
TRADE AND DEVELOPMENT BOARD
UNITED NATIONS ORGANIZATION FOR INDUSTRIAL DEVELOPMENT
UNITED NATIONS DEVELOPMENT PROGRAMME
UNITED NATIONS CHILDREN'S FUND (UNICEF)
OFFICE OF UNITED NATIONS HIGH COMMISSIONER FOR REFUGEES
REGIONAL ECONOMIC COMMISSIONS
FUNCTIONAL COMMISSIONS

ADMINISTRATIVE COMMITTEE ON CO-ORDINATION
INTER-AGENCY CONSULTATIVE BOARD OF THE UNITED NATIONS DEVELOPMENT PROGRAMME

SECURITY COUNCIL

TRUSTEESHIP COUNCIL

GENERAL ASSEMBLY

ECONOMIC AND SOCIAL COUNCIL

INTERNATIONAL COURT OF JUSTICE

SECRETARIAT

MILITARY STAFF COMMITTEE
DISARMAMENT COMMISSION

UNITED NATIONS FORCE IN CYPRUS
UNITED NATIONS TRUCE SUPERVISION ORGANISATION IN PALESTINE
UNITED NATIONS MILITARY OBSERVER GROUP IN INDIA AND PAKISTAN

MAIN COMMITTEES
PROCEDURAL COMMITTEES
STANDING COMMITTEES
OTHER SUBSIDIARY BODIES OF GENERAL ASSEMBLY

UNITED NATIONS ADMINISTRATIVE TRIBUNAL

THE SPECIALIZED AGENCIES

INTERNATIONAL MONETARY FUND
INTERNATIONAL CIVIL AVIATION ORGANIZATION
INTERNATIONAL LABOUR ORGANISATION
FOOD AND AGRICULTURE ORGANIZATION OF THE UNITED NATIONS
UNIVERSAL POSTAL UNION
UNITED NATIONS EDUCATIONAL, SCIENTIFIC AND CULTURAL ORGANIZATION
INTERNATIONAL TELECOMMUNICATION UNION
WORLD HEALTH ORGANIZATION
WORLD METEOROLOGICAL ORGANIZATION
INTERNATIONAL DEVELOPMENT ASSOCIATION
INTER-GOVERNMENTAL MARITIME CONSULTATIVE ORGANIZATION
INTERNATIONAL BANK FOR RECONSTRUCTION AND DEVELOPMENT
INTERNATIONAL TRADE ORGANIZATION General Agreement on Tariffs and Trade
INTERNATIONAL FINANCE CORPORATION

94

elect the membership of the Economic and Social Council, and to participate in the election of the justices of the International Court of Justice and the election of high Secretariat officials. It also makes this the logical organ to receive reports on the work of all other UN organs and supervise their activities and to adopt the organization's budget and establish the annual contributions needed from member states to meet the expenses of the organization.

Each state has one vote in the General Assembly. A member may send a delegation of five plus five alternates and as many advisers as it chooses to represent the state in the meetings of the General Assembly and its committees. The General Assembly meets annually. It usually begins its session in mid-September and continues through mid-December. In several instances sessions of the General Assembly have begun later in the year or have been adjourned and reconvened. The General Assembly has on occasion and may at any time be called into special session.[3]

The General Assembly may deal with any of the subjects included in the United Nations Charter. Its range of interests is as broad as the Charter itself. Dealing with matters means, in essence, the right to consider, to discuss, and to make recommendations. The only proscription placed on General Assembly recommendations is that they may not deal with matters that are under consideration in the Security Council.

The General Assembly operates through seven main Committees, each specializing in a particular area of interest. Committee One and a special committee deal with political and security matters. Because of the volume of political questions placed on the agenda of the General Assembly it has been necessary to divide the items considered between these two committees. Committee Two is concerned with economic and financial matters. Committee Three deals with social, humanitarian, and cultural agenda items. Committee Four is concerned with non-self-governing territories. Committee Five has as its area of competence administrative and budgetary matters. Committee Six deals with legal questions. At each regular session of the General Assembly, a president and thirteen vice-presidents are elected. They together with the chairmen of main Committees make

[3] Special sessions have been convened to deal with such issues as the Palestine Mandate, the Hungarian revolt, the Sinai War, the Tunisian crisis of 1961, and South West Africa.

up a general committee that proposes an agenda and steers the progress of the session from beginning to end.

Meetings of the General Assembly are devoted to a consideration of all questions that have been placed on the agenda. Each main Committee deals with agenda items in its area of jurisdiction by considering resolutions submitted by member states. Every member state may be represented on each of the main Committees. During the summer prior to the annual meeting of the General Assembly, the Secretary-General of the United Nations presents his annual report, which contains a statement by the Secretary-General concerning the significant international developments of the preceding year and proposals for a United Nation's role in these developments. In addition, the annual report also provides a comprehensive survey of the work of the organization. With the convocation of the meeting of the General Assembly, a General Debate on the Secretary-General's report takes place. Each state is provided an opportunity to make comments. In practice the General Debate has evolved as a series of policy statements by the leader of each delegation, in which he discusses his state's views on questions it considers to be of great importance.

Two types of votes are used for the adoption of motions and resolutions. Ordinary questions are passed by a majority of states present and voting, but important questions must secure a two-thirds majority.

The importance of the General Assembly derives from its composition—all member states—and from its scope of action—all subjects dealt with in the Charter. In addition, the General Assembly has gained in importance because its resolutions are not subject to veto. As action by the Security Council became unlikely because of the Soviet's practice of vetoing action it did not like, a tendency to bring matters immediately to the General Assembly and thus circumvent the veto became prevalent.

THE SECURITY COUNCIL

The Security Council has primary responsibility for peace and security. It is not concerned with any other function. The Charter denotes five states, China, France, Great Britain, the Union of Soviet Socialist Republics, and the United States, as permanent members of the Security Council. They are also given the power to veto substantive decisions of the Security Council. In addition to the five permanent members, the General Assembly elected six nonpermanent members, making the Security Council a body of eleven. On August 31, 1965, the Charter was amended to provide for a membership of fifteen, ten elected, with five elected each year for a two-year term.

The Charter provides, in Article 23, that nonpermanent members of the Security Council should be elected by the General Assembly on the basis of two criteria: first, "due regard being specially paid ... to the contribution of members of the United Nations to the maintenance of international peace and security and to the other purposes of the Organization ..."; second, such election should also be based upon "equitable geographic distribution." The second of these criteria has not been harmoniously satisfied. Nonpermanent memberships had been allotted among Latin American states (two seats) and Middle Eastern, West European, Commonwealth, and East European countries (one seat each). The East European seat has been a source of cold-war conflict. The Communist bloc objected to the election of defecting Yugoslavia to the "East European seat," in 1949. After 1949 no member of the Communist bloc was elected until 1959, when Poland and Turkey agreed to share, on a one-year basis, the seat for 1960 and 1961. During this time on occasion even the claim of an "East European seat" was denied.[4] Again, during the sixteenth session of the General Assembly, Rumania was elected to the Security Council with the understanding that she would resign on December 31, 1962, and the remainder of the term would be fulfilled by the Philippines.[5]

The increased African membership in the organization led to pressure for an amendment to expand the membership of the Security Council. For several years Moscow rejected a larger Security Council and held out for the redistribution of the West European and one Latin American seat to the Afro-Asian states. Russia threatened to veto enlargement of the Security Council unless Peking was given the China seat. When Peking disavowed Russia's stand in this matter, Soviet objections fell away and the Charter was subsequently amended. The new arrangement assigns nonpermanent seats on the

[4] The Philippines and Japan have held this seat.
[5] *International Organization,* Vol. XVI, No. 1, Winter, 1962, p. 57 and p. 61, note 3.

following basis: Africa and Asia, five; Western Europe, Canada, Oceana, two; Eastern Europe, one; Latin America, two.

The larger nonpermanent states have been elected and reelected to the Security Council. States of moderate power are infrequently elected to membership. Small states are either never or rarely elected to sit in that council.[6]

The peace and security function of the Security Council has led it to undertake activities in three broad areas: the promotion of pacific settlement of disputes; the enforcement of peace where peaceful resolution of disputes appeared to be of no avail; and in conjunction with the General Assembly control of arms.

Chapter VI of the Charter (Articles 33–38) sets out the techniques for peaceful settlement of disputes that the Security Council may employ. The Security Council may, under Article 33, call on disputing parties to negotiate. It may also propose methods by which the disputes between states may be settled, and, if it chooses, it may also propose terms upon which a dispute may be brought to an end. Whenever the Security Council is engaged in the pacific settlement of disputes its resolutions are considered recommendations. There is no legal requirement that states obey these recommendations. The moral stature of the recommendation and the authority of the United Nations and its Charter stand behind such proposals. One exception to the normal voting procedures of this organ is observed when peaceful settlement of a dispute is under consideration, namely, a state that is a party to the dispute may not vote. This means that even a permanent member of the UN, when party to such a dispute, may neither vote nor veto.

The Security Council is the only organ of the United Nations authorized to propose action for enforcement that all member states are required to accept. As we shall see below, the General Assembly has gained significant authority to act in this area.[7] However, while the General Assembly cannot require any state to carry out its resolutions, the Charter does provide that "the members of the United Nations agree to accept and carry out the decisions of the Security Council in accordance with the present charter." [8]

[6] Thus, Belgium and Columbia have been on the Security Council three times between 1945 and 1962. On the other hand, Honduras, Libya, Paraguay, and Yemen, among others, have never served.

[7] See pp. 117–118.

[8] Charter of the United Nations, Article 25.

Chapter VII of the Charter entitled, "Action with Respect to Threats to the Peace, Breaches of the Peace, and Acts of Aggression" (Articles 39–51), details the powers of the Security Council for the purpose of enforcing peace. It may order provisional measures, such as a cease-fire, when hostilities have begun. It did this in 1948 in the Palestine War. It may call on members of the organization to employ "complete or partial interruption of economic relations and rail, sea, air, postal, telegraphic, radio, and other means of communication, and the severance of diplomatic relations." [9] Should the foregoing measures prove unavailing the Security Council may propose even more drastic action of a military nature.

The Security Council as well as the General Assembly has responsibility for the regulation of arms.[10] Pursuant to this obligation the Security Council established two commissions to deal with the disarmament question, one for conventional armaments and another dealing with atomic energy. With the decline in the activity of the Security Council during the 1950's the question of disarmament became the concern of the General Assembly, which has prodded the major military powers to proceed with the task of working out a plan for arms reduction and control. Negotiations have been primarily the responsibility of the United States and the Soviet Union. The General Assembly could do little more than urge these two powers to negotiate and make concessions to achieve agreement.

Under the Charter, the Pacific Islands that Washington took over from Japan are denoted as *strategic trusts*. The Security Council is responsible for the United Nations functions in these areas.[11]

The Security Council is organized to function continuously. Its structure is simple. The Council is headed by a president; the presidency rotates monthly in the alphabetical order of states. Among the subsidiary organs reporting to the Council is the Military Staff Committee, made up of the chiefs of staff (or their representatives) of the permanent members of the Security Council. The Council from time to time makes use of *ad hoc* committees and commissions. Such bodies have been set up to deal with the Indonesian question, the Kashmir dispute, and the Congo.

One of the more contentious aspects of the Security Council opera-

9 *Ibid.*, Article 41.
10 *Ibid.*, Article 26.
11 *Ibid.*, Article 83.

tion is the use of the veto. The Charter originally provided that questions of procedure require seven affirmative votes for adoption. With the expansion of the Security Council to fifteen members in 1966 nine affirmative votes became necessary. Questions of substance may not be adopted with a negative vote from any one of the big-five members. A vote of "no" on a substantive question from any of the big five constitutes a veto. The Security Council's rules of procedure establish a number of questions that are held to be substantive and others that are to be considered procedural. However, whenever a question arises about a matter that is not within the established categories of substantive or procedural questions, the rules of procedure provide that a procedural designation can be vetoed. A permanent member may thus veto a motion that a question be considered procedural, thereby making the subject one of substance and subject to veto. This constitutes a "double veto."

THE INTERNATIONAL COURT OF JUSTICE

All members of the United Nations are "parties to the statute of the International Court of Justice." The Court consists of fifteen judges who have been elected by the General Assembly and the Security Council.[12] They are elected in their personal capacity "regardless of their nationality..." but no two of them may be nationals of the same state. Selection is based upon their qualifications and competence as lawyers, or jurists, and is made "from among persons of high moral character..." [13] Every three years the General Assembly and Security Council elect five judges to a nine-year term. This makes for overlapping terms of membership.

Only states may bring cases to the Court. The Charter provides that members of the organization must comply with the decisions of the Court. If any party to a case fails to carry out the Court's decision the other party may request the Security Council to take action to give effect to the Court's judgment.[14] The Court's jurisdiction extends over all cases voluntarily submitted to it by members of the UN, and also to such compulsory jurisdiction as has been given it under the *optional clause* by states that have accepted that provision.[15] In addition the Court gives advisory opinions on questions

12 *Statute of the International Court of Justice,* Article 4.
13 *Ibid.,* Articles 2 and 3.
14 Charter, Article 94.
15 See Chapter 3, pages 68–69.

submitted to it by any of the organs of the UN or by the specialized agencies. An advisory opinion is meant to guide the body requesting it, in its pursuit of legally constituted activity.

The International Court of Justice is in continuous session, that is, it meets on demand. Nine judges constitute a quorum and decisions are made by a majority of the judges participating.

THE ECONOMIC AND SOCIAL COUNCIL

The Economic and Social Council stands second only to the General Assembly in scope of activities. Although initially the work of the Council was to be closely related to the eradication of the causes of war, as the organization has developed the economic and social activities promoted by ECOSOC have often become ends in themselves. Under the authority of the General Assembly it may promote measures designed to raise standards of living; help develop full employment; stimulate economic development; find solutions for international economic, social, health, and related problems; and give attention to international cultural and educational cooperation.[16] Article 55 of the Charter obligates the UN to promote "universal respect for, and observance of, human rights and fundamental freedoms for all without distinction as to race, sex, language, religion." This activity has become a major ECOSOC responsibility.

The Economic and Social Council has developed an impressive number of devices for carrying out its activities. Studies, surveys, statistical compilations and reports, training seminars, technical assistance, special conferences, conventions, recommendations, and coordinating functions have all come within its province. The work of the Council need not be catalogued here. The *United Nations Yearbook* and *Everyman's United Nations,* published by the UN, provide a detailed summation of much of this labor. Illustrative of the more noteworthy studies and surveys are the annual *World Economic Survey, Current Economic Indicators,* the study of *National Legislation and Other Governmental Measures Relating to Restrictive Business Practices,* and the *Yearbook on Human Rights.* The *Demographic Yearbook* and the *Statistical Yearbook* are important reference works produced under its overall direction.

Conferences, such as those on trade and development, on the conservation and utilization of resources, and on a number of commodity problems, have been held under ECOSOC authority. Tech-

[16] Charter, Article 55.

nical assistance programs are under the general direction of the Council's Technical Assistance Committees.

The Economic and Social Council may make recommendations to member states, to other organs of the United Nations, and to the specialized agencies on matters within its competence. Recommendations are adopted to encourage action toward desired goals. With the approval of the General Assembly the Council may prepare conventions and thus gain legal obligations from member states to fulfill UN purposes. Conventions relating to the status of refugees, slavery and slave trade, and the nationality of married women are a few that have been successfully promoted by ECOSOC. Conventions on human rights are in preparation.

The Economic and Social Council is given responsibility for coordinating the work of the specialized agencies and the UN. Agreements for this purpose have been signed between each agency and the Economic and Social Council under the approval of the General Assembly. The Council makes recommendations to the agencies and it holds periodic consultations with them. Each agency has a consultative voice in the deliberations of the Council. Annual reports are submitted to the Council by them, and the Council has from time to time communicated observations on these reports to the Assembly and to the agency concerned. The International Atomic Energy Agency, which is in a somewhat special category and is not a specialized agency, is required to submit annual reports to the Economic and Social Council on matters within the competence of the Council.

ECOSOC was initially an eighteen-member body. An amendment to the Charter in 1965 reconstituted ECOSOC as a twenty-seven member organ. The larger body reflects the growth in membership of the UN and allocates a larger number of places in ECOSOC to the African and Asian countries. Nine states are elected each year to a three-year term. In contrast with the Security Council, which does not permit immediate reelection of nonpermanent members, members of the Economic and Social Council are eligible for immediate reelection. The United States, the Soviet Union, Great Britain, and France have held continuous membership on the Council. The Council meets twice a year; one of its sessions is held at the UN headquarters in New York and the other at its headquarters in Geneva, Switzerland. Decisions are made by a majority vote.

A consultative voice is given to nongovernmental organizations. Three categories of nongovernmental agencies are recognized. Category "A" consists of ten organizations which have wide-ranging interests roughly equivalent to that of the Council itself.[17] Category "B" has been established for organizations that have a high degree of competence but are concerned with only a few of the fields of ECOSOC activities.[18] In addition to the more than one hundred organizations accredited under Category "B," an even larger number of organizations, almost two hundred, have been recognized as nongovernmental organizations on register and for *ad hoc* consultations.[19] All nongovernmental organizations may send observers to public meetings of the Council and its commissions. Organizations that fall into the "A" and "B" categories may submit written statements that the UN is required to circulate as documents of the United Nations. These organizations may also present their views orally. A special prerogative of Category "A" organizations is the right to propose agenda items to the Council and its commissions.[20]

Some economic and social problems are regional in character and this led to the establishment of regional commissions of ECOSOC. In 1947 an Economic Commission for Europe was founded. It cuts across cold-war lines and includes all European UN members. It has undertaken activities in a variety of areas: housing, land transport, steel, timber, and the development of trade. In 1947 the commission for Asia and the Far East (ECAFE) was organized. Regional commissions for Latin America (ECLA) and Africa (ECA) were established in 1948 and 1958.

The broad scope of activity undertaken by ECOSOC has required the founding of functional commissions. Seven functional commissions and one subcommission were set up as expert groups. With the essential assistance of the Secretariat these commissions study problems and propose solutions on matters that have been assigned to them. The functional commissions are the Commission on Human Rights, with twenty-one members; the Social Commission, with twenty-one members; the Commission on the Status of Women, with eighteen members; the Commission on Narcotic Drugs, with twenty-

[17] *Everyman's United Nations, op. cit.,* p. 17.
[18] *Ibid.*
[19] *Ibid.*
[20] *Ibid.*

one members; the Statistical Commission, with fifteen members; the Population Commission, with eighteen members; and the Commission on International Commodity Trade, with twenty-one members. There is a twelve-member subcommission of the Commission on Human Rights dealing with the prevention of discrimination and the protection of minorities. Standing committees, such as the Technical Assistance Committee, and a number of special bodies, such as the Permanent Central Opium Board, the Drug Supervisory Body, and the well-known United Nations Childrens Fund (UNICEF), completes ECOSOC's organizational structure.

THE TRUSTEESHIP COUNCIL

When the states assembled in San Francisco in April, 1945, to write a charter for the United Nations they had no previously agreed upon proposal about colonial problems to consider. The Dumbarton Oaks Proposals contained no reference to colonial matters; it had been understood that the question would be dealt with further by Roosevelt, Churchill, and Stalin. At the Yalta Conference the matter was considered but positive agreement was not reached. Nevertheless, at San Francisco three chapters were included in the Charter dealing with Non-Self-Governing Territories, the International Trusteeship System, and the Trusteeship Council.

It was inevitable that the colonial problem would have to be considered in the drafting of the United Nations Charter. Even in 1919, when the Versailles Treaty was written, this question could not be avoided. Then, the expectation that the colonial possessions of the defeated powers would simply be appropriated by the victorious ones as spoils of war ran counter to the more idealistic demands of Woodrow Wilson and Jan Smuts for a "democratic" resolution of this problem. It seemed, especially to Wilson, that a war fought by the United States to end all wars should not result in imperialist aggrandizement, with the danger that annexations would lead to future wars. The League's Covenant spoke of "the principle that the well-being and development of such peoples (living in colonies) form a sacred trust of civilization ..." [21] This idea bespoke the need for doing something other than assigning to the victor the colonies of the loser and resulted in the League's system of mandates.

This system created a special relationship between the former

[21] Article 22.

German and Turkish colonies and their new rulers. The League's mandate relationship was by any reasonable definition a colonial relationship but it was qualified in important ways. Germany and Turkey lost their colonies. The German islands of the Pacific were apportioned among victors possessing adjacent holdings; those north of the equator became the mandated areas of Japan, the islands south of the equator became mandated areas of New Zealand, Australia, and Great Britain. Turkey's Arab colonies became mandated areas of Britain and France. The German colonies in Africa were divided among Great Britain, France, Belgium, and the Union of South Africa.

The League's system of mandates involved three parties, the mandated territory, the mandatory power that controlled the territory, and the League of Nations itself, whose responsibilities were exercised by the Permanent Mandates Commission operating under the overall supervision of the League's Council. The mandated areas fell into three categories, simply denoted "A," "B," and "C." "A" territories were those considered almost ready for self-government and independence. They were without exception Turkey's Arab colonies of the Middle East. In 1932 the British "A" mandate over Iraq was terminated and Iraq became an independent state. This was the only mandated territory to achieve independence prior to the Second World War. The African mandates with the exception of German South West Africa were all denoted "B" mandates and as such they were eventually to become independent states. They were deemed to be unready to accept the responsibilities of independence and, consequently, independence was to come in the distant future. "C" mandates were held to be unqualified for attaining independence at any time because they were too sparsely settled or were held to be unable ever to develop a viable economy.

The Permanent Mandates Commission was an expert body, and it was through this body that the League of Nations exercised its pressures on mandatory powers to live up to the spirit and letter of Article 22 of the Covenant.

The Second World War even more than the First World War juxtaposed the forces of "democracy" against those of reactionary dictatorships. During the war United Nations leaders, especially the American President, appealed to the colonial peoples of the world to support the United Nations forces against Axis aggression, promising a new deal. There was to be no return to the "good old days," which meant colonial oppression for the peoples of Africa and Asia. The ideals for which the United Nations fought, the ideals on which the UN itself was established, bespoke a need for according to peoples living in colonies that full measure of human dignity that independence alone can provide. In a word there were compelling ideological reasons for a United Nations interest in freedom for all people, including freedom from colonial oppression.

Two more practical considerations required that action be taken with respect to colonies. First, with the demise of the League the mandate system was also terminated, at least as a League of Nations operation. A new entity had to be found to take over the League's responsibility for mandated areas that were not yet independent. To be sure by 1948 all of the League's "A" mandates had become independent states, but for the larger number of mandated territories that had not become independent the question of an heir to the League's responsibility was at issue. Second, imperialist powers that had been members of the Axis coalition had to be divested of their colonial holdings. Italy and Japan had such holdings. No serious thought was given to the appropriation of these colonies by victor powers as spoils of war. The disposition of these territories on the basis of a concern for the welfare of the people living there was a generally accepted proposition.

Three chapters of the United Nations Charter have been devoted to the matter of colonies.[22] Those territories that had been mandates and had not received their independence and the Italian colonies were singled out for special treatment by being put into a trusteeship system with the objective of furthering "international peace and security" and promoting the "progressive development toward self-government or independence ... of each territory and its peoples ..." held in trust.[23] To achieve this end the system was to exact humane government over colonial populations and to ensure favorable economic, social, and educational conditions for the people. All of this, it was expected, would stimulate progress toward independence.

The trusteeship system has three component entities. First, there are the trust territories. The League's distinction of "A," "B," and

[22] See Charter, Chapters XI, XII, and XIII, Articles 73–91.
[23] Charter, Article 76.

"C" categories has been eliminated. Mandates that had not won independence and former Italian and Japanese colonies were denoted trust territories under the Charter.[24] Second, there are the trust-owning powers with responsibility for supervision of trusts. Third, there is the Trusteeship Council. The Council is made up of all states that hold trust territories and an equal number of countries that come from two categories of member states, (a) all permanent members of the Security Council who own no trust territories, and (b) enough other states elected by the General Assembly to balance the number of trust-owning states in the Council. During the 1950's the Trusteeship Council was a fourteen-member council. Seven trust-owning powers were balanced by China and the Soviet Union as two permanent members of the Security Council who did not own trust territories and five additional states elected by the General Assembly for three-year terms.

The Trusteeship Council holds semiannual sessions, in January and July. Voting is by majority. The Council is responsible to the General Assembly for carrying out the purposes of the trusteeship system. It has developed three primary modes of operation. First, trust-owning powers are required to submit to the Council an annual report concerning all developments, including political, and emphasizing those leading toward independence. Such reports are based on a questionnaire developed for the Trusteeship Council to better elicit the information it needs. These reports are reviewed and lead to recommendations being made by the Council. Second, people of trust territories may petition the Council for a consideration of their grievances. Such petitions are received in large number and reviewed by the Council. In many instances they help correct malpractices. Third, the Council sends visiting missions each year into several of the trust areas to make investigations on the spot and receive oral petitions. This provides for a meaningful check on the conduct of trust-owning powers within their trust territories.

It is useful to trace the geneology of trust territories to evaluate the work of the Trusteeship Council. German Togoland in West Africa was divided between Britain and France after World War I and each part became a "B" mandate. This division was dictated by the fact that a British colony, the Gold Coast, was to the west of

[24] Eritrea was an exception. An Italian colony through 1954, it was given to Ethiopia.

Togoland and that French West African colonies were to the east and north. With the establishment of the trusteeship system British and French Togoland became trust territories. The German Kamerun was similarly divided between Britain and France. About five-sixths of the Kamerun became a French "B" mandate, again because French Equatorial Africa was adjacent to it; the remaining one-sixth of the Kamerun became a British mandate adjacent to Nigeria to its west. With the establishment of the trusteeship system the two Cameroons became trust territories. German East Africa was divided between Britain and Belgium. The smaller area of Ruanda-Urundi was given to Belgium as a mandate because it was adjacent to the Belgian Congo, while the much larger British annexation was renamed Tanganyika and it too became a "B" mandate situated between the British colonies of Uganda and Kenya to the north and Northern Rhodesia and Nyasaland to the south. After the Second World War they too became trust territories. Italian Somaliland and Libya were never mandated areas. After Italy's defeat in the Second World War the colonies were taken from her. Libya was given to the United Nations itself as a trust territory, and the United Nations supervised the trust until its independence at the end of 1951. For want of a better solution Italy was given back its Somaliland colony as a trust, to be held, however, only for a ten-year period, after which this land, Somalia, was to become independent.

German South West Africa created special difficulties. It had been a "C" mandate of the Union of South Africa. South Africa refused to put South West Africa in trust. In 1966 the status of South West Africa was still in litigation. On the one hand, the Republic of South Africa has insisted on its right to annex this valuable territory. On the other hand, the International Court of Justice has given a decision in which it held that the Republic of South Africa could not unilaterally divest itself of the earlier mandate relationship and that, if it were unwilling to place this territory in trust, then the mandate still exists with the United Nations taking over the earlier League of Nations responsibility. With the addition of a large number of African states to the United Nations and in view of the South African racial policy, there has been increased pressure for a more satisfactory disposition of the South West African problem and a marked desire to deny the Republic of South Africa its bid for annexation.

The former German Islands of the Pacific south of the equator which had been assigned to Australia, New Zealand, and Great Britain as "C" mandates became trust territories after World War II. The German islands north of the equator which had been made Japanese "C" mandates became strategic trust territories of the United States. The United States provides its annual reports for these strategic trusts to the Security Council rather than to the Trusteeship Council.

Most trust territories have become independent. This accomplishment is telling proof that the trusteeship system has been effective in accomplishing its purposes as outlined in the UN Charter. Beginning in 1951 with the United Nations Libyan trust achieving independence, all of the trust territories in Africa had by the end of 1962 become independent. British Togoland joined Ghana in 1957 as part of that independent state. French Togoland, French Cameroons, and Italian Somaliland became independent states in 1960. In 1961 the British Cameroons divided, the southern part joining the Republic of Cameroon while the northern part was annexed to Nigeria. At the end of 1961 the Tanganyikan trust became an independent state. In July of 1962, after extensive consideration by the General Assembly, the Belgian trust territory of Ruanda-Urundi became the independent states of Rwanda and Burundi. Western Samoa became independent of its New Zealand trust relationship in 1962. With the beginning of 1963 only the trust territories of Nauru and New Guinea (both held by Australia), and the Pacific trust territories of the United States remained.

The success of the trusteeship system has created a vexing problem for the future of the Trusteeship Council. With only two *bona fide* trust-owning powers remaining (the United States and Australia), according to the Charter the other four permanent members of the Security Council should be added to the Council; however, this would upset the balance of trust- and non-trust-owning powers also required by the Charter and would no longer allow for elected members to the Council. This situation poses an additional problem in that states that have themselves been colonies (that is, most of the Afro-Asian states) doubt that former colonial powers will effectively champion the interests of the peoples of the trust territories. They are reluctant to give up the work of the Trusteeship Council and, indeed, their participation as elected members of that Council.

By the Twentieth Session of the General Assembly no permanent solution had been worked out with respect to this problem. Exploiting the somewhat ambiguous situation respecting the Nauru trust, because this small island is under the joint administering authority of Australia, New Zealand, and the United Kingdom (but, in fact administered by Australia), all three states are considered as trust owning. These three states and the United States are the trust-owning states, and they are balanced by China, France, and the Soviet Union plus one elected state. By 1964 the Special Committee on the Implementation of the Declaration on the Granting of Independence to Colonial Countries and Peoples, commonly known as the Committee of 24, was the important United Nations body working on colonial problems.

THE SECRETARIAT

A staff of over four thousand people headed by a Secretary-General make up the Secretariat of the United Nations. It is one of the principal organs of the UN. Its work is executive and administrative in function. The Secretariat is executive in the sense that it provides leadership in the political, economic, social, and other areas of UN interest. The Secretary-General is an executive in his worldwide leadership.[25] The Secretariat is an administrative organ in the sense that it carries out assignments given it by the General Assembly, the other councils, and their commissions and committees.[26]

> The importance of the Secretariat as a major institution in the International System derives mainly from the uniqueness of its function ... as such, it is intended to represent the values universally sought in the executive form of organization: unity, continuity, leadership, initiative, energy, expertness, performance. It is the Secretariat, more than any other organ, which transforms the United Nations from a series of periodic meetings of Assembly and Councils into a permanent and cohesive organization. It is the main centripetal force in the international system. Without the Secretariat, the United Nations would be deprived of its center of communication and co-ordination, its *international* core as distinct from the national character of the delegations which make up the Assembly and the Councils.[27]

[25] Carnegie Endowment for International Peace, *The United Nations Secretariat* (New York: 1950), p. 19.
[26] *Ibid.*, pp. 41–43.
[27] *Ibid.*, pp. 8–9.

The Secretariat is headed by a Secretary-General who is elected to a five-year term by the General Assembly upon recommendation of the Security Council. The Security Council's recommendation is a measure that can be vetoed. In 1950 the Soviet Union vetoed a new five-year term for the first Secretary-General, Trygve Lie, because of his strong stand in support of UN measures to repel North Korean aggression. Under these circumstances the Western powers, led by the United States, refused to permit Lie's victimization. The General Assembly thereupon simply extended his term of office.

Trygve Lie was succeeded by the late Dag Hammarskjöld. After Hammarskjöld's death in September, 1961, U Thant of Burma became the new Secretary-General. Secretary-Generals are chosen from a smaller member state. As such they are less likely, so it is believed, to represent the attitudes and serve the interests of one of the major powers.

The vast quantity and range of work that the UN must carry out has inevitably led to the need for a large and hard-working Secretariat. What do the Secretary-General and his staff do? A great bulk of the work undertaken by the Secretariat may simply be labeled *services*. This entails such pedestrian but essential functions as janitorial and clerical services. The Secretariat provides the necessary *supplies and utilities* to keep the work of the UN going. The staff of the organization includes researchers, technicians, and administrators. Over the years the Secretariat has literally produced mountains of *research and reports. Records* must be maintained; *communications with member states* and other international organizations are continuous. Speeches must be *interpreted* and documents *translated*.

The Security Council, the General Assembly, ECOSOC, and the Trusteeship Council adopt resolutions at each sitting calling upon the Secretariat to do a variety of things. In this sense the Secretary-General executes resolutions. The Charter itself lays upon the Secretary-General certain administrative responsibilities. Under Article 102 he compiles and publishes treaties and international agreements that are registered with the organization. The large and diverse staff creates a need for coordination of its work, and this is a function of the Secretary-General. As a strong leader he is likely to take the initiative for liaison with the specialized agencies. The Secretary-General can use reports that he makes to one or another of the organs of the UN to further the policy he believes best serves the interests of the organization or world peace.

The Secretary-General invariably has the major responsibility for preparing the United Nations budget. The expenditure of appropriated funds is similarly his responsibility.

The Secretariat is involved in political functions. Thus, the Secretary-General and his top officers may engage in mediation and have, on occasion, provided good offices. United Nations conventions are likely to have been drafted by the Secretary-General and his staff. Trygve Lie was chosen Secretary-General partly because his experience as Foreign Minister of Norway was political rather than purely administrative. The Charter provided the Secretary-General with ample leverage for playing a political role.[28] He has the right to recommend items for inclusion in the agenda of the Security Council. He influences the construction of agendas. From time to time the Secretary-General has circulated his own memoranda on a subject under consideration in the UN. In this way he sets out his views and proposes means by which the United Nations purposes can be advanced. Each of the Secretaries-General has carried out important consultations behind the scenes with heads of states to forward the goals of the organization. The annual report provides the Secretary-General with still another vehicle for discussing world issues and taking stands in the furtherance of UN purposes. The Secretary-General and his top assistants must represent the UN and, in general, act as spokesmen for the organization.

THE PEACE AND SECURITY FUNCTION OF THE UNITED NATIONS

We have already pointed out that the primary purpose of the UN is the maintenance of international peace and security. But the role of the organization in quest of its purposes has been disputed. Some have said that the UN is simply a mechanism—machinery— that may be used for any proper purposes which states desire. Others claim that the UN is more than machinery; it has a life of its own and has a positive obligation to undertake whatever action might be necessary to preserve peace and security. The latter attitude reflects the approach that is usually adopted when disputes or

[28] Charter, Article 99.

situations occur. A consensus seems to emerge activating the UN whenever the need arises. Yet again, the Secretary-General, speaking for the UN, intervenes on behalf of international peace. The obligation to act explains the United Nations involvement in Korea in 1950, the Middle East in 1956, the Congo in 1960, the Cuban crisis of 1962, and Kashmir in 1965.

The Charter devises for the United Nations three approaches to peace and security:

(1) The peaceful settlement of disputes;
(2) The enforcement of peace; the organization must be prepared to discourage, defeat, or punish aggression;
(3) The building of an enduring peace by eliminating the causes of war.

The Peaceful Settlement of Disputes

Under the Charter all members of the UN are obligated to settle disputes by peaceful methods and "in such a manner that international peace and security, and justice are not endangered." Member states of the United Nations agree to "refrain in their international relations from the threat or use of force against the territorial integrity or political independence of any state." [29] This Charter obligation would appear to create a built-in factor favoring the use of pacific settlement of all disputes. Yet, many disputes remain unsettled. The United Nations has not been slow to consider those disputes where its role might prove useful by utilizing techniques specifically provided for by the Charter.[30] Mediation, good offices, and enquiry have been used with some frequency. Resort to adjudication by the International Court of Justice has been tried in several cases. On the other hand, arbitration has hardly been used.

In the view of two authorities:

The general influence of the United Nations as "a center for harmonizing" the policies of its members is a significant factor in the world situation, over and above the use of specific methods of peaceful settlement in particular cases. The very existence of the United Nations as a form of multilateral diplomacy offers a resource for negotiations which

[29] Charter, Article 2, Paragraphs 3 and 4.
[30] See Chapter 3, pages 82–86, for peaceful settlement techniques.

would not otherwise be available. Furthermore, the opportunities for bilateral diplomacy are greatly increased by the facilities, continuing conferences, and contacts among delegates. The United Nations system, therefore, should not be viewed as a replacement of bilateral diplomacy but as a supplement to it and as a device of enhancing effectiveness.[31]

The Security Council and the General Assembly have been arenas for negotiating peaceful settlements. The Secretary-General, especially Dag Hammarskjöld, was more likely to use "quiet diplomacy," behind-the-scenes, unpublicized negotiation, to attain agreements.

Disputes that have come before the organization have been considered with varying degrees of success.[32] The final evaluation of the UN's work in this area should not equate success with a 100 percent batting average. Some quarrels have been settled with the assistance of the United Nations and perhaps a greater number have simply lapsed or remain but fighting has been avoided.

The UN has played a helpful role where peaceful settlement of the question at issue was mutually desired by the disputing states. UN terms allow a minimum loss of face and diminish the sense of winning or losing. Where the desire for peaceful accommodation has been lacking the United Nations has discouraged resort to force. The organization has tended to encourage settlements tempered by standards of morality and justice rather than those based on power. In this respect, the UN has been more helpful to smaller states than great powers by reducing the influence of power. Finally, it is often essential that a disinterested and authoritative third party take an active role in the resolution of conflicts. United Nations organs are an obvious choice to play this part.

THE ENFORCEMENT OF PEACE

The League of Nations failed to enforce peace. Faced with acts of aggression, the League proved impotent to curb the use of force and the outbreak of war. The League's failure notwithstanding, statesmen were agreed on the necessity for an international organiza-

[31] Amry Vandenbosch and Willard N. Hogan, *Toward World Order* (New York: McGraw-Hill, 1963), p. 135.
[32] *Everyman's United Nations, op. cit.* Contains a summary of all disputes handled by the United Nations, including those that have been considered for peaceful settlement. Current reports on disputes may be found in the monthly issues of the *United Nations Chronicle* and in the quarterly résumés of activity published in *International Organization*.

tion. It was not the idea of the League of Nations that was wrong; the trouble was that the League was too weak. Most important of all the improvements written into the UN Charter was its authority to enforce peace by preventing, halting, or punishing aggression.

Under the Charter the Security Council has been given primary responsibility for the maintenance of international peace and security. Chapter VII of the Charter (Articles 39–51) detailed its responsibility with respect to the enforcement of peace. It was to determine when peace was endangered. The Council was expected to employ measures short of armed force, calling upon parties to stop fighting or recommending "provisional measures as it deems necessary or desirable." [33] It could also decide on the use of economic and financial sanctions, the interruption of postal, telegraphic, radio, and other communications, and the severance of diplomatic relations as a means of enforcing peace. In the last analysis, the Security Council could take military action.[34]

The effectiveness of the Security Council as an enforcement agency rested on a number of expectations. First, that members would abide by their obligations under Article 25 to carry out the decisions of the Security Council. Second, that the Military Staff Committee could agree on a plan for United Nations forces based upon earmarked units and facilities which could be used by the Security Council when necessary. Third, that the Security Council would negotiate an agreement with each member state under which prior consent would be granted for the use of forces and facilities by the Council.

The Military Staff Committee was unable to agree on the plan for United Nations military forces. Consequently, there was no treaty for the Security Council to negotiate with member states. Although some areas of agreement on such a military force had been reached (by April of 1947, 25 out of 41 projected articles were accepted), the area of disagreement that remained was far more significant. The Soviet Union and the others of the big five were in basic conflict. While the four advocated that each of the big-five powers ought to contribute units in relation to their military capabilities, the Soviet Union insisted on equal contributions from the big five. The four-power plan would allow the United States, which was largely

[33] Article 40.
[34] Article 42.

demobilized, to contribute planes and perhaps the atomic bomb, inasmuch as she was the only state that had it at the time. Britain might contribute naval units; France, tanks; Russia, other types of equipment; and China, who had very little other than infantry and artillery, would provide whatever she could. In the Soviet plan the contributions of the big five would have to be reduced to the least common denominator of the weakest among them. Thus, if the Chinese were not in a position to contribute naval or air units to the United Nations force then no other of the big-five powers could contribute such forces. Contributions were to be exactly equal. There can be little doubt that the purpose of the Soviet Union was to prevent the creation of a formidable United Nations military force and to ensure that any United Nations force would be markedly weaker than that of the Soviet Union.

Other areas of East-West disagreement were equally frustrating. The West took the position that the Security Council should decide by agreement with the governments concerned the location of UN forces, while the Soviet Union wanted forces to remain within their own territory until called up by the Security Council. The West favored the establishment of military bases essential for the operation of UN forces, which the Soviet Union opposed as a violation of sovereignty. The four Western states insisted that armed forces should be withdrawn, after their use, only by Security Council decision, while the Soviet Union demanded a 30- to 90-day time limit on UN detachments remaining in theaters of operation.

Despite the inability of the Military Staff Committee to agree on a plan for a UN force, the obligations of the organization for the maintenance of peace and security remain. This has led to improvisation and evolution along lines not originally intended.

Three noteworthy developments have taken place to make up for the failure of the original design for the use of military power to materialize. (1) Beginning with the organization of NATO in 1949, a series of regional alliances were established under Article 51 of the Charter which provide for individual and collective self-defense in the event of an armed attack.[35] (2) In 1950, because the Soviet

---

[35] Article 51, "nothing in the present Charter shall impair the inherent right of individual or collective self-defense if an armed attack occurs against a member of the United Nations, until the Security Council has taken the measures necessary to maintain international peace and security.

veto made action by the Security Council unlikely, and with the specific condition that the war in Korea could not be prosecuted by the Security Council, a "Uniting for Peace" resolution was adopted by the General Assembly. Under this resolution the General Assembly was to act as a center for harmonizing actions by member states in cases of aggression, when the Security Council was unable to act because of a veto. (3) In 1956, as a result of the Suez crisis, the Secretary-General was given the authority to introduce force in defense of peace. "A United Nations presence" was created to physically separate warring states or, if necessary, to suppress warring forces.

In the days of Dumbarton Oaks and the San Francisco charter-writing conference the expectation that military force would have to be used to suppress aggression was predicated upon the belief that the defeated Axis powers might rise and try aggression again. The Charter was truly designed to suppress renascent German, Japanese, or Italian aggression. Faced with this prospect the permanent members of the Security Council would be united and support collective security against resurgent Fascist forces. The original concept of the UN Charter did not fit the postwar source of conflict. The Communist *coup d'etat* in Czechoslovakia and the Berlin blockade in 1948 ended all doubt that the Soviet Union was pursuing an expansionist policy. It became obvious that the Security Council, because the Soviet Union could veto resolutions there, was not the proper agency for maintaining security against Soviet expansion. This then led to the utilization of Article 51 as a primary device by which security from aggression could be assured. Article 51 brings NATO, SEATO, CENTO, and the ANZUS pacts within the ambit of the UN Charter. These treaties establish an organization for collective self-defense that operates in *defense* of its members "if an armed attack occurs." Reliance on Security Council action is no longer essential.

On June 25, 1950, North Korea attacked South Korea. The Soviet Union was absent from the Security Council, having walked out in

---

Measures taken by Members in the exercise of this right of self-defense shall be immediately reported to the Security Council and shall not in any way affect the authority and responsibility of the Security Council under the present Charter to take at any time such action as it deems necessary in order to maintain or restore international peace and security."

January of that year because the Security Council had refused to immediately seat the Peking government. Although the Soviet Union insisted that all action of the Security Council was illegal because it was improperly constituted, the Security Council continued to operate and, during the early days of the Korean war, authorized a series of actions under American leadership in defense of South Korea. By July, 1950, it became clear, even to Stalin, that the Soviet Union had blundered and should have its representatives in the Security Council to forestall further action. Mr. Malik, the Soviet representative to the Security Council, announced that on August 1 the Soviet Union would return to the Security Council and would under the monthly alphabetical rotation assume the president's chair. The Soviet Union's return effectively stalled all further action there on Korea.

At the regular meeting of the General Assembly in September a "Uniting for Peace" resolution was introduced, giving the General Assembly the authority to deal with a threat to peace, breach of peace, or act of aggression. The General Assembly could be called into session within twenty-four hours in the event that the Security Council failed to act *because of a veto.* Inasmuch as the General Assembly has no authority to require action but may only make recommendations, the resolution provided that the General Assembly may *recommend* military action to deal with aggression. With a desire to act by a large majority of states, indicated by a two-thirds vote, the General Assembly could be used as the authority for action and the organizer of collective security. In this way, the "Uniting for Peace" resolution allows the UN to apply force to forestall aggression.

The Suez war of 1956 presented problems that led to the invention of another technique for the enforcement of peace. In essence it involved the physical separation of combatants by a United Nations military force. By 1956 Dag Hammarskjöld was acknowledged to be a skillful negotiator, a forceful promoter of a UN peace role, and an "honest broker" among antagonistic countries. A desire to "let Dag do it" led to Hammarskjöld's useful intervention in the war. He worked out an agreement to station an emergency force in the Gaza Strip to discourage clashes between Egypt and Israel.

Again in 1960 anarchy in the Congo presented a need to enforce order but raised the danger that outside forces might come in. To forestall Belgium, United States, or Soviet intervention, and thereby prevent a cold-war intrusion into Africa, a United Nations *presence* was authorized by the Security Council. Police forces to reestablish law and order were sent by neutral states, a number of them African. They were to play a stabilizing role within the land while trying to isolate the Congo from intervention by the great powers which might have led to war. This aim was not completely fulfilled but the value of this approach was proved when similar devices were employed in Yemen and Cyprus.

THE UNITED NATIONS AND THE PROMOTION OF A PEACEFUL WORLD

The enforcement of peace and the pacific settlement of disputes provide, at best, temporary guarantees that peace will be preserved. Occasions may arise when the will to prevent aggression by collective security may be lacking. Attempts at pacific settlement may fail. The assurance of peace requires means less likely to fail. Thus, the foregoing approaches for the maintenance of peace and security should be seen as devices for "holding the ring," for preserving peace occasion by occasion as threats to international peace arise. Lasting peace requires a more basic approach to the problem. It needs attention to the causes of war and an elimination of the use of force in international affairs.

The ultimate aim of the United Nations is the fulfillment of the prophecy of Isaiah,

> They shall beat their swords into plowshares, and
> their spears into pruning-hooks, nation shall not
> lift up sword against nation, neither shall they learn
> war any more. (Isaiah I, 18)

To achieve this goal the UN has undertaken activities meant to alter the behavior of states. Everlasting peace could be brought nearer should the UN succeed in creating a world wherein peaceful resolution of conflicts replaces resort to force; international anarchy gives way to world order; friendly relations is the characteristic of interstate behavior; and the causes of war have been eliminated.

Developing the Habits of Peaceful Resolution of Conflicts. Well-established techniques for peaceful settlement of disputes have been developed (see Chapter 3, pages 82–86). The UN contains institutional entities—the General Assembly, Security Council, Court,

Secretariat—which can apply such techniques. What is then necessary is that all states as a matter of course submit their disputes to the UN for consideration.

Efforts to encourage greater recourse to pacific settlement have not been promising. The General Assembly established, in 1947, the Interim Committee, which was given responsibility for developing "general principles of cooperation in the maintenance of international peace and security" and "international cooperation in the political field." [36] This committee set out to promote the use of peaceful settlement of disputes. Its researches were fruitful and it proposed that arbitration under United Nations auspices could be promoted by a general treaty to which member states would subscribe, agreeing beforehand that certain of their disputes be submitted to arbitration. To enhance the use of peaceful settlement the Interim Committee suggested that a list of eminent persons with international reputations and who possessed the requisite qualifications might be listed as potential mediators or conciliators. The Interim Committee also considered the wisdom of eliminating the veto on matters considered under Chapter VI, in other words, on disputes that were submitted for peaceful settlement.

Unfortunately the good suggestions and proposals of the Interim Committee were not adopted. Pacific settlement is necessarily used today because of the fear of war. Peaceful settlement has gained from the good reputation of the UN, and especially its Secretary-General, as a fair intermediary. The weight of public opinion behind the Charter obligation for peaceful settlement also influences statesmen to some degree. However, one might wish that better use would be made of the organization in seeking settlement of international disputes.

Promoting World Order. The conscious pursuit of international order based upon international law, international moral and ethical standards, disarmament, and peaceful change of the *status quo* has been noted elsewhere (see Chapter 3, pages 65–73). Normative regulation of the behavior of states has at best been inadequately realized. To be sure, the International Law Commission does, year by year, record modest progress in its efforts. A genocide convention, reflecting international moral standards, has been adopted and ratified by

---

[36] Doc. A/510, *Official Records of the Second Session of the General Assembly;* Resolutions, 16 September–29 November, 1947.

a large number of states. A declaration of human rights has been unanimously voted in the General Assembly and conventions deriving from this declaration are in the offing. At best the UN has been responsible for a modest development of international law. The dangers that result from world anarchy and the revulsion against immoral and unethical behavior has heightened the popular expectation that law, order, justice, and right will guide the behavior of states, and the continued effort of the United Nations is evidence that most states desire progress in these areas.

Promoting Friendly Relations. There is an obvious relationship between peace and friendly relations between states. The UN and its related agencies are involved in a variety of efforts designed to build ties among states. These efforts are promoted on two levels, intergovernmental and peoples to peoples.

Under Article 1, Paragraph 4, of the Charter, the UN is to be "a center for harmonizing the actions of nations in the attainment of common ends." The UN brings governments together in cooperative endeavors to improve economic and social standards. It seeks to facilitate friendly contact between people from different lands. Programs sponsored by specialized agencies depend on intergovernmental cooperation.

Through international organizations countries cooperate to alleviate food shortages, reduce barriers to international trade, finance economic development, promote better transportation and communication, reduce illicit traffic in narcotic drugs, and promote improved health for children. Atomic energy, labor, food and agriculture, education, science, culture, health, aviation, postal matters, telecommunications, monetary stability, weather predictions, and maritime problems are matters which have gained international cooperation. Over and above the intrinsic merits of such cooperation, a by-product of friendly relations among states and among people is also expected.

UNESCO has a particular mission to foster international friendship. Its philosophy, eloquently stated in the preamble to its constitution, is based on the premise that the attitudes which people hold toward one another is a key to lasting peace.

> ... since wars begin in the minds of men it is in the minds of men that the defenses of peace must be constructed; the ignorance of each other's ways and lives has been a common cause throughout the history of

mankind of that suspicion and mistrust between the peoples of the world through which their differences have all too often broken into war. . . .

UNESCO's philosophy has called forth a unique approach to its work. UNESCO programs were to involve not only governments but also people. UNESCO considered itself to be a "people-to-peoples" organization. Its constitution implies that if people can learn to shed "suspicion and mistrust" they will force their governments to pursue friendship with others, preserving peace.

". . . peace based exclusively upon the political and economic arrangements of Governments would not be a peace which could secure the unanimous, lasting and sincere support of the peoples of the world and that the peace must, therefore, be founded, if it is not to fail, upon the intellectual and moral solidarity of mankind." [37]

UNESCO's programs reflect this outlook. Projects aimed at eradicating illiteracy and promoting education have high priority. The dissemination of knowledge and the encouragement of scientific and cultural activities have played a large part in UNESCO's continuing effort. The agency has helped in the establishment of libraries and museums. A wholesale attack on ignorance on the one hand and an attempt to broaden the understanding of the world on the other has been a persistent guideline for its work.

Several organizational devices have been employed to bring UNESCO to the people. Foremost among these are the national commissions or national cooperating bodies which member states must establish. These commissions are to be representative of the people or at least of its intellectual community. They are to serve as agencies for transmitting UNESCO's program and ideals to the people and, at the same time, as a transmission belt from the people to UNESCO enabling the organization to reflect the genius of the people in its program.

Another method for making an impact at the grass roots was the plan for holding annual meetings of UNESCO in different cities around the world. Over a period of time UNESCO was to have met in all of its member states. Annual meetings were to become occasions for national programs on UNESCO, the United Nations, the other specialized agencies, and for disseminating information about

[37] Preamble UNESCO Constitution.

other peoples. These ambitions proved impractical. The organization no longer holds annual meetings but instead meets biennially. They meet alternately at its Paris headquarters and abroad. The quadrennial UNESCO conferences abroad are still taking place and serve in some degree their original purposes.

UNESCO has supported international contacts among intellectual groups. It has founded organizations such as the International Political Science Association, the International Sociological Association, the International Council of Philosophy and Humanistic Studies, the International Theater Institute, and the International Music Council.

If the tensions of our time were largely a result of popular ignorance and misunderstanding UNESCO's efforts would bode well for the future. Unfortunately few conflicts are caused by blind ignorance. Much of UNESCO's work may be, therefore, irrelevant to the aim of peace. Americans may, through UNESCO's efforts, learn to enjoy the novels of Sholokhov, the music of Shostakovich, the artistry of Richter and Oistrakh. They may develop a taste for Armenian food and Ukrainian dancing. Russians, for their part, may grow to appreciate Hemingway, American jazz, variety shows on TV, refrigerators built in the United States, and lemon pie. All of this would heighten the level of mutual understanding and appreciation but would not reduce antagonism over Castro's Cuba, the status of West Berlin, or the role of the United States in Southeast Asia.

While UNESCO has not singlehandedly brought about an era of peace, its work has advanced international understanding. Its program is worthwhile because it ennobles man and makes him more humane. As such it certainly helps reduce irrational conflicts. The agency amplifies a sense of community among people and the essential unity of all mankind.

Eliminating the Causes of War. The causes of war are many and varied. Power, land, arms, economic inequity, racial, religious and national hatreds, and the quest for freedom are some of the reasons for resort to armed conflict.

Arms races are a significant cause of war. We have already said that disarmament agreements are tension-reducing agreements and that such agreements can be an important contribution to an ordered universe and some measure of international government.

Arms build-up, on the other hand, may be an excuse for war. The United Nations has played two roles in the field of disarmament. It has been an arena for negotiation of disarmament agreements. When disarmament negotiations have been conducted under other auspices, the UN has become an instrument of popular pressure upon the major powers for the unremitting quest for a disarmament agreement.

One need not be a Marxist to believe that economic conflict may lead to war. While we reject the thesis that war is an unalterable function of the capitalist system and that peace is assured in a socialist world, there are economic conditions—poverty and exploitation—which if left unattended may well lead to international conflict. Article 55 of the Charter speaks of "the creation of conditions of stability and well-being which are necessary for peaceful and friendly relations among nations . . ." The economic and social activities of the United Nations serve a dual purpose. They are meant to eliminate economic and social causes of war and at the same time bring states together in fruitful cooperation.

A catalogue of the United Nations economic activities is beyond the scope of this volume. In general these activities fall into several broad areas:

(1) At the end of the Second World War primary interest was focused on reconstruction activities.
(2) In the past decade the emphasis has shifted to economic development activities.
(3) Most recently the organization has worked at easing inhibitions upon international trade.
(4) When necessary the UN and the agencies have provided disaster relief for stricken countries.

In sum, UN and agency activities are directed to the end that all states may achieve greater prosperity through cooperation rather than at the expense of their neighbors.

Social and humanitarian issues have been at the root of some of the tensions which endanger peace. Racial hatred is probably the most serious of the social conflicts of our time. But serious tensions are also instigated by religious discrimination and the maltreatment of national minorities. International organizations have accepted the task of extirpating such conflict and reducing intolerance. Their activity has emphasized education to counter prejudice. They have also encouraged states to adopt laws eliminating discrimination based upon race, religion, sex, or nationality. The UN, the ILO, and UNESCO have exerted pressure on their members to adopt higher social standards. Spectacular or immediate improvements in this broad and complex field of activity are not to be expected. Results ought more properly to be measured over a longer period of time. Yet there are reasons for optimism that action in this area is bringing about better understanding among peoples and higher levels of concern for the conditions of man. The efforts of the United Nations and the agencies give some encouragement that these causes for tension will grow smaller.

In recent years the organization has been painfully aware of the deleterious economic and social effects of "the population explosion." Population pressure has been used as an excuse for territorial acquisition. It is still feared as a problem that might lead to desperate measures. Should the organization be able to"solve"the population question a cause for conflict would thus be eliminated. The Population Commission of ECOSOC has produced expert studies, statistics, and other data and has convened conferences of experts to devise means for helping countries to cope with their problems of overpopulation.

Refugees exacerbate hostile feelings. The preservation of peace and humanitarian considerations have kept refugee issues before th UN since its inception. In 1959–1960 the General Assembly carried through a world refugee year to draw the world's attention to the plight of refugees and to mount a campaign for the permanent settlement of refugees. Most of the refugee groups were resettled, the noteworthy exception being those in Palestine.[38] Since 1960 other areas of strife have produced new groups of refugees. An important humanitarian effort to maintain refugees has been undertaken by the United Nations High Commissioner for Refugees (UNHCR), and for the refugees of Palestine the United Nations Relief and Works Agency (UNRWA) has been active.

Lastly, in trying to eliminate the causes of war the organization has had extensive interest in colonial matters.[39] The UN through its

[38] See Chapter 9, pp. 262–264.
[39] See pp. 104–110.

Trusteeship Council had direct responsibility for trust territories.[40] But the responsibilities of the UN went beyond trust territories, and included all other colonies. In keeping with the anti-imperialist tenor of the Charter the United Nations was made responsible for overseeing implementation of the principle "that the interests of the inhabitants of these (colonial) territories are paramount," and accepted the "obligation to promote to the utmost, within the system of international peace and security established by the present Charter, the well-being of the inhabitants of these territories..." [41] If this provision was to be something other than a pious platitude, the UN had to undertake specific tasks for its implementation. Techniques and institutional devices were developed to fulfill this obligation. Members of the UN who hold territories that are not self-governing are required to submit annual reports. These reports have been made the basis for discussions which have proved an effective instrument for safeguarding the interests of the inhabitants of those territories.

The institutional responsibility within the organization for territories that are not self-governing rests with the General Assembly. A main committee, Committee Four, deals with colonial matters at the annual meetings. It was assisted by the Committee on Information from Non-Self-Governing Territories, which received the annual reports and prepared comments and studies on them.

In 1960 the General Assembly adopted a historic declaration, called the Declaration on the Granting of Independence to Colonial Countries and Peoples. A Special Committee on the Implementation of the Declaration, commonly called the Committee of 24, was set up to carry out the declaration. In 1963 the Assembly dissolved the Committee on Information from Non-Self-Governing Territories and transferred its functions to the Committee of 24. This committee has led the efforts to gain early independence for remaining colonies.

The colonial functions of the organization have not always progressed smoothly. Disputes exist about the definition of non-self-governing territories. The Portuguese have been particularly intractable on this score, refusing to accept such a designation for their overseas territories. The General Assembly has taken a strong

[40] See pages 104–107 above.
[41] Charter, Article 73.

stand, insisting that Portugal make reports on its African territories but without success. Great Britain similarly resisted reporting on Southern Rhodesia, which has been self-governing since
1923. Despite some feeling that the General Assembly is being less
than helpful on the colonial question, the evidence shows that in
this dangerous transition period the organization has played a useful role in assisting the orderly process of independence for colonies.
The handwriting is clearly on the wall; the old colonial era is
drawing to a close. The function of the UN as a midwife in the
birth of new states provides some guarantee against the danger
of world conflict.

SUMMARY

We have seen that the United Nations plays an essential role in
international relations. The UN is an institution for the development of order and the preservation of peace and security. It is the
most important stage for multilateral diplomacy. The organization
can also be used for a wide variety of economic, social, cultural, and
humanitarian activities in which states seek to cooperate and move
forward together. This is ever more true when the United Nations
is assisted by specialized agencies, regional organizations, and other
public international organizations.

The United Nations is more than a mechanism, more than a useful tool available when desired by the member states. The Charter
lays upon the UN the positive responsibility for the maintenance of
international peace and security. The record of the organization
provides hope that whenever war threatens, a large coalition of states
will align themselves under the banners of the United Nations for
the preservation of international peace. The record also shows that
the Secretaries-General and the Secretariat have taken the initiative
to make the UN an active protagonist in the quest for peace and
security. International tensions continue to exist. Dangers of war
abound. But thus far, another world war has been prevented. For
the preservation of even a tenuous peace the United Nations has
played an essential role.

The organization needs to develop its potentialities for the pacific
settlement of disputes. While the Security Council and the International Court of Justice have not fulfilled the hopes of mankind

that their efforts would bear greater fruit, the Secretaries-General have exceeded expectation on this score. The enforcement of peace through the Security Council fell victim to the cold war. The development of alternative means for acting against aggression through collective self-defense under Article 51, through General Assembly action under the "Uniting for Peace" resolution, and through United Nations forces have been among the most imaginative improvisations under the Charter. The era of permanent peace is no more than a hope. Prognosis for the future is uncertain. Codification of international law and the promotion of order based on generally accepted principles has been discouragingly slow. On the other hand, the eradication of irrational hatreds as a disruptive force in the relations among peoples appears to be giving way before the onslaught of the organization.

Among the more hopeful developments have been those associated with the elimination of economic, social, and colonial conflicts. Although reasons for optimism must be tempered by the varied record of failures as well as success, any progress in the direction of law and order, any improvement in the prosperity of mankind, and every gain in the level of human dignity should persuade even the realist that he should not despair.

PART II

The International Conflicts of Our Time

THE foregoing chapters have been concerned with an analytical exposition of the nature of international politics. We turn now to the contemporary international scene. We are living in a time of crisis. Three long-term conditions give birth to our most serious international problems. The cold war, contemporary nationalism in the underdeveloped states, and the quest for economic development provide a background as well as a root cause for the conflicts of our time.

Four chapters are devoted to a study of the cold war. Here we examine the historic antecedents of the cold war, the ideological foundations for this antagonism, the events which brought the cold war into being, and the continuing issues of this conflict. Four chapters will deal with contemporary nationalism in the Middle East, Africa, Asia, and Latin America. One chapter will be devoted to the problems of and the approaches to economic development. A concluding chapter will examine major contemporary issues of United States foreign policy.

CHAPTER 5

The Background for the Cold War

THE COLD war came hard on the heels of World War II. A convenient date for marking its beginning has been the enunciation of the Truman Doctrine on March 12, 1947. However, the cold war did not simply break out on that day; it had evolved over a period of several years during which relations between West and East became increasingly hostile. The cold war resulted from issues in which the West and the Soviet Union were in conflict. These issues will be considered in Chapter 7. It also developed because of proximate historical experiences of the Western democracies with aggressor states prior to the war. Also conducive to enmity between the Western states and the USSR was a legacy of relations that were often disharmonious. These we consider below.

NONAPPEASEMENT OF AGGRESSOR STATES

Disillusionment with the peace established by the Versailles Treaty led some scholars and statesmen to doubt an earlier opinion that the First World War was caused by German imperialism. There was a tendency to assign guilt for the war to all states. An outgrowth of this perspective was the attitude that states were neither good nor bad, aggressive or peace loving. States were states and they all behaved about the same. They all had their grievances which reasonable statesmen could consider and satisfy. Such an attitude was not prepared to understand or to cope with the phenomenon of the aggressor nations of the 1930's. There was, therefore, no consensus that Germany, Japan, and Italy were revisionist states pursuing unlimited goals by aggressive means. It took the experience of the

131

Second World War to end all doubt that Hitler, Mussolini, and Tojo pursued aggressive policies and that these policies caused the war. Prior to the war there were voices, such as those of Franklin D. Roosevelt, Maxim Litvinov, and Winston Churchill, which warned that Hitler's Germany, Tojo's Japan, and Mussolini's Italy were expansionist and had to be stopped by demonstrations of force. They warned that only collective security would preserve peace. But the counsel of the appeasers prevailed. The aggressors were not blocked.

The high point of appeasement was the Munich Agreement of 1938. By this pact Neville Chamberlain believed that German ambitions had been satisfied and a durable peace ensured. However, when Hitler occupied Czechoslovakia in March of 1939, it was plain that appeasement did not sate the appetite of German expansion. The outbreak of the Second World War proved that appeasement does not work, that is, it does not serve to preserve peace.

At the end of the Second World War the people and their leaders in the Western states were psychologically prepared to identify aggressor nations. No matter what policy might be adopted in response to the rise of a new aggressor, the experience of the 1930's ruled out appeasement as a possible answer. This outlook was relevant to the outbreak of the cold war. Soviet demands on a number of issues produced a feeling in the West that the Soviet Union had become intransigent in its negotiations. It wanted all problems settled on its own terms. By 1947 leaders in the Western democracies were sure that the foreign policy of the Soviet Union was revisionist. They then decided to face Soviet expansionist tendencies by policies other than appeasement. They perforce rejected any suggestion of attempting a new Munich. The United States led the way in the containment of Soviet expansion. This policy and the unwillingness of the Soviet Union to adopt a more tractable response resulted in the cold war.

SOVIET FOREIGN POLICY AND THE WEST

The deterioration of relations between the Soviet Union and the Western democracies at the end of the Second World War was unexpected. From 1941 to 1945 these relations were harmonious and friendly. It was generally believed that these good relations would continue into the postwar era. Nevertheless, relations between the Soviet Union and the West had not always been good but had moved in cycles with periods of considerable hostility mitigated by periods of comparative friendship. These "ups" and "downs" in Soviet-Western relations established credibility that hostile relations might yet again take place. This is not to say that alternating cycles of hostility and friendship occur in some mechanistic fashion. It is not predetermined that bad relations must improve and friendliness is temporary. Relations, good and bad, result from underlying circumstances, conflicting or cooperative interests, and the assumptions of policy makers with respect to one another's intentions.

By and large, from 1917, that is, after the Bolshevik [1] Revolution, until 1934 relations between the Soviet Union and the Western democracies were poor. Between 1934 and August of 1939 these relations improved. The signing of the Nazi-Soviet Pact in August, 1939, ushered in a period of hostility that lasted until Germany attacked the Soviet Union in June of 1941. Under the influence of fighting a common war against the Axis and attempting to arrange to their mutual advantage the postwar peace, the relations between East and West from 1941 to 1947 were on the whole good. 1947 marked the beginning of the cold-war period. Until 1953, roughly until the death of Stalin, the relations were dangerously hostile. The death of Stalin led to a thaw in the cold war that has been with us ever since, but with some fluctuations that provided months of great hostility (as during the time of the U-2 incident, the time of the construction of the Berlin wall, and again during the Cuban crisis of October, 1962). To be sure, these generalizations are not precise. Within the countries of the West, relations between each of them and the Soviet Union have not always been the same. In each of these periods, there were instances of cooperation during periods of hostility, and irritation and tension during periods of friendly relations.

SOVIET FOREIGN POLICY, 1917–1934

The Bolshevik Revolution of November 7, 1917, initiated a period of hostile relations between the new Bolshevik regime of Rus-

---

[1] The Bolsheviks were the majority wing of the Russian Social Democratic Labor Party. They functioned as a distinct party from 1903; in 1918 they took the name of Communist Party.

sia, later to be renamed the Union of Soviet Socialist Republics, and the democracies of Western Europe and North America. From the point of view of the Western democracies, their grievances were many. The revolutionary doctrine of the Bolsheviks advocated the overthrow of all of the "capitalist" regimes of the West. The governments of the Allied and Associated Powers in World War I were considered class enemies to be overthrown. Bolshevik leaders expected that within a relatively brief period of time Communists in the countries of Central and Eastern Europe would win power by revolution. They found no particular virtue in democratic systems of government and politics. Their views were conditioned by a belief in an irreconcilable class struggle that could only be extirpated through revolutionary violence.

Not only were the ideas emanating from the Soviet Union revolutionary, but they also were supported by practices intended to disturb the domestic tranquility of the Western democracies. Agitation and propaganda by Communist parties were among the lesser expressions of hostility. The use of the Red Army against the Poles in 1919 raised the specter of the Bolsheviks' use of military force to assist proletarian revolutions.

In 1919 Lenin established the Comintern. This was organized as an international Communist party with sections in most countries. The Comintern assumed the role of promoting revolutions, mobilizing support for Communist Russia, agitating against the Western democracies, and doing all of this under a single well-organized international leadership.

One of the early steps of Lenin's government was the withdrawal of Russia from the war against the Central Powers. Western statesmen considered this an act of betrayal to the Allied cause and a violation of the promises given by the Czarist regime and its successor, the Provisional Government. The publication of secret correspondence detrimental to the Allied and Associated Powers and Lenin's confiscation of foreign properties deepened hostility between the Western democracies and Communist Russia.

From the point of view of Lenin and his colleagues, the actions of the Allied Powers were alarming. Communist ideology led them to expect counterrevolution from the capitalist West against Soviet Russia, the country of the working class. An Allied occupation in northern Russia and eastern Siberia served to corroborate this expectation. The Japanese landed troops at Vladivostok on April 5, 1918, ostensibly because of the murder of three Japanese shopkeepers. The presence of Japanese forces in this part of an unstable Russia racked by civil war brought British, French, and American troops into the area. At about the same time, the British landed a small force in Murmansk for the purpose of safeguarding Allied stores stockpiled there. In addition, British and French forces were landed in nearby Archangel during the summer months of 1918. These forces were followed some weeks later by the landing of American troops. The Bolsheviks considered these Allied forces to portend the crushing of Soviet rule. When the war ended on November 11, 1918, and the Allied forces were not removed, the Bolsheviks, with some cause, credited the intervention with supporting the White Guard forces seeking to overthrow the Bolshevik regime.

For some years after the Bolshevik revolution Lenin's government anticipated similar revolutions in other European states. They had little hope that they could continue to exist as an isolated socialist regime in a capitalist world. However, as Communist revolutions failed to materialize and as those that did take place proved short-lived, the need to maintain their rule in Russia alone became increasingly compelling. By 1925 it became apparent to the Bolshevik leaders that the likelihood of revolution in the immediate future had passed and that capitalism had "stabilized itself," at least for some years to come. This new outlook led to Russian attempts to enter into formal and normal relations with other countries. The earliest success, in this respect, involved the coming together of the two outcasts of European society, Communist Russia and defeated Germany, in their agreement at Rapallo in 1922. Over a period of years the Soviet Union established diplomatic relations, but hardly friendly relations, with most states. The United States was the last large power to recognize Bolshevik Russia. This it did in November of 1933. During this period, however, the Soviet Union participated in the Preparatory Commission for the Disarmament Conference sponsored by the League of Nations, and it entered into a number of trade agreements with capitalist states. In brief, despite an intrinsic hostility between the Soviet Union and the West, during the later 1920's and the early 1930's diplomatic relations were established.

SOVIET FOREIGN POLICY, 1934–1939

The rise of Hitler in 1933 and the increasingly aggressive activities of Japan in Asia created new conditions for Soviet foreign policy. Until Hitler came to power, the Soviets believed that capitalist encirclement was the real source of danger to their security. The "line" then advanced by the Soviet Union was that a workers' paradise was in the process of construction in the Soviet Union and that the example of such a prosperous working-class country provoked a potentially revolutionary situation. Capitalists would feel compelled to eradicate the successful Soviet experiment. The Soviet Union, therefore, tried to promote policies intended to undermine the power of capitalist states. They encouraged nationalist revolutionaries in Asia to revolt against imperialist rule, a tactic which would serve to weaken the common enemy of the Bolsheviks and the nationalists—Great Britain, France, the United States, and other imperialist countries.

Communist ideology led Soviet leaders to believe that capitalism could not solve the economic problems that produced the depression of 1929. Consequently, the initial reaction of Communist parties to the rise of fascism was to see it simply as a variant form of capitalism. Just as other capitalist parties could not solve, within the context of capitalist economics, the social problems of the day, so the Fascists were doomed to failure because they would retain the capitalist system. The German Communists judged the National Socialists to be the last dying gasp of German capitalism. The Nazis would be unable to lead Germany out of the depression, and after their failure the masses would turn to the Communist Party to set things right through a socialist reorganization of society. The strength of the Communist Party rested upon its ability to win the proletariat away from the German Social Democratic Party. This became a major objective of Communist parties throughout Europe and North America. The idea that the Socialist parties were really Social-Fascists, using socialist language for the purpose of betraying the working class to fascism, became the propaganda line promoted by the Communists in their drive to win the support of the working class. Hitler's coming to power, therefore, found the Communists separated from all other anti-Nazi movements.

The expected failure of national socialism and a renewed strength for communism soon proved illusory. Hitler's advocacy of a *drang noch osten,* a drive eastward, and the successful suppression of Communist parties in Italy, Germany, and Japan led the Kremlin to reassess its outlook. It soon saw that Germany and Japan were aggressive. They threatened the interests of European countries and the United States as well as the Soviet Union. The fear of fascism coming to power within France and Spain now led to cooperative efforts between Communists and non-Communists in a united anti-Fascist effort. In 1934 the Soviet Union changed its policy, seeking alliances and collective security against the threat of the aggressor nations. Within democratic states, Communist parties dropped their more extreme advocacy of revolution and class struggle and adopted the tactic of the "popular front" of anti-Fascist organizations against fascism.

The new Soviet "line" naturally facilitated collaborative efforts with the regimes of the Western democracies. Mutual-assistance pacts were signed by the Soviet Union with France and with Czechoslovakia. The Soviet Union joined the League of Nations, and her foreign minister, Maxim Litvinov, became a foremost spokesman for collective security against Fascist aggression. Democrats like Leon Blum of France, Edouard Beneš of Czechoslovakia, and Franklin D. Roosevelt of the United States were no longer attacked but were often supported by the Communists in their efforts to prove their sincerity in advocating unity against fascism.

However, by 1937 collective security had failed to win the support of the British and French governments. The policies of the aggressor states were succeeding. Japan's occupation of Manchuria, Italy's conquest of Ethiopia, and Germany's violation of the Versailles treaty all went unchecked and unpunished. This led to doubts on Stalin's part that collective security could be achieved. Leon Blum's popular-front government fell in France, and the Chamberlain regime which favored appeasement came to power in Great Britain.[2] Spain's popular-front government faced a Fascist uprising which became a civil war in which Italy and Germany supported General Franco while the Western democracies stood by denying the democratic Republic their assistance. The Soviet Union had new cause to doubt that collective security would come to pass.

[2] A. L. Rowse, *Appeasement: A Study in Political Decline, 1933–1938* (New York: Norton, 1961), p. 123.

Communist leadership interpreted appeasement as encouraging Hitler to march eastward and engage the Soviet Union in a war which would be mutually debilitating to both states. There is no tangible evidence that this was in fact the intention of appeasement. On the contrary, from the point of view of the appeasers, the Soviet Union appeared to be a weak reed upon which a policy of collective security might be based; since 1934 it had instigated extensive purges of leadership including a purge of its general staff in 1938.

The failure of the League to assure security, the victory of fascism in Spain, the Austrian *anschluss,* and the attitude of Chamberlain and Daladier in the Sudetenland question led to a reassessment of the Soviet strategy. The Munich agreement provided a strong impetus for the articulation of a new foreign policy. Stalin used the occasion of the 18th Congress of the Communist Party of the Soviet Union for a major foreign policy statement. Speaking on March 10, 1939, he warned the Western democracies that the Soviet Union could pursue its own alternative to collective security. Believing that the policy of appeasement was designed to drive Hitler eastward and involve the Soviet Union and Germany in war, Stalin warned that the Soviet Union would not stand idly by and permit this to happen. He apparently considered the possibility of reversing Soviet policy to promote a different war in which Hitler and the Western democracies would destroy one another.[3] He warned the states of the West that the Soviet Union would not "pull the chestnuts out of the fire for them" [4] without mutually advantageous prior commitments. In other words, although the Soviet Union was willing to engage in collective-security arrangements and carry out its part of such a bargain, it would only do this on terms that were mutually beneficial. Only if such an arrangement would guarantee the security of the Soviet Union against Fascist aggression would the Soviet Union undertake to guarantee the security of Western democracies. A few days after this address Hitler tore up the Munich Pact by occupying Czechoslovakia. The British and French now signed a treaty of

[3] Arthur E. Adams, *Readings in Soviet Foreign Policy, Theory and Practice* (Boston: Heath, 1961). See Stalin's Report on the Work of the Central Committee to the Eighteenth Congress of the Communist Party of the Soviet Union, March 10, 1939, pp. 150–154.
[4] *Ibid.,* p. 154.

mutual assistance with Poland, but they were still slow to engage Russia in any collective-security commitments. For its part, Poland refused to allow the passage of Soviet troops across its territory for the purposes of opposing Hitler's *Wehrmacht*. Events moved quickly. While the German Foreign Office responded to Soviet feelers for better relations, Britain and France approached the Soviet Union with extreme caution.

On May 3, 1939, Litvinov, the Soviet Foreign Minister, a man closely associated with the Soviet advocacy of collective security, was replaced by Molotov. The British-French guarantee of Polish territorial integrity drove Hitler to seek agreement with the Soviet Union. Secret negotiations between Moscow and Berlin proceeded harmoniously through the summer of 1939. On the other hand, a military mission of rather low diplomatic standing was dispatched by London and Paris for discussions in Moscow of a defense agreement. The fact that they traveled to the Soviet Union by sea underlined the lack of urgency with which the British and French leadership viewed such an agreement. By the time the British and French delegation opened its discussions with the Soviet representatives, it was too late. The die had been cast. On August 23, 1939, Ribbentrop, the German Foreign Minister, signed a 10-year nonaggression pact with the Soviet Union. This pact not only assured the outbreak of the Second World War, which in fact began just a little more than a week later, but it also marked a new turn in Soviet relations with the West.

The Nazi-Soviet pact assured Hitler of the benevolent neutrality of the Soviet Union, and he could, therefore, with impunity, attack Poland. Even if the British and French would carry out their treaty obligations to Poland and make war on Germany, such a war would be largely a one-front fight of manageable proportions.

Now, the increasing hostility between Russia and the West that had been developing since 1938 gained momentum—August 23, 1939, to June 22, 1941, was marked by tension and hostility.

August 23, 1939–June 22, 1941

The pact was signed on August 23 and eight days later, on September 1, the Second World War began. Germany's attack on Poland, which started the war, was followed two days later by a French and British declaration of war against Germany. The Nazi-Soviet pact produced an atmosphere of enmity between the Soviet Union and Great Britain and France. The United States developed close relations with the Western democracies, and, with most Americans sympathetic to Great Britain and France, the hostility that they felt toward Germany was also reflected in a negative attitude toward the Soviet Union. There was ample basis for a cooling off of earlier friendly attitudes.

The anti-Soviet atmosphere was exacerbated by the policy pursued by the Communist Party in the United States. The feeling that the Communist Party of the United States was a foreign conspiracy, a tool of the Soviet Union, was hardly disabused by the Party's position. Almost overnight it changed from advocating collective security and anti-fascism to opposing collective security and anti-fascism as warmongering. It condemned the war as an imperialist conflict rather than one begun by an aggressor state; instead of collective security it now favored an isolationist policy. Franklin D. Roosevelt, who had some Communist support prior to this time, now became their prime target as "the worst warmonger in United States history." In a Communist-led labor union the slogan, "The Yanks are not Coming," was evidence of Communist aims. The Communists seemed to favor Nazi Germany because she was a friend of the Soviet Union. All of this produced a strong anti-Communist reaction in the United States. Communists no longer appeared to be simply extreme left-wingers but rather disloyal citizens serving the Soviet cause. The policy of the American Communist Party was clearly responding to the needs of Soviet foreign policy rather than those of the American working class. But Communist policy in the United States was not an isolated phenomenon. Communist parties in all countries quickly adopted positions favorable to Hitler's Germany and hostile to the Western democracies.

Although the Nazi-Soviet Treaty of August 23, 1939, was called a nonaggression pact, appended to it was a secret protocol that meted out spheres of influence in Eastern Europe between Germany and the USSR.[5] Under this protocol the Soviet Union lost little time in expanding westward. On September 17, the Red Army marched into Eastern Poland to reclaim land that the Soviet Union had lost to Poland about two decades earlier. This move had the effect of ad-

[5] Alvin Z. Rubinstein, *The Foreign Policy of the Soviet Union* (New York: Random House, 1960), pp. 144–145.

ministering the *coup de grace* to the Polish regime, which now had to escape and eventually reestablish itself in London as a government-in-exile. Soviet pressures on the Baltic states imposed "mutual-assistance agreements" presumably to "defend" these states against aggression and placed Soviet military forces on Baltic territories. With the armies of the Soviet Union on the soil of Estonia, Latvia, and Lithuania, plebescites were staged which incorporated these lands into the Soviet Union. In August, 1940, they became constituent republics of the Soviet Union.

The Soviet war with Finland was particularly vexing to the people of the Western democracies. The Soviet Union sought border adjustments in the area of the Karelian Isthmus, a lease of the Hangoe Peninsula, and the icefree port of Petsamo on the Arctic Sea. In return the Soviet Union offered to compensate Finland by a cession of territory twice as large but less valuable. The Soviet Union claimed that the Finnish border was too close to its second largest city, Leningrad, which could be brought under artillery fire. For the Finns, however, the satisfaction of Soviet territorial demands would have resulted in giving up their formidable Mannerheim Line, a defensive complex which they considered essential to their security. When negotiations proved inconclusive, the Soviet Union, on November 29, 1939, attacked Finland.[6]

Western sympathy for the Finns after this aggressive attack mounted to a feeling of adulation as the numerically inferior Finnish troops were able to defeat and outmaneuver Soviet forces in the Karelian Isthmus and in central Finland. Soviet aggression was condemned by the League of Nations, and Russia was expelled on December 14. Although plans for significant Western military support in the form of British, French, and American volunteers were well advanced, they did not have time to materialize, and the Finns had to capitulate in February of 1940. The Soviet stock in the West fell to new depths.

The fall of France to Germany in June of 1940 brought Soviet pressure on Rumania to cede to it Bessarabia and northern Bukovina. Each step of Soviet expansion produced greater hostility in the West. Official relations between the Soviet Union and the Western

[6] *Ibid.*, pp. 128–129. However, in the Soviet version of the Finnish War of 1939–1940 it was the Finns who committed the aggression and left the Soviet Union with no choice but to defend itself!

democracies conformed with this mood. Nor did the attitude adopted by the Soviet Union toward Germany in the early months of 1941 do much to change this situation.

Now it was the Soviet turn to appease Hitler. It repeatedly asserted its indestructible friendship for Nazi Germany. Warnings from the United States and Great Britain that a German attack on the Soviet Union was impending were brusquely rejected. In. Churchill's words, Stalin's policy, on this occasion was one of

> ... error and vanity of cold-blooded calculation of the Soviet Government and enormous Communist machine, and their amazing ignorance about where they stood themselves. They had shown a total indifference to the fate of the Western Powers, although this meant the destruction of that "Second Front" for which they were soon to clamour. They seemed to have no inkling that Hitler had for more than six months resolved to destroy them. If their Intelligence Service informed them of the vast German deployment towards the East, which was now increasing every day, they omitted many needful steps to meet it. Thus they had allowed the whole of the Balkans to be overrun by Germany. They hated and despised the democracies of the West; but the four countries, Turkey, Rumania, Bulgaria, and Yugoslavia, which were of vital interest to them and their own safety, could all have been combined by the Soviet Government in January with active British aid to form a Balkan front against Hitler. They let them all break into confusion, and all but Turkey were mopped up one by one. War is mainly a catalogue of blunders, but it may be doubted whether any mistake in history has equalled that of which Stalin and the Communist chiefs were guilty when they cast away all possibilities in the Balkans and supinely awaited, or were incapable of realizing, the fearful onslaught which impended upon Russia. We have hitherto rated them as selfish calculators. In this period they were proved simpletons as well.[7]

On June 15, Tass published a communiqué authored by Molotov claiming as absurd rumors to the effect that Germany and the Soviet Union were close to war and asserting that such allegations were "clumsy propaganda maneuver (s) of the forces arrayed against the Soviet Union and Germany, which are interested in a spread and intensification of the war." [8] Again, on the eve of the German attack Molotov was reported by the German Ambassador to the Soviet

[7] Winston S. Churchill, *The Second World War. The Grand Alliance* (Boston: Houghton Mifflin, 1950), pp. 352–353.

[8] *Ibid.,* p. 365.

Union to have stated that "There were a number of indications that the German Government was dissatisfied with the Soviet Government. Rumours were even current that a war was impending between Germany and the Soviet Union ... The Soviet Government was unable to understand the reasons for Germany's dissatisfaction . . .[9] It has been noted that "Molotov could grovel as well as growl. . . ." [10]

Hitler's legions struck the Soviet Union with disastrous impact on June 22, 1941. The Soviet Union suffered grave losses from the beginning of the fighting. The warnings given Stalin did not prevent the Germans from surprising the Soviet Union with their attack. Stalin was inadequately prepared. His Communist fifth columns around the world were still mouthing the phrases of struggle against the "imperialist war" and working to undermine the fight of the democracies against Hitler. As the war between the USSR and Germany began, relations between the Soviet Union and the West were at their worst. However, in view of their need to fight together against Hitler's aggression, their hostility gave way to friendly relations almost overnight.

SOVIET PARTICIPATION IN THE UNITED NATIONS COALITION AGAINST THE AXIS, 1941–1945

The German attack on the Soviet Union produced an immediate decisive change in the relations between the Soviet Union and the Western democracies. Extreme hostility changed to feelings of warm friendship and cooperation. In a sense the "slate was wiped clean." That which had gone before was quickly forgotten in the need for cooperation. Hitler was too formidable and too victorious a foe to permit recriminating debate about who was at fault for the antagonisms of the preceding two years. In a speech to the Russian people on July 3 Stalin referred to the American and European peoples as the "loyal allies" of the Soviet peoples. He assured his people that "in this war of liberation we shall not be alone," and expressed Soviet gratitude to the British and United States Governments for declarations signifying their intention to render aid to the Soviet Union.

[9] *Ibid.*, p. 366.
[10] Herbert Feis, *Churchill, Roosevelt, Stalin. The War They Waged and the Peace They Sought* (Princeton, N.J.: Princeton University Press, 1957), p. 6.

For his part, Churchill was resolved even before the German attack on Russia actually began that Great Britain would come to the support of Russia. His private secretary, Colville, reports that when he questioned Churchill about the propriety of an association between the arch anti-Communist Churchill and the Communists, Churchill replied, "... I have only one purpose, the destruction of Hitler, and my life is much simplified thereby. If Hitler invaded Hell I would make at least a favourable reference to the Devil in the House of Commons." In a radio address on the B.B.C. the night of the German attack Churchill, after calling attention to his long record of opposition to communism and his own feeling that his anti-Communist sentiments were well-founded and required no apology, went on to assert a policy of assistance to, "any man or state who fights on against Nazism . . ." and assurances, "that we shall give whatever help we can to Russia and the Russian people. We shall appeal to all our friends and allies in every part of the world to take the same course and pursue it as we shall faithfully and steadfastly to the end . . ." for, said Churchill, "the Russian danger is our danger and the danger of the United States, just as the cause of any Russian fighting for his hearth and home is the cause of free men and free peoples in every quarter of the globe. . . ." [11]

The early expressions of common cause against Nazi aggression quickly led to more tangible steps of unity. When Roosevelt and Churchill drafted the Atlantic Charter the Soviet Ambassador to Great Britain, Maisky, quickly asserted Soviet agreement and support for this statement of principle. With the Japanese attack on Pearl Harbor and the creation of a United Nations coalition the Soviet Union became a part of this alliance. Missions between the Soviet Union and the United States and the Soviet Union and Great Britain were exchanged to further cooperation in fighting the war. Public opinion in the West responded to this new alliance. In the United States and Great Britain the Soviet people were considered heroes. The Soviet Union got a good press. Hollywood's movies showed Russians most favorably. For their part the Soviet press and radio emphasized the solidarity of the American and British peoples and their governments with those of the Soviet Union. The valor of the Soviet people in the face of massive German blows and the reso-

11 Churchill, *op. cit.*, pp. 370–373.

luteness of Soviet defense against German aggression could not but
have been admired by all in the West.

Hidden from view by the consciously propounded official declarations of unending friendship and harmony were a variety of minor
irritations and increasing clashes of interest. From the Soviet's point
of view the Western Allies were not doing enough to help defeat
German armed might. The Soviet clamor for an early second front
and Stalin's impatience with the interruption of Allied North Atlantic convoys because of losses suffered from German U-boat and air-
plane attacks reflected not only the feeling that the Soviet Union was
bearing an inordinately large share of the burden but reflected also
lingering suspicion that the Western democracies were trying to
bleed the Soviet Union while in the process of defeating Hitler.
Perhaps it bespoke a Soviet desire that the war become more costly
to the United States and Great Britain and that they emerge from
the conflict measurably weakened. From the point of view of the
Western Allies it was the difficulty of negotiations with the Soviets,
the secretiveness of Soviet leadership, and the suspicion which
greeted all United States and British initiatives that was troubling.
A situation that was most irritating to the United States was the
difficulty of negotiating implementations of lend-lease agreements.
Soviet negotiators refused to acknowledge the importance of demands on United States supplies other than their own. They objected
to the provision of supplies for the Pacific front, which they considered a sideshow. They troubled American negotiators by their attitudes of ingratitude and by their clamor for more and more.[12]
Most objectionable was the failure of the Soviet Union to credit the
United States after 1942 with any significant role in aid for the
Eastern front, at least so far as the Russian public was concerned.
However, these were, in retrospect, minor irritations. The future of
Poland and the countries of Eastern Europe, the problem of German
reparations, and other Soviet interests of a more enduring nature
were to bring on the cold war. These we shall consider in Chapter 7.

By and large, from the time of Soviet entry into the Second World
War until its termination, the relations between the Soviet Union

[12] This situation is well described in the book by General Gordon R.
Deane entitled *The Strange Alliance: The Story of Our Efforts at War
Time Cooperation with Russia* (New York: Viking, 1946).

and the Western democracies were good. They appeared in the public eye far better than they had been in actuality. During the time when the Soviet Union was in its most difficult straits cooperation was easiest. As the war turned in favor of the Allies the relations between the Soviet Union and the West became increasingly difficult. In retrospect the Yalta Agreement of February, 1945, appeared as the high point in the close collaboration between East and West. That agreement was, by and large, an agreement in broad principle. The arrangements accepted at Yalta quickly broke down in their implementation. From then on relations between East and West progressively deteriorated. It took the Western democracies some time— several years—before their leaders were finally satisfied that the Soviet Union demanded not merely reasonable concessions but something more than its own security needs. This reaction of the West to Stalin's excesses brought on a virulent anti-Communist atmosphere.

In the United States, especially, anti-Communist attitudes hardened. Perhaps because the American people felt they had been so open and generous with the Soviet Union they also now felt a strong sense of having been betrayed. Because of Soviet intransigence and because the Soviet Union violated any acceptable interpretation of treaties to which it was a party, its credibility and honor in the eyes of the West became worthless. The expectation that East and West, having cooperated well together to win the war, would maintain their unity to preserve the peace was frustrated. It was this sense of frustration and this sense of betrayal that led not only to the outbreak of the cold war but also, in the United States, to a single-minded and often exaggerated anti-communism.

SUMMARY

The cold war must be seen against a background of the events which preceded it. The failure of appeasement in the 1930's precluded any likelihood that it would be attempted in the 1940's. The alternating cycles of hostile and moderated relations between the USSR and the Western democracies allowed a psychological preparedness for the cold war. However, the harmony brought on by close collaboration against a common enemy led many in the West to expect enduring friendship between East and West. Soviet leaders frustrated agreements after the war with unrelenting demands. In communizing Eastern Europe they violated agreements which they had made. To the people in the West, Soviet behavior was a betrayal of their good faith and generosity. It led to feelings of outrage, expressed as bitter anti-communism.

CHAPTER 6

The Theory and Practice of Communism and the Cold War

WHAT is the cold war, a contest between two antagonistic ideologies or a struggle for power between the United States and the Soviet Union? Marked disagreement exists about the basic causes of the cold war. Some have perceived it to be a struggle for the minds of men. There are those who believe that countries have become Communist because of the wily appeals of the Marxist doctrines. Communists themselves have said that the cold war is rooted in a clash of systems, the socialist versus the capitalist, and that ultimately the Communists must win because their system provides the masses with a better life than capitalism.

Another approach holds the cold war to be a struggle for world supremacy by great powers. In this view ideology is nothing more than rationalization after the fact. It is an attempt to justify amoral action in moral terms. It is used for propagandistic purposes. Ideology provides the appropriate scripture to be quoted in support of a desired course of action, any desired course of action. The cold war would hardly be different if Russia were still ruled by the czars. The czars conceived Russian national interest in revisionist and messianic terms and also would have had to be contained by a *status-quo* West.

To understand the relevance of Communist ideology to the cold-war conflict, there is little to be gained in insisting that the conflict is entirely ideological or wholly a drive for power. Communist behavior cannot be explained solely in terms of the writings of Marx, Engels, Lenin, Stalin, or more contemporary leaders. The corpus of writings known as Marxism-Leninism is not quite a catechism provided by the bearded prophets of communism that can be looked into for answers to day-to-day problems. It would, however, be a gross exaggeration to say that ideology is mere "window dressing" and serves the function of justifying rather than directing the action Communists take. A wiser view would seek to establish the way in which the actions of Communists derive from their theoretical suppositions and are molded by these presuppositions. The fact is that Communist leaders all over the world study the writings of Marx and Lenin. Some influence must therefore be presumed to exist. For Communists, ideology becomes a frame of reference for viewing the world, for viewing themselves, and for viewing "the enemy." Ideology is a tool useful to the Communists for explaining their actions to themselves and to the world at large.

Not all aspects of ideology have continuing significance, however. Even if one took the extreme position that all of the moves of the Soviet Union are directed by Marxism-Leninism, one would be confronted with the fact that Marxism-Leninism constitutes a large body of writing, some of it contradictory. The "scriptures" offer many varying lines of action. One can, without too much trouble, find justification for almost any policy—revolution or peaceful coexistence, strict adherence to legal means or clandestine illegal activity, proletarian internationalism or narrow Russian nationalism. It follows that at any point in time differing aspects of ideology serve to direct or influence Communist activity.

Not all component elements of ideology do, as a matter of fact, serve to inform us about Communist or Soviet policies and intentions. Many ideas and interpretations propounded in the writings are irrelevant to the things that Communists do today. For instance, Marx posited a goal to which all Communist activity was ultimately to be directed. He called that goal a Communist society. This society would be marked by two characteristics. First, it would be a society of plenty, the only society in all human history to have enough of everything for everyone. Marx anticipated that the productivity of capitalism and the even greater productivity of socialism would increase products and services to the point where man would produce enough to satisfy everyone's needs. With plenty of goods people could simply take whatever they needed. "From each according to his ability to each according to his need" [1] would govern the production and distribution of goods in a Communist society. A second characteristic of the Communist society was the absence of a state. We shall consider the Communist position on the state below; here we only point out that Marx predicted that as a result of the continuing class struggle the proletariat (factory workers) would eventually liquidate the capitalists (employers-owners of industry) and create a society in which only one class existed, a classless society. According to Marx the state is an essential product of a class-divided society. It is necessary only where classes are in conflict with one another. Once a classless society had been established there would be no basis for class conflict and consequently no need for the state. He, therefore, predicted that the state would just wither away.[2]

It may be worthwhile to learn the meaning of communism as an ultimate goal, but this predicted course of development is irrelevant to the current problems and policies of the Communists. Knowledge of this goal does not serve to inform us about the policies that the Soviet Union or Red China pursue today or are likely to pursue in the foreseeable future. In no sense does the activity of the Communist Party or Soviet state derive from the aim of creating the ultimate ideal Communist society.

The utopian goals of Marxist communism tell us little about what Communists do. There are other concepts, however, that are very much to the point in explaining the action of Communists. The more important of these are: the belief that Marxism-Leninism is a science; the concept and the role of class struggle; the Communists' view of the state; their views concerning social change; the function and the nature of the party; the strategy and tactics of present-day communism.

COMMUNISM AS A SCIENCE

In an article appearing in the October, 1959, issue of *Foreign Affairs*, Nikita S. Khrushchev wrote of the inevitable victory of communism. "Our confidence in the victory of Communism . . . is based

[1] Karl Marx, *Critique of the Gotha Programme* (New York: International Publishers, 1933), p. 31.
[2] *Ibid.*, pp. 102–104.

on a knowledge of the laws governing the development of society. Just as in its time capitalism, as a more progressive system, took the place of feudalism, so will capitalism be inevitably superseded by Communism—the more progressive the more equitable social system." [3]

Communists believe that the course of history and the social, cultural, economic, and political condition of any society is determined by underlying laws of social development. The structure of society, the events of the day, and the developments which take place are determined by pervasive "laws." Marxism-Leninism "lays bare" the "laws" governing the organization of society and the nature of social change. In this sense it is considered to be scientific. The writings of authoritative Communist leaders, from Marx to the present, are subsumed under the rubric Marxism-Leninism and constitute the articulation of this science. Just as we are able to explain by the law of gravity why the apple falls down and not up when it drops off the tree, so the Communist believes that he can explain the nature of society as deriving from social-class relationships. Just as we predict that next year and the year following and for millions of years hence apples will fall down and not up because we understand the scientific law determining this phenomenon, so the Marxist asserts that "scientific" laws make inevitable a given historic process.

DIALECTICAL MATERIALISM

The hallmark of the Marxist science is its theory of *dialectical materialism*. Fundamental to this concept is the observation that all phenomena are in a state of constant change. Dialectics explains the cause of change as due to an inherent internal conflict. Dialectics is not an invention of Karl Marx. Marx inherited from Hegel the dialectical method. Indeed ancient Greek philosophers sought to arrive at truth through dialectical disputes. Their method was based upon a statement of truth, called a thesis, against which was ranged a counterstatement, called an antithesis. Both the thesis and the antithesis had in them aspects of truth, and in the conflict between the two a synthesis was developed in which the valid aspects of the thesis and the antithesis statements were included. However, each new synthesis became a thesis that begot its antithesis which in turn

[3] "On Peaceful Coexistence," Vol. 38, No. 1, p. 6.

led to a new synthesis. In this way some thinkers expected to reach higher and higher levels of truth.

Hegel adopted the dialectical method to explain and to predict historic change. He believed that such change resulted from thesis-antithesis conflicts. Every age had its dominating idea against which an opposite idea arose. In the conflict of ideas which then took place a "higher" idea, a synthesis of both, eventuated. This produced a historic process in which each new stage of history constituted a perfection of the preceding stage. The Hegelian concept of continuous change through thesis-antithesis conflict was adopted by Marx to explain historic change. However, Marx rejected the view that the conflict was in the realm of ideas. For Marx the thesis-antithesis conflict took place in the material realm.

The concept of materialism begins with the belief that the world is real, that is, matter exists. To this concept is affixed the idea that all thought, all ideas, derive from matter and are bound to matter. Man's thoughts reflect the world around him and cannot transcend the limits of the world of reality. Dialectical materialism, therefore, is a view in which the world is seen as in a state of constant change as a result of conflict inherent in all phenomena. This thesis-antithesis conflict, producing change, takes place first of all in the material universe. Ideas merely reflect and express this clash. The application of dialectical materialism to history, the belief that historic change results from forces in conflict and that these forces are to be found in the material realm of man's being, is the essence of the scientific approach of the Marxists. This concept is called *historical materialism*.

HISTORICAL MATERIALISM

Historical materialism views history as a dialectical process. Dialectical conflict producing the flow of history takes place in the material realm of man's existence, which, according to Karl Marx, is found in the economic life of a society. It is the economic life of the community that influences all human relations and therefore is the source for "scientific" explanations. The Marxist approach is sometimes labeled "economic determinism," a term that Communists dislike. Although economic determinism is an exaggeration of the Marxist view concerning the role of economic factors, it is an exaggeration of their actual outlook on social questions. In the sense that

Marxists hold that economic forces determine social relations they are economic determinists.

Material reality, according to historical materialism, rests upon particular tools of production or, as the Marxists call them, "means of production," in use at a given time. In all societies other than the Socialist and Communist means of production are privately owned. Distinct social classes arise based upon ownership and nonownership of means of production; some people own the means of production while others—most—do not and must "sell their labor power" to those who do. Each class in a class-divided society seeks its gain and makes such gains at the expense of other classes. This generates class conflict, another thesis-antithesis relationship which, according to the "laws," must be synthesized.

The materialist interpretation of history is based on the pervasive influence of economic factors on society. They constitute a substructure upon which superstructures are erected. Class struggle is the determining element in the substructure. A superstructure consisting of ideas, politics, government, culture, art, etc., is molded by the underlying class struggle. Thus, under capitalism, religion (a part of the superstructure) becomes a necessary opiate for the masses used by the capitalist class to distract the people from their misery and from the class struggle, to promise them "pie in the sky when they die" if they behave and obey their capitalist masters. Class-struggle explanations are thought up by Communists for such diverse phenomena as United States federalism, French parliamentary institutions, the British crown, abstract art, romantic period music, beatnik poetry, and modern architecture. Every element in the superstructure is determined by the needs of the class struggle.

The Marxist science claims to give an infallible explanation not only for what is but also for what will be. The class struggle provides the motive force for history. When Khrushchev tells us in his article in *Foreign Affairs* that the victory of communism is inevitable, when we are told that our grandchildren will live under communism, or when Communists say "we will bury you," what they mean is that the class struggle must end in a victory by the proletariat and the liquidation of the capitalist system. The victory of the proletariat is, in their view, an inevitable result of the dialectical process of history, and this provides them with assurance that socialism will triumph. By understanding the nature of the class struggle the Marxists believe they can predict its outcome and thereby the future shape of history.

Communists also believe that socialism is not only scientifically preordained but also morally necessary. What promotes socialism is good. That which inhibits it is evil. This reasoning leads to a very curious interpretation of peace-lovingness and aggression. Acts of defense against Communist take-over, as in Vietnam, Korea, or the Congo, are labeled aggression. North Vietnamese invasion of South Vietnam, Soviet suppression of the Hungarian revolution, and Pathet Lao attacks on the Laotian government are examples of peace-loving behavior. Aggression is not determined by who initiates the use of force but by the purpose of its use. The use of force to promote socialism, the next stage of history, is an act of peace. Defending the *status quo* is the "truly aggressive" conduct. Thus Communist countries are peace loving no matter how they act. "Capitalist" countries are aggressors whenever they clash with Communist efforts to implement "the course of history."

How true is the claim that Marxism-Leninism is truly a science? There is good reason to question the scientific character of Marxism if only by observing the not infrequent disagreement among its practitioners, the Communist leaders. As a science it is neither accurate nor simple. Marxist laws do not operate under controlled conditions with few variables. Communists cannot apply the relevant Marxist laws of social development to a set of circumstances and always agree on the outcome. In other words, Marxism-Leninism suffers a lack of accuracy and predictability as do all of the social sciences, in that controlled conditions and a limited number of variables are not representative of the nature of social relationships. The skilled social scientist may be able to explain why certain outcomes may develop, but he will be less than sure that they will in fact occur.

Even knowledgeable Communists apply different laws and propose different policies. Yet, as they see it, the application of the right law to any situation should ensure agreement on one correct solution. Communists therefore cannot allow for disagreements. Disagreement implies error. This consideration has given rise to two typical explanations for clashes in points of view. Either somebody is mistaken or there is a deliberate intention to betray through misleadership. On occasion Communists in the spirit of "self-criticism" revile themselves for having made erroneous assessments and promise to restudy the "classics" so that such errors will not be made in the future. At times leaders have been accused of treason, a deliberate attempt to mislead the working class. The capitalists, the imperialists, have insidious means to seduce and buy off leaders of the proletariat who have won the confidence of the working class. Misleadership here is deliberate. The only solution for this is the execution of the traitor and the denunciation of his treason.

The record of the Communists with respect to the accuracy of their predictions has been mixed. Their predictions have been no better than those of non-Marxists. Beginning with Marx himself and his expectation that the working class will be forced to live in conditions of increasing misery, through Lenin and his expectations of spreading proletarian revolution at the end of the First World War, to Stalin with his predictions of depression in capitalist countries at the end of the Second World War, and to Khrushchev's expectations that the West would back down in Cuba and West Berlin, Communist predictions have neither been scientifically accurate nor particularly good. Historical materialism has provided no laws which foretell political and social developments.

The fact that Communists consider Marxism-Leninism a science is a matter of great significance. In the first place it gives them a belief in their infallibility. They believe that Marx, Engels, and Lenin discovered the inexorable course that history must traverse. Communists view themselves as "handmaidens" of history. Even when things go badly, the feeling that their triumph is inevitable and can no more be inhibited than the change from night to day and day to night provides them with a confidence in the future.

In the second place the theory has enough flexibility in it to justify any line of conduct.

Third, the belief that their positions are scientifically correct also fosters confidence in the skill of their leaders. Leaders tend not to be questioned. Leadership is presumed to be too well grounded in the mastery of the Marxist-Leninist science to be questioned by mortal men. Just as one does not question the calculations of mathematicians or the results of experiments by chemists and physicists, so the Communists tend not to question the pronouncements of their "scientifically" apt leaders. This is invariably true when the leaders themselves maintain a high degree of unity in the positions they adopt. Then the Communist tends to be so self-assured that he becomes impregnable to views critical of the Party and its line.

The attitude of the Communist toward his party and Marxism-Leninism is essentially religious. Indeed communism has been called a secular religion.[4] The Communist would deny that his attitude is in any sense religious. He believes that the rationalization he goes through in support of the party position is really a scientific explanation. He tends to confuse the mental skills of working out explanations for all manner of policies with an inductive scientific exercise. In fact Communist thought is anything but scientific. The Communist typically begins with the assumption that the party's position is correct. His only task then is to find the proper Marxist explanation, making imaginative reference to the Marxist-Leninist writings to convince himself the party has adopted the scientifically correct "line."

Finally, the belief in Marxism-Leninism as a science also serves to promote a unity of outlook and appearance. All problems are viewed as having one correct solution. The task of Marxism-Leninism is to discover that solution and declare it to be the party "line," the scientifically correct position to which all Communists must affirm their undeviating acceptance.

THE DOCTRINE OF THE CLASS STRUGGLE

To comprehend the "scientific" qualities of historical materialism one must understand the concept of class struggle. In the Communist view history "is the history of class struggles."[5] It was the contest between classes that brought about stages of historic development. The slave-owning society gave way to the feudal society; the feudal society was succeeded by the capitalist society; and capitalism will give way to socialism. Class struggles brought about each successive change of society.

Communists consider the Western states to be capitalist. Capitalist

[4] Massimo Salvadori, *The Rise of Modern Communism. A Brief History of the Communist Movement in the Twentieth Century,* Berkshire Studies in European History (New York: Holt, Rinehart, and Winston, 1952), pp. 44–52.

[5] Karl Marx and Friedrich Engels, *The Communist Manifesto,* published in 1848. Reproduced in Emile Burns, *A Handbook of Marxism* (New York: International Publishers, 1935), p. 22.

(bourgeois) society is a class-stratified society but stratification is simple. Classes are few in number and only two of them are really important. The chief protagonists in the class struggle are the capitalists (bourgeoisie) —the class that owns the means of production and takes away from (exploits) workers a substantial portion of the fruits of their toil and the workers (proletariat) —the class that owns nothing and is forced to sell its labor power to the capitalists. Other classes, the peasantry, the *petit bourgeoisie* (a class that owns its own means of production but does not exploit workingmen), the aristocracy, are classes that are either passing from the scene or are drawn to one or another side of this overriding class struggle.

Class conflict is inevitable under capitalism because the capitalist seeks greater profit which can be gained, mainly, through more intensive exploitation of labor. Capitalists drive down the standards of living of the working class to the barest minimum "absolutely requisite to keep the labourer in bare existence as a labourer." [6] The outlook for the worker is exceedingly bleak. Competition among capitalists results in the bankruptcy and ruin of many of them who are driven to the level of the working man. Capitalism increasingly assumes the form of huge monopolies. Labor-saving machinery displaces many workers. A gap between wages and the cost of commodities creates periods of overproduction and consequent depression. Capitalism means increasing misery for the working class.

Workers have no choice but to organize and fight for their interests. Thus class struggle is an inevitable consequence of the capitalist economy. Workers unite because they "have nothing to lose but their chains. They have a world to win." [7] Just as the antithesis "overthrows" the thesis, the working class shall overthrow the capitalist class and establish a new order, a socialist society.

The Marxist image of the capitalist society is grossly overdrawn. The central position of the class struggle in capitalist society is an exaggeration of one aspect of Western society. Yet Marx's concepts are not simply the hallucinations of a cloistered and imaginative intellectual. The preeminence that Marx gives to the class struggle is valid in relation to the nineteenth-century capitalism in England and Western Europe which he observed. His explanations and his predictions were logical for the society in which he lived. But they hardly

[6] *Ibid.,* p. 39.
[7] *Ibid.,* p. 59.

seem appropriate to our own time. Least of all are they appropriate to Western Europe and the United States today where the capitalist economy has proved to be responsive to man's needs and remarkably flexible in meeting the economic problems of society. The pervasive influence of social classes and their struggle is questionable. Man acts not only on the basis of his economic interests but also as a Catholic, a rural resident, a member of a close-knit family, a Negro, a devotee of classical music or modern art, and as a member of many groups in a plural society. At best, economic conditions and the class struggle are two of many motivations that influence the ways of men and the course of history.

Class conflict in which each side seeks its advantage and aims to defeat the other tells one a great deal about the way in which Communists look at society and at the world. The struggle is everywhere. There are always enemies, neutrals, and allies. Enemies, within the state and on the world plane, must be overcome. Lenin instructed his followers that in politics the strategically crucial question is: "Kto kogo—Who whom?" The stands which Communists take on every issue must be decided with reference to who gains and who loses.[8] There is our side and their side. There are no moral absolutes. Communists do that which strengthens them and weakens the enemy. The logic of the concept of class struggle is to perceive the West as the class enemy which must be defeated.

Communists envisage the cold war as a conflict of economic systems, socialism versus capitalism. They promote the myth that socialism provides the greatest prosperity and social justice for the greatest number and is consequently a superior system. The fact of abundance in capitalist America and Europe is discounted and the broad sharing of this wealth denied. Believing in the superiority of socialism Communists then assert that capitalists must suppress socialism or the example of socialist prosperity will cause the working class everywhere to seek a socialist solution to their problems. In this sense they consider the cold war to be an expression of the attempt by capitalism to hold back the inexorable surge of history and assure its own preservation.

Communist statements to the contrary, the cold-war conflict is not

8 This concept is effectively developed by Bertram D. Wolfe in "Communist Ideology and Soviet Foreign Policy," *Foreign Affairs,* Vol. 41, No. 1, October, 1962, pp. 164–167.

one between economic systems. It is not that the West would like to impose upon the East a capitalist system while the East seeks to promote a socialist economy. In the main, the struggle is not even a clash of political systems. Although the West holds that men can live better in democratic states and stands against dictatorships, the goal of the West is hardly one of freeing the East from their totalitarian rulers. The cold war is a conflict between the Soviet sense of mission, the belief that universal communism, hopefully led by Moscow, is an unavoidable future, and the resistance of the West to the accomplishment of this objective, with perhaps a hope that eventually the Communist sense of mission will erode and then be replaced by democratic rule. In this conflict, differing economic systems play at best a minor role.

THE COMMUNIST VIEW OF THE STATE

The Marxist-Leninist theory of the state molds Communist attitudes toward the states of the West. This theory also serves to inform us about the role they expect the state to play in socialist societies.

Friedrich Engels, Marx's collaborator, observed that not all societies had organized states. Primitive man lived in a tribal society devoid of any state. This stage of development Engels called primitive communism. The characteristics of the primitive Communist society were common (rather than private) ownership of the means of production—canoes, bows and arrows, cooking implements—a food-gathering (rather than food-producing) society, and the absence of a state with authority to compel desired behavior.[9]

With the development of agriculture and animal husbandry, man learned to produce more than he could himself consume. Commodities, land, and animals now had value and were worth possessing. But not all men possessed such things. Those who did held their possessions as their property. Thus began the institution of private property. The development of private property marks the beginning of both historical society and the state.

Private property gives rise to a class-stratified society. Men are divided into property-owning and propertyless groupings. Class

[9] Friedrich Engels, *The Origin of the Family, Private Property and the State.* Reproduced in Burns, *op. cit.,* pp. 301–308.

stratification leads to class struggle. It is in the nature of things that those possessing property want to retain possession of it and of the advantages which can accrue from this ownership. Those who own nothing want to take away property from the owning class and deny them the advantages which their possessions give them. Hence the struggle of classes becomes unavoidable, creating the need for the state. Marxists define the state as police power. It is set up to protect the property-owning class and does so by putting down all threats to the sanctity of private ownership. In this sense the Marxists speak of a slave-owning state, one which preserves for slave owners their possessions in slaves; a feudal state, which enforces feudal landowning relations; a capitalist state, which ensures the possession and the advantages of capital; and a socialist state, which protects the social ownership of the means of production against private interests. To borrow a phrase from Engels, the state is an executive committee "of the most powerful, economically dominant class, which by virtue thereof becomes also the dominant class politically, and thus acquires new means of holding down and exploiting the oppressed class." [10]

A word is in order about the Communist concept of democracy. Inasmuch as political structure and political form are a part of the superstructure of a state and are an outgrowth of an underlying economic reality, democracy and dictatorship are considered to be mere forms of governments chosen by the capitalist class as most useful for its rule. Democracy, in this view, is simply a useful means for exploiting the working class.

Profit is "more *secure* in a democratic republic . . . A democratic republic is the best possible political shell for capitalism . . . it establishes its power so securely, so firmly that *no* change, either of persons, or institutions, or parties in the bourgeois republic can shake it . . . universal suffrage . . . (is) a means of bourgeois domination. . . ." [11]

Marx and Lenin believed that the class struggle would ultimately lead the proletariat to the revolutionary overthrow of capitalism and to the organization of a state of their own. This state was to be a dictatorship of the proletariat. Its purpose was ensuring proletarian rule by liquidating the class enemy. Bourgeois democracy was a

---

[10] *Ibid.,* p. 330.
[11] V. I. Lenin, *The State and Revolution* (published 1918), quoted in Burns, *op. cit.,* p. 731 (author's italics).

sham because behind it lay capitalist exploitation and inequality. Lenin argued that "the Soviet form of the dictatorship of the proletariat ... (is) a million times more democratic than the most democratic bourgeois republic." [12]

The proletarian dictatorship was to be a majoritarian dictatorship. In this sense Lenin considered it to be democratic. His concept of democracy leaves no place for minority rights and freedom of thought and expression. Coercion was to be directed against the enemy classes which in practice meant those who disagreed with the self-appointed spokesmen for the proletariat. In fact, the dictatorship of the proletariat in the Soviet Union quickly became a dictatorship of the Communist Party *for* the proletariat. Such a state was said to be "democratic" in the sense that it served the interests of the proletariat, the progressive class of society and the most numerous (this was often not the case) class.

The claim that the dictatorship of the proletariat, in the Soviet Union, is a superior form of democracy also rests on the representative character of the elected bodies of the state. At every level of government, from local to the national, Soviets (councils) are elected. They perform at the higher levels of government, in a most limited manner, legislative and some executive functions. Soviets are elected by universal suffrage, for those eighteen or older, and by secret ballot. However, candidates for the Soviets run uncontested. There is no choice, only the single ticket. Through a device of electoral commissions, which nominate all candidates, a rough cross section of Soviet society is put forward for election to the Soviets. Thus, the Soviets will contain men and women of all ages from all walks of life and will not consist primarily of lawyers. It is in this sense that Soviets are considered representative and hence democratic. By way of contrast, the Western democracy centers on the responsiveness of government to the popular will. It does not matter what the occupation, sex, or age of the elected official might be; as long as he responds to the will of his constituency, the purposes of democracy are thereby served.

The Communist meaning of democracy also rests upon broad participation in government. Citizens in Communist countries are encouraged to join groups and participate in government activity.

[12] V. I. Lenin, *The Proletarian Revolution and Kautsky the Renegade* (published in 1919), quoted in Burns, *ibid.*, p. 831.

There are "street committees," mass organization "deputy groups," and committees which take an interest in, may criticize, and may even perform voluntary services for governmental agencies. A measure of popular control is attained through letters to the editors and articles on wall newspapers criticizing red tape, administrative bungling, inefficiency, and inattention to local needs. Control is exerted upon the work of administrative agencies but people avoid criticism of policy.

Despite the Marxist devaluation of democracy in theory, for tactical reasons the Communists have always claimed the mantle of "true democrats." From the nineteenth century, democracy has had popular appeal. It was held in reverence by the people because it served their desire for freedom and a control of their destiny. Communist appeal for mass support would fail if it opposed democracy. It was wiser, therefore, for the Communists to claim that they were the true democrats.

The Communist-led state has never disavowed its coercive character. The dictatorship of the proletariat was to usher in a period of repression. The capitalist class was to be liquidated. It is not only hostile classes that have been liquidated but also ideas and activities considered hostile to proletarian class interests, as decided by the Communist Party, that have been suppressed.

With the liquidation of the capitalist class the class division of society ends and a one-class society remains. There will no longer be an enemy class to suppress. With no one to suppress, the state loses its function and it simply withers away.

In 1936 a new constitution was adopted for the Soviet Union. In the discussion that took place in connection with its adoption, the question of the status of the dictatorship was a matter of interest. According to Stalin the enemy classes had been liquidated and the Soviet Union had become a society of "toilers." This situation naturally raised the question of the withering away of the state. The "prophecy" led one to have anticipated the imminent demise of the state. Yet the Soviet state was obviously a most coercive dictatorship. Secret police, purges, and concentration camps were at the very heart of the instruments of Soviet administration. Stalin developed a theoretical elaboration to explain away the reality of Soviet repressive society. He denied that the "withering away" takes place gradually and over a period of time. He insisted that the state must get stronger and more repressive. As it grows more repressive it is better able to more rapidly bring about the liquidation of all the remnants of capitalism. It can better eliminate the spies, wreckers, and saboteurs that capitalism sends into the Soviet Union to bring about its downfall. He predicted that the time would come when all the remnants of capitalism would be removed from Soviet society by the dictatorship and the threats of capitalist aggression would vanish with its overthrow in other lands. Then overnight the state would wither away.

Along with much else that Stalin said, Khrushchev disavowed this Stalinist position. The past decade has seen the removal of some of the most irrational aspects of coercion in Soviet society. Prison labor camps and the denial of due process have been reduced. Expression has become freer, especially in nonpolitical fields. The new program of the Communist Party of the Soviet Union, adopted in November, 1961, anticipates the creation of a Communist society during the decade of the 1980's.[13]

Certain practical consequences derive from the Marxist-Leninist theorizing about the state. (1) All capitalist states represent the interests of the capitalist class, the enemy of the Communists. (2) Capitalist democracy is nothing more than a convenient way of promoting the exploitation of the working class. (3) The workers can through struggle gain some concessions to their benefit, but they cannot recast the purposes of the capitalist state. That state must preserve its class interests. To forestall worse consequences, concessions and palliatives are permissible, in capitalist eyes, but change of purpose, the establishment of a state that stands above the class struggle, is impossible. Only revolution, the destruction of the capitalist state, and the establishment of a new state, a dictatorship of the proletariat, will suffice for the working class. In the meantime the working class should fight for democratic reforms. Such reforms may have some merit. More important than the intrinsic merits of the reforms which may be won is the fight itself. In this fight workers develop greater militancy and unity. (4) The dictatorship of the proletariat represents the class interests of the proletariat—as the Communist Party interprets their interests—and because the proletariat is more numerous than the capitalists its dictatorship is inherently

---

[13] Dan N. Jacobs (ed.), *The New Communist Manifesto and Related Documents,* 2nd ed. (Evanston, Ill.: Row, Peterson, 1962), pp. 241–245.

more democratic than any capitalist state. (5) For tactical reasons the use of the term dictatorship should be deemphasized and the claim that the Soviet Union is an advanced democracy asserted. (6) The fact of coercion, terror, censorship, and absence of freedom is irrelevant. What is important is the class nature of the state. Because the dictatorship of the proletariat is the state of the workers (and other toiling classes) and functions in their interests, the suppressive actions of that state are applied in the interests of the working class. All who oppose, all who object, are enemies and their suppression is entirely "democratic." Freedom *per se* cannot be permitted; only the right to assert that which serves the interests of the working class as the Communists interpret that interest may be tolerated. Coercion and terror must be used when they serve the interest of the working class.

THE COMMUNIST VIEW OF SOCIAL CHANGE

In 1949 the leaders of the American Communist Party were convicted of violating the Smith Act. This law makes it illegal to conspire to teach and advocate the revolutionary overthrow of the United States government. The conviction rested on the finding that the Communist Party and its leaders illegally advocated or conspired to advocate revolution. The party's position on this matter appeared ambivalent. On the one hand, since 1940 the Communist Party of the United States has not come out for the revolutionary overthrow of the government in any of its policy statements or in the positions adopted by its authoritative spokesmen. To be sure, at one time the party had not only favored revolution but insisted that failure to openly urge revolution was a betrayal of the cause. In 1940, however, the Communist Party Constitution made advocacy of the violent overthrow of the government grounds for expulsion from the party.[14]

[14] This position has been retained in the present Constitution. The CPUSA theoretical organ, *Political Affairs*, Vol. XXXVI, No. 3, March, 1957, "Report on the Draft Constitution," p. 22. "Our new draft Constitution, in its Preamble and various clauses, reiterates and makes clear that we have no room in our ranks for those who advocate force or violence or terrorism, or who by word or act seek to subvert, undermine or overthrow the institutions of American democracy through which the majority of American people can maintain their right to determine their destinies."

On the other hand, the party did not disavow the Marxist-Leninist position that only through revolution can capitalism be liquidated. At the 1949 trial, the defendants, Eugene Dennis and his colleagues of the United States Communist Party's National Committee, took the position that a time would come when the American people would want to establish a socialist system, and, if the capitalists denied the people the right to make such a change by their use of force, then, and only then, would the Communists urge the use of counterforce to bring about the will of the people. In this manner both the theoretical precepts of Marxism and United States law concerning revolution were reconciled.

The United States Government's case against Dennis *et al.* was based on evidence provided by persons who left the party after some years in positions of leadership and by FBI operatives in the party.[15] This evidence showed that the disavowal of revolutionary violence was a tactical masking of the true position of the party, and that higher levels of party leadership secretly affirmed the need for a revolutionary solution.

The Communists propose to reorder society and end the capitalist system. To achieve this aim a revolution will be necessary because capitalists will refuse to give up their advantageous position and will have to be driven from power by force. In the Marxist view no capitalists would give up their favored position by agreeing to the democratic will of the people should they desire socialism. In the long run the revolution would put an end to the terrors, the inequities, the inevitable wars, and the social costs of the capitalist system, and even the most violent revolution will be an act of mercy.

The present Soviet position on this matter is that the proletariat, led by the Communists in each country, "has a right and is in a position to specify the tactics of a revolution and the forms and methods of its struggle . . ." [16] Revolution is not disavowed, it is soft-pedaled.

No Communist-led dictatorship has ever been elected by the people. The Communists have never abjured the use of force to bring about their proletarian dictatorship when the results of violence appeared promising. As Khrushchev said, "Specific preconditions are

[15] Herbert A. Philbrick, *I Led Three Lives* (New York: McGraw-Hill, Inc., 1952).

[16] N. S. Khrushchev, "The New Content of Peaceful Coexistence in the Nuclear Age," Speech to the Socialist Unity Party of Germany, January 16, 1963. (New York: Crosscurrents Press, 1963), p. 37.

required for the revolution to win ... An accurate analysis of the concrete situation and a correct appraisal of the balance of forces are essential to the revolutionary tactics of the working class ..." [17]

The Marxist position is that capitalism has outlived its usefulness and has become a regressive system. It should be replaced. Revolutions, however, can succeed only during periods of crises—war, depressions, social and political upheaval—and only when a well-organized Communist Party has achieved an adequate measure of strength to carry out the revolution.

THE ROLE AND NATURE OF THE COMMUNIST PARTY

Closely related to the Marxist-Leninist concept of the state is the special position of leadership that is accorded to the Communist Party. The Communist Party plays the central role in the development of the socialist state as well as in promoting the overthrow of the capitalist state.

A PARTY OF PROFESSIONAL REVOLUTIONARIES

The Communist Party is conceived as a party of professional revolutionaries. Lenin articulated this concept of the character of the party. He gathered a coterie of devoted and singleminded revolutionaries who agreed to operate with military efficiency to effect the overthrow of the czar and establish their own rule. Professional revolutionaries exhibit two characteristics. First, each must prove himself devoted above and beyond everything else to the tasks of the party. At a minimum, party members are expected to actively participate in party work. But, above and beyond that, for those who are to be more than rank-and-file members of the party, an extra measure of devotion is expected. They must accept party assignments and carry them out to the best of their ability. They are to go where the party sends them, do what the party wishes. Nothing comes before the obligations of party activity. In the United States members of the party have been assigned work in trade unions and other mass organizations. On occasion college careers of young Communists were cut short by party directives ordering them to seek work in steel mills, auto factories, or in the transportation industry to carry out

[17] *Ibid.*

party purposes. All Communist parties give their members assignments which they are expected to carry out. A second quality, no less
important than the first, expected of each party member is mastery of
the Marxist-Leninist "science." Inasmuch as the party is a leadership
body, to lead with unity of purpose and to lead correctly requires
that Communists know well the writings of Marx, Engels, Lenin,
and other leaders.

Vanguard Role of the Party

Communists believe that they constitute a vanguard of the proletariat. Lenin's concept of the vanguard role meant that the party
arrogated unto itself decision-making for the proletariat. As a fellow-
ship of men devoted to the cause of the proletariat and guided by
Marxism-Leninism, the party would lead without error, providing
an almost infallible leadership to the working class. Its role is one of
chosen leadership only where it does not have the power to impose
its decisions. Where, as is true in Communist-controlled countries,
power is in the hands of the party, it enforces a monopoly of decision-making for itself, presumably in the interest of the workers.

The effectiveness of the Communist Party is enhanced by its rules
of operation and organization. The party aspires to be a monolithic
body. Members of the organization must agree with all decisions and
act in concert with one another. Party rules outlaw factions. Dissent
and discussion take place only under carefully prescribed rules. Once
a decision is made by a majority vote (and the majority has proved
completely receptive to leadership suggestion), then all debate
comes to an end and everyone is to carry out the decision.

Party Organization

Party organization is governed by the principle of *democratic
centralism*. Most important among the several aspects of this principle is the rule that decisions of higher party bodies and leaders are
binding on the lower. The rule that all higher bodies are to be
elected by those immediately below them is given effect by leaders
submitting a slate of candidates to be elected which is invariably
unanimously approved.

Communist parties are organized on a series of levels. Each higher
level is elected by the one below. The constitution names the con-

gress of the party (in the Soviet Union it meets every four years) as the highest authority of the party. In fact congresses of the party have become mere rubber stamps for the top leadership. Leadership in the Soviet Communist Party is lodged in its Presidium [18] of about fifteen members. The rules of democratic centralism ensure that the decisions of this body will be carried out by the membership as orders from above.

Within one year after the Communists came to power in Russia the dictatorship *of* the proletariat assumed the character of a dictatorship *for* the proletariat by its vanguard, the party. Somewhat later the dominating role of party leadership resulted in the conversion of the dictatorship to one by the Central Committee of the Party. The Central Committee became, in this sense, a vanguard of the vanguard of the proletariat. Stalin's domination of the Communist Party led to the passing of the leading role from the Central Committee into the hands of the Communist Party Presidium, then called the Politburo.

Communist states are dictatorships of party leaders. This practice was first established in the Soviet Union and has been duplicated in China and the satellite states as well. The government, trade unions, and other representative bodies are used as transmission belts for carrying out the party's policies. Within each organization the party organizes a fraction of party members to carry out action which the party deems necessary. National legislatures do not legislate. Their function is unrelated to decision-making. In the Soviet Union the highest legislative body, the Supreme Soviet, meets twice a year for five to seven days at most. Its members listen to speeches and applaud, but make no real attempts at legislating. Their role is to acclaim their leaders. Membership in the Supreme Soviet is a reward to those who have labored hard for the welfare of the Soviet state. Over the years the Supreme Soviet has discussed few laws but has

[18] There are three distinct leadership bodies named Presidium in the Soviet Union. In addition to the Communist Party's Presidium, the Supreme Soviet elects a Presidium of thirty-three members which acts as an interim legislative body between meetings of the Supreme Soviet. An inner committee of the Council of Ministers consisting of the Premier, his deputies, and first deputies make up a Presidium of the Council of Ministers. At the 23rd Congress of the CPSU which met in 1966, the name of the party Presidium was changed back to its original one of Politburo and the First Secretary was once again called General Secretary.

simply rubber-stamped, without discussion, laws promulgated by leadership bodies.

Major executive offices, such as premiers and their deputies, are held by members of the party Presidium. The executive organs of government carry out party decisions emanating from the Presidium.

Khrushchev and Stalin while serving as First Secretaries of the Communist Party and having no function in the government would on occasion countersign the more important laws. This would serve to underline the importance of the law. In 1954 and 1955 there took place in Geneva summit meetings. It would have been futile for President Eisenhower to have met with the Soviet premier of those years, Bulganin, rather than with Khrushchev, who had no governmental post. The plain fact is that only Khrushchev as Party Secretary was in a position to make commitments for the Soviet Union. This anomalous situation is entirely explicable in terms of the Communist doctrine which makes the party leadership the repository of unfailing wisdom because its members have mastery of the Marxist-Leninist science.

Even in states that are not controlled by the Communists, mass organizations in which the Communists are active are used to project party positions and to assist the party in carrying out its policies on current issues. Such organizations are also exploited as a source of recruits into the party. There, persons who exhibit leadership talents and support party stands become prime targets for recruitment into party cells.

INTERNATIONAL ORGANIZATION OF COMMUNISM

The Communist Party is unique in one important respect. Throughout its history it has operated as an international movement. In 1919, Lenin established the Third International as the international Communist Party. Sections were organized in most states. The Comintern, as the Third International was called, conceived itself to be an international party that established one line to be followed by all Communist parties. With the rise of Stalin's leadership in the Communist Party of the Soviet Union the Comintern itself became Stalinized. After 1928 it clearly served as an arm of Soviet policy.

In 1943, the Comintern was officially dissolved to eliminate an irritant in United States-Soviet relations. But in 1947 a new international Communist organization, the Cominform, bringing together the Communist parties of the Soviet Union and the Peoples Democracies and also including the parties of Italy and France, was established. The Cominform also was a device for Soviet control. The defection of Tito from the satellite empire, and the active role of the Cominform in the anti-Tito fight, made necessary the liquidation of that body when the Soviet Union set out to mend its fences with Yugoslavia.

Sharp dissension wracked the Communist movement in 1956. This occurred chiefly for two reasons. First, Khrushchev denounced Stalin in a secret speech he made to the Twentieth Party Congress. In this speech Khrushchev told of the irrational purges of loyal members of the Communist Party by Stalin's rule. He revealed the terror of Stalin's rule and frequent instances of his poor leadership. For the international Communist movement which had worshiped Stalin as the equal of the immortal Marx and Lenin, this speech came as a shock. Not only was the speech disturbing but the fact that it also had been leaked and reproduced in the press of the West rather than candidly issued by Soviet sources lent credence to the oft-repeated assertions of the "capitalist press" that the Soviet leadership did not let their followers know what was really happening in Russia. In any event, this speech served to undermine the most fundamental affections and most strongly held loyalty of Communists around the world. Communists had been accustomed to twists and turns in the Soviet position, and, although each new change of direction, each new change of friend to foe and foe to friend, caused a toll of disaffiliation in the ranks of the Communist Party, a loyal corps of Communists remained. Communist parties in the West had suffered large losses of membership because Soviet policies disaffected significant numbers in their ranks. By 1956 it appeared that Communist parties in the West were reduced to a membership that was unshakably loyal to the Soviet Union. But even this membership was jolted by the disclosures of Khrushchev.

Almost immediately after Khrushchev's disclosures about Stalin came the shock of working-class rebellions against their Communist regimes in Poland and Hungary. The latter was treacherously suppressed by Soviet tanks. These events gave rise to more defections from Communist ranks and led a few parties to advocate polycentrism. Some parties, such as the Italian Communist Party, asserted a measure of independence of Soviet control with respect to the line they might adopt. But even for these parties, the polycentrist posture is concerned with tactics to be pursued rather than the aims of the movement. Polycentrism has not led parties to disavow the aim of communizing the world or the need for supporting the Soviet Union.

THE SINO-SOVIET DISPUTE

More recently the conflict between the Soviet Union and China has come to the fore. This has been a conflict over policy and leadership. It has forced most Communist parties to take sides either in support of the Soviet Union or China.

Differences over policy have emerged on several vital issues. Moscow asserts that world war can be prevented by the "forces of peace" —the Communist-led states and the neutrals—who are strong enough to block the moves of the imperialist aggressors. Peking denies that peace can be maintained as long as imperialist countries bestride the world. Its line holds war inevitable and nuclear war likely. What is more, the Chinese reject Moscow's claim that nuclear war would destroy all countries, socialist as well as capitalist. They contend that imperialism alone would be annihilated but socialism would endure or at worst be reborn.

Mao Tse Tung has said that "the east wind prevails over the west wind" and that Soviet leadership has failed to exploit this advantage. Peking's language has been belligerent, extravagant, and intemperate but its action in face of United States power has been cautious. It urges greater boldness and military confrontation with Washington—a paper tiger—on Moscow. For itself it is well aware that the "paper tiger" has atomic teeth. Moscow's caution in face of United States military strength is condemned as covert collaboration with American imperialism.

Russia and China disagree over the utility of local wars. Moscow considers them unnecessary for the victory of socialism and dangerous because they can escalate into a thermonuclear conflagration. Peking contends that they are unavoidable, can be contained if necessary, and are essential to socialist advances.

Peking accuses Moscow of betraying national liberation movements by hesitating to risk expanded conflicts. China has proved more ready to support revolutionary elements preparing to over-throw existing regimes.

Positions diverge on the question of disarmament. Moscow favors disarmament and believes that agreements can be reached. Peking opposes disarmament until imperialism has been defeated and looks on it as a handicap in the development of its military strength.

Peaceful coexistence has become a cornerstone of Russian foreign policy. It helps preserve the advances of socialist construction and permits the superiority of socialism to expose the decadence of capitalism according to Russia's spokesmen. Chinese leaders say that the important aim is the defeat of imperialism, and, consequently, struggle must be emphasized and not peaceful coexistence.

The Sino-Soviet dispute is also a clash of leaderships. Peking considers itself to be the inheritor of Lenin's mantle of militant leadership. It rejects a leading role for the Soviet Union. It suspects that Russia's withdrawal of assistance and denial of aid in manufacturing atomic weapons stems from the Kremlin's desire to continue to be communism's foremost country and leading party. In the Communist movements of Asia, Africa, and Latin America, Russia and China are actively lining up support. The fight is a bitter one with compromise ruled out.

In the beginning, many of the acrimonious accusations exchanged between the Soviet Union and China passed as euphemisms. The Kremlin attacked Albania in stern tones meant for China. China replied in kind with vituperative statements against Yugoslavia, but the real target was the party leadership of the Soviet Union. Later euphemisms were dropped and charges were exchanged directly between the Communist parties of the Soviet Union and China.

This conflict broke the monolithic unity of the international Communist movement and reduced Soviet domination of other party leaderships. It enhanced a measure of independence in policies the parties pursue. Yet this dispute is unlikely to realign Communist countries to make common cause with the Western states, nor will Communists give up their promotion of communism by all means that may succeed. Communist internationals no longer exist, but periodic consultation and continuing cooperating among Communist parties, at least within the Moscow and Peking camps, respectively, continues.

THE STRATEGY AND TACTICS OF
PRESENT-DAY COMMUNISM

In order to win power Communists devise strategic objectives and day-to-day tactical steps for carrying out these objectives. A distinction is made between strategic goals and tactics. Strategic goals are long-term goals designed to implement ultimate aims. Communists want a socialist world and this requires the universal defeat of capitalism. This ultimate aim is promoted through a series of intermediate goals—building a monolithic party, organizing labor and encouraging strikes, fighting the growth of military strength in capitalist lands, and undermining the positive image of capitalism and of democratic parties—designed to achieve this objective. These intermediate goals we call strategic goals. The day-to-day devices designed to achieve these intermediate goals are tactics.

In 1917 and for about a half a dozen years thereafter, the primary strategic objective was the revolutionary overthrow of capitalism. The tactics designed to accomplish this goal were the establishment of Communist parties in all states and the fomenting of demonstrations, strikes, and uprisings. Somewhat later the major strategic objective of the Communists was the preservation of the Soviet Union against hostile forces. For this aim popular fronts, Soviet friendship societies, and anti-fascism were the tactics that were fostered. Since the end of the Second World War, the strategic objective of the Communist world appears to be the reduction and eventual eradication of United States power. As we have seen, the last years of the war and the early postwar years were a period in which the Soviet Union established its authoritative power over almost all areas that had been physically occupied by the Red Army. The further march of Soviet communism was stalled by the overwhelming might of the United States. Therefore the Soviet Union adopted the strategy of undermining United States power so that Soviet objectives might be attained without effective challenge. To carry out this strategy the Communists adopted a number of tactical steps. They reconstituted the United States Communist Party. The Communist Party of the United States had been dissolved under the leadership of Earl Browder. A looser association that disavowed revolutionary intentions had been established. In 1945 the French Communist Duclos denounced Browder's dissolution of the party. He spoke for Stalin in this matter, and the party within the United States was reestablished and Browder was expelled from the organization. This step signaled the promotion of a harder line, for among the objections to Browder's leadership was his advocacy of continued cooperation between liberal capitalism and the Soviet Union. Browder's line and leadership were not geared to an impending assault on United States power.

Other tactics have been developed to attack the United States. The United States was denoted the most reactionary and leading imperialist state. The Soviet Union used the halls of the UN as a propaganda forum to seek support of Asian and African states against "United States imperialism." Disarmament tactics were more concerned with weakening the United States militarily than in promoting disarmament. Soviet leaders encouraged and supported all manifestations of anti-Americanism. Castro in Cuba, Nasser in Egypt, Sukarno in Indonesia, Nkrumah in Ghana, and others who at one time or another spoke out against the United States were encouraged, assisted, and befriended.

THE TACTIC OF PEACEFUL COEXISTENCE

Thermonuclear war would not spare the Soviet Union from devastation beyond recovery. Khrushchev reported that by 1963 the United States possessed about 40,000 H-bombs. By his estimate, "the first blow alone would take a toll of 700 to 800 million human lives. All the large cities would be wiped out or destroyed—not only in the two leading nuclear countries, the US and the USSR, but in France, Britain, Germany, Italy, China, Japan and many other countries of the world. The effects of a nuclear war would continue to tell throughout the lifetime of many generations, causing disease and death and the worst deformities in the development of people." [19]

The reality of thermonuclear devastation has required a reassessment of the doctrinal stand that under capitalism war is inevitable and that war can be utilized to promote proletarian revolution. A new version of the Marxist-Leninist position on war has been enunciated. In this view war is no longer inevitable because the forces of peace, composed of the socialist states and the African and Asian

[19] Khrushchev, *op. cit.,* p. 34.

neutralists, are strong enough to frustrate capitalist warlike aims and with it wars initiated by capitalist states.[20]

In place of Lenin's insistence that imperialist wars provide the working class with a golden opportunity to use the guns put in their hands by their capitalist governments for the overthrow of those governments, distinctions are made about the kinds of wars that are to be promoted and those that are to be avoided. Russian Communists today want to avoid thermonuclear war because it would be devastating for the socialist states. They also seek to prevent conventional wars because of the danger that they might escalate into thermonuclear wars. Wars of national liberation against colonial powers and civil wars to overthrow capitalism are still to be promoted. As long as nuclear war would devastate Communist-led states, peaceful coexistence will continue to be the policy that the states led by the Soviet Union will pursue.

[20] "Statement by 81 Marxist-Leninist Parties," *Political Affairs,* Vol. XL, No. 1, January, 1961, pp. 1, 13.

CHAPTER 7

The Origins and Development of the Cold War

ON JUNE 10, 1963, in a commencement address at American University, President John F. Kennedy called for an end to the cold war. He said, "History teaches us that enmities between nations, as between individuals, do not last forever. However fixed our likes and dislikes may seem, the tide of time and events will often bring surprising changes in the relations between nations and neighbors."

This chapter is devoted to a study of the origins of the cold war. As such this study is not intended as an exercise in anti-Soviet recrimination. Nor are we concerned simply with a historical exercise. There is need to know the reasons for this struggle. This understanding should enable us to better ascertain whether the conditions that produced the cold war have changed and whether the time may not have come for the solution of some cold-war issues.

In the Western view, as we shall see, the cold war was a product of Soviet expansionist ambitions. It is reasonable to assume that the cold war will give way to more friendly and peaceful relations only when the West becomes convinced that the Soviet Union no longer seeks such ends. A study of the enduring issues of the cold war will provide us with a clue to the goals, old and new, which the Soviet Union seeks to achieve. Evidence of change should alert us to the usefulness of new initiatives designed to reduce cold-war antagonisms. Evidence that the revisionist aims persist should lead to an evaluation of the effectiveness of the West in discouraging Soviet pursuit of hostile ambitions.

In the Eastern view the cold war was caused by American imperialism and the insoluble problems inherent in capitalism. As such it was an inevitable manifestation of capitalism. It is important to

176

know whether in the Soviet view any meaningful reduction of cold-war antagonism can take place as long as capitalism exists. Does the leadership of the Communist world see an end to the cold war only when the West makes the "necessary" concessions? Are accommodations of Soviet and American aims possible?

Not least of our concerns in analyzing the cold war is to seek answers to the question of whether the United States, and to a lesser extent Great Britain, appeased the Soviet Union. This matter has been of continuing concern to Americans, and it appears as part of the quadrennial dialogue in each of the Presidential elections.

From another standpoint, the cold war is deemed to be a result of ignorance and misunderstanding by all the participants. If this should be the case a study of the cold war might identify those issues that were misunderstood and help clear up misapprehensions.

A more realistic view recognized that while ignorance and misunderstandings between East and West have never been lacking, neither have knowledge and clear understandings served to reduce the conflict. Indeed, the clash of interest becomes clearer with greater understanding. The cold war developed from a number of situations in which the Soviet Union, on the one hand, and the Western democracies, on the other, were seriously at odds. The most important of these issues concerned (a) Poland, (b) the development of a satellite empire by the Soviet Union in Eastern Europe, (c) the role of the Soviet Union in the Middle and Near Eastern areas, (d) the *coup d'etat* in Czechoslovakia, (e) the future of Austria and Germany, and (f) the war in Korea.

THE POLISH QUESTION

Poland became a touchstone of East-West relations. The Soviet approach to the Polish question would be the key to her image of postwar Eastern Europe. For almost two years after Germany's attack on the Soviet Union, the future looked promising. It was generally agreed that a reconstituted Poland would have a regime friendly to Russia. It was also assumed that the Polish boundaries might be altered from those existing when the war began. A Soviet-Polish border roughly that of the Curzon line proposal was acceptable to the major powers at war with Germany. Compensations on Poland's west at Germany's expense were to be a part of the bargain. Within

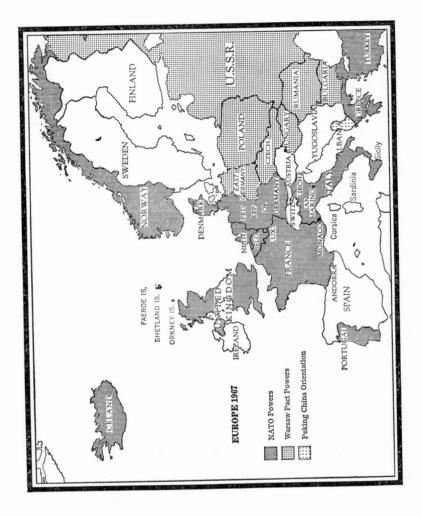

EUROPE 1967

NATO Powers

Warsaw Pact Powers

Peking China Orientation

ICELAND

FAEROE IS.
SHETLAND IS.
ORKNEY IS.

UNITED KINGDOM

IRELAND

PORTUGAL

SPAIN

ANDORRA

Corsica

Sardinia

NORWAY

SWEDEN

FINLAND

U.S.S.R.

DENMARK

NETH.
BELG.
LUX.

FRANCE

FED.
REP.
OF
GERMANY

EAST
GERMANY

POLAND

CZECH.

AUSTRIA

HUNGARY

SWITZ.

LIECH.

SAN
MARINO

MONACO

ITALY

YUGOSLAVIA

RUMANIA

BULGARIA

GREECE

TURKEY

ALBANIA

Sicily

this new configuration the Polish people would through self-determination dispose of their future.

From 1943 negotiations over the future of Poland became difficult. As events unfolded doubts increased that the Soviet Union would permit real self-determination to take place. Too many incidents—the Katyn-Forest Massacre, the executions of Ehrlich and Alter, the Soviet performance in connection with the Warsaw uprising, and Soviet promotion of a Lublin government—bespoke Soviet intention to undermine the reestablishment of a non-Communist regime.

BOUNDARIES

The secret protocol appended to the pact between the Nazis and the Russians [1] dealt with the "territorial and political rearrangement in the areas belonging to the Baltic States..." and raised the question "of whether the interests of both parties make desirable the maintenance of an independent Polish state and how such a state should be bounded..." [2] On September 17, 1939, the Red Army entered Poland, and eleven days later Germany and the Soviet Union concluded a secret agreement partitioning Poland.

Diplomatic relations between Poland and Russia were severed and did not resume until after the Nazi attack on the Soviet Union in 1941. The agreement between the Russian government and the Polish government-in-exile on July 30, 1941, formally reestablished relations. The desperate military situation in Russia at that time undoubtedly necessitated a conciliatory attitude toward the Poles on Stalin's part and led the Soviet Union to disavow Polish territorial changes brought about in the Nazi-Soviet Pact. Stalin also agreed "to the formation on the territory of the USSR of a Polish Army under a commander appointed by the Polish Government in agreement with the Soviet Government..." [3]

The Polish-Soviet agreement was short-lived. Stalin's commitment with respect to Polish boundaries remained a dead letter. The Soviet Union never entertained serious proposals for negotiation of the boundaries question. While the United States and Great Britain

[1] See Chapter 5, pp. 140–141 above.
[2] Alvin S. Rubinstein, *The Foreign Policy of the Soviet Union* (New York: Random House, 1960), pp. 144–145. (Document reproduced.)
[3] *Ibid.*, Agreement Between the Government of Poland and the Union of Soviet Socialist Republics, London, July 30, 1941, Article 4, p. 187.

did not seek to reimpose prewar boundaries, it was agreed at Yalta that this question would be settled in connection with the German peace treaty, a procedure that Soviet action disallowed. However, other issues led to the breakdown of diplomatic relations between Poland and the Soviet Union in 1943.

KATYN-FOREST MASSACRE

Large numbers of Polish soldiers fleeing the German blitzkrieg found themselves in the area of Russian occupation when the Red Army advanced in September, 1939. The Russians interned almost 250,000 of them, and these were the forces which were to be formed into a Polish army under the Russo-Polish Agreement of July 30, 1941. The Polish General Wladyslaw Anders was freed from imprisonment to assume command of the troops. The Polish soldiers were asked to assemble in camps specially set aside for the purpose of organizing this new force. As they arrived, it soon became apparent that officers rarely appeared. Subsequent attempts to locate them proved unavailing.[4] Fourteen generals were known to have been captured by the Soviet Army but only two reached the assembly camp. Approximately three hundred high-ranking officers were interned in Soviet camps but only six appeared at the assembly point. In all about 15,000 persons were missing, 8,300 to 8,400 of them officers.[5] Over a period of a year or more the Polish government, with occasional assistance from the United States and Great Britain, sought to establish what had happened to the missing persons. The officials of the N.K.V.D. (Soviet secret police) were either evasive or claimed to have no information. On one occasion Stalin told General Sikorski, Premier of the Polish government-in-exile, that the missing men escaped to Manchuria.[6] At another time, Stanislaw Mikolajczyk, who later became Premier, was told by a Soviet officer that the missing men were executed as a result of a mistaken interpretation of Stalin's order: Stalin had directed the N.K.V.D. to liquidate some camps and the N.K.V.D. understood this directive to mean the liquidation of the prisoners in these camps. Nevertheless,

---

[4] See the study of the Katyn-Forest Massacre written by J. K. Zawodny, *Death in the Forest: The Story of the Katyn-Forest Massacre* (Notre Dame, Ind.: University of Notre Dame Press, 1962). This volume contains an exhaustive bibliography on this subject.

[5] *Ibid.*, p. 6.

[6] *Ibid.*, p. 10.

men had disappeared and no information concerning their fate could be uncovered.

In April, 1943, the German government announced that they had discovered a mass grave in which a number of the missing officers' bodies had been buried. The Germans claimed that the men had been gunned down in cold blood and that an international commission drawn from twelve countries other than Germany had investigated and corroborated the truth of the German allegation. Based upon the evidence at hand—the conditions of the men's bodies and the documents found on the bodies of the slaughtered victims—it was ascertained that the executions had taken place in April and May of 1940. In a word, the executions took place at a time when the area was under Soviet control. Subsequent study of this situation [7] has proved that the deed was perpetrated by the Soviet government.

The Polish government insisted on an International Red Cross investigation of the German charge. Stalin's immediate response was a severing of diplomatic relations, accusing the Poles of collusion with Hitler. He took the position that the failure of the Polish government to reject out of hand the German charges was sufficient evidence that they were in the camp of the Hitlerites. With relations severed, a few days later the Soviet Union established an organization known as the "Union of Polish Patriots." Later this body became the Soviet-sponsored Lublin government.

A design of Soviet policy toward Poland was beginning to become evident. First, the massacre dealt a grievous blow to Polish military might by destroying the flower of her officer corps. Second, the massacre created a reasonable suspicion that the Soviet Union sought to undermine future Polish opposition to Soviet control. Finally, Stalin quickly exploited the event by organizing a body to serve as a future Soviet-dominated regime, which the Soviet Union in due course proceeded to recognize as the government of Poland.

THE EHRLICH AND ALTER AFFAIR

Evidence that the Soviet Union consciously moved to undermine Polish independence was borne out by the execution of two leaders

[7] *Ibid.*, see the judgment of the Select Committee on the Katyn-Forest Massacre of the U.S. House of Representatives, 82nd Congress, First and Second Sessions, 1951–1952.

of the General Jewish Workers' Union, a Jewish socialist organization in Poland popularly known as the "Bund." The Bund was the largest Jewish workers' organization in Poland. Among its more important leaders were Henryk Ehrlich and Victor Alter. With the occupation of eastern Poland by Soviet forces both Ehrlich and Alter found themselves in the Soviet zone. In September of 1939 they were arrested and imprisoned in Russia for treasonable activities. Although imprisoned for almost two years neither man was formally charged nor tried until July of 1941, when each was tried and sentenced to death by a court-martial. However, in a matter of a few days their sentence was commuted to ten years of hard labor. Then, in September of 1941, both men were released from prison under the amnesty granted to all Polish citizens. Their liberation from prison was accompanied by expressions of regret from the Soviet government for the mistake which had been committed by those members of the N.K.V.D. who had detained them.[8] With a request to let bygones be bygones the Soviet government urged these men to organize world Jewry against Hitler's Germany. They agreed and set up a Jewish anti-Hitler committee, which was chaired by Ehrlich while Alter served as secretary.

On December 4, 1941, Ehrlich and Alter were once again arrested by the N.K.V.D. The fact of their arrest became known, and over a period of fifteen months intercessions on their behalf from the Polish Ambassador to the Soviet Union, by American Jewish groups, and by labor organizations interested in their fate brought no satisfactory response. Information concerning their incarceration and the progress of their case could not be secured from the Soviet authorities. In autumn of 1942, Wendell Willkie, on the occasion of his visit to Russia, inquired about them and was assured that this matter would be worked out in a satisfactory manner.[9] Finally Maxim Litvinov, the Soviet Ambassador to the United States, announced that Alter and Ehrlich were executed for "active subversive work against the Soviet Union and assistance to Polish intelligence organs in armed

[8] *The Case of Henryk Ehrlich and Victor Alter* (New York: The American Representation of General Jewish Workers' Union of Poland, 1943), a pamphlet.

[9] I. Hart, *Henryk Ehrlich Oon Victor Alter, A Labn Fon Kamfer—A Toit Fon Martirer (Henry Ehrlich and Victor Alter, a Life of Fighters—A Death of Martyrs)* (New York: The American Representation of General Jewish Workers' Union of Poland, 1943), in Yiddish.

activities." To add a dubious measure of legality to these executions the Soviet government claimed these men were Soviet citizens rather than Poles. The original notification of this execution in 1943 announced that it had taken place in December of 1942. It was subsequently admitted by the Soviet Union that the execution took place in December, 1941. No evidence of anti-Soviet subversive action was ever produced. Nothing more than an allegation to that effect had been made. Under the conditions of wartime cooperation the Soviet Union appeared to assume that its word was beyond question. For fifteen months the Soviet government gave the impression that the affair of Ehrlich and Alter was still a matter of litigation. In fact these men had been executed. The significance of this happening, designed to disrupt the "Bund," an important organization independent of Communist control, could not be lost upon those seeking to assess Soviet intentions.

WARSAW UPRISING

In 1944 the Soviets advanced into Poland. By August the Russians reached the Vistula River across from Warsaw. A new act in the Polish drama was about to be played. The Polish underground army gathered for a revolt. It had every expectation that the Soviet offensive would continue. A revolt behind German lines would serve to draw off German attention and help make crossing of the Vistula easier and less costly. General Komarowski (Bor) led the Polish Home Army in an uprising. Five German divisions in the area were concentrated to defeat the revolt.

At first the Soviet Union refused to take notice of this insurrection. General Bor's appeals for help went unanswered. No Soviet offensive and no Soviet planes appeared to assist the uprising. Stalin claimed he had neither men nor supplies to spare. He insisted that the Polish struggle was an irresponsible action uncoordinated with the Red Army advance. Appeals for Russian assistance were unavailing.

The British attempted to assist the rebels by night bombings of Warsaw mounted from Italy but with little effect. Churchill and Roosevelt, receiving Polish appeals for assistance and intercession, asked Stalin's aid, again without success. Churchill then proposed that the American and British Air Forces fly bombing runs in support of the uprising and leave the Russians with the decision of barring the landing of their planes.[10] Roosevelt was unwilling to go that far. Airplanes did not have the range to undertake a round-trip bombing mission from either Italy or France over Warsaw and had to land at Russian bases to refuel. Only when it was too late and the uprising was effectively suppressed did the Russians begin flights on behalf of the Warsaw revolution. American and British missions undertaken from Western Europe also were too late. Thus, a force loyal to the London government, the Polish Home Army, was substantially decimated. With this organization out of the way the establishment of a satellite became ever more possible.[11]

The Question of the Polish Government

The Soviet advance into eastern Poland enabled the Russians to establish their Polish regime. The "Union of Polish Patriots," later renamed the Committee of National Liberation, became the core of the Lublin (Communist) regime. With the Soviet Union recognizing the Lublin government while the United States and Britain continued to recognize the London government an impasse developed.

This matter was given considerable attention at the Yalta Conference. Two crucial questions had to be settled. The first involved the political composition of the provisional government. The second dealt with rules for the election of a popularly chosen government. The Yalta agreement recognized the need for a "more broadly based" provisional government than that provided by the government-in-exile. A new government was to be established combining the "democratic leaders from Poland itself and from the Poles abroad." This government would be pledged "to the holding of free and unfettered elections as soon as possible on the basis of universal suffrage and secret ballot. For these elections all democratic and anti-Nazi parties shall have the right to take part and to put forward candidates . . ." [12]

[10] Winston S. Churchill, *Triumph and Tragedy* (Boston: Houghton Mifflin, 1953), pp. 128–145.

[11] Herbert Feis, *Churchill, Roosevelt, Stalin. The War They Waged and the Peace They Sought* (Princeton, N.J.: Princeton University Press, 1957), pp. 378–390. Also Hugh Seton-Watson, *The East European Revolution* (New York: Frederick A. Praeger, 1951), pp. 115–118.

[12] Yalta Conference, Statement of Churchill, Roosevelt, and Stalin. Feis, *op. cit.,* p. 528.

It soon became apparent that serious weaknesses inhered in this agreement. The difficulty of getting the government-in-exile to combine with the Lublin group had been underestimated. Few of the London Poles were willing to give up their legal authority as the Polish government, and they certainly did not want to fuse their government with a Communist regime. Also, agreements in broad principle had proved too vague to provide application in practice. In this respect, the meanings of "democratic parties" and "free elections" were not spelled out, and consequently the Soviet Union defined these concepts in ways totally unacceptable to the West and in clear violation of any ordinary definition of these terms. The expectation, or perhaps the hope, that the Soviet Union would live by these agreements proved illusory. With Soviet forces on Polish soil to enforce the will of the Soviet Union, there was little, short of the use of force, that could have changed the Polish situation. The hope that in the interests of peace the Soviet Union would pursue a policy to which the United States and Great Britain could agree was overrated.

The provisional government that was finally put together in July, 1945, was created with great difficulty. Few of the London-based ministers-in-exile succumbed to American and British pressure to fuse governments. Only Mikolajczyk, who became Vice-Premier and Minister of Agriculture, and Kiernik, Minister of Public Administration, joined.[13] The elections that were subsequently held in January, 1947, were not at all "free." They were held under conditions of terror. The Communists and their puppets were permitted to appeal for popular support. Other parties were hindered and their leaders imprisoned. Mikolajczyk estimated that over 100,000 of his party members and 142 of his party's candidates were jailed.[14] Before the year was out Mikolajczyk had to flee Poland or suffer the fate of Petkov and Maniu (see below).

ESTABLISHING A SATELLITE EMPIRE

The communization of Eastern Europe was a major cause of the cold war. Communism was forced on the peoples of Eastern Europe by the Soviet Union. Their methods outraged public opinion in the

[13] Seton-Watson, *op. cit.,* pp. 171–172.
[14] *Ibid.,* pp. 175–179.

West. In the process of imposing their will they violated agreements that they had signed. It had been generally anticipated that postwar governments would be set up in conformity with two agreements, the Churchill-Stalin understanding concerning the Balkans and the Yalta "Declaration on Liberated Europe," accords perhaps incompatible with one another, but acceptable to all concerned.

The Soviet advance in the summer of 1944 drove the Germans from the soil of the Soviet Union. By fall Rumania and Bulgaria were held by the Red Army, and Hungary and Yugoslavia were the scene of fighting. Churchill thought it useful to consider with Stalin the future of the Balkans and flew to Moscow in October for conversations. An agreement was readily arranged, giving the Soviet Union a 90 percent interest in Rumania, but allowing 10 percent to the Western allies. In Greece, Britain (with United States accord) was to have a 90 percent interest and the Soviet Union would be allowed 10 percent. Bulgarian interest would be shared 75–25 percent, the Soviet Union having the larger part. Yugoslavia and Hungary were to be shared 50–50 percent.[15]

The Yalta Conference issued a "Declaration on Liberated Europe," which established the principles that would govern the composition of governments in liberated states.

In general, the declaration promised to help the people of Europe organize governments in harmony with the principles of the Atlantic Charter and to "solve by democratic means their pressing political and economic problems." It affirmed "the right of all peoples to choose the form of government under which they will live" and more specifically the right "to form interim governmental authorities broadly representative of all democratic elements in the population and pledged the earliest possible establishment through free elections of the governments responsive to the will of the people . . ."[16]

These principles were patterned after earlier Italian arrangements. The "Declaration Regarding Italy" signed on November 1, 1943, by the foreign ministers' meeting in Moscow was meant to re-establish democracy there. An Italian regime would be "based upon the fundamental principle that Fascism and all of its evil influences and emanations shall be utterly destroyed and that the Italian peo-

[15] Churchill, *Triumph and Tragedy,* p. 227.
[16] Yalta Conference Statement, reproduced in Sigrid Arne, *United Nations Primer* (New York: Farrar and Rinehart, 1945), p. 105.

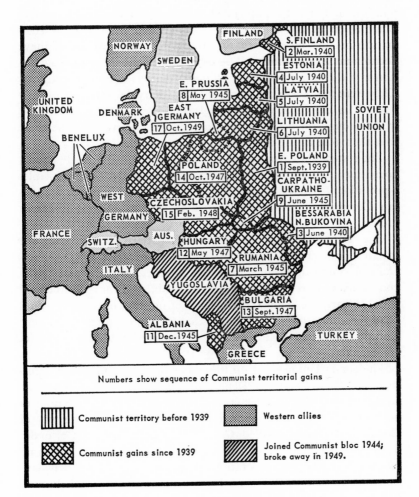

FINLAND	
NORWAY	**S. FINLAND** 2 Mar. 1940
SWEDEN	**ESTONIA** 4 July 1940
E. PRUSSIA 8 May 1945	**LATVIA** 5 July 1940
EAST GERMANY 17 Oct. 1949	**LITHUANIA** 6 July 1940
UNITED KINGDOM DENMARK	SOVIET UNION
BENELUX	**E. POLAND** 1 Sept. 1939
POLAND 14 Oct. 1947	**CARPATHO-UKRAINE** 9 June 1945
WEST GERMANY **CZECHOSLOVAKIA** 15 Feb. 1948	**BESSARABIA N. BUKOVINA** 3 June 1940
FRANCE SWITZ. AUS. **HUNGARY** 12 May 1947	
ITALY **YUGOSLAVIA**	**RUMANIA** 7 March 1945
ALBANIA 11 Dec. 1945	**BULGARIA** 13 Sept. 1947 TURKEY
GREECE	

Numbers show sequence of Communist territorial gains

▮▮▮	Communist territory before 1939	▨	Western allies
▨▨	Communist gains since 1939	▧	Joined Communist bloc 1944; broke away in 1949.

ple shall be given every opportunity to establish governmental and other institutions based upon democratic principles . . ." All Fascist and pro-Fascist elements and organizations were to be barred from political activity. To implement this decision an Allied Control Commission of the three powers was created in which the commander-in-chief of military operations for the area would have decision-making authority. The other two members of the commission would be informed about all policy matters other than military. They were to observe the operation of military governments in Italy and advise the commander-in-chief. This device appeared to work well although the Soviets raised some initial objections to the effect that their role in the commission was too small.

The system thus established was to operate until a freely chosen government was elected by the Italian people. Under these principles a provisional government for Italy was established in which the Italian Communist Party participated as well as other anti-Fascist groups.

The Yalta Declaration repeated this pattern by providing for interim governments representative of non-Fascist organizations. Control commissions in which the America, British, and Soviet commands were represented would be established for each liberated state. In each the commander-in-chief of military operations would head the commission. This meant that for the countries of Eastern Europe the Allied Control Commissions were headed by a Soviet commander.

The Soviet Union lived up to neither the Churchill-Stalin agreement nor the declaration. "Democratic elements" were denied a role in the political life of their land. The promise of "free elections of government" were not honored because they stood in the way of Communist control. Allied Control Commissions (ACC) under Soviet control allowed the American and British representatives no effective voice in their operation. In Eastern Europe the Russians operated in callous disregard for the principles which had been agreed upon.

NONFULFILLMENT OF THE DECLARATION ON LIBERATED EUROPE

The Churchill-Stalin understanding and the Declaration on Liberated Europe were first violated in Rumania and Bulgaria. No Western "interest" was permitted there despite the agreement of

October, 1944. In Hungary and Yugoslavia the declaration was at best briefly implemented. Coalitions of Communist and non-Communist parties enjoyed short tenure.

The Impotence of Allied Control Commissions. Allied Control Commissions for East European states existed in name only. In Rumania and Bulgaria the Soviet commanders refused to consult with their American and British members at critical junctures, when changes of government impended. In Hungary, Voroshilov, the Russian chief, although friendly with the American and British members of the commission allowed them no advisory voice and gave them little information about the operation of the Russian military government. Where the Russians had at one time complained that their role in the Italian commission was too small, they allowed no role to Great Britain and the United States in the commissions under their control.

Communization of Interim Governments. The Declaration on Liberated Europe called for interim governments "representative of all democratic elements." Before the Yalta Conference met, liberated Rumania was ruled by a representative coalition. The government led by Nicolae Radescu was not to the liking of the Soviet Union. Communist agitation against this regime assumed a measure of violence, and on this pretext Vice-Commissar Vishinsky arrived in Bucharest on February 27th to "correct" the situation. He demanded a new government headed by Petru Groza, a pro-Communist, and gave King Michael two hours and five minutes to announce the change. While the two-hour ultimatum was not accepted, the pressures were too great to withstand, and on March 6th a Communist-dominated government headed by Groza came into office. Protests by the American and British ambassadors in Moscow could not even be made because Molotov refused requests for consultation on this question, claiming that American and British members of the Allied Control Commission were talking with Vishinsky in Bucharest.[17] The State Department protest that the Groza government did not meet the requirements of the Declaration on the Liberation of Europe did not change Soviet policy.

The Fatherland Front established as the government of Bulgaria after the Nazi defeat was a coalition which included the Commu-

---

[17] Feis, *op. cit.,* pp. 564–567.

nist, Social Democratic, Agrarian Union, and Zveno parties.[18] However, the Fatherland Front was controlled by the Communists; during 1945 they purged those forces in the coalition which became increasingly restive under their dictation.

In Hungary, elections in 1945 resulted in a coalition regime. The Small Farmers' Party, having received 57 percent of the vote, led the coalition. However, they had promised the Russians that, regardless of the outcome of the elections, they would bring the other parties into the government. Over the next two years the Communists, on Russian authority, were able to gain control by purging the government of those who refused to act as their stooges.

The Yugoslav situation was distinctly different from those considered above. Yugoslavia was largely liberated of German control by Tito's partisan forces. Tito was the president of the National Committee of Liberation which united several anti-Fascist organizations but was under the firm control of the Yugoslav Communist Party. A royal Yugoslav government-in-exile did exist. Its Prime Minister, Subasic, agreed to the establishment of a united government for Yugoslavia. A cabinet for such a government was worked out in which Tito's National Committee of Liberation held a dominating number of posts. The United States State Department objected to these British-Soviet supported arrangements for the composition of the Yugoslav government. In the end, however, Roosevelt retracted his objection, and a Tito-Subasic cabinet was installed in March, 1945, containing a few representatives of the government-in-exile but dominated by Tito's committee.[19]

Liquidation of Non-Communist Parties. In all the countries which the Soviet Union controlled those parties which refused to bend to the will of the Communists were arbitrarily labeled Fascist and suppressed. In this manner the two largest parties of Rumania, the Peasant and the Liberal, were debarred from activity.

Iuliu Maniu, the leader of the National Peasant Party and one of the leading Rumanian statesmen of this century, was imprisoned and charged with counterrevolutionary activity. In 1947 he was sentenced to a long term in prison, where he eventually died.

In Bulgaria the Socialist Party and Agrarian Union were driven underground through terror. Trumped-up charges and confessions

[18] Seton-Watson, *op. cit.,* pp. 213–214.
[19] Feis, *op. cit.,* pp. 543–545.

secured by torture laid the groundwork for staged trials, which gave "legal" excuse for repression. Nikola Petkov, the leader of the Agrarian Union, was tried, sentenced, and executed, over world-wide protests, in 1947.[20] The Small Farmers' and Socialist Parties of Hungary were purged for "harboring Fascist elements." The leader of the Small Farmers' Party, Bela Kovacs, was accused of espionage, arrested in disregard of his parliamentary immunity by Russian soldiers, and never again seen alive. In Yugoslavia false charges of collaboration with the Germans led to show trials and purges of opposition by Tito.

Infiltration of Liberal Parties. Hand in hand with the suppression of non-Communist parties went attempts to capture some of these parties by infiltration. When successful, the techniques of "boring from within" and of terrorization of opposition leaders installed leaderships of Socialist, Agrarian, and middle-class parties that were pliant tools of the Communist Party or actually Communists in disguise.[21] The Agrarian Union and Social Democratic Parties in Bulgaria had Communists in positions of leadership. There were instances of some leaders in Czechoslovakia succumbing to pressures and serving as agents for the Communist Party. To overcome a weak position in Hungary, Communists organized other parties, such as the National Peasant Party, to exploit them as "fronts." Purges of the chosen leaders of the Small Farmers' and Socialist Parties left the field to the supporters of the Communists. However, similar tactics in Czechoslovakia boomeranged. Pro-Communists were defeated in their attempts to win the leadership of the Social Democratic Party.[22]

Suppression of Elections. The promise of free elections fared no better under Russian control. Bulgaria's elections of 1945 were conducted under conditions of terror. In the opinions of the American

[20] Seton-Watson, *op. cit.*, pp. 211–219.

[21] This is not an unheard-of technique in the Communist Party. The device of "boring from within" was a well-established tactic and adopted by the Communists in the 1920's and 1930's. In many countries Communists would hide their party affiliation and seek leadership of "mass organizations." This was a favorite technique of the American Communist Party in the 1930's and 1940's. Not only were organizations such as labor unions, religious organizations, and youth groups infiltrated, but in some instances political parties, such as the Democratic Party in California, became targets for Communist penetration.

[22] Seton-Watson, *op. cit.*, pp. 186–187.

and British missions there, not only were the elections not free but the results were also falsified on a large scale.[23] Two elections conducted in Hungary after the war were free. In the city of Budapest the Small Farmers' Party received 51 percent of the vote and later this party won 57 percent in a national election. Despite their majority the Small Farmers' were forced by the Kremlin to accept a coalition—the alternative was to agree to Voroshilov's demand for a single-slate election with other parties given a portion of the seats beforehand. Later the Russian command supervised a purge of the Small Farmers' leadership using pretexts of "conspiracy" with foreign powers, "reactionary affiliations," and treason to force cancellation of parliamentary immunity and to imprison them. New elections were then ordered in which those "convicted" of "crimes" against the state and their relatives residing with them were disenfranchised. Opponents of the Communists and their collaborators were curbed in their campaign, and the stuffing of ballot boxes was used to allow the Communist Party to emerge as the leader of a ruling coalition. The 22 percent of the vote which the Communist Party received was the largest attained by any party.[24]

Yugoslavia did not permit any contested elections. The voting of November, 1945, was for a single slate.

Control of Ministries of Interior. Possibly the tactic which most effectively brought Communist reign to Eastern Europe was control of the ministry of interior. Every country occupied by Soviet forces was forced to appoint a Communist as minister of interior. This placed a Communist in charge of the police power of the state and made the police an agency for eliminating all competition to Communist rule.

The Clash over Satellites. At the Potsdam Conference Stalin and Molotov attempted to secure British and American approval for the governments that had by then been established in Rumania, Bulgaria, and Hungary. Truman refused. He considered these governments puppets and complained that even information concerning them was unavailable to American and British sources.[25] Discussions at Potsdam concerning Russia's occupation were among the most

[23] *Ibid.,* p. 216.
[24] *Ibid.,* pp. 190–202.
[25] Harry S. Truman, *Memoirs. Year of Decisions,* Vol. I (Garden City, N.Y.: Doubleday, 1956), p. 384.

acrimonious of the conference. They apparently served to encourage non-Communist forces in each of the East European countries. In 1945 only Bulgaria could properly have been considered a satellite of the Soviet Union. While the Soviet Union sought United States and British approval for their new order in Eastern Europe, the Americans and British fought for a democratic order based upon the principles of the Atlantic Charter and the Yalta Declaration on the Liberation of Europe. On the occasion of the second meeting of the Council of Foreign Ministers it was agreed that the Rumanian and Bulgarian governments ought to be broadened to include parties that were in opposition to the existing government. However, this "intervention" produced no meaningful change in the character of the governments for either state. They remained satellites. Stalin made no real concessions which would give democracy a chance.

Diplomatic pressures were insufficient to alter Soviet behavior. Peace treaties obligated Bulgaria, Hungary, and Rumania to assure their peoples the enjoyment of "human rights and fundamental freedoms." These guarantees were violated. The General Assembly of the UN condemned the "willful refusal" of these three countries to live up to their treaty obligations. However, the imposition of a Communist dictatorship was not thereby forestalled.

The oft-repeated charge that Eastern Europe was given to the Communists at Yalta hardly describes the situation. It is true that the United States and Great Britain may have held illusions concerning the peaceful and cooperative role they expected the Soviet Union to play at the end of the war. However, by February, 1945, Eastern Europe was outside of Roosevelt's and Churchill's effective disposition. The course of Eastern European history was determined by Soviet military occupation of the East European states.

In all likelihood the rapid demobilization of United States military forces at the end of the war contributed to the disregard by the Soviet Union of Western sensibilities. The Churchill-Stalin agreement on spheres of influence in Eastern Europe may have encouraged the Soviet Union to believe that as long as they did not interfere in British activity in Greece in 1944 they would enjoy a free hand in Rumania and Bulgaria in 1945. The small role assigned the Soviet Union with respect to military government in Italy could well have touched off retaliation, denying Great Britain and the

United States a voice in the government of lands under Soviet control. Stalin may have assumed that the meanings of the words "free" and "democratic" were sufficiently flexible to be perverted to suit Russian interests.

By contrast, the United States and Great Britain operated within the letter and spirit of the Atlantic Charter and the agreements made at Yalta. In territories liberated by them people were provided an opportunity to choose governments in accordance with their "freely expressed wishes . . ." In the areas under Soviet control no such freedom was permitted. The Kremlin seemed to feel that in the areas under the control of Britain and the United States Western-style democracies would be established and that this was a function of Western rule. By the same token, in areas under Soviet military domination Communist-style "democracies" would be established. In point of fact democracy was never imposed. It was chosen in free elections through broad participation in the political process. On the other hand, Communist regimes were nowhere freely elected but were imposed.

The communization of Eastern Europe was a major cause of the cold war. It affronted the conscience of the West and, in their eyes, destroyed the credibility of Stalin's word. Stalin's rule was harsh. Satellites were forced to reorder their economies for Moscow's benefit. Through intrabloc export and import "agreements" and through joint holding companies of East European enterprises controlled by Russia, the wealth of the satellite lands was extorted for Russia's gain.

THE DEVELOPMENT OF THE COLD WAR
IN THE MIDDLE AND NEAR EAST

Russia's behavior in Eastern Europe appeared clearly aggressive in Western eyes. Pressure which she exerted upon Iran, Turkey, and Greece fortified this impression. Treaties and understandings were violated here too. The sum total of Soviet efforts in the Middle East was to confirm the need for containment of her expansionist proclivities by the Western powers led by the United States.

IRAN

At the end of the war a troublesome conflict arose in Iran. The country had been occupied by the Soviet Union and Great Britain in August-September of 1941 by joint agreement. A serious military crisis prompted this action. The Nazis were advancing eastward in the southern Ukraine while simultaneously Rommel's Afrika Corps was driving eastward in North Africa. Arab leaders in the Middle East tried to exploit the adverse fortunes of war to overthrow British rule there with German help. At the same time in neighboring Iran the Persian (Iranian) Shah was openly pro-German. Under these circumstances, Great Britain and the Soviet Union decided to occupy Iran with Soviet forces in the north and British troops elsewhere. This move was deemed essential to forestall a uniting of German forces driving south through the Ukraine and east from North Africa or through Turkey. The Shah abdicated and his son, the present ruler of Iran, known to be sympathetic to the Allies, was put on the throne.[26]

On January 29, 1942, the Treaty of Alliance was signed allowing United States, Soviet, and British forces on Iranian territory to protect Iran and in addition to channel lend-lease assistance from the Persian Gulf to the Soviet Union. The Treaty of Alliance also provided for the withdrawal of the allied forces from Iran within six months after Germany and her allies had been defeated.[27]

Iran was discussed at the Potsdam Conference at which time Stalin dismayed Truman by announcing that the Soviet Union would not depart from Iranian soil until six months after the termination of hostilities with Japan. It had been assumed that six months after May 8, 1945, the date of Germany's surrender, the occupation of Iran would come to an end. It should be remembered in this connection that during the early days of the Potsdam Conference when negotiations concerning Iran were held it was expected that the war against Japan would last for a year or more. The atomic bomb had not yet been exploded on the sands of New Mexico. The collapse of Japan within a month of the Potsdam meeting could scarcely have been anticipated. In view of these considerations there was some fear that Stalin meant to communize that part of Iran which was under Soviet occupation.

By the end of 1945 both American and British troops had left

[26] Winston S. Churchill, *The Grand Alliance, op. cit.,* pp. 476–486.
[27] William Eagleton, Jr., *The Kurdish Republic of 1946* (London: Oxford University Press for the Royal Institute of International Affairs, 1963). This volume contains useful data on Soviet activities in the Kurdish areas of the Middle East and northwestern Iran.

Iran. Soviet troops, however, were still in full occupation of Azerbaijan, a province of Iran, and forbade Iranian authorities entry into the province.

The Tudeh Party, the Communist Party of Iran, advocated autonomy for Azerbaijan. When the central government refused autonomy, a rump government under Tudeh leadership assumed power in Tabriz, capital of Azerbaijan. Iranian Azerbaijan had been long abused by the Iranian government. Absentee landlords residing in Teheran exploited the people. Britain and the United States, nevertheless, feared that this was a first step in the attempt to detach this province and annex it to the Azerbaijan republic of the Soviet Union.[28]

At Potsdam, Stalin had said that Russian troops were entitled to remain in Iran until six months after the end of the war with Japan (March 2, 1946). In the interim Stalin had expected the Tudeh Party to solidify its control over Azerbaijan. The March 2nd deadline was not observed. Soviet forces remained in Azerbaijan. Iran complained to the Security Council on March 18, charging the Soviet Union with the illegal occupation of Iranian territory and with interference in the internal affairs of the land. However, shortly after the complaint was made, the government withdrew its action because its negotiations with the Soviet Union were in progress. Despite the official withdrawal of the complaint the Iranian Ambassador to the United States, Hussein Ala, came to New York to press Iran's case before the Security Council. Over Soviet protests and a Soviet walkout the Security Council considered the question. On April 4 the Soviet government reversed itself and agreed to evacuate Iranian soil. By May 9 all Russian soldiers were withdrawn.

Security Council pressure reflecting world public opinion contributed to the decision to evacuate Iran. The Soviet Union may also have felt that it obtained valuable concessions for joint exploitations of Iranian oil and for Azerbaijan autonomy through a treaty negotiated with Iran. Later the Iranian parliament (Majlis) refused to ratify the treaty and it failed to go into effect. The hope that the Tudeh movement would spread throughout Iran and that Premier Qavam would be a friendly dupe and place Iran into the

[28] *Ibid.*, pp. 72–74.

Soviet fold may well have been another miscalculation that induced the Soviets to leave Iranian territory.

Stalin's policy in Iran increased suspicions that the Kremlin harbored expansionist goals and that to gain them she was prepared to disregard treaties she had signed.

GREECE AND TURKEY

Concurrent with Russia's expansionist ventures in Iran, pressures were building against the independence of Greece and Turkey. We have already seen that the Stalin-Churchill agreement put Greece in a British sphere of influence. British troops landed in Greece in October, 1944. The country had then been largely in control of the EAM-ELAS forces.[29] The British Commander, General Scorbie, was recognized by both the Greek government-in-exile and the ELAS, opposed to that government, as the Commander-in-Chief of all Greek forces.[30]

Unity among the various political groups broke down. Greek Communists bid for power, appealing for popular support but also staging riots and finally a rebellion. In the end an EAM-ELAS uprising was suppressed by the British. During 1945 Stalin refrained from assisting the Communist rebellion.[31] In 1946, right-wing parties won the parliamentary elections, and Soviet demands in the Security Council for the exit of British forces because they "threatened the peace of the area" came to naught. Greek Communists now commenced a new round in the civil war supported by the Communist-led regimes of the countries to the north. Albania, Yugoslavia, and Bulgaria provided privileged sanctuaries for Communist forces as well as sources of supply.

Greek and British armies were unable to end the civil war. Soviet support for the rebels and the general weakening of Great Britain during the war forced the British to urge the United States

[29] EAM—National Liberation Front, a Communist-dominated attempt at popular front organization. ELAS—Peoples' Liberation Army, a Communist-led guerrilla force.

[30] These forces included the Royal Greek Army, ELAS, and a smaller National Democratic Union (EDES) guerrilla force.

[31] However, at San Francisco, during the United Nations Conference on International Organization, Molotov advised the Greek foreign minister that he should no longer place reliance upon the British. Stephen G. Xydes, "The 1945 Crisis over the Balkan Straits," *Balkan Studies*, Vol. I., 1960, p. 70.

to take over the traditional British responsibilities for Greek and Turkish security. Unless Truman did so, London asserted, the area might well fall under Soviet control.[32] On March 12, 1947, the President addressed a joint session of Congress and announced a policy since named the Truman Doctrine. Truman wrote:

> Greece needed aid, and needed it quickly and in substantial amounts. The alternative was the loss of Greece and the extension of the iron curtain across the Eastern Mediterranean. If Greece was lost, Turkey would become an untenable outpost in a sea of Communism. Similarly, if Turkey yielded to Soviet demands, the position of Greece would be extremely in danger.
>
> But the situation had even wider implications. Poland, Rumania, and other satellite nations of Eastern Europe had been turned into Communist camps because, in the course of the war, they had been occupied by the Russian Army. We had tried, vainly, to pursuade the Soviets to permit political freedom in these countries, but we had no means to compel them to relinquish their control, unless we were prepared to wage war.
>
> Greece and Turkey were still free countries being challenged by Communist threats both from within and without. These free peoples were now engaged in a valiant struggle to preserve their liberties and their independence.
>
> America could not, and should not, let these free countries stand unaided. To do so would carry the clearest implications in the Middle East and in Italy, Germany, and France. The ideals and the traditions of our nations demanded that we come to the aid of Greece and Turkey and that we put the world on notice that it would be our policy to support the cause of freedom wherever it was threatened.[33]

The Truman Doctrine provided for economic, financial, and military assistance to Greece and Turkey. Four hundred million dollars were appropriated, and a team of military instructors was sent to Turkey to help with the organization and training of its armed forces. The President stated that "... it must be the policy of the United States to support free peoples who are resisting attempted subjugation by armed minorities or by outside pressures. ..." [34]

[32] Truman, *Memoirs. Years of Trial and Hope,* pp. 98–100. The British ambassador to the United States informed the Secretary of State, Marshall, that Britain would have to pull out of Greece by April 1.

[33] *Ibid.,* pp. 100–101.

[34] Norman A. Graebner, *Cold War Diplomacy 1945–1960* (Princeton, N.J.: Van Nostrand, 1962), Truman's speech to Congress, March 12, 1947, p. 151.

Not only did the Truman Doctrine play an essential role in preserving the independence of Greece against the Communist onslaught but it also put the Communist world on notice that the United States would not allow additional territory and populations to fall to Communist aggression. A new policy, *containment*, of Soviet expansion became a basic precept of United States foreign policy.

Parallel with the events in Greece a crisis developed over Turkey. The nub of this crisis involved control of the Turkish Straits, which were governed by Turkey under the Montreux Convention of 1936.[35] The Soviet Union had been a signatory of that instrument. During the war Stalin stated his dissatisfaction with the Montreux Convention on several occasions to both Churchill and Roosevelt. On March 19, 1945, the Soviet government denounced its Treaty of Friendship with Turkey which had been signed twenty years earlier. Russia wanted a new treaty which would allow her to share control of the Turkish Straits. Stalin also demanded that the provinces of Kars, Artvin, and Ardahan be ceded to the Soviet Union. These provinces in the northeastern part of Turkey had once been a part of greater Russia. While Stalin and Molotov, on several occasions, reaffirmed their interest in the acquisition of the provinces of Kars and Ardahan, it was the Turkish Straits that was their real goal.

There was general agreement by all concerned that the Montreux Convention gave Turkey too much control over the straits in an unregulated manner. Washington favored revision of the convention to the effect that no power not on the Black Sea should be permitted to send warships through the straits into the Black Sea whenever one or more of the Black Sea states were at war, unless the United Nations authorized such a move. Great Britain and the United States held, and the Turkish government agreed, that the Soviet Union had legitimate security interests here which ought to be recognized without endangering Turkey or violating her sovereignty.

Moscow asked for two things: a military presence on Turkish

---

[35] Herbert Feis, *Between War and Peace. The Potsdam Conference* (Princeton, N.J.: Princeton University Press, 1960), p. 337, Supplementary Note 6, extracts of the Montreux Convention pertinent to the Soviet demands for revision.

soil in the area of the Turkish Straits and a new agreement restricted, however, to the Black Sea powers—the riparian states Turkey, Rumania, Bulgaria, and the Soviet Union. Soviet demands for
a share of control over the straits and for the acquisition of Kars
and Ardahan were rejected by Turkey, Great Britain, and the
United States. A new war of nerves against Turkey ensued which
led to the inclusion of Turkey in the Truman Doctrine. Turkey, as
well as Greece, was "saved" by the assistance provided it under the
Truman Doctrine.

The Soviet Union has never receded from its demands for a
larger role in the Turkish Straits. However, after Stalin's death,
a Soviet note sent to Turkey informed her that it no longer had
any claim on Kars and Ardahan, provinces which it recognized as
being purely Turkish.[36]

NAZI-SOVIET CORRESPONDENCE

In the last weeks of the war, American and British forces captured
the archives of the German Foreign Office. A study of these documents followed. Among the documents were found those relating
to the Soviet-German relations during the period of the Nazi-Soviet
Pact. In 1948 the Department of State issued a collection of the
documents under the editorship of Raymond J. Sontag and James
S. Beddie.[37] Several memoranda documented Soviet ambitions in
Southeastern Europe and the Middle East. One reported a conversation between the Italian ambassador to Moscow and Molotov in
which Molotov agreed to Italian hegemony in the Mediterranean in
return for Italian acceptance of Soviet hegemony in the Black Sea.[38]
Others dealt with Molotov's visit to Berlin in November, 1940, for
the purpose of reviewing and solidifying the relations between the
Soviet Union and Nazi Germany. They showed that in conversations
concerning the division of territories among the Axis powers and
the Soviet Union Molotov strongly pressed a Soviet interest in the
Balkans, involving Rumania, Bulgaria, and Hungary, and the Turk-

[36] A comprehensive review of the diplomatic interchange concerning the
question of the Turkish Straits, Kars, and Ardahan may be found in
Stephen G. Xydis, "The 1945 Crisis over the Turkish Straits," *Balkan
Studies,* Vol. I., 1960, pp. 63–90.
[37] *Nazi-Soviet Relations, 1939–1941* (Department of State, Publication
3023).
[38] *Ibid.,* see document of June 26, 1940.

ish Straits. The Germans had competing interests in this area and pressed on the Soviet Union expansion southward in the Middle East and South Asia. While Molotov was unwilling to give up Soviet interests in the Balkans he put forward Russian aspirations in "the area south of Batum and Baku in the general direction of the Persian Gulf. . . ." [39]

Publication of the documents concerning Nazi-Soviet relations strengthened the well-developed impression of Soviet expansionist interest. Iran, the sponsorship of a Kurdish rebellion disadvantageous to the security of Iran and Turkey, and Soviet pressure on Greece and Turkey all served to enforce Moscow's imperialist image. Stalin's claim for the Dodecanese Islands and a trusteeship over Tripolitania, made in connection with negotiations of the Italian peace treaty, were hardly calculated to build confidence regarding Soviet intentions. Nor was faith restored by a later Soviet offer to give up its claim to the aforementioned territories, which of course it did not possess, in return for the cession of Trieste to Yugoslavia, then a Soviet satellite. [40]

CZECHOSLOVAK COUP

The decision to contain the Soviet Union did not bring about any redirection of Soviet policy. To the contrary the cold war was intensified. A Communist take-over in Czechoslovakia in February, 1948, aggravated the deepening hostility which marked the cold war. Of all the countries of Europe Czechoslovakia had been the most friendly toward the Soviet Union prior to the Second World War and indeed during that war. The Czechoslovak government appreciated the Soviet offer for assistance at the time of the Munich agreement. While the Nazi-Soviet Pact led to the severing of ties between the Soviet Union and the Czech government in London and while Czech Communists supported Hitler in conformity with Soviet policy and were thus despised by many Czech patriots, the Czechs were quick to restore diplomatic relations after Hitler's attack on Russia. [41] A treaty of friendship between the two govern-

[39] Ibid., p. 259.
[40] Benjamin Rivlin, The United Nations and the Italian Colonies (New York: Carnegie Endowment for International Peace, 1950), pp. 9–14.
[41] Josef Korbel, The Communist Subversion of Czechoslovakia: 1938–1948 (Princeton, N.J.: Princeton University Press, 1959).

ments followed. There could be no question of Czechoslovakia's friendly intentions toward the Soviet Union and this made the Communist coup appear so grotesque.

Most of Czechoslovakia was liberated from the Germans by Soviet forces. The Soviet occupation of Czechoslovakia was brief. Under the occupation a people's front government composed of the Communist Party, the Social Democratic Party, the National Socialist Party, and the Catholics was established. Within Czechoslovakia the Communist Party enjoyed great prestige based upon its association with the victorious Soviet armies and its own role in partisan activity which began after Hitler invaded the Soviet Union. The Communist Party held several ministries in the people's front government including, of course, the Ministry of Interior, thereby giving it control of the police. Elections were held in May, 1946, from which the Communist Party emerged as the largest party of the country. It received 38 percent of the vote, and a coalition government was then established headed by Clement Gottwald, the leader of the Czechoslovak Communist Party, who became premier.

During 1947 disagreements within the cabinet became increasingly irreconcilable. Non-Communist members of the coalition feared the aggressiveness with which Nosek, the Communist Minister of the Interior, policed the country. The Communist police were accused of injustice and brutality. Stalin's ban on Czechoslovakia's participation in the Paris conference for setting up the Marshall Plan turned public opinion against the Communist Party. The blatant attempt by the Communists to capture the Social Democratic Party, an operation reminiscent of Communist procedures in Hungary, Rumania, and Bulgaria, also diminished the party's popularity. In the Social Democratic Party Communist agents were defeated and a non-Communist leadership was elected.

The Soviet Union wanted a Communist-controlled parliament. With elections scheduled for May, 1948, the outlook for Communist victory in a free election appeared dim. Such an election therefore had to be circumvented.

In the last months of 1947 Nosek began a purge of non-Communist elements in the police, and by February, 1948, the Communist Party enjoyed control of the police. The crisis which led to a *coup d'état* was touched off by the demand of the non-Communist majority in the cabinet that Nosek cease his purge of the police. This cabinet decision Nosek declined to carry out, and in this he was supported by Premier Gottwald. The National Socialist and the Slovak Democratic ministers resigned in protest of this illegal behavior. The Communists responded by staging their coup. They armed detachments of factory workers under their leadership, sent their gangsters into the ministries of the resigned ministers, and invaded the headquarters of non-Communist parties. They organized street demonstrations demanding the exclusion of the parties whose ministers had resigned from the government and established action committees to take over local government. During all of this the pro-Communist Minister of Defense, Svoboda, ordered the armed forces to remain neutral. While Soviet forces were not within Czechoslovakia, their presence on the borders of the land served to ensure that the coup would succeed.[42]

The objectives of the coup were evident. In the first place, the Communists wished to avoid free elections because they would record a recession of Communist strength. When elections were finally held, a single-list unopposed ticket was presented. In the second place, the Soviet Union wanted more than friendship and security. The Beneš government was friendly to Russia but Stalin wanted satellites and not merely friends. In the third place, democracy was to be destroyed and supplanted by Communist totalitarianism.

It was also becoming clear to the West that the existing instrument for the maintenance of peace and security, the Security Council, was not adequate when the threat of aggression emanated from the Soviet Union. New organs of multilateral defense were necessary. The Czech *coup d'état* led to deliberations which a year later resulted in the establishment of the North Atlantic Treaty Organization.

GERMANY

Perhaps the most important problem facing the big three in respect to postwar Europe concerned the future of Germany. During the war general agreement on the German question was not difficult to achieve. As long as military considerations were primary, the need to maintain unity to defeat Hitler dominated the planning of the big-three leadership. Churchill, Roosevelt, and Stalin

[42] Seton-Watson, *op. cit.,* pp. 179–190.

agreed that they must act in concert to end the German threat to world peace, possibly by dismembering that state. They agreed that the German war criminals should be tried and punished. There was no difficulty in reaching an accord on the principle that the Germans should pay reparations for the destruction which their aggression had wrought. At Yalta decisions were made regarding the division of Germany into three zones, one each for the United States, the Soviet Union, and Great Britain—later to become four zones with a French zone pieced out of the British and the United States areas. It was also decided that an Allied Control Council be appointed to carry out the big-three administrative responsibility in Germany. A special arrangement was signed with respect to Berlin which provided for a three-zone (later to become a four-zone) occupation of the city. Berlin was, nevertheless, deep in the Soviet zone.

Concurrence on the details of reparations was not reached at the Yalta Conference and therefore was left to a separate commission. Later at the Potsdam Conference a reparations agreement was signed. Reparations were to be paid in goods produced in excess of a level determined by pegging German living standards at a level no higher than those of the poorest countries of Europe. Production over and above this level was to be used for reparations purposes. Essential imports which were required for subsistence were to be paid for out of her exports. The Soviet Union was to collect reparations from the Soviet zone and share them with Poland. In addition Russia was to receive 10 percent of the reparations available in the Western zones and another 15 percent in capital goods would be traded for exports from the Soviet zone.[43]

This agreement was never implemented. From the first Americans, including President Truman on the occasion of his trip to Potsdam, observed the wastefulness of wholesale reparations taken in the Soviet zone of occupation.[44] Reparations were seized without proper accounting. There was some anxiety that Soviet demands were excessive and would force the United States to subsidize the Germans in its zone to prevent wholesale starvation. By taking the position that it would not be permissible for the United States to support

---

[43] J. Eugene Harley, *Documentary Textbook on the United Nations* (Los Angeles: Center for International Understanding, 1947), Ch. XXIV, "The Potsdam Declaration," pp. 770–779.

[44] Truman, *Year of Decisions,* p. 357.

Germans so that they might pay reparations, the Potsdam formula provided that "payment of reparations should leave enough resources to enable the German people to subsist without external assistance." [45]

The Yalta and Potsdam agreements called for a unified economic and administrative policy for Germany. A Yalta statement referred to "coordinated plans and uniform decisions for Germany as a whole" at the same time that it agreed that each state would supervise its own zone of occupation. A central administrative agency, an Allied Control Council, was established to standardize administrative policy and unify the economy for all of Germany. To be sure, control council policy decisions were subject to the veto of each of the four zonal commanders. For Berlin a special four-power Allied Kommandatura was established with responsibility for unifying the administration and the economy of greater Berlin. The unifying principles also were never implemented. Almost from the beginning the Soviet zone was administered without regard to a common policy. Attempts to administer greater Germany as a single economic unit were frustrated. In 1946 the United States administrator, General Lucius Clay, offered a pact on the level of German industry to be used as a basis for reparations payment. He had hoped that concurrence on level of industry could be used as a lever for unifying the German economy. Agreement in this matter did not change the Soviet's policy of isolating its zone or its rigid intransigence on all proposals for economic cooperation. Clay therefore suspended advance reparations delivery to the Soviet Union on May 3, 1946. Reparations issues and administrative and economic dissociation caused continuing discord.

The issue of Germany's boundary illustrated the yawning gap between agreements on broad principles and their translation into practical details. In general Roosevelt, Churchill, and Stalin were agreed that Soviet boundaries in Eastern Europe ought to be those held by the Soviet Union at the time of the German attack in 1941. They also favored compensating Poland for loss of territory at German expense. Churchill proposed an Oder River boundary between Poland and Germany, but Stalin wanted to include German Silesia in Poland and demanded that the border be the Oder-Neisse.

[45] Harley, *op. cit.*, p. 774.

Furthermore, while the United States and Great Britain proposed to endorse and support these boundary agreements, they also insisted that they come into force as part of a German peace treaty. A treaty of peace with Germany has never been negotiated. The Soviet Union unilaterally determined the present boundaries of East Germany and Poland, incorporating Silesia into Poland.

In the long run the most important issue concerning Germany is unity of the German state. The Potsdam Conference approved the principle of a united Germany. Implementation of this undertaking remains unfulfilled. The Soviet Union wanted unity only under the condition that Communist domination of East Germany be assured. The Western stand based on "free elections" would have spelled certain defeat for the Communists. It was, therefore, rejected by the Soviet Union.

In July, 1946, Molotov proposed joint operation of the industrial Ruhr Valley. In the eyes of the West this seemed an ominous initiative; Moscow sought entry to the industrial might of Western Germany to advance its power position. Western statesmen have always been sensitive to any indication of Soviet ambition for control of the Ruhr. Molotov's proposal was rejected.

From 1946 on, the Kremlin implemented the Sovietization of its zone, making East Germany a Soviet satellite. It had, during the early years of the war, begun preparations for this purpose.[46] German Communists living in Russian exile were brought together and trained for a future leadership role in Germany. Stalin thereby assured himself of operatives who would be loyal to the Soviet Union.

As in the countries of Eastern Europe, Communists attempted to capture the opposition parties. In Germany the Social Democratic Party was a special target. In the Soviet Zone an enforced unity of the Social Democratic and Communist Parties took place. The new Socialist Unity Party was from the beginning dominated by the Communists and pursued the Communist line. As in the other satellite countries genuine opposition parties were eliminated. When the first East German local elections went poorly for the Communists and when free elections in Berlin gave less than 20 percent of

[46] Wolfgang Leonhard, *A Child of the Revolution* (Chicago: Henry Regnery, 1958).

the votes to the Socialist Unity Party, the all-Berlin government was terminated in 1948 and Soviet-style single-slate elections became the rule for East Berlin and East Germany.

Sovietization of East Germany brought about unification of the Western zones. This move was all the more necessary as West German recovery moved ahead, making it a considerable asset in the growing struggle with Soviet might. As the cold war grew in intensity it became increasingly apparent that danger to the security of the European states and to world peace emanated from revisionist Russia rather than a rehabilitated Germany. West German participation in a Western alliance was welcomed as it became evident that the German people had wholeheartedly adopted democratic practices. A democratic, peace-loving, prosperous, and powerful Germany was a welcome partner to the West, but such a Germany proved to be a poor candidate for reunification with the East German state in the view of the Soviet Union.

East-West exchanges on the German question held little promise that German reunification on terms acceptable to the West would soon take place. The alternative adopted by the West was the recognition of the unified zones as the Bonn Republic and the cultivation of close ties with it. By mid-June of 1948 both the Allied Control Council and the Berlin Kommandatura had ceased its operations. On June 24, Stalin instituted a blockade of West Berlin as Soviet retaliation for the unification of the Western zones, the dissolution, for all practical purposes, of the Allied Control Council and the Berlin Kommandatura, and the circulation of a new West German currency by the Western zonal powers over a Soviet veto.[47] The blockade was intended to achieve a dissolution of the unified zones, the ouster of the United States, Britain, and France from Berlin, and a visible defeat of Western prestige in Europe. The West reacted effectively by mounting an airlift that kept West Berlin supplied. The population of West Berlin was tough and steadfast. Stalin could have no doubt that the West was ready to face war

[47] The USSR first imposed rail and road restrictions to traffic from West Germany to Berlin on April 1. On June 24, the day after the currency reforms, all land and water routes between West Germany and Berlin were severed. The blockade became fully effective on August 4. See *International Review Service,* "Berlin and Germany," Vol. VIII, No. 71, 1962, pp. 6–7.

on this issue. Eleven months later the blockade was defeated and withdrawn. Yet this did not mitigate the cold-war struggles. That experience, if anything, served to intensify hatred.

AUSTRIA

An even more exasperating, although less critical, situation evolved in Austria. Austria was also governed by a four-power occupation. However, the Austrian people were permitted to elect a government, and the Second Austrian Republic came into being on December 19, 1945. Two parties, the Peoples Party (in favor of democracy and capitalism) and the Socialist Party, emerged as the major parties. They had won one hundred and sixty-one of the one hundred and sixty-five seats in parliament, the Peoples Party being somewhat stronger. A coalition government of these parties was installed. The Communists were a weak minority as they had won only four seats.[48]

Agreement on an Austrian state treaty proved frustratingly elusive. The three Western powers, anxious to end the Austrian occupation, met virtually every Soviet condition. Each concession brought forth additional Russian demands, and there were long periods during which the Soviet Union simply refused to sign a treaty. It was evident that the Russians were simply disinclined to depart Austrian soil. Soviet occupation did not prevent the Austrians from establishing a democratic regime, and it failed to help the Austrian Communist Party grow. Nevertheless this occupation facilitated Moscow's influence in Central Europe.

DISPLACED PERSONS

The end of the war found many Soviet citizens in Austria and Germany. Some had been taken there by the Nazis to work as "slave labor" on German farms and in factories. Others had luckily escaped death in the concentration camps and at the war's end roamed the German and Austrian countryside. A number of Russian prisoners of war had fought with the forces of General Vlasov, a defector from the Soviet army who raised a division to fight against the Soviet Union and her allies. All of these displaced persons were to be returned home but many refused to go. Often they were forced to

[48] Philip E. Moseley, *The Kremlin in World Politics* (New York: Random House, 1960), p. 267.

enter trains destined for Russia at gunpoint. It became difficult for American and British officials responsible for camps for displaced persons to decide whether to honor commitments to return displaced persons to Russia as Soviet representatives insisted, or to allow themselves to be swayed by humane inclinations to permit these persons to remain behind. The wartime image of the Soviet Union as having the undivided support and loyalty of its people and of Stalin enjoying the affection of the masses was thereby undermined.

About 1,500,000 displaced persons remained in Germany, Austria, and Italy unwilling to return to their East European homelands. By 1946 American, British, and French policy allowed the individual freedom of choice in this matter. This position was endorsed in a General Assembly resolution passed on February 12, 1946. An even larger number of German refugees resulted from the expulsion of Germans from East European states and the flight of Jews and others from areas under Russian control after the war.

THE KOREAN WAR

War in Korea might easily have touched off a third world war. Even before the Korean fighting broke out, the Korean situation itself engendered deep United States and Russian antagonism. Soviet occupation of North Korea enabled it to impose a puppet regime upon the people in violation of agreements which it had made.

The Korean question can be traced back to a decision of Roosevelt, Churchill, and Chiang Kai-shek at the Cairo Conference of November, 1943. Roosevelt and Churchill were then *en route* to Teheran for their first meeting with Stalin. The occasion for the Cairo Conference was the need to consider new steps in the war on Japan. The war in the Pacific had been going well. The Battle of Midway and the Battle of the Coral Sea had ended in United States victories. Therefore the time had come for initial consideration of postwar arrangements for Asia. It was decided that Japan would be divested of its colonial holdings. With respect to Korea it was agreed "that in due course Korea shall become free and independent." [49] This statement implied that a period of tutelage would be necessary for the Koreans to learn the arts of government and how to

[49] The Department of State, *The Record on Korean Unification. 1943– 1960*, Publ. 7084, Far Eastern Series 101, October, 1960, p. 42.

rule themselves. Stalin was apprised of this agreement during the Teheran meeting and appeared to subscribe to its intent.

Korean policy was affected by the United States desire for Soviet assistance in the war against Japan. Until the first atomic bomb was exploded on July 17, 1945, at Alamogordo, New Mexico, it was believed that Japan's defeat would necessitate an invasion of the Japanese homeland. Considerable casualties were anticipated, and to facilitate final victory at a minimum of cost in American lives it was considered vital that the Soviet Union make war on Japan, pinning down Japanese forces in northern China. At the Yalta Conference Stalin confirmed earlier undertakings that the Soviet Union would commence hostilities against Japan two to three months after Germany's surrender. The atomic bomb made Soviet participation in the Asian engagement unnecessary, but by that time it was too late to call off the agreed-upon Soviet operation. In the opening days of the Potsdam Conference Russian representatives said that they would attack Japan late in August, but when the first atomic bomb was dropped on Hiroshima the Soviet Union apparently ordered an attack that came on August 9th. Molotov then explained that the Soviet Union had met its commitment with great exactness in timing its attack on Japan exactly three months after VE Day.[50]

It took several weeks from the time the Japanese announced that they would surrender (on August 14) to arrange the shipping needed to bring American forces to South Korea. In the meantime Russian soldiers entered Korea. An improvised arrangement designated the 38th parallel as a dividing line. North of the parallel the Japanese were to surrender to Soviet forces and south of the parallel to the Americans.

Japan's surrender brought on feverish nationalist activity on the Korean Peninsula and many exiles returned. Some came from Nationalist China, others from the United States, and still others from their exile in the Soviet Union. All were ready to renew Korea's place in the family of sovereign states.

It had been agreed that the 38th parallel was to have no significance other than to provide for the acceptance of surrendered arms.

---

[50] The Soviet government recognizes VE Day as May 9th rather than May 8th, when the Germans surrendered in Berlin to the Russian as well as other commands.

More specifically it had been determined that the country was to be treated as an economic whole. Nevertheless the Soviet military command very quickly turned the 38th parallel into an international frontier. On-the-spot effort by the American commanders to overcome this division of the land failed as the Soviet commander refused to integrate the Korean economy.[51]

The Potsdam Conference established a Council of Foreign Ministers of the big-five powers with responsibility for writing treaties of peace with the defeated Axis powers. Korea was considered at the meetings of the Council in Moscow in December, 1945, as an aspect of the Japanese peace settlement. The foreign ministers agreed that a five-year trusteeship should be instituted for Korea, to operate under the authority of four powers—all of the big five except France, who had no interest in this area. The ministers reasoned that the lengthy period of Japanese rule had left Korea unprepared for self-government. They believed that a period of tutelage, up to five years, would be advantageous to the Korean people. Pending independence a provisional government was to be established by a joint commission of the United States and Soviet commanders in Korea. This "provisional Korean democratic government was to be composed in consultation with the representatives of the democratic parties and social organizations" of the Korean people.[52]

The announcement of a five-year trusteeship received a hostile reaction from the Korean people. They demonstrated for immediate independence in all of the major cities. Significantly, however, the Communists withdrew from these protest demonstrations. They alone accepted the five-year trusteeship provisions without complaint.

Between March 20 and May 8, 1946, the American and Russian commanders met for consultations with the representatives of the democratic organizations of Korea for the purpose of composing a provisional government. At the first meeting of the Joint Commission the Soviet commander announced that he would not consult with the representatives of organizations which were opposed to the five-year trusteeship, proposing consultation with leaders of organizations that accepted trusteeship. Aside from violating the Moscow agreement to consult with democratic organizations, this decision

[51] *The Record on Korean Unification . . . , op. cit.,* pp. 4–5.
[52] *Ibid.,* p. 47.

would have the effect of limiting all consultation to Communist organizations or groups controlled by the Communists. Such a proposal was out of the question as far as Washington was concerned, and the American representative refused to use acceptance of the trusteeship as the criterion for a "democratic organization." From 1946 on, negotiations between the American and Russian commands proved sterile. Even when agreement seemed to be arranged in an exchange of letters between Secretary of State Marshall and Foreign Minister Molotov, it failed to be implemented at the level of the negotiations in Korea. The Soviet spokesman never did accept consultation with non-Communist Koreans for the establishment of a provisional government.

Eventually Marshall decided that no acceptable progress could be made through bilateral negotiations. By 1947 the 38th parallel had become an international boundary, yet the desire for reunification remained and made for a volatile situation that endangered the peace of Asia. It was with this in view that Marshall referred the Korean question to the General Assembly over Soviet objections. Russian objections were based on the premise that all postwar settlements, of which the Korean was one, were reserved to the Council of Foreign Ministers. There was little hope that the General Assembly could solve the Korean dilemma; still an international consensus supporting Washington's position could wring some advantage from the situation.

The General Assembly appointed a commission to facilitate the creation of a duly elected government and bring the occupation to an end. The commission was not permitted north of the 38th parallel. The General Assembly's Interim Committee thereupon directed that elections go forward wherever they could be held and observed by the commission. They took place in the southern zone. A national assembly was elected with one-third of the seats left open for North Korea on the basis of the proportion of population resident there.

The Soviet position on the Korean question and the negotiations over Korea once again impressed the West with the intransigence of the Soviets and the impunity with which they twisted the plain language of treaties for their purposes.

During 1950 the goal of Korean unification seemed more remote than ever. South Korea's President, Syngman Rhee, favored unification by force if necessary. Because of the sometimes provocative position adopted by Rhee, the United States was reluctant to give the Republic of Korea large quantities of modern arms which left it relatively unprepared for North Korea's attack.[53]

The war in Korea made plain that the Soviet Union was ready to utilize force, at least by its satellites, for the purpose of further expansion of the area under Communist control. It also tested the willingness of the United States to contain, by force if necessary, Soviet-sponsored expansion. In retrospect Korea showed that there was to be no relaxation in the probing efforts of the Soviet Union wherever promising results appeared likely; that limited war was an ever-possible probing tactic; and that the Soviet Union appreciated the limitations of its own power and would avoid a nuclear confrontation or a third world war.

SUMMARY

The above review suggests that the major cause of the cold war was the revisionist policies of the Soviet Union. The issues which we reviewed detail the imposition or attempts to impose unwanted Communist rule. Other situations that might have been considered would in no way change this basic conclusion. Soviet pressure for a greater role in Japan's occupation, the attempt to destroy the Marshall Plan conference in Paris, the anti-American pro-Soviet position of Communist parties around the world in encouraging strikes harmful to the economy of their own countries but serving the interests of Soviet policy all serve to confirm that irreconcilable goals lay at the root of the cold war. The Soviet refusal to join most of the specialized agencies of the United Nations indicated the limited arena for negotiation and contact. The "iron curtain" closed off the Soviet East from the democratic West.

Soviet expansion was characterized by the attempts to control provisional governments through the elimination of non-Communist elements and control of those ministries that were the key to power. Where Soviet military forces were in occupation this was effectively done. Free elections in which all democratic political organizations

[53] In the Russian version it was the South Koreans who attacked North Korea. This ludicrous allegation is denied by United Nations observers who observed the aggression on the spot, by the willingness of the South Koreans and the refusal of the North Koreans to accept the cease-fire proposal of the Security Council on the day that war began.

were to participate and only Fascists were to be excluded became, under Soviet control, elections in which only the Communists and their tools qualified as the "democratic organizations" and all other groups were suppressed as Fascist. With staged elections went terror and finally liquidation of non-Communist elements.

Soviet policy was aggressive rather than oriented toward security. At the war's end America and Britain were prepared to ensure Russia's security. Governments of countries near the Soviet Union had to be friendly to Russia and no responsible official in the West wished it otherwise. The Kremlin could have assured its security through friendly collaboration with the West and by fulfilling its pledge in the Declaration on Liberated Europe. Stalin chose to exploit his military advantage to set up a satellite empire. With few exceptions, where Russia's armies were in occupation, communization under Stalin's agents was carried out and democracy was extirpated, an exercise going far beyond Russia's security needs. In areas where Moscow's writ did not extend, the Kremlin tried to expand its sway. After 1945 East-West settlements were usually impossible to negotiate.

CHAPTER 8

Continuing Issues in the Cold War

THE WORLD has experienced two decades of cold-war conflict. During these two decades there have been years when antagonism abated. There have also been times when the struggle verged on war. Despite the ebb and flow of hostility there is little hope that the cold war will soon end. The issues in conflict are too incontractible. A realistic prognosis of the situation leads one to expect that this conflict will continue indefinitely, and the world will continue to experience periods of relaxation as well as intensified hostility.

No region of the earth has escaped the cold war. Each continent has its points of tension where the Communist and non-Communist forces have been arrayed. We shall examine the most important of these conflicts in Europe, the Middle East, Africa, Asia, and Latin America, but some cold-war issues are international in scope. The most important of these are disarmament, and the proper role and function of the United Nations.

INTERNATIONAL ISSUES

DISARMAMENT

Since 1946 the world has witnessed a continuing dialogue on the question of disarmament. The goal of disarmament is universally accepted. The means for achieving this goal have been the subject of this dialogue. The question appears, in the main, as a two-sided debate. Of course not only the Communists and the West have put forward schemes for disarmament. Neutralist states have also made proposals. They have on occasion been helpful in voicing an international concern, and they have acted to curb both sides when their proposals have been overly self-serving. Neutralist states have constituted an important pressure group to keep the United States and the Soviet Union negotiating. In the main, however, the disarmament question has involved the United States and Russia as protagonists offering significantly different approaches. The military imbalance in the world has virtually dictated that the United States and the Soviet Union, the two states without which disarmament would be meaningless, take the lead on this issue.

Too much of the disarmament dialogue has been concerned with scoring points in the cold-war debate, with putting the onus for lack of progress on the other side, and with advocating disarmament for propaganda purposes rather than in quest of solid agreements. When the position of each side is evaluated it becomes clear that neither side is adverse to promoting its power advantages through disarmament agreements. The Soviet Union has proposed measures designed to weaken the West. Thus, during the period of the United States A-bomb monopoly they advocated unconditional destruction of atomic bombs, and the prohibition of their manufacture. At the same time they urged a one-third reduction of armed forces to take effect simultaneously with the agreement to destroy A-bombs. At a time when Soviet forces totaled 175 divisions to 12 for the United States such a proposal would have served only to increase Soviet superiority in conventional forces.[1] Later with the build-up of United States bases around the world to deal with threats of Soviet aggression, Soviet disarmament plans included dismantling of foreign bases. United States superiority in long-range bombers led Moscow to demand a ban on the use of nuclear weapons, except on agreement of the Security Council where the veto could be used. Proposals to "freeze" or "thin out" conventional forces in Europe or to restrict the number of men under arms of certain other nations (West Germany to 200,000) were aimed mainly at reducing NATO's effectiveness.

The West has, for its part, put forward proposals to serve its military advantage. Thus, the Baruch Plan of 1946 would have en-

[1] The American Assembly, Louis Henkin (ed.), *Arms Control Issues for the Public* (Englewood Cliffs, N.J.: Prentice-Hall, 1961), p. 145.

abled the United States to retain its position of nuclear superiority during the period in which the disarmament agreements were in the process of fulfillment. Western plans for inspection would have required nothing less than the opening of the closed society of the Soviet Union. United Nations policing of disarmament agreements would give the West a working majority with which to operate, while the Soviet Union could not hope to escape its minority position for the foreseeable future.[2]

Disarmament proposals of both sides are made with consideration for the resulting military posture. Even when resolutions are tabled in a sincere desire to disarm, they contain assurances for military security at every stage. Such considerations have not prevented some recent agreements, such as the banning of nuclear tests in the atmosphere and under water, and the agreement to reduce the danger of accidental war through direct telephonic communication between the White House and the Kremlin. There is some willingness to station observers at one another's airfields, ports, and rail depots to guard against surprise attack. Nevertheless, disarmament proposals have led to bitter disputes. The Soviet emphasis on general and complete disarmament (GCD) to be completed within a brief time period (four years was Khrushchev's proposal) has been refused by the West. Under the Soviet proposal states would disarm to the level of local militias necessary to maintain order within the land. This would enhance Soviet preeminence in Europe and American superiority in the Western hemisphere but require a consequent departure of United States forces from Europe. The Soviet Union has been vague about inspection and verification of performance on agreements. It proposed limited inspection. It is tremendously concerned with the preservation of its closed society. Inspections therefore appear as espionage. The Soviet Union takes the position that it would accept inspection along with disarmament provided that the opportunity for espionage is impossible and that inspection is subject to veto within the Security Council.

The United States, as the major spokesman for the West on disarmament questions, has placed greater emphasis on measures of arms control. Washington's emphasis is on assurances that agreements are meticulously checked with continuing proof against

[2] *Ibid.,* pp. 68–75.

cheating. It assesses disarmament measures in terms of long-term or temporary imbalance in military power. For the United States, disarmament can occur when security is assured. Security means guarantees against cheating, protections against surprise attack, and step-by-step reductions in arms during which the West would not be faced with an unfavorable balance in military power. Eventually a democratically controlled UN would enforce security in a disarmed world.

The United Nations

It is ironic that the United Nations, an organization established to mitigate conflict among states and reduce tensions between them, has become an arena in which both protagonists in the cold war seek to build their strength and defame the position of the other side. The UN has itself become the subject of bitter conflict between the Communists and the West.

The UN has provided a forum for propagandistic appeals. For the Soviet Union this involves the exploitation of colonial issues. Russia has strengthened its ties with newly independent states and encouraged anti-Western positions by assuming the role of champion for the liquidation of West European and American colonialism on terms most favorable to the colonial states. In addition, the Soviet Union has been a vociferous spokesman for "peace" against the threats of "imperialist aggression."

The West has used the UN forum to assume the mantle of spokesman for human freedom and dignity and to condemn countries behind the iron curtain for enslaving their people. In meetings of the General Assembly and Security Council the West has hammered away at the aggressive behavior of Communist states in Europe and Asia. The West has underlined its ready acceptance of United Nations peace-serving decisions, and has pinned the failure of these decisions and most especially that of the Security Council to promote peaceful settlements upon the Soviet Union and its abuse of the veto.

The cold-war conflict within the United Nations derives in part from differing conceptions about the proper role of the UN. The Soviet Union believes the UN ought to be an institution for discussion and negotiation. Yet it is not loath to use the organization for putting the West in the dock on colonial issues. In true Leninist fashion it envisages its own role as one of propaganda in the parliamentary debate of this institution. From the beginning, the Soviet Union wished to limit United Nations action to only such matters as are acceptable to both the East and the West—perhaps to the states of the world in between as well. The Soviet Union, deeply conscious of the fact that it is almost always outvoted on cold-war issues, would like to extend its veto by denying the General Assembly competence to help enforce peace and security and by tying up action in the Secretariat through a "troika" arrangement that would give it a veto over the work of that body.

From the point of view of the West the UN has many useful functions to perform. Some of these functions are directly related to the cold-war conflict. It utilizes the forum provided by the organization for carrying on the cold-war dialogue. In this respect it feels that it has certain natural advantages because of its *status-quo* interests. It sees the organization as one that ought to be able to make more majoritarian decisions, knowing full well that in most instances the decisions would be favorable to it. The UN has been used to point out the isolated position of the Communist bloc through votes cast on many questions. The West does not exclude the possibility that the United Nations may become an anti-Communist coalition in the event of Communist aggression.

The UN has had to deal with many cold-war issues. These issues have been debated and voted. Few, if any, of them have been solved in the process. Often they have exacerbated hostility. For almost a decade East and West fought over the admission of new states to the United Nations. While this is still an issue with respect to the admissibility of the two Germanies, the two Vietnams, and the two Koreas, by and large this question is now of minor importance. The Hungarian revolution, the presence of British forces in Syria, the conflict between the Netherlands and Indonesia over Western New Guinea, and the settlements with respect to the sinking of British ships in the Corfu Channel have all had their day in court and produced their harvest of antagonisms. Today these issues are finally at rest. The cold-war conflict is presently waged on such questions as the seating of Communist China and the financing of United Nations peace-serving forces.

Chinese Representation. The question of the Chinese seat in the United Nations has been a perennial issue. The West is not united in favoring the Nationalist government's retention of the China seat. Some states voted with nonaligned and Communist states to seat the Peking government.[3] Nevertheless, the conflict has its cold-war overtones.

The main arena for this battle is the General Assembly which has requested other councils of the United Nations and the specialized agencies to permit it to give the lead on this question. In this way the United Nations system can preserve a consistent approach on this matter.

Debate on this question has introduced a mixture of legal, moral, and political arguments. Some states have favored the seating of the Peking regime on the grounds that it is in effective control of most of the country, all of China except the island of Formosa, and therefore only it can legally and in fact represent the Chinese people. The United States has opposed the seating of the Communist regime on the grounds that it was warlike and unfit for membership. Many states see this as a political question. In voting on this matter, they ask themselves what is to be gained by replacing the Formosa government with the Peking government. Whose advantage will be served by this change? What consequences would flow from such a change? For the Soviet Union the issue itself has proved most useful. There is good reason to believe that the deliberately provocative approach of the Russians at the first instance when this matter was brought before the Security Council in January, 1950, was intended to prevent Peking's being seated. It was Soviet insistence that Red China be given the Chinese seat immediately before any other business was considered, the abusive Soviet presentation of this demand, and the stating of the matter in such a light that it would appear to be a Soviet victory, that precluded the early seating of Peking. Had the Soviet Union really wanted the seating of Peking, it is entirely likely that this could have been attained by postponing the question for a month or so, until Mr. T. F. Tsiang, the Chinese representative to the Security Council, had retired from the chairmanship by

[3] *United Nations Monthly Chronicle,* Vol. III, No. 11, December, 1966, p. 43. On a resolution favoring the seating of the Peking government, a resolution that was defeated, a number of states allied with the United States in NATO and SEATO voted in favor, among them Denmark, Norway, Pakistan, and the United Kingdom.

monthly rotation. The United States had at the time taken the position that the question of whose credentials were to be accepted as representative of a state was a procedural question and consequently its negative vote on this matter would not have constituted a veto. Under these circumstances the seven votes needed for seating the Peking government could have been forthcoming. Since then the Kremlin's antagonizing behavior gives substance to the belief that the Soviet Union has been more interested in being able to argue the issue than in winning the seat. Alternatively, should the seating of Peking take place, it would be in Moscow's interest that it appear as a Soviet victory and a United States defeat.

The cold-war aspects of this question also derive from the fact that Peking is Communist, and the Soviet Union wants to establish the precedent for seating competing Communist governments in the UN. It castigates Chiang Kai-shek as an American puppet. The elimination of his regime from the China seat would therefore seem a blow to American prestige. The intrinsic merit of expelling the anti-Communist Nationalist government would be a gain to the Soviet Union. In addition, on this question the Soviet Union enjoys a position of being at one with most of the states of Asia.

For the United States the question of the Chinese seat has also been significant. The United States appears as the leading antagonist of Red China, and it has led the fight against seating her in the UN and the agencies. When this question was first considered by the Security Council, it was the provocative and intractable behavior of the Soviet Union that denied Peking the Chinese seat. Later the Chinese Communists were excluded by becoming active partners in the North Korean aggression against United Nations forces. Peking was named an aggressor by the General Assembly and most members felt that Red China ought not to be permitted to "shoot her way into the UN." In 1956 and in 1960 the United States presidential elections dictated that it would be most unwise for the General Assembly to approve the seating of Red China and allow it to become an issue in the campaign with dangerous consequences for the United Nations.

The Chinese Reds have done very little to help their case. Their behavior has been anything but peace loving. The shelling of Nationalist-held islands off the Communist mainland, the seizure of

Tibet, their aggressive behavior *vis à vis* India, and their belligerent posture on Vietnam have made the seating of Peking appear inappropriate in the eyes of the majority of the members of the UN. Finally, the consequences of giving Peking the Chinese seat create problems for which palatable solutions have not been found. Communist China has insisted upon the possession of Formosa, presently controlled by the Nationalist government. Therefore it would not agree to a UN membership for the Formosan regime. States opposed to Communist occupation of Formosa and the expulsion of the Nationalists from the UN feel compelled to vote against seating Communist China because Peking has been unwilling to offer concessions.

Financing UN Peace Forces. United Nations activity in the Congo touched off another cold-war crisis in the organization. The UN shouldered the burden of pacifying this strife-ridden new state, thereby discouraging the intrusion of national forces which might exploit for their benefit the chaos in the Congo. Both the Security Council and the General Assembly authorized the United Nations mission there. However, UN Congo forces were specifically organized under the General Assembly. The creation of the United Nations Operation in the Congo (ONUC) carried with it an authorization for expenditure of funds.[4] By the end of 1961 the United Nations faced depletion of its treasury. Ordinary UN resources were inadequate to fund continued operations in the Congo and the United Nations Emergency Forces (UNEF) in the Middle East. The General Assembly therefore moved to include these expenses in the regular budget. An advisory opinion from the International Court of Justice sustained the legal authority of the General Assembly to do so under Article 17 of the Charter and to penalize by suspending voting rights in the General Assembly any state whose "arrears equals or exceeds the amount of the contribution due from it for the preceding two full years." [5]

Russia objected to the shared financing of ONUC and UNEF. She held that decisions to enforce peace can only be made by the Security Council. Inasmuch as both UNEF and ONUC involved

---

[4] "Issues before the 16th General Assembly," *International Conciliation,* No. 534, September, 1961, pp. 197–198.

[5] Charter, Article 19.

General Assembly sponsored actions, they were illegal. The Soviet Union took the position that the countries responsible for the conflict, France and the United Kingdom in the Middle East and Belgium and the United States in the Congo, must pay for the UN operations there. The Soviet Union also said in effect that it alone is competent to decide the legality of activities undertaken by the organization, decisions of the General Assembly and World Court notwithstanding. Finally, in the case of the Congo the United Nations operations were disadvantageous to the Soviet Union. It refused to finance operations hostile to it. (For the substance of the Congo dispute, see pages 233–235 below.)

The West favored the Middle East and Congo operations and upheld the competence of the UN to act there. With the significant defection of France on this question, the Western states asserted that the UN as a peace and security organization must finance from its regular budget peace-enforcing activity.

The UN faced a crisis of dues delinquency. The Soviet Union refused to pay the part of its contribution which was apportioned to the maintenance of United Nations forces in the Middle East and the Congo and by 1964 had become delinquent for two years. At first the General Assembly insisted on full dues payments. Faced with Moscow's threat to withdraw from the UN should it be deprived of its vote under Article 19, members of the UN hesitated. A special committee sought unsuccessfully to find a formula which could be satisfactory to Moscow and Washington. The Nineteenth Session of the General Assembly barely met, and took only such action as commanded unanimous consent to avoid a showdown over Russia's and France's right to vote. The organization could not carry on with these impediments. In the end the Soviet threat to leave the UN led a majority of members to give way. The United Nations would be emasculated without its Communist bloc. The United States reluctantly gave way to the majority will. The UN can no longer force a country to pay for peace-enforcement operations not authorized by the Security Council. In the future, actions taken by the General Assembly under the "Uniting for Peace" resolution will require special methods for funding. Despite financial handicaps the peace-enforcing role of the UN under the "Uniting for Peace" resolution remains.

THE COLD WAR IN EUROPE

At the end of the Second World War Europe provided the main arena for the cold war. By contrast in the 1960's Europe is prosperous and stable and the cold war is muted. Yet within the continent three questions continue to excite cold-war passions: (1) the reunification of Germany, (2) the future of West Berlin, and (3) the future of the satellite states.

GERMANY

In principle both East and West favor reunification of the two German states. At issue are the terms upon which such reunification should take place. The West favors an all-German government and conclusion of a treaty of peace which would normalize Germany's place in the family of states. A sovereign Germany would then be free to order her internal life and pursue a foreign policy according to her likes. Russia insists that Germany's unification is now a bilateral matter to be decided by the German Democratic Republic (East Germany) and the Federal Republic of Germany (West Germany), which are sovereign states. Reunification should take place on the basis of bilateral agreement and it should take the form of a confederation of West Germany, with its fifty-six million people, and East Germany, with its population of seventeen million. The East German province would remain a Communist dictatorship, now enjoying international recognition. The West German province could retain its democratic ways. The Soviet Union demands that a reunified Germany must not be associated with either NATO or the Warsaw Treaty Organization.

The reunification of Germany on the basis of free elections would certainly remove East Germany from Soviet control. The Communists could not win an all-German, or for that matter, a democratic East German election. The flocking of refugees from East Germany to the West bears more than mute testimony to communism's unpopularity with the German people.

Bonn contributes a large share to NATO's forces and constitutes a vital asset to Western defense. It might be an overstatement to say that the exit of Germany from NATO is not negotiable. But it should be clear that the price for such a weakening of NATO would be very high. Perhaps only reunification on the basis of free elections could justify Western agreement to a neutral rather than a NATO Germany.

BERLIN

Closely related to the German question is the status of West Berlin.[6] West Berlin, 110 miles from West Germany, is in a logistically exposed position. Yet the United States and the NATO powers are deeply committed to the retention of West Berlin within the "free world." Berlin's location offers the Soviet Union a tempting opportunity to eliminate a Western outpost and raises serious doubts respecting the credence of Western commitments under conditions of Communist pressure. It is not just an opportunity to make mischief for the West that motivates Soviet pressures here. Khrushchev had said that West Berlin was a bone in his throat. It is an attractive showcase for democracy. The contrast between affluent, happy, and free West Berlin and a drab, sullen, and oppressed East Berlin had given the lie to Communist propaganda about life under socialism. A large number of German refugees fled westward through East Berlin demonstrating the unpopularity and the failures of satellite states. East Germany was being drained of skills essential to its economy. The Russian claim that West Berlin is a hub of espionage, sabotage, and a source of hostile appeals to peoples living in satellite lands is an excuse rather than a reason for Soviet pressures.

Between 1958 and 1962 Berlin held the center of the international stage. The Kremlin threatened to sign a peace treaty with the East German government giving it full control of lines of communication and transportation on its soil between West Germany and West Berlin. The Berlin agreement could be cancelled because all other Potsdam arrangements had lapsed. Twice Khrushchev announced a six-month ultimatum from which he later withdrew. Often motor and rail transport between West Germany and Berlin was obstructed, and Moscow and Washington neared the brink of war.

It is estimated that between 1949 and 1962 almost three million persons fled East Germany. During 1961 the flood of defectors

[6] For the early history of the Berlin conflict and the first Berlin blockade see Chapter 7, pp. 204–208, and "Berlin and Germany," *International Review Service*, Vol. 8, No. 71.

greatly increased. In July, for instance, 30,000 people crossed into West Berlin, a number twice the previous monthly average.[7] On the 13th of August, 1961, the East German government barricaded its Berlin border. With troops, police, armored cars, and tanks deployed, 68 of the 80 crossing points were closed to East-West traffic. A few days later a solid wall of cement blocks replaced the barbed wire barrier. Western protests could not reverse this action and the wall stood.

The confrontation over Cuba in October, 1962, established America's readiness to stand behind its commitments even to the point of nuclear war. Thereafter Soviet pressures on Berlin were moderated. The *status quo* appears unalterable. The association of West Berlin with the free world is not negotiable. At stake is Washington's unambiguous promise to defend the city at any cost and Europe's assumption that United States power is adequate for the task. At present the Soviet Union is unable to expel the three-power occupation. Enforced unification by NATO powers is not even considered because it would certainly mean war. Reunification of Berlin is as unlikely as the reunification of Germany. Until both sides reassess their approaches in the cold war the *status quo* in Berlin will continue.

Future of the Satellite Empire of the Soviet Union

The Western powers have never been reconciled to a Soviet satellite empire in Eastern Europe. Russian rule there is a violation of treaties and a subjugation of peoples. Mastery of Eastern Europe was a foundation of Soviet might. As *status-quo* states, the West will not use military force to free the satellites. It is generally agreed that forceful liberation of the satellite states would result in a third world war. These considerations compel the West to seek peaceful liberation of satellites but do not allow it to become reconciled to permanent control of Eastern Europe by the Soviet Union.

Acceptance of the East European *status quo* has been an important objective of Soviet foreign policy. It has reacted vehemently to "captive nations" resolutions, propaganda broadcasts of Radio Free Europe, and UN resolutions condemning oppression in Eastern Europe. The threatened Hungarian defection in 1956 was drowned in blood by Russian tanks. To ensure its sphere of control Moscow

[7] *International Review Service, ibid.*, pp. 13–14.

has sought legal ratification of communized East Europe as part of a German peace treaty. Alternatively, it has tried to gain this end through proposing a nonaggression pact between NATO and the Warsaw coalition.

The Western powers are not reconciled to the permanence of a satellite empire. Acceptance of the communization of East Europe as final while Communists at the same time seek to take power everywhere else would be a one-sided bargain. Through Communist parties all over the world the Soviet Union would continue to pursue the goal of world communism. While the Russians insist that the future of Eastern Europe is settled and no longer open to debate, they consider the future of the non-Communist world unsettled and one in which Communist activity must go forward uninhibited. As President Kennedy remarked, the Kremlin has the attitude "that what's mine is mine but what's yours is negotiable."

Unpopularity of satellite regimes provides the West with certain advantages that may not be lightly conceded. Soviet control over its satellites is potentially unstable, and it must therefore divert its energies to control them. The possibility of war makes it important for the West to encourage potential disloyalty within the Soviet empire. It is likely that only in the larger context of a general cold-war settlement would the West agree to give up these advantages. The difficult task of the West, in this respect, is the maintenance of a spirit of hope for freedom among the oppressed masses of the East without encouraging premature revolts which could readily be put down.

Stalin's rule of Eastern Europe was harsh and unrelenting. An "iron curtain" isolated it from West European contact. Since his death the terror of Communist government has lessened and the satellite states have been better able to rebuild their economies in their own interest. Soviet political and economic institutions need no longer be slavishly copied. Recently there have been growing signs of greater independence from Moscow's decisions. National communism and polycentrism have attained a measure of approval within the Communist camp and marked erosion of satellite status is clearly evident.

The desire for freedom is a durable sentiment. It is perhaps not everlasting. Eventually the people of Eastern Europe may reconcile themselves to Communist rule. Nevertheless, the spirit of human freedom dies hard and this is an important obstacle to Soviet domination. For the West, power considerations merge with moral concerns. There is little advantage to the West in an acceptance of Soviet domination of Eastern Europe. No democratic government in the West could survive the popular outcry against acknowledged surrender of the peoples of Eastern Europe to Soviet rule. Neither can one contemplate the liberation of satellites by force. In time the gradual assertion of independence from the Kremlin's dictates and growing ties with the West may allow this issue to disappear.

THE COLD WAR IN THE MIDDLE EAST

Russia's desire for a warm-water port on the Mediterranean and on the Persian Gulf did not start with the Bolshevik succession to power in 1917. It has had a long history. During the nineteenth century and the first half of the twentieth century the British kept Russia penned up in its land-locked area. Soviet attempts to break out of its land-locked position by diplomatic means at the end of the Second World War through pressure on Iran, Turkey, and Greece and in asserting an interest in the Dodecanese Islands and Tripoli, proved unsuccessful.[8] Nevertheless Russia's desire to become a major Middle Eastern power continued.

Soviet interests in the Middle East were not only strategic and commercial. A major consideration was the existence of a power vacuum in the area once the British departed which the Soviet Union wanted to fill. Control of the Middle East would have given her domination of an area of crucial strategic significance and would have provided her with an opportunity to deny Western Europe the all-important resource of oil. The economic consequences of such a development could have assumed the proportions of a major debacle for the West.

The general weakening of Great Britain during the Second World War required that she reduce her commitments in the Middle East. In 1947 she terminated her responsibilities for Greece and Turkey, and the United States took over the British responsibilities there.[9] In the same year Britain informed the United Nations that she would surrender her Palestine mandate on May 14, 1948, and urged

[8] See Chapter 7, pp. 194–201.
[9] See Chapter 7, pp. 197–200.

the General Assembly to adopt a plan for the future arrangements in this area. After 1948, British responsibilities in the Middle East were limited mainly to the security of Jordan and the sheikdoms around the southern and eastern edge of the Arabian Peninsula.

BUILDING DEFENSES AGAINST COMMUNIST AGGRESSION

The United States took over primary responsibility for maintaining the Middle East free from Soviet penetration. American policy toward this end was originally conceived largely in military terms. In 1955 the United States organized a defensive alliance known as the Baghdad Pact. This pact established a "northern tier" of defense against Soviet penetration southward. While the United States was not a member of the organization of the Baghdad Pact it was a member of a number of its committees including the highly important military committee. Members of the pact originally included Great Britain, Turkey, Iraq, Iran, and Pakistan. Iraq withdrew in 1959 and the organization has been renamed the Central Treaty Organization for the Middle East (CENTO). Although the military capabilities of the CENTO powers could hardly match those of the Soviet Union, American SAC bases available in Turkey, Pakistan, Saudi Arabia, and Libya served to check whatever Soviet aggressive intentions may have existed for this area.

Closely related to the CENTO approach was an Eisenhower doctrine for the Middle East. Following the war of the Sinai Peninsula in 1956, for which a lack of United States leadership was considered to be somewhat to blame, President Eisenhower enunciated a doctrine for the defense of the Middle East against Communist aggression. Middle East states could, under this doctrine, request American assistance against such attack. The President as Commander-in-Chief would use American forces to prevent a Communist take-over. In support of this policy the Sixth Fleet was stationed in the eastern Mediterranean available for immediate action. For the states which accepted this doctrine a program of economic assistance was made available.

CENTO and the Eisenhower Doctrine enjoyed, at best, limited success in preventing Soviet penetration of the area. The fact is that the Soviet Union is today a major Middle Eastern power. If CENTO may be deemed to have established a wall against Russian invasion, the Soviet Union vaulted over the wall. It was able to become a Middle Eastern power through its exploitation of the Arab-Israeli conflict. Since 1950 the Soviet Union has used every opportunity to come forward as a champion of the Arab cause. This posture led Arab states to request Russian aid in arms, technical assistance, and funds for economic development. The Soviet Union was thus able to successfully "play the Arab card."

THE ARAB-ISRAELI CONFLICT AND THE COLD WAR

The Soviet Union was among the first states to recognize Israel after its establishment in May, 1948. Perhaps the existence of a small but not insignificant Communist Party within Irsael gave the Soviet Union some hope of influence upon Israeli policy. The large Mapam Party, sympathetic to the Soviet Union, also allowed hope for swaying Israeli positions in foreign affairs. However, such influence never materialized. The mistreatment of the Jews within the Soviet Union impaired the Russian image in Israel. In 1951 the Soviet Union thereupon took up the Arab cause. With ninety million Arabs to two million Jews the shift of appeal from Jews to Arabs was an attractive alternative. Moscow embraced the Arab "line," castigating Israel as a tool of Western imperialism. (For a discussion of the Arab-Israeli dispute, see Chapter 9.)

ANTI-IMPERIALISM AND THE COLD WAR

Anti-imperialism is a popular emotion in the Middle East. The days of British and French rule, and in some instances Turkish rule, are well remembered. The Soviet Union has been able to establish its image as a champion of colonial peoples against imperialist rule. During the 1950's the Arabs, probably with little reason, feared Western imperialism. The Soviet Union encouraged the belief that Arabs were being exploited by American, British, and French imperialists. They pointed to the Israeli, British, and French attack on Egypt in 1956 as evidence of the West's desire to reimpose imperialist rule. Khrushchev's threat to send volunteers to fight for Egypt was credited with forcing the British and French withdrawal, the falseness of this claim notwithstanding. Later, Turkish army maneuvers were played up as a prelude to an invasion of Syria which Moscow fortuitously prevented by warning the Turks to back down. In this manner the Soviet Union appeared as the defender and friend of the Arab people.

The growing desire for modernization in the Middle East provided the Soviet Union with other opportunities to further its interests. It posed as the generous giver of foreign aid with no strings attached. Western assistance, the Arab countries were warned, was simply a device for exploitation and control.

The confrontation between East and West in the Middle East has therefore become inextricably intertwined with the Arab-Israeli antagonism and with the issues of colonialism and modernization.

THE COLD WAR AND AFRICA

It is only in recent years that Communists have turned their attention to Africa south of the Sahara. Until the later 1950's the Soviet Union enjoyed little diplomatic contact with Africa, and there were few African Communists to provide an entry to the African scene. Small Communist parties were set up in the Republic of South Africa and in the North African states, but forces for winning adherents to the Soviet Union were lacking. Africans were interested in Africa. The great international cold-war issues commanded little attention and could not be effectively exploited to the detriment of the West. Africans' consuming concern with colonialism was the best issue available to the Soviet Union as it sought to eliminate Western influence on the continent.

COLONIALISM AND THE COLD WAR

Soviet attempts to win African support have had varying success. The issue of colonialism is not clear-cut since both the United States and the Soviet Union favor its liquidation. The Kremlin's attempt to picture the West as unrepentant imperialists is belied by the British, French, and Belgian policy of giving their colonies independence. Russian spokesmen, therefore, try to convince Africans that the West is at one with Portugal's and South Africa's exploitation of the African people. In the United Nations, North American and West European states have supported orderly and peaceful decolonization which may have appeared too slow to some African spokesmen. Few African leaders believe, however, that the United States is secretly in league with the Portuguese and South African colonialists. Portugal's membership in NATO and in 1960 Belgium's membership in that organization have been embarrassing to the Western states. The Soviet Union has been able to gain advantage from this situation by proposing extremist measures to provoke United States opposition so that she may then denounce the United States as protecting Portuguese imperialists and the South African racists.

Communism naturally utilizes the class struggle. Traditional African society was devoid of classes, and class struggle. Industrialization is not yet adequately advanced for widespread class conflict to occur. The Soviet Union has been unable to speak for an African "proletariat" against their "bourgeoisie." The class enemy has had to be identified as Western capital. Yet foreign capital is too useful for the developing economies of African states to be attacked irresponsibly. Despite Communist warnings that Western programs of economic aid and foreign investment are signs of neo-colonialism, this has not lessened African desire to secure aid from the West and entice its foreign investment capital into their lands. Nevertheless Africans are wary of the role which Europeans mean to play in their countries. Russia itself derives some benefit from the fact that it has never been an imperialist power in Africa.

The Soviet Union has had no great success in exploiting the race issue. The Communists accuse the West of chauvinism. There is a good measure of credibility in this charge as Africans have experienced European race prejudice at home and abroad. Discrimination against Negroes in the United States is well known in Africa. However, Soviet attempts to gain advantage thereby are handicapped because the Soviet Union is itself white. Reports of prejudice against African students in Communist countries have been well publicized in the African press. This shortcoming does not exist for Chinese Communists. The Soviet Union has been careful to send among its representatives to African conferences leaders from Soviet Central Asia.

The oppression of Africans in southern Africa gives Communists their best opportunity to build support in Africa. Majority rule for Rhodesia, Portuguese Africa, and South Africa may very well be favored by the West, but Western states are not willing to use force to facilitate the transfer of power to Africans. In their frustration independent African states have threatened to turn to the Communist world for aid in deposing white man's minority rule. As the issues of Rhodesia, South Africa, and Portuguese territories in

Africa build in international importance, the danger grows that this conflict could become linked to the cold war.

Russia has devoted little effort to the building of Communist parties on the African continent. They have been more concerned with winning the support of African elites for anti-Western nationalist movements. In their appeals they emphasize their anti-colonial stand and say little about their other goals. They seek to promote the Soviet Union and the Eastern camp as the only champion of African liberation. They invariably support African stands in the UN. They have selectively given economic and technical assistance.

THE CONGO

The issue of the Congo provided the most direct cold-war confrontation in Africa. The Belgians gave the Congo its independence on June 30, 1960. Almost immediately the Congo was reduced to chaos. Tribal dissension and bloody conflict threatened the existence of the Congo as a single state.

The new Premier, Patrice Lumumba, sought foreign assistance to pacify internal conflict and to hold together the seceding provinces. He turned first to the United States in quest of such aid.[10] President Eisenhower urged action within the UN framework, preferring in this way to insulate the Congo from the cold war. The Congolese then turned to the United Nations for help, which was rapidly forthcoming. Within a week after Lumumba's request UN forces and material assistance began arriving in Leopoldville.

UN efforts were limited to the pacification of the land, to facilitating the expulsion of Belgian forces from Katanga province, and to economic and technical assistance. Lumumba wanted something more. He wanted the UN forces to reunify the Congo, and most especially to bring Katanga back into the fold. The terms of the Security Council resolutions did not authorize the action he desired. Hammarskjöld said the UN would not be helping the "Congolese people by actions in which Africans kill Africans, or Congolese kill Congolese..."[11]

Lumumba then requested Russian aid. The Soviet Union responded by sending 100 military trucks, 29 transport planes, and 200

[10] Colin Legum, *Congo Disaster* (Baltimore: Penguin, 1961), p. 127.
[11] *Ibid.*, pp. 134–135.

technicians.[12] Aid was provided directly to Lumumba's government rather than through United Nations' channels and was used to suppress the revolt in the "Diamond State." In supplying aid directly, the Russians disregarded the General Assembly resolution that all members "refrain from direct and indirect provision of arms" outside UN facilities. It frustrated the hope of Nkrumah that the Congo not become "a battleground between East and West" and went counter to the desire of the African states that aid for the Congo be channeled through the UN.[13]

The threatened involvement of the Congo in the cold war on the side of the Russians led the Chief of Staff of the Congolese Army, Colonel Joseph D. Mobuto, to take over the reins of government and expel "technicians" sent in by the Soviet, Czechoslovak, and "other socialist" embassies. With this action a promising base for Soviet operations came to an end. The Secretary-General's refusal to acquiesce to the Kremlin's intrusion and his tacit assent to the expulsion of Communist personnel caused Khrushchev's furious assault on Hammarskjöld and the United States at the 1960 meetings of the General Assembly. In this fight the Soviet Union was in a substantially isolated position. Neither her demands for a three-headed Secretary-Generalship nor for Dag Hammarskjöld's resignation won support.

Congolese instability is conducive to mischievous exploitation by major powers. The financial crisis forced the UN to end its stabilizing operation, and once again opened the Congo to rebellion. The Organization of African Unity was unable to compose the warring factions and save the Congo from cold-war involvements largely because important African states also sought to exploit Congolese dislocations to their advantage. Rebel movements were aided by some African states and by Communists, while other African states and the West supported the Leopoldville government. The Congolese rebels overplayed their hand by holding as hostage foreigners in areas under their control. They hoped to gain an end to the government army's offensive, which was led by mercenaries, against them. This blackmail failed when Belgian paratroops were

[12] *Ibid.*, p. 141.
[13] *International Review Service*, Vol. VI, No. 16, "Congo and the United Nations," Hammarskjöld protested unilateral Soviet assistance. See p. 13.

dropped on Stanleyville to free the hostages, thereby dealing grievous defeat upon the rebels. In 1966 rebel activity virtually ceased
and with it a possible Communist foothold was brought to naught.
Apprehension endures that other opportunities to find agents who
can be elevated to power will yet arise.

THE COLD WAR IN ASIA

The Japanese collapse of 1945 left a power vacuum in the Far
East and Southeast Asia. Asia, which had been an area of colonial
possessions, now quickly began to throw off imperialist rule. Not
unwillingly the British and Americans freed their colonies. Less
willingly the Dutch and the French agreed to Indonesian and In-
dochinese freedom. The new nationalist regimes were unstable and
inexperienced. In 1948, Communists, probably on direction from
Moscow,[14] began a series of insurrections aimed mainly at over-
throwing the nationalist governments. In Indonesia and Burma the
Communists struck during the summer of 1948. The Philippines
faced a Communist-led Hukbalahap rebellion. In the spring of 1948,
the Communist Party of Malaysia, with an almost exclusively Chinese membership, launched its insurrection. The Communist-led
Viet Minh and Pathet Lao had already been in revolt against
French rule in Indochina. Meanwhile the Chinese civil war was
reaching its climax in Communist victory. Of the states of Southeast Asia, only Thailand escaped a Communist uprising.

The Communist attempt to take over through revolution the
countries of Southeast Asia succeeded only in North Vietnam where
the Communist character of the Viet Minh rebellion could not be
separated from the nationalist desire for freedom from French
colonialism.[15] In the rest of Indochina, in the Philippines, Indonesia,
Burma, and Malaya, Communist rebellions failed.

In the 1950's the cold war in Asia took on new dimensions. With
the Soviet Union's emergence from the Stalinist period, the tactic
of Communist revolution was scrapped. Communists made their
peace with Asian nationalists and sought to establish an "anti-

[14] Hugh Seton-Watson, *Neither War Nor Peace* (New York: Frederick
A. Praeger, 1960), p. 85.
[15] The Communist-led Pathet Lao were partly successful in Laos. They
held the northern provinces against efforts to dislodge them.

imperialist" peoples front. To this end they limited their appeal to advocacy of freedom, democracy, and socialism. Ironically, the concepts of democracy and modernization came from the West. However, without the handicap of an imperial heritage and attitudes of racial superiority, the Communists have been able to appear as defenders of Asian nationalism. They have encouraged hostility to the West by fostering the belief that Asia faced the threat of renascent Western colonialism. The Soviet Union has been able to build its own influence among the new states of Asia by cultivating expanded trade relations, promoting cultural exchanges, providing economic and technical assistance, and by supporting the neutralist states in the UN whenever possible. In the short run, weaning Asian states from their Western connections and building ties of friendship and cooperation were adequate for Moscow's purposes.

ANTI-COMMUNIST ALLIANCES

Western efforts to fight Communist imperialism engendered little enthusiasm among the Asian masses and their leaders. Russian imperialism had little meaning in South and Southeast Asia. Anti-Communist alliances were often seen as diversions to perpetuate reactionary rule and the favored position of privileged groups who sold out to the imperialists. Nevertheless, the rise of Communist China, given to belligerent postures, has caused growing apprehension.

In the Far East, Korea, and Formosa, the threat of Communist aggression was real. Mutual-assistance pacts between the United States and Japan, the Republic of Korea, and the Republic of China (Formosa) were signed to meet the visible threat of Communist China's aggression. Communist shelling of Nationalist-held islands off the mainland seemed to be a prelude for an invasion of Formosa. In face of this President Eisenhower was authorized by Congress to use American forces to defend Formosa and the Pescadores Islands,[16] and the Seventh Fleet was interposed there to frustrate Mao Tse Tung's threat.

[16] Dorothy Bume Goebel, *American Foreign Policy. A Documentary Survey, 1776–1960* (New York: Holt, Rinehart and Winston, 1961), Text of Joint Resolution authorizing Presidential action, January 29, 1955, pp. 400–401.

A Southeast Asia Treaty Organization (SEATO) was set up in 1954 under the leadership of John Foster Dulles to forestall Communist aggression.[17] Of the countries of Southeast Asia, only the Philippines, Thailand, and Pakistan joined. Other states perceived no special Communist threat of a military character. Communist danger, to the degree that it existed, appeared to stem from the opportunity to take advantage of popular dissatisfaction over the lack of economic development, wide-ranging social inequality, gross inefficiency, graft, corruption, and injustice so common in Asian countries. Conditions enabled Communist organizations to build popular support. The military emphasis of SEATO appeared poorly suited to meet this situation.

The 1960's have witnessed another change of Communist tactics, probably at Peking's instigation. Aggression in the form of guerrilla attacks was commenced in Vietnam and Laos, and an abortive insurrection in Indonesia took place in 1965. The Geneva settlement of 1954 broadly set a course based on self-determination for the peoples of Indochina. The agreement was never more than partially implemented. Elections for the unification of Vietnam were barred by Ngo Dinh Diem in South Vietnam, and freedom of choice was banned through Ho Chi Minh's Communist dictatorship in North Vietnam. The Pathet Lao never laid down their arms or permitted reintegration of the northeastern provinces of Laos under their control. The time came when the Pathet Lao saw its opportunity to win all of Laos. In coalition with neutralist forces they gained control of much of the country, but when they demanded an ascendant position in the coalition, that unity ended. The neutralist Premier Souvanna Phouma rebuilt his ties with a chastened right wing, and with American support forced the Pathet Lao to retreat. The fight against the Pathet Lao is handicapped by a lack of popular enthusiasm for either side. In this country of impoverished, illiterate peasants the stakes in this fight have little meaning. Several years of stalemate have allowed the Laotian government to begin a program of economic development which may bring to it a greater measure of popular backing.

The war in Vietnam has become a decisive confrontation between

[17] *Ibid.*, Text of Treaty, pp. 397–400.

the United States and Communist power in Asia. At stake is containment of Peking-led forces on the continent. Just as Europe under Russia's sway would have undermined United States security, so Asia under Peking's command would have equal ramifications. The struggle has been complicated by being fought as a guerrilla action. The Geneva settlement called for the removal of Communist forces from South Vietnam; this was not fully honored when some remained behind and others infiltrated back when the Communist Viet Cong resumed the attack. Guerrilla fighters merge with the peasant masses; sometimes they are welcomed, often Vietnamese peasants have had to accept them at the point of a gun. Counter-insurgency battles, therefore, may seem to be waged against the people.

Defeat of the Communist forces in Vietnam involves superiority in the field of battle and winning the loyalty of the masses by giving them hope for a better life when victory is won. The battles are a test of arms and soldiers between anti-Communist and Communist powers. The political sphere of this confrontation necessitates that the forces led by the United States convince world public opinion that the United States will resolutely fight Communist aggression, that it wishes no Asian empire of its own, that force is used only because negotiations are shunned by Hanoi and Peking, and that war is not Washington's chosen means for dealing with issues. In the long run security of democratic states must rest on support of the masses who believe that the government has their interests at heart. If democracy is to have this chance aggression must be repelled.

THE SINO-SOVIET SPLIT AND THE COLD WAR

The split between Russia and China has proved to be a most far-reaching development. A division of purpose within Communist ranks has taken place. Communists in Asia, some pro-Peking and others pro-Moscow, pursue contradictory goals and no longer present a unity of purpose. The image of China as an aggressor nation and the evidence of Chinese aggression against India has lessened unity between Communists and nationalists. The Soviet Union maintains the ties she has established with the neutralist states of the continent, but fears of Chinese aggression have strengthened associations with the West as well as the Soviet Union. There will be less mileage to be squeezed out of beating the anti-imperialist drum.

THE COLD WAR IN LATIN AMERICA

As long as the United States viewed the cold war primarily in military terms Latin America appeared safely insulated from the conflict. Soviet emplacement of missiles on Cuban soil in October, 1962, and enforcement of their withdrawal by the United States introduced ever so briefly a military dimension to the conflict. The Organization of American States (OAS) Charter of 1948 provided for hemispheric defense under Article 51 of the UN Charter (see Chapter 4, pp. 116–117 footnote). In terms of its activity the OAS had only passing concern with extracontinental aggression.

Small wonder, therefore, that the Latin Americans were little occupied with the cold war. To be sure, Latin American dictators made phony protestations that they were essential in the fight against communism, statements which the United States appeared to accept uncritically. In reality dictators like Batista were likely to tolerate the Cuban Communists but suppress the democrats and liberals. In this way conditions were created for a Communist upsurge when the dictators were overthrown, and internal conditions within many Latin American states practically guaranteed that the dictators would be overthrown.

The cold war came to Latin America not as a confrontation between the United States and Russia or a face-down between West and East but primarily as a battle for men's minds. In this conflict the Communists have tried to picture Washington as a reactionary and exploitive oppressor of the Latin American people. They have sought to establish themselves as leaders in programs of economic development, believers in social justice, fighters against graft and corruption, champions of the poor, the oppressed, the colored masses, and the abused and downtrodden peasants and workers. With such appeals the strength of indigenous Communist movements has grown.

CUBA

In January, 1961, the United States severed diplomatic relations with Cuba. This action marked a culmination of more than eighteen months of growing hostility. Castro claimed it was America's action that precipitated Cuba's response: since Batista's overthrow in 1959 the Cuban government undertook programs of land reform, nationalization of inefficient industries, abrogation of colonial exploitation of its resources and manpower, and this led the United States to adopt anti-Cuban policies to which the Cubans retaliated. Above all America resented the Cuban refusal to continue to accept United States domination, they said.

The evidence belies these assertions. Castro's revolution in its earlier stages demonstrated all the characteristics of an uprising to overthrow a brutal, reactionary, and self-serving dictatorship. In the final stages of Batista's overthrow the United States gave oblique support to Castro by denying Batista's regime military assistance.[18] The United States was not unsympathetic to the stated aims of Castro and his July 26th movement. President Eisenhower was prepared to assist Cuba in its efforts for economic development and for improving the standards of the poorer classes. There was little reason to doubt that Castro would carry out his promises to restore constitutional processes, order free elections, and institute representative government.

The promises that brought Castro to power were betrayed. The July 26th movement that made the revolution was suppressed.[19] Within one year the Communist Party was the only party tolerated in Cuba. During the last months of 1959 and through 1960 men who had fought with Castro in the Sierra Maestra Mountains and held important posts in Castro's government were imprisoned or forced to flee for opposing communism and continuing to believe in the principles of the revolution. Cuba became a land of repression devoid of civil and political freedom.

During 1960 Castro stepped up his expressions of American hostility and moved Cuba decisively into the Soviet camp. All of this occurred before the United States stopped buying Cuban sugar in the summer of 1960 and long before the United States closed its embassy in Havana.

The revolution that brought Castro to power was also betrayed by his rejection of United States assistance which could have most easily facilitated the modernization of Cuba's economy. Castro de-

[18] Theodore Draper, *Castro's Revolution. Myth and Realities* (New York: Frederick A. Praeger, 1962), p. 39.
[19] *Ibid.,* Ch. 1 and pp. 160–162.

liberately tied the Cuban economy to the Communist camp. In this way he served Soviet interests rather than Cuba's. These blatant steps of deliberate communization encouraged democratic Cubans to organize, as exiles, Castro's overthrow and to attempt, with limited United States support, an invasion at the Bay of Pigs in April, 1961. The invasion failed as United States assistance proved inadequate to guarantee its success. But the aid was visible enough to earn for the United States the disadvantages of complicity without the benefits of success.

Castro has served the interests of the Soviet Union far better than the interests of the Cuban people. He did this not only in suppressing anti-Communist expression, in tying the Cuban economy to Eastern Europe, in becoming the leading spokesman of anti-Americanism, but also in the autumn of 1962 by providing the Soviet Union with missile bases to threaten the hemisphere. In the process of doing this he came dangerously close to inviting the destruction of Cuba.

The crisis of October 22, 1962, exposed the nature of the Cuban role in the cold war. Adlai Stevenson, as United States Ambassador to the United Nations, expressed America's grievance.

Let me make it absolutely clear what the issue of Cuba is. It is not an issue of revolution. This hemisphere has seen many revolutions, including the one which gave my own nation its independence.

It is not an issue of reform. My nation has lived happily with other countries which have had thorough-going and fundamental social transformations, like Mexico and Bolivia. The whole point of the Alliance for Progress is to bring about an economic and social revolution in the Americas.

It is not an issue of socialism. As Secretary of State Rusk said in February: "Our hemisphere has room for a diversity of economic systems."

It is not an issue of dictatorship. The American republics have lived with dictators before. If this were his only fault, they would live with Mr. Castro.

The foremost objection of the states of the Americas to the Castro regime is not because it is revolutionary, not because it is socialistic, not because it is dictatorial, not even because Mr. Castro perverted a noble revolution in the interests of a squalid totalitarianism. It is because he has aided and abetted an invasion of this hemisphere—an invasion just at the time when the hemisphere is making a new and unprecedented effort for economic progress and social reform.

The crucial fact is that Cuba has given the Soviet Union a bridgehead and staging area in this hemisphere—that it has invited an extracontinental, antidemocratic and expansionist power into the bosom of the American family—that it has made itself an accomplice in the Communist enterprise of world dominion.[20]

The missile crisis and President Kennedy's decisive action isolated Cuba. The OAS unanimously adopted a resolution in support of the United States blockade. The cold war in Latin America now turned against the Communists.

Castro's efforts were intended to capture the support of the Latin American masses for the Communist movement. Democratic alternatives for modernization and social justice were ultimately the most serious competition to Castro's appeal. To undercut such competition Castro made the target of his attack not the remaining dictators on the continent but the democratic modernizers such as Presidents Betancourt of Venezuela and Figueres of Costa Rica. By mid-decade the bankruptcy of Castro's leadership in Cuba had become common knowledge and Latin American Castroites had lost much of their appeal.

The aftermath of the crisis of October, 1962, when thermonuclear war hung in the balance, has been a relaxation of tension. The threats of war inherent in the situation in Berlin and Cuba abated. The desire to avoid thermonuclear war is strong. It led to an agreement for direct telephonic communication between Kennedy and Khrushchev and to a ban on nuclear testing in the atmosphere and under water. However, the big issues of the cold war remain. Neither side appears ready to make the concessions necessary for their resolution and, until agreements on issues are reached, the world may know neither war nor peace.

[20] Speech of Ambassador Adlai Stevenson delivered to the Emergency Session of the Security Council on October 23, 1962. Reproduced in *Headline Series*, No. 157, "The Cuban Crisis: A Documentary Record," January–February, 1963, p. 43.

PART III

Contemporary Nationalism:
THE LEGACY OF IMPERIALISM

In the underdeveloped countries of the world nationalism ranks high as a major influence of contemporary life. In some respects this nationalism is significantly different from the earlier European variety. It is not necessarily democratic. It does not even require the existence of a nation in the sense of a people who have undergone a long period of historic development together. It does not seek the establishment of a state by gathering within it separated nationals, but instead most often independence from colonial rule constitutes the immediate aim of the nationalist movements. What it does have in common with the earlier European nationalism is its extensive popular support. It has now become a movement that has by and large secured its immediate goal: national independence through freedom from colonial rule.

Chapters 9, 10, 11, and 12 will be devoted to a study of contemporary nationalism and its problems in the Middle East; Sub-Saharan Africa; South, Southeast, and East Asia; and Latin America, respectively.

One of the characteristics of contemporary nationalism is its evolution in colonial territories and in states that considered themselves to be only nominally independent but, in reality, economically exploited by imperialist powers. Another characteristic of this nationalism is that it has appeared as a unifying force in a negative sense. People were united *against* imperialism and *for* the most rapid destruction of imperialist control. Until recent times the states of Asia and Africa were, in most instances, colonies. The nationalist movements that developed there perforce sought independence from colonial rule. The constructive task of nation-building would come later and often produce dissension within the nationalist movements.

Countries like China, Nicaragua, Iran, and Thailand felt that they were far from free agents. They viewed their existence as colonial in fact if not in form. Nationalist movements of an anticolonial nature were established there as well as in the territories that were explicitly colonial. States of Latin America, legally independent, felt a deep sense of economic exploitation. Anti-imperialist movements arose in Latin American states largely for the purpose of fighting United States imperialism. Nationalism and anti-imperialism were no more than the head and tail of the same coin.

Colonial oppression instigates nationalism. A sparsely settled area of nomadic tribes such as Trucial Oman—a British protectorate on the Persian Gulf—has, as yet, no nationalist movement because the tribesmen of the area have no sense of a British presence, let alone British oppression. Syria, by contrast, oppressed first by the Turks and later by the French, evolved revolutionary nationalist organizations against Turkish and French oppression. Similarly, Yemen, a backward and isolated state in the southwestern part of the Arabian Peninsula, was *given* its independence from Turkish rule after World War I. Turkish suppression was too spasmodic to call into being popular Yemeni anti-colonialist forces, and Yemeni independence was a product of the postwar settlements. To this day, there is little that could probably be designated as Yemeni nationalism. The contrast with Algeria need hardly be commented on. French colonialism was deemed to be oppressive enough that Algerians became fervent nationalists and fought a long and bloody revolution to end French rule.

In the newer national states most or all social classes share the nationalist feeling. The middle class, the workers, often the peasantry, and sometimes the upper classes unite under its banner. Invariably, however, they are led by the intellectual elite of the land. By virtue of their education this group enjoys great prestige. Their education is by and large Western; many leaders of this elite have been educated in the universities of Europe and the United States.

They are the young men from Asia, Africa, and Latin America like those whom college students in the United States and Europe meet in their classrooms and laboratories.

This leadership group is often disaffected by the conditions at home. In many instances their knowledge and training cannot be utilized. They are trained for the professions utilized by an industrialized society but find little use for their knowledge and skills in their preindustrial civilization. Even when their training can be usefully exploited, as in the cases of doctors and lawyers, a paying clientele does not exist in adequate numbers to make professional practice remunerative. Underdeveloped lands simply lack the industry, laboratories, advanced students, and clients to fully employ the engineers, scientists, college professors, lawyers, and doctors whose services, therefore, find inadequate outlet. These conditions alienate intellectuals from society. Intellectuals also see the need for modernization of the economy and the social life of their country. They lead organized efforts seeking social change. This often brings them into conflict with the traditional leaders of their society, the chiefs, sheikhs, orthodox religious hierarchs, and the hereditary monarchs. The evidence of the last decade leads to the necessary conclusion that the modernizers are winning the support of the masses away from the older leadership.

Colonial rule not only deprived an indigenous people of their sense of dignity, but was also considered to be a cause for their backwardness. All manner of improvements—political, social, and economic—would come with independence. As Nkrumah of Ghana said, "seek ye first the kingdom of politics and all other things shall be added unto thee."

Imperialism and colonialism have been phenomena more easily alluded to than defined as they are words laden with emotion. Both terms have been used as a gambit in propaganda offensives and in the ideological conflict between East and West. Thus a favorite Communist phrase is, "the aggressive circles of U.S. imperialism." The Soviet Union seeks to win support and drive a wedge between the Western democracies and the underdeveloped countries by labeling the West imperialist. In a speech to the Sixth Congress of the Socialist Unity Party of Germany Khrushchev championed the cause of anti-colonialism:

The Soviet Union supports the just wars of peoples not only through its declarations and statements; its support has more than once taken the form of concrete assistance. Many peoples have used our arms in their liberation struggles and have won, and freed themselves from colonial oppression. The colonial peoples' wars for their liberation are holy wars, and it is for this reason that we have been, are and always will be on the side of the peoples fighting for their independence.[1]

However, the Communists enjoy no monopoly in calling the other side imperialist. In recent years the term "Communist imperialism" has become a stock phrase of Western spokesmen. Frequent recourse to the terms "imperialism" and "colonialism" is often a debater's trick rather than an attempt to categorize in a descriptive way the policies that states actually pursue.

The terms imperialism and colonialism are used interchangeably. Should a distinction be made, the word *imperialism* would denote the process by which one state establishes control over another. The state exercising control is the imperialist state. *Colonialism* is the same phenomenon viewed from the point of view of the victims of imperialism. The maintenance of this control is called colonialism. This usage lacks precision, however. All powerful states exert a measure of influence over other lands. Yet such influence does not constitute imperialist control. Imperialist control is enforced control. Canada, even though strongly influenced by the United States, is an independent state, while Hong Kong is a colony because that island is run by Great Britain. But there is a continuum of gradation between the independent state and that colony which is devoid of all decision-making authority. At a point on the continuum the loss of decision-making power in foreign relations renders a territory a semicolony; when a territory rules itself internally but does not have foreign relations it has a narrower range of decision-making and becomes an autonomous or self-governing colony; with the loss of internal authority it becomes a full-fledged colony.

There are several types of colonies. The term *colony* is a generic term and refers to all "distant territor(ies) dependent on a ruling power...."[2] The British make some of these territories, in a formal

---

[1] "The New Content of Peaceful Co-existence in the Nuclear Age," speech delivered in Berlin, January 16, 1963 (New York: Crosscurrents Press, 1963), p. 36.

[2] Webster's New International Dictionary, 2nd ed., Unabridged.

sense, possessions of the crown, and they are called *crown colonies.* When a powerful state extends protection over a weaker state and exacts control over its foreign relations the protected state is a *protectorate.* The terms of the protectorate relationship are set out in a treaty which establishes the relationship. No two protectorates are identical. Invariably, however, these treaties provide that all third parties must deal with the protectorate through the mother country, and allows the mother country to intervene in the internal affairs of the protectorate when it believes it necessary. *Spheres of influence* are a form of semicolonialism; the powerful state enjoys preferential or exclusive authority in the sphere of influence, and asserts the right to deny the area to other interests. Another form of imperialist jurisdiction is the use of *concessions* or *franchises* which involve rights of economic exploitation of an area.[3] When along with the right to economic exploitation there exists a right of political control over the area, this is called a *leasehold.*[4] On occasion two states jointly control a colonial territory. Such colonies are called *condominiums.* Under the League of Nations the colonies lost by Germany and Turkey after the First World War over which the League exerted a limited supervisory authority were called *mandates.* (See p. 105, Chapter 4.) Under the UN they became *trust territories.* (See pp. 105–107, Chapter 4.)

The concept of imperialism is confused by what is sometimes called the "salt-water theory." In this outlook imperialism can only take place when the imperialist power crosses a body of salt water to impose its rule on the colony. Imperialist policies, therefore, are pursued only by the British, French, Dutch, Belgians, Portuguese, and the United States. It is different when a power like the Soviet Union moves eastward, bringing under Russian control the nations and races of Central and Eastern Asia. In a similar vein there is the feeling that imperialism must involve the white man's governing of colored races. A good working definition of imperialism identifies the phenomenon with control by any state over a backward people. As such this phenomenon can take place in areas contiguous to or remote from one another and among all races without exception.

Imperialism is not only difficult to define, but the causes for its de-

[3] Louis L. Snyder, *The Imperialism Reader: Documents and Readings on Modern Expansionism* (Princeton, N.J.: Van Nostrand, 1962), p. 55.
[4] *Ibid.*

velopment are in dispute as well. Nineteenth- and twentieth-century imperialism was promoted for military, moral, religious, economic, and political reasons. Some say it was not a conscious policy—it just happened. It is evident that the motives and purposes of imperialist expansion have been manifold. The United States and Russia expanded into sparsely populated areas, areas constituting a power vacuum inviting expansion of vigorously growing states. Military needs led powers to seize strategically situated points, places such as Gibraltar, Aden, Singapore, and Hong Kong. The Japanese, Germans, and Italians have justified imperialist ventures ostensibly to relocate surplus population. In point of fact, however, relatively few nationals from the imperialist country emigrated into the areas which were seized. More Italians have come to the United States than went to the Italian colonies of Libya, Eritrea, and Somaliland. Relatively few Japanese emigrated into North China and Southeast Asia when the Japanese conquered those areas. Surplus population is more an excuse than a reason for conquest. States seeking new possessions encourage large families so that armies can be raised to acquire colonies, at the same time pleading population pressure.

There are psychological motivations for imperialist expansion. Colonies can serve as a visual demonstration of power and prestige. Victorian England was afflicted with "mapitis." Englishmen took satisfaction in seeing so much of the world, especially on Mercator projections, colored in red. National prestige also required that when one imperialist power added a new territory other powers would have to do the same to "keep up." European powers tried not to fall behind in laying claim to African areas. In Asia when Germany obtained a naval base from China at Tsingtao, Russia insisted on the right to Port Arthur. It seemed "only right" when France got Kiaochow that Britain got Weihaiwei.[5]

At the end of the nineteenth century altruistic motives were offered as an excuse for imperialism. Kipling's celebrated poem "The White Man's Burden" portrayed imperialism as a moral obligation to civilize the backward peoples of Asia and Africa, "half-devil and half-child." Senator Beveridge demanded that the United States annex the Philippines. He said we must "not renounce our part in the mission of our race, trustee, under God, of the civilization of the

[5] Parker T. Moon, *Imperialism and World Politics* (New York: Macmillan, 1947), pp. 334–335.

world.... God had not been preparing the English-speaking and Teutonic peoples for a thousand years for nothing but vain and idle self-contemplation and self-admiration.... He has made us adept in government that we may administer government among savage and senile peoples. Were it not for such a force as this the world would relapse into barbarism and night...." [6] President McKinley gave voice to the same sentiment when he said, "there was nothing left for us to do but to take them all, and to educate the Filipinos and uplift and civilize and Christianize them, and, by God's grace do the very best we could by them, as our fellow men for whom Christ also died...." [7]

Exploration and adventure brought Europeans to Africa. This led to the feeling, at least in England, "that England acquired an empire in fits of absence of mind." [8] Explorers came to Africa and once there simply claimed large areas for their homeland, almost without premeditation.

In the twentieth century explanation of the scramble for colonies in high moral and psychological terms appeared unrealistic, untrue, and unsophisticated. Interpretations resting on strategic interests and surplus population were held to be superficial. After all, why should states need strategic bases? Economic motivations appeared to provide a more sophisticated and insightful basis for analysis. John A. Hobson, an English economist, wrote an authoritative study of imperialism as a phenomenon deriving from economic factors.[9] Hobson wrote that imperialism resulted from the malfunction of the capitalist system. It came about because of a need for markets brought on by the inability of the working class to consume the commodities produced, an endemic situation caused by excessive profits and rents. Imperialism was also useful to guarantee sources of raw materials. Then, too, it fitted the need for safeguarding profitable investment of surplus capital.

Hobson was against imperialism because it was expensive and led inevitably to wars. Only the small group of investors benefited. He believed that the need for imperialism would not exist if a greater

[6] *Congressional Record*, XXXIII, Part I, January 9, 1900, pp. 704–707. Quoted in Snyder, *op. cit.*, pp. 393–395.

[7] Snyder, *op. cit.*, p. 396.

[8] Moon, *op. cit.*, p. 34.

[9] J. A. Hobson, *Imperialism, A Study*, 3rd ed. (London: Allen and Unwin, 1938). This book was written in 1902.

share of the wealth went to the poorer classes. Greater purchasing power would eliminate overproduction and with it the need for colonial markets.

In 1916, Lenin wrote his book on imperialism.[10] Lenin's views were largely based on Hobson's earlier study, but he emphasized the development of imperialism as an aspect of monopolistic capitalism. The distinguishing characteristic of this phase of capitalism was "the export of capital, as distinguished from the export of commodities . . ." [11] The crucial amendment that Lenin made to Hobson's point of view was his conclusion that imperialism was an inevitable outgrowth of capitalism in its last stage of being. It was beyond reform. Capitalists were driven by the falling rates of their profits to seek the exploitation of the working classes of Asia, Africa, and Latin America. It was here that large profits could be made. Capitalism needed imperialism because it was essential to its profit position. The class struggle dictated that capitalism must reject attempts to give a greater share of wealth to the masses as a solution to the dilemma of overproduction. Capitalism could not be reformed, and Hobson made a fatal mistake in trying to convince capitalists to pay higher wages. Imperialism would only end with the overthrow of capitalism. Under capitalism imperialist powers would divide the world among themselves and would then be driven into war against one another to redivide colonial real estate.

At a somewhat lower level of intellectual sophistication a third economic theory of imperialism has been propounded, what Charles A. Beard called the "devil" theory.[12] According to this theory imperialist policy is favored by those who gain from war. War means great profits to the munitions makers, certain industrialists, and "Wall Street." These forces become a warmongering pressure group for imperialist ventures and for large military budgets. Senator Nye's investigation in 1934–36 of United States participation in World War I attempted to prove this point. While it was shown that profits were made from arms production and the House of Morgan had much to lose if Britain were defeated, the Nye investigation failed to prove—as, indeed it could not prove—that Wilson's decision

[10] V. I. Lenin, *Imperialism, the Highest Stage of Capitalism,* new revised translation (New York: International Publishers, 1939).

[11] *Ibid.,* p. 89.

[12] Cited in Hans J. Morgenthau, *Politics Among Nations,* 3rd ed. (New York: Alfred A. Knopf, 1960), pp. 48–49.

to go to war was even slightly influenced by such factors as bailing out the House of Morgan or serving the interests of "Wall Street." The truth of the matter is that the decisions to go to war in 1917 and again to rearm in 1949 were made because the Presidents involved believed this essential to United States security. Neither President was inordinately responsive to munitions makers or "Wall Street" as pressure groups.

For about one hundred years most of Asia, Africa, and possibly Latin America constituted the imperial domains of the great powers of Europe, the United States, and Japan. Since the end of the Second World War imperialism has rapidly receded, most often without colonial uprisings.

Liquidation of colonial rule stems from the ideals of democracy espoused by the imperialist powers themselves. It was acknowledged that colonialism constituted a degradation of human dignity and was exploitive of human and material resources in the colony. As people became conscious of this exploitation they gravitated toward nationalist organizations. Here again the democratic ideology asserted the right of organization and political action. Demands for self-determination, voting rights, free speech, and freedom of the press were consonant with and indeed inspired by the tenets of democracy.

The "benefits" of imperialism were rejected by indigenous populations. They recognized their economic and social backwardness and this too was a fault of colonial rule. Rapid modernization would come only when national leaders made the decisions in the interest of their people. The economic development of colonies was inhibited by the requirement that the economy must benefit the imperialist exploiters.

Reluctance of the imperialist power to accept the nationalists' demands brought forth a struggle for freedom. Struggle inevitably produces martyrs and martyrs rally new forces to the struggle. Conflict is further intensified when imperialists and colonial peoples are of different races.

It is no accident that the great movement of freedom from imperialism took place after the Second World War. Wartime leaders of the Western democracies appealed to the peoples of Asia to help defeat Japanese imperialism with the promise that after Japanese aggression was repelled freedom would be given to all peoples.

Franklin D. Roosevelt voiced "... determination to restore these conquered peoples to the dignity of human beings, masters of their own fate, entitled to freedom of speech, freedom of religion, freedom from want, and freedom from fear. I am sorry if I step on the toes of those Americans who call that kind of foreign policy 'crazy altruism' and 'starry-eyed dreaming.' " [13] He spoke of "decency and greater justice throughout the world." [14]

The liberalizing ideals of democracy and of the war aims of the United Nations coalition, which were continued in the Charter, and the activity of the United Nations, have been a powerful influence for colonial independence.

Most colonies have become independent states. The predictions that colonial peoples would be unable to rule themselves have proven false. The success of independence for one colony became a new stimulus for others to claim the same right. The logic that people ought to be able to control their destiny and that they can serve their own advantage better than their foreign rulers seems beyond contradiction.

[13] Basil Rauch (ed.), Franklin D. Roosevelt, *Selected Speeches, Messages, Press Conferences, and Letters* (New York: Rinehart, 1957), p. 330.
[14] Ibid.

CHAPTER 9

Nationalism in the Middle East

AMERICAN involvement in the Middle East is recent but this should not obscure the fact that the Middle East has been important in international politics since ancient times. Its location has made it the hinge between the continents of Asia, Europe, and Africa. The great powers of the world have at almost all times had involvements in this area. This is the area from which three major religions have sprung. Judaism, the first of these, took form more than three thousand years ago. It gave root to Christianity and later Islam, which were also born in the Middle East. Western civilization came out of the Middle East. In recent decades the exploitation of extensive oil resources around the Persian Gulf added a new measure of importance to this region.

There are no generally accepted boundaries for the area. Even scholars delimit the Middle East differently. Historically, the term Middle East evolved in European usage. The areas far from Europe, from India east, were called the Far East. The lands of the Eastern Mediterranean had been called the "Near East." It seemed logical that the region between the Far East and the Near East should simply be designated the "Middle East." During the Second World War, United States and British military activities for Turkey, Iran, and the countries of the Arabian Peninsula were placed under the British Middle East Command. Thus the habit of designating these territories as the Middle East has continued since that time.[1] (See map, p. 254.)

[1] Don Peretz, *The Middle East—Today* (New York: Holt, Rinehart and Winston, 1963), p. 3.

Some of the confusion in delimiting this region arises from the assumption that the Moslem faith and the Arab peoples and the Middle East are different aspects of one and the same thing. The Arab world and the world of Islam have occasionally been mistakenly considered to be coterminous with the Middle East.

Not all countries of the Middle East are *Arab* states. Turkey, Israel, and Iran are not Arab states. North Africa includes Morocco, Algeria, and Tunisia, which are Arab states collectively denoted as the Maghreb (west), but is not part of the Middle East.

Not all Middle Eastern states are preponderantly *Moslem*. Israel is a Jewish state and Lebanon is about half Christian. The world of Islam extends far beyond the Middle East. North Africa and the countries along the southern perimeter of the Sahara, Chad, Niger,

Mali, Mauretania, etc., are predominantly Moslem. In Asia, Afghanistan, Pakistan, Malaya, and Indonesia are all Moslem states.

Four major groups of people live in the Middle East. The largest in numbers are the Arabs, who inhabit Egypt, Sudan, Lebanon, Syria, Jordan, Iraq, Saudi Arabia, Kuwait, Yemen, and the British protectorates along the Indian Ocean, Arabian Sea, and the Persian Gulf. The Turks and the Iranians are distinct national groups. About two million Jews residing in Israel constitute a fourth major group within the area. Smaller minorities, such as the Kurds, the Armenians, and the Bedouins, also live in the Middle East. Religious minorities such as the Druzes, Bahais, Zoroastrians, and others maintain their ancient homelands in the region.

THE ARAB WORLD

There are about seventy million Arabs in the Middle East. Another twenty-eight million live in the Maghreb states of Tunisia, Algeria, and Morocco. Many Arab spokesmen claim that the Arabs are a nationality. Certainly they have a cultural similarity and speak one language. However, they are politically divided and are often in sharp conflict with one another. Under these circumstances one is justified in speaking of Arab nations and Arab nationalisms, both in the plural.[2] Nevertheless, the creation of a pan-Arab nation state holds a strong emotional appeal.

UNITY AND DISUNITY IN THE ARAB WORLD

The creation of a single Arab state is a goal and not a reality. Presumably the articulate Arab intellectuals are imbued with feelings of Arab nationalism. The aims of Arab nationalism were succinctly stated in a letter to The New York Times by a member of the Palestine Arab delegation to the United Nations, who said "nothing will ever stop the Arab nation from reuniting. This determination exists in the heart and soul of every Arab from the Atlantic in the West to the Arabian Gulf in the East."[3]

The most compelling separative force within the Arab world is to be found in the conflict of nationalisms. Writing in 1952, Professor Hurewitz spoke of "state nationalism" as distinct from a larger

[2] John B. Christopher, "Middle East—National Growing Pains," *Headline Series,* No. 148, July–August, 1961, p. 46.
[3] Letter to the editor, *New York Times,* Western Edition, May 26, 1963.

Arab nationalism. He pointed out that "None of the 10 sovereign states existed in its present form prior to the peace settlement of 1919–23 and four have won their independence only since the end of the Second World War." [4] It appeared, therefore, that state nationalisms were of such recent origin that the dissolution of existing states and the reorganization of the Arab community into a single state might prove feasible.

In March, 1945, the Arab League was set up with Egypt, Iraq, Lebanon, Saudi Arabia, Syria, Trans-Jordan, and Yemen as founding members. It was conceived as an organization promoting coordination and collaboration among Arab states. But it was nevertheless a league of sovereign states. Members pledged to "respect the systems of government established in the other member states and regard them as exclusive concerns of those states." [5] This pledge has been imperfectly redeemed. The United Arab Republic (UAR), Syria, Iraq, and Saudi Arabia, have all been charged with interference in the affairs of other Arab lands and with good reason. On the other hand, the Arab League has made no progress in creating the unified Arab state. Since assuming control over their destinies each Arab state has developed its own local brand of nationalism. Arabs think of themselves as members of the Iraqi, Syrian, Lebanese, Sudanese, or Egyptian nations. Each national group is jealous of its prerogatives and interests. Even when the concept of greater Arab nationalism is accepted in principle, as was true in 1962 in the case of Egypt, Iraq, and Syria, the concrete problems of integration have proved insoluble and the states remained sovereign "national" entities. Each national leader seeks advantages for his state. The construction of the Arab superstate moves no closer to actuality. The evidence to date is compelling. The Arab League has been unable to bring about the unification of the Arab states. The UAR, despite its lofty proclamations,[6] joined only Syria and Egypt and lasted less than four

[4] J. C. Hurewitz, "Unity and Disunity in the Middle East," *International Conciliation*, No. 481, May, 1952, p. 205.

[5] Pact of the Arab League, Article 2. Reproduced in B. Y. Boutros-Ghali, "The Arab League, 1945–1955," *International Conciliation*, No. 498, 1955, pp. 444–447.

[6] The Proclamation of the United Arab Republic, February 1, 1958, states, "... the participants declare that their unity aims at the unification of all the Arab peoples..."

years, being dissolved in 1961. Sudan did not opt for integration with Egypt when it became independent and had the opportunity to do so. The efforts of Egypt, Syria, and Iraq to form an Arab federation foundered in negotiation. The Maghreb states have considered the formation only of a united Maghreb. Only Algeria pays more than lip service to the ideal of one Arab nation. Even the limited proposal for a Maghreb national state has been nowhere near implementation. Effective national unity lies within each of the existing Arab states and not *among* them.

The difficulty of overcoming the local nationalisms of the Arab states in favor of greater Arab nationalism is compounded by a conflict over leadership. Between 1958 and 1962 Kassem of Iraq and Nasser of Egypt, both advocates of Arab national unity, fought for leadership of a united Arab world. Neither was willing to accept the other's leadership. The vigorous and at times dictatorial bearing of President Nasser of Egypt has provoked fear among Arab leaders that a united Arab state would be dominated by Nasser. Many leaders in Arab countries prefer to retain their leading positions within smaller domains than lose their positions of leadership as would be inevitable in one all-inclusive Arab state.

Conflict among Arab leaders is more than a clash of personalities. It sometimes derives from incompatible positions on the nature of the state that should be established. The modernizers visualize the Arab state as a modern republic. They might prefer democracy or dictatorship, either capitalism or socialism, but they will not accept continuation of the feudal edifice of earlier times. Traditional leaders, the sultans, imams, sheikhs, and beys, see in the modernized republic an end to their way of life and the advantages that it offered them. Arab states led by traditional forces, states like Saudi Arabia, Libya, and Jordan, therefore tend to oppose tangible steps in the direction of unification of the Arab world.

The cold war has provided still another influence making for disunity. Some Arab leaders, on occasion Nasser and the Iraqi leaders prior to the revolution of 1962, carried out a neutralist foreign policy that "leaned toward the East." They saw danger of renewed imperialism from the former colonial powers of the West. They embraced the Soviet Union as a friendly and helpful power. Against the posture was the position taken by Bourguiba of Tunisia, Malik of Lebanon, and King Hussein of Jordan, whose neutralism "leaned toward the West." They saw in the West a source of defense against Communist imperialism, a new imperialist force which they believed potentially threatened the Arab's independence. Western imperialism, they observed, was a receding phenomenon. Although all Arab states favor a neutralist foreign policy this similarity is insufficient to unify their stands or to reduce the frictions resulting from "East-leaning" and "West-leaning" policies.

Arab lands sometimes have divergent economic interests. When Syria withdrew from the UAR in 1961, Syrian leaders claimed that their economy was being harmed for Egypt's benefit.[7] During the Sinai War of 1956, the oil-producing countries of the Arab world took a dim view of Egypt's sabotaging of the Suez Canal, making it temporarily unusable and forcing oil tankers to sail around Africa, a more costly procedure which reduced their oil revenues.

In sum, barring conquest of the Arab states by one Arab power, such as Egypt, the creation of a single unified Arab state is remote. Divisive factors make unity and cooperation among them on a broad range of issues unlikely. Agreement among them is limited to their hostile stand *vis-à-vis* Israel, their opposition to colonialism, and their encouragement of UN assistance programs.

The defeat of the Arab armies by the small Israeli force in the Palestine War in 1948 did much to stimulate Arab nationalism. This event was a blow to Arab pride. Officers at the higher ranks were drawn from the conservative upper strata in Arab society. They wanted to preserve the *status quo*. It was the junior officers drawn from middle- and lower-middle-class families who were shamed by this event and moved to redeem Arab power. Resentment of French and British imperialist domination had converted many in this strata, as well as Arab intellectuals, to nationalism. Military coups placed these elements in power in Egypt, Iraq, and in Syria.

Israel has become the focus of Arab hostility. Taken at their word, the Arab states would organize a *jehad* to destroy her. For this end the Arab states are in agreement. On this subject the Arab League has been most successful in promoting unity. Unity against imperialism ranks second only to that in force over Israel.

[7] *New York Times,* September 20, 1961.

With the important exception of the traditional elements in Arab society who wish to maintain the *status quo,* colonial rule anywhere brings forth opposition to it from the Arab states. The leaders of these states are especially sensitive to even the remotest danger of renewed colonial rule. Kuwait upon becoming independent faced the threat of Iraq's invasion from the north and the sheikh asked the British to help defend his country. The Arab League thereupon moved quickly to organize Arab forces to replace the British.

As is true of all underdeveloped countries, the Arab states have through their group in the United Nations pressed for economic development programs in the Middle East. They have advocated greater UN investment in economic development and technical assistance. Desire for economic improvement has not, however, been great enough to overcome their hostility to Israel and permit establishment of economic development programs in cooperation with the Israelis. For this reason they have rejected the joint development of the Jordan River and the creation of a regional council of the Economic and Social Council.

THE ARAB-ISRAELI CONFLICT

The most serious conflict within the Middle East is that between Israel and the Arab states. This quarrel has caused two wars and almost continuous crisis. As we have seen, it has provided the Soviet Union with an issue which she could exploit to become a major force in the area (see Chapter 8, p. 230). While the wars have ended in armistices, peace between Israel and the Arab states has yet to be established. Hostility on a broad range of specific issues provides the raw material for continuing antagonism.

ISRAEL'S EXISTENCE

The most important cause for the Arab-Israeli conflict is the existence of Israel. The Jews and Arabs both laid claim to Palestine. For the Jews the creation of a national homeland there marked a fulfillment of a biblical prophecy, a reconstitution of an ancient nation still conscious of its identity though dispersed for two millennia, a refuge from religious oppression and anti-Semitism—most recently carried to unparalleled extremes with the destruction of six million

Jews by Hitler—and the fulfillment of a promise by the British government, in control of the Palestine mandate, to facilitate the establishment of a homeland for the Jewish people in Palestine.[8] For the Arabs the formation of an independent Arab Palestine was a matter of national self-determination. About two-thirds of the population of Palestine at the end of 1946 was Arab.[9] An Arab Palestine was considered to be a "natural right" based upon the long-term residence of the Arab people in this area.[10]

The British, as the mandatory authority, tried to get both sides to agree on a solution for the future of Palestine. When this effort proved unsuccessful the United Nations was asked to make its proposals for the disposition of the mandate. After a thorough investigation of this matter by a special committee and after discussion by the General Assembly, that body adopted, over bitter Arab opposition, a plan for the partition of Palestine into a Jewish state, an Arab state, and an international zone for Jerusalem.[11]

The General Assembly decision was rejected by the Arab Higher Committee, which demanded that the whole of Palestine be made into an independent Arab state. It promised "before God and history, that they will never submit or yield to any power going to Palestine to enforce partition. . . ." and that "the only way to establish partition is to wipe them [the Arabs] out—man, woman and child. . . ." [12]

Shortly after the UN resolution was adopted, fighting broke out between Arabs and Jews within Palestine. The British, reluctantly complying with the General Assembly action, terminated their mandate on May 15, 1948. One day earlier the Jewish Agency announced

[8] This promise was conveyed in the Balfour Declaration of November 2, 1917. "His Majesty's Government view with favour the establishment in Palestine of a national home for the Jewish people, and will use their best endeavours to facilitate the achievement of this object. . . ." The ideas of this pledge became a part of the Palestine mandate agreement and in this sense a British obligation as the mandatory power. L. Larry Leonard, "The United Nations and Palestine," *International Conciliation*, No. 454, October, 1949, pp. 744–745 and Appendix C, "The Jewish Case."

[9] *Ibid.*, p. 754.

[10] *Ibid.*, Appendix B, "The Arab Case."

[11] Adoption of the partition plan required a two-thirds majority. The plan was adopted by a vote of 33 in favor, 13 opposed, with 10 abstentions. *Ibid.*, p. 644.

[12] *Ibid.*, p. 651.

the establishment of the state of Israel. This brought on an immediate invasion of Palestine by Egypt, Lebanon, Syria, Jordan, and Iraq. The fighting resulted in an Israeli victory and the Arabs eventually accepted a truce.

Arab leaders have never reconciled themselves to the existence of Israel.[13] They claim Palestine as their own homeland, which must be liberated and resettled by its "original" population as soon as the Israelis are "pushed into the sea."

It is entirely likely that other issues in dispute would be more easily solved if the basic fact of the existence of Israel were accepted by her neighbors. Once the security of all states in the area was no longer threatened, accommodations on outstanding disputes would become attractive to all parties. Peace could be of benefit to the Arab states and to Israel. Israel cannot be expected to "commit suicide." During the first eighteen years of Israel's existence the Arabs did not have the power to bring an end to the Israeli state. There is substantial question as to whether the Western democracies would permit a war of extermination against Israel to succeed.[14] While most of the Western states have tried to avoid involvement in the purely Arab-Israeli issues, they recognize that Israel is a successful, stable, and relatively prosperous democracy. Its existence has permitted a measure of reassembling of the long-suffering Jewish people for the first time in two thousand years. The fact that Israel is very small, about the size of the state of Massachusetts, and the Arab states do not suffer land hunger and are not overpopulated tends to reduce worldwide sympathy for the Arab position.

[13] Agitation for the destruction of the Israeli state is virtually continuous. A summit meeting of Arab leaders issued a concluding statement on January 17, 1964, which spoke of "organizing the Palestine Arab people to enable it to play its role in liberating its country...," a clear restatement of the goal of destroying Israel. *New York Times,* Western Edition, January 18, 1964.

[14] The United States, Great Britain, and France signed a tripartite declaration designed to promote peace based upon the *status quo* in the area. Tripartite declaration of May 25, 1950. See Emil Lengyel, *The Changing Middle East* (New York: John Day, 1960), pp. 114–115. In 1963, the Kennedy Administration, in response to an Israeli request for a big-power guarantee, rejected any unilateral pledge to Israel, but promised to defend against aggression any Middle Eastern state. *The United States and the Middle East,* Georgiana G. Stevens (ed.), (Englewood Cliffs, N.J.: Prentice-Hall, 1964), p. 116.

THE ISSUE OF ISRAEL'S BOUNDARIES

In the course of the war of 1948, Israeli armies occupied territories not assigned to them under the partition resolution. These areas remain a part of Israel and constitute approximately 30 percent of its land area. Arabs have demanded that Israel give up land won in the war. This has led to suggestions that border modification might lead to a general peace agreement. Arab leaders have not encouraged any hope that boundary rectifications would win their acceptance of a truncated Israel.[15] These demands are not meant to imply that the existence of Israel in any form would secure their agreement. For her part, Israel does not consider major changes in her boundaries a negotiable question.[16]

Today more than half of Israel's population is composed of recent immigrants from Europe, North Africa, and Asia. The land must support a population larger than that of 1948. While Israel had given assurances that she has no territorial ambitions, she has been unwilling to surrender any of her territory. Israel proposes to use all of her lands to support her present population and to provide refuge for Jews from other parts of the world.

THE ABAB REFUGEES

Of all the outstanding issues, the Arab refugee question has probably been the most contentious one. In the course of 1948, about 700,000 Arabs fled to neighboring Arab countries. Most of them sought refuge in Jordan and in the Gaza Strip. Lesser numbers arrived in Syria and Lebanon. The cause of their flight is in dispute. According to Israel, Arab refugees fled their homes at the urging of Arab leaders who promised that they would return to reclaim their homes and lands in the wake of the victorious Arab armies and ob-

[15] In 1949 Israel was willing to negotiate on frontiers as part of overall peace negotiations. Leonard, *op. cit.*, p. 740.

[16] Statement of Prime Minister Eshkol reported in *The Israel Digest of Press and Events in Israel and the Middle East*, Vol. VI, No. 16, August 2, 1963. After comparing the size of Israel with that of the Arab states, which are more than five hundred times larger, he said, "Is there any sense in countries with such vast spaces at their command still waiting for development, to begrudge us this small corner which is the basis for our independence?

"Of course, if it should be found necessary, in the course of negotiations, to make certain minor and mutual adjustments we should be willing to discuss problems of that kind."

tain a share of Jewish properties left behind.[17] The Arabs blame the refugee problem on the Israelis, who, they say, drove the Arabs out by force. There may well be a measure of truth in both versions of the story.[18] In any case, establishing the degree of veracity in this situation is unlikely to contribute at all to the solution of the problem.

The inescapable facts are: these refugee camps exist; the number of refugees cared for has increased to 1,210,170 in 1964 by official count; [19] the refugees are not integrated into any of the states in which they find themselves; and they assert, in the strongest terms, their desire to reclaim their old homes in Israel. Since 1948, the United Nations Relief and Works Agency (UNRWA) has been providing a basic ration, housing, some limited training, and other forms of assistance to sustain these people. A permanent solution for this problem has proved unattainable.

Two basic approaches on this matter have been pressed in the General Assembly. The Arabs propose that the refugees be repatriated—returned to their homes, lands, and farms. They have refused to accept other solutions. Their stand rests on the belief that their position is morally right, legally sanctified by Paragraph 11 of the General Assembly Resolution 194 (III), which declares "that refugees wishing to return to their homes and live at peace with their neighbors should be permitted to do so at the earliest practicable date, and that compensation should be paid for property of those choosing not to return . . ." Arab statesmen are not unaware of the political advantages that would accrue to them through the "hard" position which they have adopted on this issue. They benefit from popular sympathy for refugees. By remaining adamant on this question they hope to wear down the positions of states which have differed from their stand. It is likely that public opinion in Arab lands will tolerate no compromise on this issue. Without the refugee population to occupy Israeli lands, the whole fight to bring an end to Israel could be undermined.

[17] Statement of Abba Eban, Israel's Permanent Representative to the United Nations to the Special Political Committee of the General Assembly, November 17, 1958.

[18] Peretz, *op. cit.*, pp. 277–278. This writer believes that atrocities on both sides topped by the massacre of Arabs at Dier Yassin led to panic in Arab towns and villages and the consequent flight to neighboring countries.

[19] Stevens (ed.), *op. cit.*, p. 135.

The Israelis propose that the refugees be resettled, in Arab lands or elsewhere. They believe that Arab refugees are pledged to the destruction of Israel, and with good reason. They refuse to consider the reabsorption of this large Arab mass, which they believe would function as a fifth column. To further their proposal for resettlement, the Israeli government has offered compensation for refugee properties. The level of compensation was to take into account the value of Arab properties and the claims of Israeli citizens against Arab states for property which they left behind in taking refuge in Israel.[20] They underscore the "live at peace with their neighbors" phrase in the General Assembly resolution to give legal basis for nonimplementation of Paragraph 11.

Israel itself is largely a country of refugees. About two-thirds of its population is composed of refugees who have arrived there from European, Asian, and North African lands since Israel's creation. It, therefore, feels that with the absorption of Jewish refugees it has played its "natural" role in accepting refugee population. In the process Jews have settled upon Arab refugee properties which can no longer be reclaimed.

The quest for a solution of the refugee problem approached through repatriation versus resettlement has produced an impasse. The Arabs will settle for nothing less than repatriation. The Israelis insist on resettlement.

United Nations efforts to settle this matter through compromise and indirection and in the humanitarian interests of the refugees have failed to budge either side in the "hard" lines which they have adopted. Disinterested parties have suggested that if the Israelis would accept, in principle, the repatriation of the refugees, few of them would actually agree to return to Israel. The Israelis have their doubts on this score and decline this solution. Perhaps over a period of time the refugees will gradually be integrated into the surrounding Arab communities. The history of refugee populations shows that they almost never go back. Refugees tend to integrate in their place of refuge. In the short run, however, this problem may lead to a serious clash before the years have given it time to wear away. United States support of UNRWA—at the rate of 70 percent of the agency's budget—dictates Washington's close attention to this issue.

[20] Statement of Eban, *op. cit.*

The Gulf of Aqaba

When Israel attacked Egypt in October, 1956, it sought, as a major military objective, the opening of the Gulf of Aqaba. This body of water provides Israel with an outlet to the Red Sea and facilitates trade with the countries of East Africa and Asia. The gulf is about one hundred miles long. Its coastline is shared by four states. Almost all of the west coast of the gulf is Egyptian territory (the Sinai Peninsula) and most of the eastern coast is Saudi Arabian territory. At the northern head of the gulf are the Israeli port of Elath and the Jordanian port of Aqaba. At the mouth of the gulf lie the islands of Tiran and Sanafir. From the Red Sea the gulf is entered through a narrow channel between the islands and the Sinai Peninsula.[21]

Israeli plans for trade with Asia and Africa involved the development of its six-mile coastline into a major new port. From 1949, however, the Egyptian government maintained an effective blockade on all shipping in and out of Elath. The Egyptian blockade was made possible by its policing of the channel between Tiran and Sanafir and the Sinai Peninsula. These islands, although Saudi Arabian territory, were occupied with Saudi Arabian permission by the Egyptians. Military installations were erected. A narrow passageway through the Straits of Tiran, only some 500 to 600 yards wide, permitted Egypt to interdict Israeli shipping. It was only after Israel had captured and destroyed the military installations on Sanafir and Tiran and on a promontory, the Sharm el Sheikh, on Sinai that the blockade was brought to an end. The Arab states claim a right of riparian control over the use of the gulf. The Security Council, the Secretary-General, and the unanimous opinion of the major maritime powers, however, allow no interference with "the right of innocent passage through the Straits of Tiran and the Gulf . . ." [22] Since 1957, the blockade has not been reimposed.

The Suez Canal

After the war with Israel in 1948, the Egyptian government prohibited Israeli commerce and shipping in the Suez Canal. It is gen-

[21] Paul A. Porter, *The Gulf of Aqaba: An International Waterway. Its Significance in International Trade* (Washington, D.C.: Public Affairs Press, 1957), p. 2.

[22] Statement of the Secretary-General on January 15, 1957. *Ibid.,* p. 4.

erally agreed that this constituted a violation of international law. The Constantinople Convention of 1888 guaranteed freedom of passage through the canal.[23] The Security Council, in a resolution passed September 1, 1951, called on Egypt to end its interference with Israeli trade through the canal.[24] After the war of 1956, President Nasser committed Egypt to live up to the terms of the Constantinople Convention.[25] For two years, Israeli cargo in non-Israeli ships passed through the Suez. In 1959, however, Egypt reimposed its blockade on all forms of Israeli trade.

Since the blockade has been reimposed, the Israelis have done little more than make formal protests claiming the legal right to use the canal. They have not pressed this claim, probably because the use of this waterway is of minor significance to Israeli commerce now that the Gulf of Aqaba is in full use.

OTHER CONFLICTS

Other conflicts between Israel and the Arab states from time to time bring on additional crises. Border raids by Egyptians, Jordanians, Syrians, and Israelis have periodically endangered the armistice.

The exploitation of water resources plays a crucial role in the development of agriculture in the area. Several schemes for the development of the Jordan River system have been proposed.[26] A United States-sponsored Jordan Valley plan was put forward by Eric Johnston, President Eisenhower's special Ambassador. In 1955, agreement on the Johnston plan between Arab and Israeli engineers was reached on a technical level but foundered on an Arab League veto because the plan would imply recognition of Israel and would be of benefit to the Israelis.[27]

In 1964, the Israelis completed a pipeline drawing water from the Sea of Galilee, in the north, to irrigate the Negev Desert. Arab leaders voiced fear that if Israel should create a habitable "south-

---

[23] "The Suez Canal," *International Review Service,* Vol. III, No. 30, February, 1957, p. 38. Article I, "The Suez Maritime Canal shall always be free and open, in time of war as in time of peace, to every vessel of commerce or war, without distinction of flag."

[24] *Ibid.,* pp. 41–42.

[25] Stevens (ed.), *op. cit.,* p. 132, Nasser's declaration of April 24, 1957.

[26] Georgiana G. Stevens, "The Jordan River Valley," *International Conciliation,* No. 506, January, 1956.

[27] *Ibid.,* p. 245.

land" in the Negev Desert this would open Israel to a new wave of Jewish immigration on a large scale. The area would then see the organization of additional military installations near the Sinai threatening Egyptian security. Israel's water diversion plans call for the drawing of water from the Sea of Galilee, which is wholly within her territory, in amounts below the quantity which she would have received under the Johnston plan. Bringing the Negev into production would enable her to support a larger population; this is her aim.

The ultimate fate of Israel in the Arab Middle East may depend on her ability to survive, perhaps for a generation or more, until new generations of Arabs become reconciled to her existence. Worldwide stability would be strengthened if the great powers would accept the responsibility for forestalling new acts of aggression.

THE ROLE OF OIL IN THE MIDDLE EAST

The area around the Persian Gulf contains the largest known oil reserves of the world. Tiny Kuwait, the Middle East's largest producer of oil, is estimated to have twice the oil reserves of the entire United States, about 20 percent of the world's total reserves.[28] Western Europe is dependent on these oil supplies, importing 90 percent of its oil from the Middle East.[29] When the Suez Canal was shut down in 1957, as a result of the Sinai fighting, the resulting oil shortage brought rising prices, unemployment, and gas rationing.

Oil provides the backbone for the economy of the oil-producing lands of the Middle East; 85 percent of Saudi Arabia's income and 90 percent of the income of Kuwait, Qatar, and Bahrain Island come from oil royalties.[30] In 1940, these sheikhdoms received $28 million in oil income. By 1960 Kuwait alone received $550 million a year income from its oil production. All of the large oil-producing states in the area, Kuwait, Saudi Arabia, Iran, Iraq, Qatar, and Bahrain, receive hundreds of millions of dollars annually in oil revenues.[31] When Suez was closed they too suffered a drop in in-

[28] "Kuwait-Iraq Dispute 1961"; "Role of Oil in the Middle East," *International Review Service,* Vol. VII, No. 66, 1961, Appendix F, p. 60.
[29] *Ibid.,* p. 16.
[30] *Ibid.,* p. 25.
[31] *Ibid.,* p. 56, Appendix C.

come. Iraq had to negotiate a $70 million loan to meet budgetary deficits, and revenue to the governments of oil-producing states fell by as much as 40 percent.[32] Even pipeine rentals provide as much as 10 percent of the budget of Syria, Lebanon, and Jordan. Tolls paid by tankers using the Suez Canal provide Egypt with an important source of revenue.

The Kuwait-Iraqi dispute of 1961 probably arose because oil-rich Kuwait is a major economic asset.

Middle East oil is produced by foreign-owned companies. Eight companies [33] owned by interests in the United States, Great Britain, France, and the Netherlands produce a major share of this oil. The United States is the largest foreign investor in the area; its companies owned 58.8 percent of the oil produced in 1960.[34]

By and large the arrangements concerning oil have been mutually profitable to the Middle East oil-producing states as well as the foreign companies engaged in this business. A secure source of abundant oil supplies was highly important to the West European states, and this is, therefore, in the American interest as well. The oil profits have an advantageous effect on the economy of states whose companies are engaged in the exploitation of this resource.

Foreign exploitation of oil in the Middle East has not always gone smoothly. In 1950, an agreement of the British-owned Anglo-Iranian Oil Company with the Iranian government failed to gain ratification of the Majlis (Iran's Parliament) because it did not include a profit-sharing arrangement. Under Premier Mohammed Mossadeq, a fervent nationalist, Iran nationalized the Anglo-Iranian Company. All oil companies responded by boycotting the Iranian facility. Shipments fell and the refineries had to be shut down. Iran faced bankruptcy. Mossadeq's government fell in a coup in August, 1953, and a new government proceeded to establish the National Iranian Oil Company which then was associated with a consortium of United States, British, French, and Dutch oil companies.

[32] "World Oil," *International Review Service,* Vol. V, No. 52, 1959, p. 1.
[33] "Kuwait-Iraq Dispute 1961," *op. cit.,* p. 23, lists them as Standard Oil of New Jersey, Standard Oil of California, The Texas Company, Socony-Vacuum and Gulf—from the United States; Royal Dutch Shell, 60 percent Netherlands and 40 percent British; British Petroleum Company, 56 percent owned by the British government; and Compagnie Française des Petroles, owned 35 percent by the French government.
[34] *Ibid.,* p. 24.

In this consortium the British interest was reduced to 40 percent and the United States obtained an equal share.

The apportionment of oil wealth between the producing states of the Middle East and the foreign operators has engendered controversy, if no major dislocation in supply. In most instances royalties are paid only on crude oil with 50 percent of the profit accruing to the oil-producing state. In 1957, Italy broke the 50–50 profit-sharing arrangement by agreeing to an Iranian share of 75 percent. Later that year, Japan signed an agreement with Saudi Arabia in which profit sharing was to cover not only the sale of crude oil but also the marketing of finished oil products. These agreements also provided for local representation on the governing bodies of the oil companies. An agreement between Kuwait and Japan incorporated profit sharing on crude oil and oil products with 57 percent assigned to Kuwait.[35] Italy and Japan were both more interested in an assured supply of oil than in the maximization of their profit.

[35] "World Oil," *op. cit.*, pp. 11–13.

CHAPTER 10

African Nationalism

THE MOST important and the most spectacular development in Africa since 1957 has been its rapid transformation from a continent ruled by European powers into one of independent states (see maps below). At the beginning of the twentieth century there were only two independent states; Ethiopia had existed since ancient times and Liberia was set up as a state for manumitted American slaves in 1847. In the early years of this century South Africa and Egypt won sovereignty, and during the 1950's the countries of North Africa, except Algeria, became free. It was not until March 6, 1957, that the first sub-Saharan African colony acquired independence. On that date, the British Gold Coast and the trust territory of Togoland became the state of Ghana. By 1967, almost all of the colonial empires had been liquidated.

Britain's extensive empire has been reduced to a High Commission territory—Swaziland—which will become independent soon. The large French holdings in Africa no longer exist. Only French Somaliland, that little enclave on the Red Sea, remains. Belgium and Italy have given up their African possessions. Only Portugal remains a stubborn holdout of European imperialism on the continent.

What has brought about this pervasive recession of imperialism? A number of causes clearly stand out. Nationalism gained popular support among the African [1] peoples after World War II. Led largely by an educated and westernized elite, nationalism became a

---

[1] In Africa, one commonly refers to indigenous people as Africans, whites as Europeans, South and Southeast Asians as Asians, and persons of mixed white and black ancestry as Coloreds.

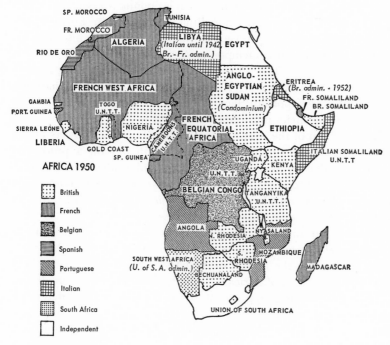

SP. MOROCCO

FR. MOROCCO

TUNISIA

RIO DE ORO

ALGERIA

LIBYA
*(Italian until 1942,
Br.-Fr. admin.)*

EGYPT

ANGLO-
EGYPTIAN
SUDAN
(Condominium)

ERITREA
(Br. admin. - 1952)
FR. SOMALILAND
BR. SOMALILAND

FRENCH WEST AFRICA

GAMBIA
PORT. GUINEA

TOGO
U.N.T.T.

NIGERIA

SIERRA LEONE

LIBERIA

GOLD COAST

SP. GUINEA

CAMEROONS
U.N.T.T.

FRENCH
EQUATORIAL
AFRICA

ETHIOPIA

ITALIAN SOMALILAND
U.N.T.T

UGANDA

KENYA

U.N.T.T.

BELGIAN CONGO

TANGANYIKA
U.N.T.T.

AFRICA 1950

	British
	French
	Belgian
	Spanish
	Portuguese
	Italian
	South Africa
	Independent

U.N.T.T.   U.N. Trust

ANGOLA

N. RHODESIA

NYASALAND

MOZAMBIQUE

MADAGASCAR

SOUTH WEST AFRICA
(U. of S. A. admin.)

S.
RHODESIA

BECHUANALAND

UNION OF SOUTH AFRICA

271

mass movement seeking freedom from foreign rule. At the same time, from the point of view of the European imperialist powers, the demand for freedom was quite in keeping with their own professions of democratic ideals necessitating a positive response, at least in principle. Attainment of independence by Asian states stimulated the nationalist demands of African leaders. When some African countries won their freedom the demands for independence grew more insistent. Imperialist policy as an economic necessity for European powers became less compelling. Prosperity in Europe grew despite the diminishing overseas empires. In one of the most famous speeches made about contemporary Africa, Prime Minister Macmillan pointed out: "The wind of change is blowing through this continent, and whether we like it or not this growth of national consciousness is a political fact. We must all accept it as a fact, and our national policies must take account of it." [2]

The division of the continent among the European powers in the latter part of the nineteenth century set in motion a process of change. Settlers, missionaries, explorers, and traders made a profound impact upon Africa. In their wake came new crops, new religions (Islam and Christianity), a *lingua franca* (Swahili), the beginnings of industry, and, above all, new ideas.

Africa is no longer the dark continent. To be sure much of the life in rural areas has changed little in a thousand years, but with each passing day the impact of modern society influences the lives of a widening circle of Africans. Tribal organization, largely devoid of class division, is giving way to urban life where the interests of the industrial working class, the business and intellectual middle class, and the more traditional authorities are in contention. The growth of transportation and communication has widened and multiplied the contact of Africans within each national unit. Over a period of time, this breaks down tribal separation. Urban centers, populated by members of different tribes, serve to erode tribal distinctiveness and promote a sense of national identity. Furthermore, detribalization is actively promoted by the educated elite which views the tribe as the fount of backwardness and superstition.

Not only do urban centers draw from a wide area of different tribal composition, but also more formal opportunities for cross-

[2] Speech to the Parliament of the Union of South Africa in 1960.

AFRICA
1967

Rabat
Algiers Tunis
TUNISIA
MOROCCO
Tripoli
Benghazi
Sidi Ifni
IFNI
(Sp.)
El Aiún
SPA
S. ARA
Cairo
ALGERIA
LIBYA
UNITED
ARAB
REPUBLIC
Nouakchott
MAURITANIA
Dakar
SENEGAL
THE
GAMBIA rst
PORT.
GUINEA
Conakry
Freetown
SIERRA LEONE
Monrovia
LIBERIA
MALI
NIGER
CHAD
Khartoum
Niamey
Bamako
Ouagadougou
UPPER VOLTA
DAHOMEY
NIGERIA
IVORY
COAST GHANA
Lomè
Accra
TOGO
Porto-Novo
Lagos
Fort-Lamy
SUDAN
FRENCH
SOMALILAND Dj bouti
Addis
Ababa
ETHIOPIA
SOMALIA
Mogadiscio
CAMEROON
Yaoundé
EQUATORIAL
GUINEA
(Sp.)
FERNANDO PO
Santa Isabel
PRÍNCIPE
(Port.)
SÃO TOMÉ
(Port.)
ANNOBÓN
MUN
Libreville
GABON CONGO
Brazzaville
Kinshasa
CENTRAL
AFRICAN REPUBLIC
Bangui
DEMOCRATIC
REPUBLIC
OF THE
CONGO
UGANDA
Kampala
Kig
Bujumbura
RWANDA
BURUNDI
KENYA
Nairobi
PEMBA
ZANZIBAR
Dar es Salaam
TANZANIA
Luanda
ANGOLA
ZAMBIA
Lusaka
MALAWI
Salisbury
SOUTHERN
RHODESIA
(U.K.)
MOZAMBIQUE
(Port.)
Tananarive
MALAGASY
REPUBLIC
POLITICAL DIVISIONS

★ Capital

SOUTH-WEST
AFRICA
Windhoek
BOTSWANA
Gaberones
WALVIS BAY
(Rep. of S. Af.)
Pretoria
Mbaban
Maseru
LESOTHO
Lourenço Marques
SWAZILAND
(U.K.)
REPUBLIC
OF
SOUTH AFRICA

0   500   1000 MILES
0   500   1000 KILOMETERS
54825 10-66

TERRITORIES UNDER COLONIAL CONTROL

273

tribal associations are frequently available. The African city has its occupational associations and entertainment and recreational groups as well as political organizations in which tribal groups are mixed. New identities are established. As tribal associations become less binding new associations within the city and increasingly within a nation take their place.

Social changes result from an understanding of the potentialities of modern society. Better standards of health, the elimination of diseases which have plagued Africans for centuries, and the extension of the life span are avidly sought by those who know that modern science has made this possible. Perhaps more than anything else Africans seek education. Budgetary allocations for education are high. Universal primary education is a goal actively sought and in some instances nearly achieved. Of Africa's fifty-one universities and colleges (existing in 1964), nineteen have been established since 1960.[3]

The United Nations has been an important influence in Africa. It has encouraged the devolution of power into African hands, the development of national political institutions, and has helped countries become stable and viable through promoting programs of economic and technical assistance.

Perhaps the most important external influence upon the development of African states has been the administrative policies of the former European colonial rulers. Four colonizers shared control of most of the continent since the end of the First World War: Great Britain, France, Belgium, and Portugal. The Spanish and Italian holdings were of lesser significance. Germany was divested of its colonial possessions after the war. Each administering power pursued a different colonial policy. The British policy was based upon a system of local autonomy and an expectation that eventually its colonies would become independent. France conceived its policy in terms of a civilizing mission, raising her African wards to be Frenchmen. Belgium perceived the future development of the Congo and Ruanda-Urundi in terms of economic and social development. Portugal claimed that eventually all of her African subjects would be integrated into the Portuguese community through a policy of *assimilado*.

[3] *Africa Report,* Vol. 8, No. 10, November, 1963, p. 56.

ADMINISTRATIVE POLICIES IN AFRICA

Of the four administrative policies, the British policy appeared
to provide the smoothest transition from colony to independent
state. British success influenced other colonial powers. As we shall
see, the French and the Belgians changed their own approach, having learned from the British example.

BRITISH POLICY

British policy was based upon local autonomy for its African
subjects. Even in its earliest stages, the British found a role for
local African leadership in their administrative organization. British administration was hierarchically structured. At the highest level
stood the governor and his staff. In the earlier years the staff was
entirely British. Territories were often divided into provinces. Each
province was headed by a provincial officer, the staff being made up
of British Colonial Office personnel. Provinces were subdivided into
districts headed by a British District Commissioner; however, districts often contained several tribal groups for which district officers
bore responsibility. Their contact with each tribe was generally
through the tribal chief. The tribal chief thus acted as the spokesman for his tribe to the district officer as well as serving as the
British government's on-the-spot representative to his people, transmitting to them the desires and expectations of British rule.

Britain employed fewer overseas colonial officers in proportion
to the population than other colonial powers. No doubt an important reason for this was the expectation that colonies should be
economically profitable. To run a "cheap administration" the number of officers brought from the British Isles was kept to a minimum
and consequently African personnel were employed.

Local autonomy also took another form, the use of local customs.
British law was not ordinarily imposed upon Africans. Local custom was suppressed when it was deemed essential for domestic tranquility or when indigenous customs outraged British sensibilities.
Robert Ruark's novel *Something of Value* is based upon such a
situation: colonial authorities outlawed the Kikuyu tribe's custom
of killing babies born by breech birth because they believed them

to be bewitched. Animistic rituals and polygamous marriage, though not tolerated in Great Britain, were among the accepted local customs in British colonies.

After World War II, local autonomy was implemented through a greater utilization of self-government, allowing over a period of years a step-by-step accretion of African responsibility and control. Development of self-government took many forms. Invariably it meant tolerating the organization of political parties by Africans. These parties in turn served as pressure groups for speeding up independence. It also led to the establishment of legislative and executive councils. The earliest legislative councils had a majority of European members who were appointed by the governor. In a series of steps the African component, elected rather than appointed, came to dominate the legislative councils until these bodies were entirely elected and African in composition. Changes in the basis for voting from restricted franchise, or from schemes permitting a few Europeans to overbalance the mass of Africans gave way to one-man one-vote arrangements. Similarly the earliest executive councils would be formed as an all-European body; at a somewhat later stage, it would become partly European and partly representative of the African political party controlling the legislative council; eventually, in the last stage before independence, the executive council was entirely Africanized and made representative of a majority party or a ruling coalition.

Growing skills in self-government were also marked by the ruling authorities permitting the legislative and executive councils an increasingly wider scope of subject matter for their decision-making. At its last stage prior to independence, only questions of foreign policy, defense, and budget remained under London's control.

Educated Africans in the British colonies were brought into administration. With the growth in trained African lawyers, the courts came under African control. A gradual Africanization of the civil service took place.

The goal of British policy was the eventual independence of the African colony. With this in view the conflicts between Britain and the Africans were over a date of emancipation. There was no question as to whether a colony would become independent. It was entirely a matter of when. Consultations and often heated interchanges between the British authorities and African leaders eventually resulted in a mutually acceptable date. In the last stages of colonial rule the African colony was substantially directed by an elected indigenous government. The legislative council was African as was the executive council. Each British minister had an African deputy prepared to take over upon the granting of independence. The techniques of party organization and election campaigns had been part of the experience of the people. With a minimum of violence and by a constitutional process African colonies became independent states.

FRENCH POLICY

The *mission civilisatrice* was a policy which sought to make Frenchmen of Africans living under French rule. In the French view, the task of France was not simply one of civilizing the indigenous population but one of also providing them with the highest of civilizations, French civilization. Through instruction in the French language, the propagation of French values and culture, and, after World War II, through providing for African representation in the French Parliament, France hoped to integrate its African empire into a tightly knit French Union. French aims, in this respect, were not entirely without success. Some of the African leaders in French territories had in fact been converted to the superior attributes of French culture. They supported integration of their territories into the French community and the French Union. Leaders like Houphouet-Boigny of the Ivory Coast, who won high office in the French National Assembly,[4] and Nikolas Grunizky of Togo favored close association with France. Others, on the other hand, fought for independence. Léopold Senghor, the President of Senegal, who served as the official grammarian of the Constitutional Convention of 1946 [5] as well as a deputy to the National Assembly from 1946 to 1959, Sékou Touré of Guinea, and Modibo Keita of Mali, who were also deputies in the National Assembly, believed that African states must go their own way. They argued that they had no wish to help rule France through the National Assembly but wanted to govern their own countries.

[4] He served as a minister in the French government between 1956 and 1959. Rolf Italiaander, translated by James McGovern, *The Leaders of Africa* (Englewood Cliffs, N.J.: Prentice-Hall, 1961), p. 254.
[5] Immanuel Wallerstein, *Africa, The Politics of Independence* (New York: Random House, A Vintage Original, 1961), p. 65.

In 1956, the National Assembly adopted a law, the *loi cadre,* granting their overseas territories authority to administer their internal affairs. Under this law, Africans gained universal suffrage. They elected territorial assemblies with legislative powers. These assemblies appointed government councils which enjoyed administrative authority in internal matters. Africans were brought into higher echelons of administration. Grand councils for the eight territories of French West Africa, the four of French Equatorial Africa, and the six provinces of Madagascar played a coordinating role in matters of common concern.

The *loi cadre,* though it extended local self-government, was not aimed at ultimate independence. Ties with France were to be preserved. African deputies, greeting the *loi cadre,* spoke of "Africa's chance for the future (lying) in its cooperation with France, a country of great culture and great civilization. We wish to build the Franco-African community and no other...." "Africa's chance and future depend on its working side by side with France—these two peoples understand each other and will always understand each other..." [6] Some rejected independence as reflecting "the selfish interests of a small minority of intellectuals..." and "most of the time merely a maiden's veil virtuously thrown over base designs..." [7] Despite such expressions of satisfaction with the *loi cadre,* the growing sentiment for freedom from French rule could not be blunted.

In 1958, with de Gaulle's coming to power, a new constitution establishing the Fifth Republic came into being. In voting on the Constitution, African territories were offered four choices:

(1)   immediate independence;
(2)   status as a department of France;
(3)   status as an overseas territory with administrative autonomy;
(4)   status as a member state of the community.

Only Guinea voted for immediate independence. The Guinean leader Sékou Touré favored independence even if it resulted in a severing of French ties. De Gaulle's response to Sékou Touré's de-

[6] Statements of Hammadoun Dicko, Deputy from Sudan (F.W.A.) and N'Daw Mamadou of Guinea, respectively. Quoted in Ambassade De France, *Service De Presse Et D'Information,* African Affairs, No. 18, May, 1957.

[7] *Ibid.* Statements of Joseph Conombo, Deputy from Upper Volta, and Maxmilian Quenum, Senator from Dahomey, respectively.

mands were not in the least conciliatory. He said: "No one will prevent you from taking independence ... If you prefer it, take the
consequences. ..." [8] Virtually all of France's four thousand administrators were withdrawn within a few days of Guinea's rejection of
the de Gaulle Constitution.[9] French Somaliland voted to remain
an overseas territory. Madagascar and all of the other French territories in Africa voted to accept the status of member state in the
community.

The community gave each territory a greater degree of self-
government. Foreign policy, national defense, economic and financial policy, and policy concerning strategic raw materials and higher
education remained under the jurisdiction of the community, whose
president was the President of France. He presided over the community assisted by an executive council composed of the premiers
of all of the states and the ministers of the French Republic concerned with community matters. French West Africa and French
Equatorial Africa as entities were dissolved. The community con-
sisted of thirteen republics: France and her overseas departments
and territories, the Central African Republic, Chad, the Republic
of the Congo, Ivory Coast, Dahomey, Gabon, Upper Volta, Malgasy,
Mauritania, Niger, Senegal, and the Sudan.

The autonomous republics and France's two trust territories,
Togoland and the Cameroons, became independent in 1960. Autonomous status did not go far enough to satisfy the African's desire
for complete independence. As autonomous republics these territories were not eligible for membership in the United Nations, which
was keenly desired. The French Constitution was amended to allow
the autonomous republics to attain their independence without
sacrificing close ties with France. As independent states they have
retained intimate contact with France. France has sponsored them
for associate status with the European Economic Community. They
have, for the most part, followed French leadership in the United
Nations.

Professor Herbert J. Spiro has observed that "In this way France,
in contrast to Great Britain, on French initiative, without a long-
range plan of constitutional advancement, pushed her sub-Saharan

[8] Gwendolen M. Carter, *Independence for Africa* (New York: Frederick
A. Praeger, 1960), p. 123.
[9] *Ibid.*, p. 120.

colonies into independence by means of several large but irregularly timed leaps."[10]

BELGIAN POLICY

In the Belgian view, a people were not ready for self-government until they had achieved maturity. Nations were conceived as organic entities. They undergo a birth, a period of maturation and growth, and they eventually achieve full maturity, and, perhaps, pass into a time of senescence. During the period of birth and growth and until maturity, nations need guidance and control. They should be wards of the "parent" who makes decisions for them. Therefore, in the Congo no one voted until December, 1957.

Belgian responsibility for the evolution of Africans was carried out through programs of economic, social, and cultural development.

The peoples of the Congo and Ruanda-Urundi were taught skills and trades. Primary education and with it basic literacy was provided for at least half of the children.[11] This was essential to support the progress in economic and cultural life promoted by the Belgian government. On the other hand, education beyond the primary level tailed off sharply. Secondary education was very difficult to get and college education was virtually unknown. When the Congo became independent on June 30, 1960, there were probably no more than twelve college graduates.[12] There were no Congolese doctors, engineers, administrators, or lawyers.

The Congo compared favorably with other African territories in economic and social development. Housing developments, hospitals, clinics, roads, railways, airports, and bicycles were visible evidence of Belgian efforts. While in neighboring Northern Rhodesia Africans were denied opportunities to learn skilled trades, such opportunities were given in the Congo. Africans drove trains over Congolese tracks while only Europeans were considered responsible enough and intelligent enough to practice such skills in Northern Rhodesia.[13]

The expectation that only after economic, social, and cultural de-

[10] *Politics in Africa* (Englewood Cliffs, N.J.: Prentice-Hall, 1962), p. 137.
[11] Colin Legum, *Congo Disaster* (Baltimore: Penguin, 1961), pp. 40 and 43.
[12] *Ibid.*, p. 44.
[13] Spiro, *op. cit.*, p. 137.

velopment had taken place would the Congolese demand political rights proved shortsighted. It should have been assumed that as some Congolese, the *évolués,* adopted the ways of western civilization in the economic and social realm they would seek political powers commensurate with their social status. As late as 1958, responsible Belgian officials believed it would be thirty years before a Congolese elite would have been created ready for independence and self-government.[14]

From 1950 on, *évolués* demanded political, economic, and social reforms. By 1956, advocacy of nationalism and independence became important enough to require Belgian attention. Joseph Kasavubu organized the Abako Party of the Bakongo people of the Lower Congo region. Others expressed impatience with Belgian reluctance to undertake political reforms and began to organize other nationalist-oriented political parties. Belgian concession to this agitation took the form of authorizing elections in Congolese municipalities in December, 1957.

For all of Belgium's paternalism toward her Congolese wards, and after almost nine decades of occupation, she never really understood the aspirations of Congolese leaders. Where Belgium expected that the *évolués* would be sympathetic with Belgian plans for slow but orderly reform, this elite moved instead toward revolutionary action. While Belgium hoped to resolve the impending crisis with plans for a Belgo-Congolese community under the Belgian crown, the Congolese leadership pressed for independence. Until 1960, Belgium vacillated between accommodation and the use of force. "When it came to the test the Belgians had no stomach for tyranny. They tried but failed to change their attitude; and they ended up muddled, defensive, resentful, and ineffectual." [15]

Belgium had to choose between repression or accession to the demands of Congolese leaders. The specter of a long, costly, and inconclusive war of suppression, such as that fought by France in Algeria, tipped the balance in favor of satisfying the Congolese demands. On January 20, 1960, a round table conference began on the future of the Congo. Meeting with the Belgians were the leaders of Congolese parties: Kasavubu of the Abako Party, Lumumba of the Movement National Conglais (MNC), Moise Tshombe of the

[14] Legum, *op. cit.,* p. 44.
[15] *Ibid.,* p. 75.

Conakat Party in Katanga, Kalonji of the Baluba division of the MNC, Sendwe of the Balubakat, Bolikango of the Parti de l'Unité National Africaine (PUNA), Bolya of the Parti National du Progrès (PNP), the most pro-Belgian of the Congolese parties, and others.[16] Agreement on independence came quickly. A motion to give the Congo its freedom on June 30, 1960, was adopted by a large majority.[17] With all too little preparation, and with the Congolese leaders deeply divided among themselves about the future of their country and the place of tribal groups in the state, the Congo began its turbulent history as an independent entity.

The dislocations which commenced with independence need not be repeated here. For this situation a large measure of blame can certainly be attributed to Belgium. By failing to develop an African *national* elite, the Congo came into being not as a nation, but as a state with competing tribal groups. The Congo lacked a nationalist leaven that only an educated elite could provide. In this sense the Congo was unready for independence. The Congolese wanted freedom but were not agreed on what was to come after Belgium abdicated its responsibility. Had it begun a few years earlier, it might have proposed a date for independence some years hence and used the intervening period to train the Congolese and to allow them to take over, step by step, the responsibilities of government.

PORTUGUESE POLICY

Portugal was the first of the European powers to occupy African territory. Since the beginning of the sixteenth century there has been a Portuguese presence in Angola and Mozambique. Over the centuries Portuguese rule has gone through benevolent and repressive periods. But at all times, the possession of an African colonial empire loomed large in Portugal's vision of her status as a world power. Her policies are intended to preserve possession of the African territories. Even in recent times when the other large colonial states have accepted African independence, Portugal has resisted all concessions in this direction.

Portugal has pursued two complementary policies in Africa. First,

[16] *Ibid.*, Ch. 8. There were 82 Congolese delegates in attendance, 62 representing about 20 parties and the rest, tribal groups.
[17] *Ibid.*, p. 57.

the retention of her African empire has led her to structure Portugal as an ultramarine state rather than a purely European entity. Under the law, Angola, Guinea, and Mozambique are overseas provinces. Therefore independence presumably was not even germane to the status of these territories. Under the law they are as independent as Portugal itself—they are part of Portugal. Secession or self-determination might be more to the point. However, advocacy of such steps are treason and are sternly suppressed.

Lisbon's position has failed to win international acceptance. Portugal refused to report to the UN on her territories, denying that they were non-self-governing within the meaning of the Charter. (See Chapter 4, pp. 126–127.) The General Assembly, nevertheless, considers Portugal's African territories to be colonies, and in no sense self-governing.

Angolans have been in revolt, however, since March, 1961. In Mozambique, African leaders have begun guerrilla operations and since 1962 guerrillas have been in revolt in Portuguese Guinea. The policy of treating African territories as overseas provinces has won little popular support among indigenous people or on the international scene.

A second policy, cultural assimilation of the Africans into the Portuguese civilization, has also been a matter of law. This policy had its roots in the belief (largely devoid of concrete evidence) in a traditional paternal Portuguese concern for the well-being of the native people. The Portuguese historian Bahia dos Santos asserts that assimilation is a natural consequence of the Portuguese character.

> Endowed by nature with exceptional qualities of sympathy and attraction for their fellow men, the Portuguese were fortified in these sentiments by the sublime doctrine of Christ, which was the maximum stimulation for these very qualities.... The gradual integration or assimilation, which today is said to have been the characteristic of Portuguese native policy ... was nothing more ... than a way of following the dictates of our moral and religious sentiments. It is a question then of a native policy more spontaneous than deliberate.[18]

Lisbon's rule was therefore presumed to appeal to the African people. Portuguese settlers would get along well with their African

[18] Quoted in James Duffy, *Portuguese Africa* (Cambridge: Harvard University Press, 1959), pp. 291–292.

brothers because ". . . they do not assume either superiority or inferiority on any basis. . . ." [19] Miscegenation was never discouraged, if not actively encouraged. Mulattoes, it was believed, would propagate Portuguese values among the native population. Some miscegenation has taken place over the years. Portuguese spokesmen have given this phenomenon an undeserved ideological significance.[20]

Until a recent change in the Portuguese law, citizenship in her African territories was automatically bestowed on the European settler population but Africans were divided into two classes, *indegenas,* "backward" black men who were not eligible for citizenship, and *assimilados,* "advanced" Africans who were citizens. Africans had to qualify for citizenship. The African had to be at least eighteen years old, speak Portuguese, give up his native customs and ways, be of good character, and earn income sufficient to support himself and his family. Africans who did not meet these criteria or who did not go through the assimilation procedure were classed as *indegenas.*[21] In theory the aim of Portuguese policy was to uplift all *indegenas* to the class of *assimilados.*

Under Salazar's dictatorship none of the people living under Portuguese rule—European or otherwise—enjoy very much freedom and liberty. For the *indegena,* Portuguese rule is particularly harsh. African males over the age of eighteen and all African females employed in urban areas must carry a pass book at all times to show to any official on demand. The pass book contains a record of taxes paid and work assignments. Labor codes require that *indegenas* between the ages of 18 and 55 be gainfully employed. Should the pass book contain no evidence of such occupation the "idle" *indegenas* are put to work by the government on state work projects or, despite Portuguese affirmation of its illegality, assigned to private employers. Work is recompensed at the legal minimum wage, which makes for cheap forced labor.[22]

Travel between districts requires prior permission. The pass book

[19] F. Clement C. Egerton, *Angola in Perspective* (London: Routledge & Kegan Paul, 1957), p. 15.
[20] Duffy, *op. cit.,* p. 261.
[21] *Ibid.,* p. 295.
[22] Marvin Harris, "Portugal's African 'Wards.' A First-Hand Report on Labor and Education in Mocambique," *Africa Today,* November–December, 1958, pp. 17–25.

must state the purpose and the destination of the journey. *Indegenas* must report to the administrative authorities within three days of arrival at their destination. If the pass book is not in order the *indegenas* must be denied employment.

In urban centers *indegenas* have been subject to curfews after dark. Corporal punishment is a feature of law enforcement for the *indegena*. For minor infractions the *palmatorio,* a wooden paddle with five or six holes, is used. The "culprit" must hold his palms up and be struck on each hand. The holes "suck up the flesh" and leave visible welts. To humiliate the *indegena,* this punishment is administered in the presence of other Africans. Offenses punished by the *palmatorio* are rarely registered as crimes and are carried out simply by the decision of the official.[23]

Few Africans have qualified as *assimilados* over the decades during which this policy has been in effect. Of an African population of 4,000,000 in Angola in 1950, only 30,089 had become *assimilados.* The accomplishment of the Portuguese in Mozambique presents an even less favorable picture: only 4,353 in an African population of 5,733,000 had become *assimilados.*[24]

From the point of view of the African, the Portuguese have, in recent times, been the most backward of all imperialist administrations. Under Portuguese rule Africans have little opportunity for education and training. Political expression is rigidly denied and opportunities for learning the arts of self-government are nonexistent. To meet the rising tide of criticism Salazar's government promulgated a reform law in 1963. Under this law the distinction between *indegenas* and *assimilados* has legally been put to an end. There have been some improvements in the conditions of labor and Africans have been given citizenship. It seems certain, however, that this law will fail to satisfy the growing unrest of Africans living under Portuguese rule. What they want is not citizenship in a Portuguese state, but independence and the opportunity to govern themselves.

[23] *Ibid.,* pp. 10–14.
[24] Duffy, *op. cit.,* p. 295. The situation has hardly changed since 1950. According to *African Report,* November, 1963, only a small fraction of the African population were legally recognized as *assimilados.* Illiteracy among Africans in both territories was 99 percent, so fewer than 1 percent of the Africans could be eligible for assimilation.

AFRICAN NATIONALISM

African states are not only a product of the influence of a colonial administration but also of indigenous forces. Nationalist organizations, often well organized and led by talented men, have played a significant role in gaining independence and in molding policies of the newborn state. The names of new leaders, difficult to pronounce but increasingly well known, are appearing on the front pages of newspapers around the world. Nkrumah of Ghana, Houphouet-Boigny of the Ivory Coast, Touré of Guinea, and Nyerere of Tanzania have all appeared on the covers of *Time* magazine.

Developing National Unity in Face of Tribal Loyalties

Traditional leaders, tribal chiefs, and religious authorities have often opposed national independence. They feared the new leaders and the groups which they represented as forces alien to tribal traditions. The society such men sought to create was different in its values and destructive of the old ways. Imperialist rule, while objectionable in many ways, usually allowed and often encouraged the preservation and the importance of the tribe. Indirect rule put a level of government into the hands of the chief. In some instances, traditional leaders sought guarantees of tribal privilege. If independence must come, they felt, at least the importance of the tribe must be assured and its role in society preserved. Because the nationalist leadership was invariably hostile to these interests a conflict between the traditional leaders and the nationalist modernizers arose during the time when the African colonies were moving toward their independence. They have continued into the era after independence and many African states today face internal disunity because of this conflict.

In some cases certain tribal groups feared the loss of a favored position that they had enjoyed under foreign rule. The Ashanti of the Gold Coast, the Buganda of Uganda, and the Watutsi of Ruanda-Urundi were all reluctant to accept independence without securing the favorable position of their tribe. Such tribes feared the creation of a unitary state in which their area would be controlled from a national capital. They preferred federal or confederal structures.

In Kenya it was the smaller tribes which organized a political party to protect their interests. They feared domination by the Kikuyu and Luo peoples who constituted about 35 percent of the population and who controlled the Kenya African National Union (KANU). An opposition party, the Kenya African Democratic Union (KADU), was established and it tried to win power by making an alliance with the more liberal elements in the European population. In Northern Rhodesia African rule under the United National Independence Party brought the threat of secession of Barotseland by its Paramount Chief, Sir Mwanawina Lewanika, should the traditional autonomy of the Barotses be threatened.

Traditional incompatibilities disrupt national unity. Hostility between the Kikuyu and the Masai in Kenya or the Baluba and the Lulua in the Congo are not yet terminated. When tribal groups evolve toward modern ways at different rates of development, then this too increases the likelihood of tension and internal disunity. Anti-Ibo feelings led the people of the Southern Cameroons to reject integration with Nigeria and vote for annexation to the Republic of Cameroun.

While a great leader may unify the people, the emergence of competing leaders, each having great appeal to a part of the masses, tends toward internal conflict. Such has been the case in Senegal where Senghor and Dia fought for power; in Nigeria where Azikiwe and Awolowo fought one another; in Zambia where a struggle between Kaunda and Nkumbula took place; and in Rhodesia where Nkomo and Sithole were at odds.

The Bakongos fought the establishment of a unitary Congolese state. They wanted to retain a large measure of control over their area. Their spokesman, President Kasavubu, and their party, the Abako, hoped to reestablish the ancient Bakongo Kingdom by reuniting the tribe living in Congo-Brazzaville, Congo-Leopoldville, and Northern Angola.[25]

UNITY AND RELIGIOUS DIFFERENCES

Religious differences also make for potential division within some African states. A belt of states along the southern reaches of the Sahara, from Senegal to Somalia, are overwhelmingly Moslem. Mauritania is 98 percent Moslem. Moslems make up 70 percent of the

[25] Legum, *op. cit.*, p. 70.

population of Senegal, 75 percent in Niger, and 60 percent in Mali. States to the south of this belt have large Moslem minorities.[26]

Arab states, especially Egypt, have actively fostered the spread of Islam in Black Africa. These efforts have met with success in terms of the number of converts to the faith. Perhaps a third or more of Africa's 275 million people are Moslems. Islam is the fastest growing faith among the pagan population. In many ways the Moslem faith is more easily accepted than Christianity and conversion is easy. Profession of the faith is all that is required. The Africans often adopt their own version of the tenets and ways of Islam. Islam gains some advantage over Christianity because the faith is usually propagated by black men whereas Christianity tends to be associated with white European colonial powers. One African leader characterized the African attitude toward religion as deriving from their "habitual desire for change. We adhere to a religious faith only so long as it is the only faith we know. If some other faith comes our way we do not insulate ourselves against its influence. The result is that often we are reconverted, to the dismay of those who converted us first. . . . That we behave in this way is no proof that we are fickle; rather it is an indication of the fact that in each one of the religious faiths which we encounter there is an element of divine truth whose fascination we fail to resist. . . ." [27]

Nigeria has had to overcome religious division and tribal rivalries in setting up its regime. In three of the four regions [28] there is a dominant tribe. The Northern region is Moslem by a large majority; however, each region has minority religious and tribal groupings from the other regions. There are also a number of smaller tribal groups in the Nigerian population of fifty-five million.[29]

[26] Jacques Baulin, *The Arab Role in Africa* (Baltimore: Penguin, 1962), pp. 12–13.

[27] Dunduzu Chisiza, "The Contemporary Outlook," *The Journal of Modern African Studies,* Vol. I, No. 1, March, 1963, p. 32.

[28] July 13, 1963, a fourth region was established by a plebiscite. Called the Mid-West region, it takes in the Benin and Delta provinces between the Western and Eastern regions. In territory it is the smallest of the regions. Its official 1963 population of 1.5 million people compared with the 22 million from the North, 10 million in the East, and 6.5 million in the West. A more recent census revealed larger populations within each of the regions.

[29] The December, 1963, census put Nigeria's population at 55.6 million with more than 50 percent in the North. Nigerians in the south dispute the accuracy of this census report.

Regional differences have been especially strong because they intertwine tribal-religious-political associations. The Eastern region is dominated by the Ibos, who belong to the National Convention of Nigerian Citizens (NCNC) Party, led by Dr. Nnamdi Azikiwe ("Zik"). The Western region is Yoruba country, where most supported the Action Party, led by Chief Obafemi Awolowo until his arrest for sedition in 1962. The North is Moslem with the Fulani-Hausa tribal influence prevalent. Its politics have been controlled by the Northern Peoples Congress (NPC) whose leaders, assassinated in 1966, were Sir Ahmadu Bello, the Sarduana of Sokoto, and Sir Alhaji Abubakar Tafawa Balewa, Prime Minister of Nigeria.

The significance of Moslem growth in sub-Saharan Africa is difficult to assess. Even the Arab Moslem states rarely adopt a united political stand despite all of them being Sunni Moslems. Religious affinities are no more likely to produce unity among Moslem populations than it has among the Christian. Among the African states, association with blocs such as the Brazzaville bloc, the Casablanca bloc, and the Monrovia bloc have been more meaningful on international issues than the religion of their people. In the United Nations Moslem states do not necessarily adopt an Arab position on most questions. A number of the Moslem states enjoy diplomatic and commercial relations with Israel.

Local separatism in the "north" and concern for domination by the "south" or "east" delayed Nigerian independence. In terms of its political sophistication and economic viability, Nigeria had been "ready" for independence some years before October 1, 1960, when it became an independent state. The major stumbling block to early independence came from the Moslem North. The Moslems constituted about 40 percent of Nigeria's population.[30] Their party, the NPC, is largest in the land. The Northern region is the largest of the three. Despite this statistical advantage, the conservative and tradition-bound Northern leaders feared leadership of the more advanced and progressive south.[31] Ibos were unpopular with other groups in Nigeria who thought them too aggressive a people. On the

[30] Baulin, op. cit., pp. 12–13. Under the December, 1963, census they constitute over 55 percent.
[31] George W. Shepherd, Jr., The Politics of African Nationalism. Challenge to American Policy (New York: Frederick A. Praeger, 1962), pp. 41–48.

other hand, Ibos and Moslems displayed some antagonism toward the Yorubas, who possessed a higher standard of living and appeared to consider themselves to be more highly civilized.

National unity, the requisite for Nigerian independence, did not evolve until 1958. It was only then that the Moslem North gave way in its opposition to a unified Nigerian state and agreed to independence. It was said that Balewa changed his mind about southern domination after his tour through the United States where he observed Americans of different faiths, national origins, and ethnic groups living together in a cohesive federation. Balewa became convinced that Nigeria as a federal state could be a united but a pluralist democracy without any tribe or faith exerting domination over the other.

THE FORCES OF NATIONALISM

The fact is that most African territories are independent and this has been achieved despite the potent divisive forces which exist in every African state. This is not to say that independence and nationalism are one and the same phenomenon. The desire for independence can be quite separate from feelings of nationalism. Those seeking independence may only wish to be rid of foreign rule or may be expressing their hostility "against the disruptive and disorganizing stranger-invaders. . . ." [32] Nationalist aims go beyond mere independence from imperialism—they seek a national state.

James S. Coleman, in an article which has become a classic in the field of African studies, asserts that true nationalism requires a period of "considerable gestation." Some of the constituent elements of national development have been: economic factors such as the transformation of a subsistence economy into a money economy; the development of a working class, and the rise of a new middle class; sociological factors such as urbanization, broadened contact among the people within the nation, and Western education; religious and psychological factors such as the spread of Christian doctrine and a "neglect or frustration of Western-educated elements"; political factors such as the "eclipse of traditional authorities" and the "forging of new 'national' symbols." [33]

[32] James S. Coleman, "Nationalism in Tropical Africa," *The American Political Science Review*, Vol. XLVIII, No. 2, June, 1954, p. 410.
[33] *Ibid.*, pp. 410–412.

Where such a period of national gestation has taken place, as for instance, in Ghana, Guinea, and Tunisia, the territorial integrity of the state has not been called into question. In the Congo, it is precisely because such a process had not occurred that the state was disrupted upon attaining its independence. The Angolan revolutionary movements show signs of seeking independence without having developed a sense of Angolan nationalism. Should Angola become independent before binding nationalism has evolved, it too might face disintegration from within by the centrifugal force of tribalism.

Nationalism is a rapidly developing force in Africa. Nationalist parties are one of the dynamic elements in the building of national patriotism. In addition there has also been revival of interest and of pride in African culture, a growth of an African literature, and a renewed attention to precolonial African history.

The time has passed when it could be said—as Lord Lugard did— that African nationalism is an "esoteric pastime of the tiny educated minorities of Lagos, Accra, Freetown, and Dakar..." [34] Nationalist leadership is lodged in an elite, but today this elite enjoys a mass following. Powerful parties and popular leaders are to be found in most African states. In most cases one united nationalist independence movement is built. The quest for independence is so dominating a concern that disparate elements are able to maintain a high degree of unity in one organization to pursue with singlemindedness the goal of national independence. African national congresses were set up in several territories. Later all-embracing political parties, such as the Convention Peoples Party (CPP) in Ghana, the Malawi Congress Party of Nyasaland, the Kenya African Union (KAU) of the early 1950's, the Istaqlal of Morocco, and the Neo Destour of Tunisia, were organized. It remains to be seen whether these parties which continue to hold a monopoly of partisan activity will split once the unifying influence of national independence from European colonialism is no longer at issue. Independence for most African states is too recent to make an accurate prediction on this score. The feeling that economic ties with the former metropolitan powers are a form of neo-colonialism serves to inflame some of the old sentiments even though the imperialist power has left the political scene. Leaders such as Kenyatta of Kenya, Nyerere of Tanzania,

[34] *Ibid,* p. 408.

and Kaunda of Zambia have encouraged a continuing spirit of mobilization for an all-out effort in economic development, demanding hard work by all the people to overcome the country's backwardness. The slogan "Uhuru"—independence—has been replaced by "Uhuru na kazi"—independence and work.

African states are undergoing a birth of national consciousness. Yet at the same time many voices are heard urging the elimination of the many nationalisms of Africa in favor of an integrating all-African nationalism. The nature of Pan-African development we shall consider below. For the present African nationalism is the growing and decisive social force.

THE PROBLEMS OF AFRICAN NATIONALISM

Generalization about an area so vast and varied as Africa is difficult and subject to many exceptions. Each African state and each region is unique, perhaps more so than in other continents, because communication between and contact among Africans from different countries has been so limited and recent. However, some issues are of moment throughout the continent and shape the dialogue of contemporary Africa. Most significant among these are (1) Pan-Africanism; (2) race relations and related to this the racial policies of the Republic of South Africa, Portugal, and Rhodesia; (3) neutralism in international affairs; and (4) modernization through socialism.

PAN-AFRICANISM

In its earliest stages, African nationalism was Pan-Africanist. Originally, Pan-Africanism was a racial concept which gained its initial support from American and West Indian Negroes. It had two chief objectives, equality for the black man living under white man's rule and self-government and independence. Pan-Africanist sentiment paid little attention to the mechanics of creating a United States of Africa or of more limited regional federations. Little time was devoted to discussion of forms of government and the character of a constitution. There was a feeling among Africans that they were involved with one another and interested in one another's well-being. There did exist a feeling of "African-ness" and some perceived the existence of an "African personality."

Independence, when it came, came piecemeal. First there was

Ghana (1957), then came Guinea (1958), later Cameroun (January, 1960), the Republic of Togo (April, 1960), and the Belgian Congo (June 30, 1960), and later all the others. States once established were reluctant to give up their national being. All African leaders embrace African unity in principle, but few have been ready to risk more than some initial steps of cooperation for fear that their country would suffer disadvantages. Nkrumah has emerged as the leading spokesman for the immediate creation of a united Africa. He found little support for bold steps among his fellow statesmen when they met in Addis Ababa in May, 1963, to establish the Organization of African Unity (OAU). Some felt that Nkrumah envisioned himself as the leader of such a union, and there was considerable opposition to Nkrumah's leadership.

Nigerian leaders argued that a united Africa had to be built slowly. They believed in economic cooperation and consultation as first steps toward ultimate unity. They argued that African states needed to deal with the practical problems of nation-building and could spare little energy to construct a United States of Africa.

Yet, as the number of independent states grew, many Africans were troubled by the "Balkanization" of the continent. Several states were exceedingly tiny (Togo, Rwanda, Burundi); others (Gabon, Mauritania, Congo [Brazzaville], and Zanzibar) had a very small population. Most of these states could not defend themselves, could make little impact in the international arena, and could not build a viable economy. While some advantage could be gained from the thirty-five or so votes cast by African states in the General Assembly, the inherent weakness of little countries minimized the real power of this African vote.

Concrete efforts toward Pan-African unity have produced varying results. One line of approach aimed at building popular support for Pan-African unity took the form of the All-African Peoples Conferences (AAPC), which met in Accra in 1958, in Tunis in 1959, and in Cairo in 1961. The meetings of the AAPC were nongovernmental. Representatives came from political parties, trade unions, and other African membership organizations. A secretariat, with headquarters in Accra, was established. George Padmore, a West Indian who was one of the fathers of the Pan-African movement after World War I, acted as the first secretary-general of the organization. Almost all African states were represented but delegations enjoyed no official status. In a number of instances delegates represented organizations outside the mainstream of the political life in their homeland, and in some instances delegates came from exile groups. By and large the resolutions adopted represented positions far to the left of those acceptable to governments. AAPC influence was at best marginal for merging the peoples of Africa into a nation.

A second line of approach to Pan-African unity involved agreements between governments. As the French West African territories approached independence an effort was made to bring them together (with the exception of Guinea) into the Federation of Mali. Only four of them, Sudan, Senegal, Dahomey, and Upper Volta, found the idea acceptable. The Ivory Coast was opposed. As the state with the highest standard of living in French West Africa, it was unwilling to be "the cow that the other territories never tired of milking."[35] Eventually the Federation of Mali came into being as a union of Senegal and Sudan, Dahomey and Upper Volta having withdrawn before independence. After the Federation of Mali attained its independence the relations between the Senegalese and Sudanese leaders deteriorated, and two months later the federation was dissolved. Senegal resumed its role as an independent state and Sudan adopted the name Republic of Mali. The Senegalese claimed that the federation was dominated by Sudanese leaders, a claim which in itself gives evidence that national integration of the two peoples had not occurred.

Nkrumah, Touré, and Keita had taken steps to unite Ghana, Guinea, and Mali. Few tangible evidences of this union can be noted. Geography and language—Nkrumah speaks English and no French while Touré speaks French and no English—were only two of many practical deterrents to effective union. The sovereignty of each party continues undisturbed.

The first substantial measures of supernational integration tended to undermine all-African unity. Two conflicting regional groupings emerged after 1960. In January, 1961, the Casablanca bloc was formed, including Ghana, Guinea, Mali, Morocco, and the UAR; later Algeria joined. The bloc, with the possible exception of Morocco, showed a measure of ideological affinity and took a similar

[35] Elliot Berg, "The Economic Basis of Political Choice in French West Africa," *The American Political Science Review,* Vol. LIV, No. 2, June, 1960, p. 403.

position on a number of important issues. They were pro-Lumumba in the Congo crisis. They were closer to the East than the West though officially nonaligned. They supported Morocco's claim against Mauritania. They condemned Israel and opposed French nuclear tests in the Sahara and demanded Algerian independence.[36]

A second grouping, the Brazzaville powers, officially called the Union of African and Malagasy States (AMU), included the former French colonies except Guinea, Mali, and Togo. AMU states joined together with eight other powers, Ethiopia, Tunisia, Nigeria, Sierra Leone, Somalia, Togo, Congo (Leopoldville), and Tanganyika, in forming a Monrovia–Lagos Conference.[37] The Monrovia-Lagos powers were more conservative. Although neutralist they took a far more sympathetic position toward the West than did the Casablanca states. The conference was primarily concerned with acceleration of economic and social development, furthering economic cooperation, and raising standards in education and health.

The Casablanca powers favored Pan-African unity. The Monrovia-Lagos states opposed political integration of sovereign African states and stressed voluntary cooperation, solidarity, and good-neighbor relations.

Nationalist movements in East Africa initiated the Pan-African Freedom Movement of East and Central Africa (PAFMECA). Their goal was freedom and the establishment of a federation among the independent, African-ruled stated in the area. Nyerere offered, on behalf of TANU, to delay Tanganyikan independence to enable Kenya, Uganda, and Tanganyika to acquire independence simultaneously in the hope that in this way the federation of these states might be more possible. PAFMECA was unable to bring into being such a federation but it gave impetus to cooperation. Its area of activity was extended at the Addis Ababa Conference of February, 1962, to include southern Africa, Ethiopia, and Somalia and its name was amended to the Pan-African Freedom Movement of East, Central, and Southern Africa (PAFMECSA).

[36] Thomas Hovet, Jr., *Africa in the United Nations* (Evanston, Ill.: Northwestern University Press, 1963), pp. 52–60.

[37] The Monrovia-Lagos powers met twice, first in Monrovia and later in Lagos. There was some difference in the states which attended each conference. Libya and Tunisia attended the Monrovia meetings but not those at Lagos. Congo (Leopoldville) and Tanganyika attended the Lagos Conference but were absent at Monrovia.

All-encompassing African unity took on tangible form with the establishment of the Organization of African Unity (OAU) at a summit conference of African states in Addis Ababa on May 22–25, 1963. The OAU is not a supernational state. It has been designed to "reinforce the links" and "establish and strengthen common institutions." [38] It furthers the "unity and solidarity" of its members. OAU powers are to "coordinate and intensify their cooperation." Through the organization, "the Member States shall coordinate and harmonize their general policies." [39] The limitations on the role of the organization is made clear in its principles which affirm the sovereign equality of the member states: noninterference in the internal affairs of others; respect for the sovereignty and territorial integrity of each state; and the requirement of peaceful settlement of disputes among the member states.[40] The OAU has four major institutional entities: the Assembly of Heads of State and Government; the Council of Foreign Ministers; the Secretariat; and the Commission of Mediation, Conciliation and Arbitration. During its first year of operation it has had to deal with two border clashes, one between Morocco and Algeria which was settled, and the second between Ethiopia and Somalia over the disputed Ogaden area, which though unsettled was not allowed to deteriorate into war. An intractable dispute between the African nationalist parties of Rhodesia, the Zimbabwe African Peoples Union (ZAPU), and the Zimbabwe African National Union (ZANU) could not be composed by the OAU.

The Charter of the OAU does not preordain the eventual elimination of national boundaries and the creation of a Unites States of Africa. Only when most states are prepared to surrender their sovereign rights will the United States of Africa come into being. On the face of it African states appear no more prepared for bolder steps of unification than do the states of the Organization of American States or those of the Atlantic Community.

There is reason to expect that more limited federations may provide a countervailing influence to the "Balkanization" of Africa. In East Africa, Tanzania and Kenya have at various times favored a federation of East African states which would at the very least also include Uganda. A single university system among these three states

[38] Charter of the OAU, Preamble.
[39] *Ibid.*, Article II.
[40] *Ibid.*, Article III.

is in existence. The successful pooling of resources in higher education could produce confidence for undertaking new steps of federation.

Regional federation is not accepted by all African leaders. The
Ghanaian Times in all likelihood was speaking for Nkrumah when
it condemned the plan to set up the East African Federation as a
"creation of the colonialist Power" to destroy African unity. The
plan for this federation was castigated as an attempt to set up a
buffer zone between the "rich mining areas, Congo, Northern Rhodesia, etc., and the avalanche of African nationalism represented by
the Organization of African Unity, coming across from West Africa
and down from North Africa." [41] Kenyatta and Nyerere were severely
reproved for pressing forward in this direction. While attacks on
limited federations are not likely to prevent their establishment,
they will serve to disturb the harmonious relations of African leaders and postpone serious consideration of concrete steps toward Pan-
African unity.

African unity is developing slowly. In principle no one is opposed
to it. Intellectuals are its fervent champions while the masses appear
to be little concerned with its development. It remains to be seen
what the closer cooperation and unity of effort agreed to by the OAU
will produce. United action to fight the legacies of colonialism—the
Portuguese and South African oppression of the African population
—is not difficult to achieve. The test of Pan-Africanism will come
when the states face economic competition and differences in their
political and ideological views. These differences are surely developing. Pan-African unification is most significantly tested by conflicting ambitions of the forceful and dynamic personalities of those who
lead the African nations.

THE PROBLEM OF RACE RELATIONS

West Africans are fond of saying that they had a valiant ally in
their battle against European settlement, the anopheles mosquito.
In contrast to the highland areas of East and Central Africa and the
more temperate South Africa, the malarial lowlands of West Africa

[41] Wednesday, February 5, 1964, issue, article by Charles P. Howard,
"Colonial Powers Aim at Strangling OAU." The author of this article also
writes for *The African Communist,* a periodical published by the South
African Communist Party.

have been unattractive as a home for white men. British policy prohibited Europeans from buying land for agricultural purposes in
West Africa. As a result few white men established themselves there
and those who did were not engaged in agriculture or wage labor,
that is, in occupations competitive with the indigenous population.
There is a larger white population in West Africa today than during the years of colonial rule. Racial problems were of minor effect
in the West African states. The issue was independence and never
white minority rule. The European without roots in an African
homeland could, if the situation became unpalatable, leave.

Where Europeans are few in number and where they have not
become permanent residents, race conflict is not a significant factor.
It is in those lands where relatively large numbers of Europeans
have come and settled and have themselves developed a strong identification with an African land that race conflict has taken place and
been difficult to accommodate.

In West Africa, Equatorial Africa, Uganda, and most of the Congo
there are about 80,000,000 people of whom about 220,000 are European, a ratio of 350 to 1.[42] In East, Central, and Southern Africa
(Kenya, Tanzania, Zambia, Malawi, Rhodesia, Angola, Mozambique,
and the Republic of South Africa), on the other hand, there are
about 42,000,000 Africans and 3,640,000 Europeans, a ratio of 12 to
1.[43] Some of these states have a sizable European population. The
Republic of South Africa, with about 20 percent, has the largest
white population. Other states such as Malawi and Tanzania have
only a fractional part of 1 percent European population and consequently have few internal racial problems (see Table I).

Kenya, Northern and Southern Rhodesia, and the Republic of
South Africa have been the lands of racial strife. European domination of the political, economic, and social life and the demands for
equality and majority rule by the African majority led to clashes
between the black and white communities. In South Africa, Europeans have been in residence for over 300 years. The Afrikaaners, a
people of Dutch and Huguenot ancestry, trace their ancestry in South

[42] The American Assembly, *The United States and Africa,* William O.
Brown and Hylan Lewis, "Racial situations and issues in Africa." (New
York: Columbia University, June, 1958), p. 145.
[43] L. H. Gann and P. Duignan, *White Settlers in Tropical Africa* (Baltimore: Penguin, 1962). See appendix for data concerning European population in East and Central African states.

Africa back to the early seventeenth century. South Africa is their land and they have no other home. Their occupation of the territory is as old as that of the African. The aboriginal population (the Bushmen and Hottentots) was driven out by both the Afrikaaners coming up from the south and the Africans coming down from the north. Afrikaaners insist that they have the right to the lands which they conquered in wars with African tribes in the nineteenth century. English settlers arrived later in the nineteenth century.

TABLE I

Population of African States with a Significant European Settler Population [a]

Country	Total Population	Europeans
Kenya	8,676,000	55,000
Tanganyika	9,538,000	22,300
Angola	4,800,000	215,000
Mozambique	7,000,000	80,200
Nyasaland	3,500,000	9,300
Northern Rhodesia	3,496,000	76,000
Southern Rhodesia	4,013,000	224,000
Republic of South Africa [b]	16,122,000	3,106,000
South West Africa	572,000	73,000

[a] Population statistics compiled from *Africa Report*, "Africa: A country-by-country situation report," Vol. 8, No. 10, November, 1963, and from Gann and Duignan, *op. cit.*, appendix.

[b] There are two additional groups living in the Republic of South Africa in significant number: Coloreds, persons of mixed race, 1,522,000, and Indian-Pakistanis, 487,000.

European settlement in the Rhodesias and in Kenya began at the end of the nineteenth century but most of the present population of settlers in these countries arrived more recently. European settlement in Portuguese colonies has been greatly increased in recent years to provide Portugal a base of support for the continued possession of its African territories.

Race difference in and of itself need not lead to racial antagonism. It is because racial identification is ramified by economics, political, and social factors that these physical differences take on such important consequences. In short, it is because the Europeans have acquired certain benefits which they seek to preserve against the aspirations of the African people that the clashes between black men and white men have occurred.

Conflict Over Land. In Kenya, possession of the best lands situated in a most favorable climate, the "White Highlands," has exacerbated the conflict between black and white. The most directly involved were the European farmers of the "White Highlands" and the Kikuyu people, but the conflict involved other Europeans and other Africans in Kenya as well. The settlers claimed this land because it was unoccupied, or in some instances purchased from Kikuyus. The Kikuyu, the largest, and most progressive tribe in Kenya, considered the "White Highlands" their land. They had temporarily left the land because of widespread rinderpest disease in cattle and a small-pox epidemic among humans. Africans provided no outward signs of land possession such as fences or deeds and perhaps for these reasons the Europeans believed the land to be unoccupied. The Kikuyu cannot conceive of the sale of tribal lands. For them, transactions with Europeans involved temporary use of land rather than permanent possession. The land belonged to the tribe in perpetuity. How could the Kikuyu give up land which belonged to the tribe through the centuries and was as much a possession of generations yet unborn as of the living? Title to the "White Highlands" was therefore in dispute. The land was leased to European farmers for as long as 999 years. Under the Crown Lands Ordinance of 1938 lands could not be sold to, managed, or otherwise occupied by non-Europeans. The "White Highlands" were underfarmed. At the same time the population of the Kikuyu was increasing and need for new land became more pressing. Too much of the land in the "White Highlands" area was permitted to lie fallow and at the same time denied to Africans for their use.[44] Tom Mboya, second in command to Kenyatta in Kenya, wrote that the Mau Mau uprising which took place in the areas around the "White Highlands" and in which some Kikuyus were the major participants was due to the European exclusive possession of the "White Highlands." Not only did the European hold this land but he also exploited the African in his demand for cheap labor.[45] Limitations were also placed on the agricultural

---

[44] John Hatch, *Africa Today—And Tomorrow. An Outline of the Basic Facts and Major Problems* (New York: Frederick A. Praeger, 1960), pp. 68–73.

[45] Tom Mboya, *Freedom and After* (Boston: Little, Brown, 1963), pp. 40–42.

activity of the Africans who were not permitted to grow cash crops like coffee, tea, sisal, and pyrethrum.

In Rhodesia a similar system of land allocation prevails. Under the Land Apportionment Act almost 40 percent of the land is reserved for European ownership. Africans may not own property in any form in European areas and in the larger cities not even live in European zones in family units. Europeans, on the other hand, may not own land in the Tribal Trust or Native Purchase Areas. However, the pressure for more land comes from the Africans who constitute almost 95 percent of the population and who are preponderantly peasants. Reservation of such a large portion of Rhodesian land for Europeans has been justified on the economic grounds that European farmers are more productive and this makes the country prosperous. The Act is defended on the cultural ground that Europeans and Africans are better off segregated, that is, living among their own peoples, and on the political ground that land must be available for European immigrants, if a larger white population is to be encouraged to move to Rhodesia.

Land apportionment is condemned by the African people. They believe that Rhodesian land is their land and that the white man is a recent intruder who has taken their ancestral land from them and all too often has ousted them from lands which were tilled by their people for generations. The law is especially brutal when African domestics are not permitted to bring their families to live with them but must take up single residence on their "masters'" property.

Another disadvantage for the African farmer comes from the scheme of taxation and pricing of commodities. Development Fund taxes and special charges reduce his income in comparison with his European counterpart.[46]

The Portuguese government has encouraged farmers and landless peasants living in Portugal to emigrate to Angola and Mozambique, where the government helps them establish themselves. Exclusively white communities competitive with the African villages are being set up. African well-being is restricted by fixed prices for cash crops that are then processed in Portugal and returned for sale to the colonies at high prices.[47]

[46] George W. Shepherd, Jr., *op. cit.,* pp. 132–133.
[47] James Duffy, "Portugal in Africa," *Foreign Affairs,* Vol. 39, No. 3, April, 1961, pp. 491–492.

The Republic of South Africa, upon completion of its program of racial separation, *apartheid,* will have relocated its entire African population, almost 80 percent of the whole, upon a small fraction of the land area of the country (see map, p. 303). In 1963, the Transkei, the first of the separate areas—known as Bantustans—was established.

Conflict Within Labor. Mboya wrote that the Mau Mau uprising "was the child of economic and social problems which had accumulated over the years and which had not found any solution through constitutional channels. They were nearly all problems of discrimination against Africans in different forms . . ." Listed first among the concrete instances of discrimination were those "in employment and in salaries." [48] Racial tensions were aggravated when Africans wanted the better jobs and higher wages which were denied them.

South Africa has a sizable skilled and semiskilled working class, largely composed of Afrikaaners. The government is committed to the preservation of a superior position for the white worker in face of competition from African and other non-European workers. Nevertheless, European employers are dependent upon African labor. With industrialization, "the wants and aspirations of the Africans inevitably rise and tend to be defined in terms of the way of life enjoyed by the Europeans . . . the need for African workers makes it increasingly difficult to prevent their rise on the economic scale." [49] To reduce dependence on African labor the South African government has reserved for Europeans certain occupations. It has tried to prevent Africans from practicing higher skills. Managerial positions have been given to Europeans only.

Competition between black and white miners also existed in the Northern Rhodesian copper belt. About 8,000 white miners had been brought into this area enticed by wages equal to the best paid American workers. They felt their position threatened by some 50,-000 African miners who wanted better jobs and better pay. The European Miners Union fought the organization of an African miners union, but nevertheless the African Miners Union was established. In 1955, with the assistance of the copper companies and the international labor movement, the color bar in the copper mining industry was substantially moderated. As Kenya and Northern Rho-

[48] Mboya, *op. cit.,* p. 40.
[49] American Assembly, *op. cit.,* pp. 149–150.

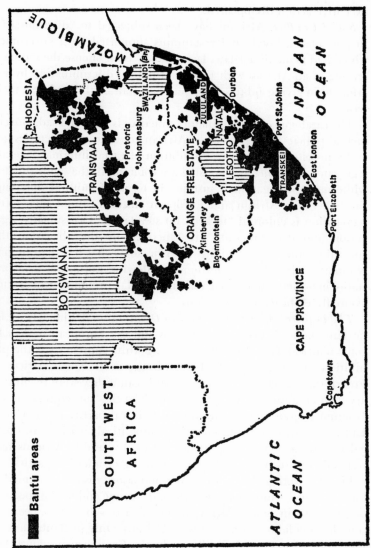

SOUTH AFRICA 1967

Bantu areas

MOZAMBIQUE
RHODESIA
TRANSVAAL
Pretoria
Johannesburg
SWAZILAND (Br.)
ZULULAND
NATAL
Durban
Port St.Johns
INDIAN OCEAN
East London
TRANSKEI
LESOTHO
ORANGE FREE STATE
Kimberley
Bloemfontein
BOTSWANA
SOUTH WEST AFRICA
CAPE PROVINCE
Capetown
Port Elizabeth
ATLANTIC OCEAN

desia approached independence, discrimination through law and
executive action disappeared.

Social Conflict. Africans have been subjected to "discrimination
in post offices, hotels and restaurants supported by a government
which had made liquor laws laying down as an offense the selling or
serving of an African with European liquor; discrimination by government in giving aid to schools and hospitals established on a racial
basis . . ." [50]

The catalogue of discriminatory practices is long and sad. Governmental policies have proscribed African access to the amenities generally provided Europeans. Prohibition of racial intermarriage and
segregated schooling and housing are common in the lands ruled by
white men. Segregation is justified in terms of cultural difference,
the belief that African and European cultures cannot mix. Often
segregation is enforced "to keep up standards." Occasionally segregation and discrimination are sanctified by the allegation that
colored people are biologically inferior, somewhat less than human.
No matter what the justification for allowing Europeans a favored
status in society, at its root one finds racial prejudice which must
assuredly embitter race relations.

The Political Aspects of European Domination. Ultimately all important clashes between the Africans and the European settlers become political. One device for ensuring white supremacy is the prohibition of African political organizations. In North Africa the
French suppressed local parties, more because they were revolutionary than because they were African. Only at the "eleventh hour" did
Belgium tolerate the organization of political parties in the Congo.
Until then Africans could join only nonpolitical associations. Portugal has forbade African political parties. Invariably Africans have
responded to such limitation by organizing clandestine parties.

Limiting voting rights of the African majority is a typical method
for ensuring a white men's government. At one end of the spectrum
of practices—in South Africa in recent years—there has been the
complete denial of voting rights to Africans. Only in Bantustans are
they allowed to elect their officers. In the Capetown province Africans were assigned separate representation of three white representatives in the House of Assembly of South Africa's Parliament.
But even this voting "right" has been taken away.

Weighted representation in which the African majority votes on a

[50] Mboya, *op. cit.*, p. 40.

separate roll to elect a minority of the Legislative Council while the European minority elects the majority has been used to maintain the political supremacy of the Europeans.

African participation in elections is kept down by too steep qualifications for voting. In this way only a tiny fraction of the African population is allowed to vote in Rhodesia and, in the past, in Northern Rhodesia as well. Little wonder that at the center of African demands for independence stood the demands for elections by "common roll"—rather than separate European, Asian, Colored, or African rolls—and "one man, one vote." When these demands are satisfied African majorities in legislative and executive councils will become the rule rather than the exception.

The Republic of South Africa. The most ambitious and far-reaching program of racial separation and subordination has been developed in the Republic of South Africa. There, race relations are governed by a system known as *apartheid* (see Table II). *Apartheid* is an Afrikaaner expression meaning "separateness." The system aims at the complete separation of the European and non-European (mainly African) population.[51] In addition, the European government enjoys supremacy. These objectives are to be attained through a number of laws that have been adopted since the Afrikaaner Nationalist Party came to power in 1948 and that have been enforced with harshness. Among the more important of them have been:

1. The Mixed Marriages Act, which prohibits interracial marriage.
2. The Immorality Act, which makes sexual intimacies between Europeans and non-Europeans a crime.
3. The Population Registration Act, which classifies persons according to their race.
4. The Separate Amenities Act, which strengthened segregation in transportation and public places.

---

[51] See note b on p. 299 for the composition of the non-European population. None of these groups is one homogeneous mass. The Africans stem from different tribal groupings—Zulu, Xhosa, Northern and Southern Sotho, etc.—and live at differing levels of social development. Some live in tribal compounds on native reserves while others farm. An increasing number have moved to urban centers, most often working in industry. Coloreds vary from almost Negro to almost white. The Europeans, on the other hand, are composed of 60 percent Afrikaaner and 40 percent British stock. *Apartheid* is, in the main, the policy of the Afrikaaner Nationalist Party.

5. The Group Areas Act, which grants the government authority to establish separated racial zones within which residence and the ownership of property or business is limited to persons of the assigned race.

6. The Bantu Education Act, which strengthened segregated education mainly by withdrawing the traditionally granted financial support from schools administered by church missions. These schools were not segregated and most African children in school attended them.

7. The Separate Universities Education Act, which set up a program of separate colleges for each racial group and debarred non-Europeans from attending the two unsegregated—"open" —universities.

8. The Bantu Self-Government Act, which abolished African representation in parliament and established separate African states—"Bantustans"—with a measure of internal autonomy but under the government's control.

TABLE II

This Is Apartheid

	White (Europeans)	Black (Africans)
Population (millions)	3	11
Per capita income (1959)	$1,819	$109
Average wage in mining (1962)	$3,587	$216
Ages subject to tax	21–60	18–65
Income exempt from tax	$ 840	None
Education expenditure per pupil (1962)	$ 182	$ 18
Infant mortality per 1,000 births	27	200+
Percentage of population (balance: Asian and mixed)	19	68
Percentage of land reserved	87	13
Persons in registered trade unions	340,000	None
Persons convicted of pass offenses (1962)	None	384,000

SOURCES: *State of South Africa: Economic, Financial and Statistical Yearbook for the Republic of South Africa,* Johannesburg, 1962; also *Report of the Special Committee on the Policies of Apartheid of the Government of the Republic of South Africa,* United Nations General Assembly, September 16, 1963.

Police control of the non-European population is meant to discourage effective opposition. Movements by non-Europeans within South Africa are controlled through pass laws which require the non-European to justify his presence anywhere at any time to the police. Activities can also be controlled through the Riotous Assembly Act and the Suppression of Communism Act. Under the latter law any opposition to the government's policies may be suppressed as acts of communism.

The racial policy of the Nationalist regime is heading South Africa toward violence and revolution. African protests which resulted in the Sharpeville Massacre in 1960 gave evidence that a bloody conflict is shaping up. In the end, the African will rule his homeland because he constitutes an overwhelming majority, because this development falls into the stream of history, and because international pressures will isolate the Nationalist regime and support efforts to win freedom and equality for the non-European peoples.

Pressures against South African policies are building up. Not only has the policy of *apartheid* come under sharp attack within the UN and elsewhere, but the South African intentions toward South West Africa are also a matter of international anxiety.

South West Africa became a Union of South Africa "C" mandate after World War I. At the end of World War II, South Africa refused to change its status to a trust territory. Prodding to this end by the General Assembly was to little avail. At best it served to delay South Africa's avowed intention to annex the territory. In 1950, the International Court of Justice gave an advisory opinion, in answer to a General Assembly request, which held that while South Africa was not compelled to place South West Africa in trust, neither could it unilaterally abrogate the League's mandate. The mandate was legally in force with the United Nations as the inheritor of the League's responsibility. Liberia and Ethiopia instituted an action against South Africa in November, 1960, before the Court. Its purpose was to prove that South Africa had defaulted on its mandate agreement and that the UN should have a voice in the administration of the land.

Spokesmen for some of the African peoples of the territory have appealed to the UN for support against South African policies in the territory and for freedom from the harsh rule of the Republic. Meanwhile the Republic has recently taken a big step toward incorporating the territory into the Republic. The Commission of Inquiry into the Development of South West Africa proposed the division of the territory into a number of Bantustans, leaving about half of the land to the whites who constitute 12 percent of the population. It also proposed closer administrative direction of the territory by the Republic.

The Republic of South Africa is a prosperous land. Even the Africans who live at a standard far below that of any European enjoy opportunity for some education and benefit to a degree from the general prosperity of the Republic. In this sense they are better off than most other Africans living to the north. This situation notwithstanding the peoples of Basutoland, Swaziland, and Bechuanaland were opposed to incorporation into the Republic. The question of incorporation arose from the fact that all three territories are landlocked and either adjacent to or, in the case of Basutoland, wholly within the land area of the Republic. Each territory has vital economic ties to the Republic. When South Africa attained its independence, Britain retained control over these territories but agreed to their eventual incorporation into the Union of South Africa after seeking an expression of the popular will. South Africa had pressed London to allow annexation of the territories and to assess African opinion as purely a matter of information, in no way binding upon Great Britain. Nevertheless, African objection to being governed by a system of *apartheid* caused Britain to reject South African proposals for incorporation. On September 30, 1966, Bechuanaland gained its independence and took the name Botswana. About a week later, Basutoland became the independent country Lesotho.

At the Fifteenth Session of the General Assembly a declaration on decolonization was passed. Subsequently a special committee was elected to oversee the implementation of this resolution. Strictly speaking, the issue is not a matter of decolonization but mainly one of the white man's minority rule. Gradually African majorities are taking over their countries even where a white settler population is in residence. In December, 1963, Kenya became independent under an African majority. The Federation of Rhodesia and Nyasaland was dissolved in response to African antipathy to European control. In 1965, Northern Rhodesia and Nyasaland became independent states (Zambia and Malawi) under majority rule. In each case the transition to majority rule was smoothly effected and most Europeans were learning to live as a nonruling minority.

Less tractable has been European control in Rhodesia, Portuguese Africa, and the Republic of South Africa. In response to mounting pressures from Africans for their rights, the Rhodesian Front government of Ian Smith tried to reverse the trend of African rule by a unilateral declaration of independence from Great Britain. Smith's government hoped to ensure permanent (or to accept his words at face value, long-term) European control in southern Africa. The future of the white man's rule of southern Africa is dim. Population statistics and historic trends indicate that Africans will reclaim their birthright. African demands for democratic rights grow stronger and are becoming inexorable. White supremacists are increasingly isolated. It would seem that accommodation by moderates of both races who wish to create lands where all may live in freedom and justice should win broad support. However, few Europeans are ready to concede that their good life will continue under governments which they do not dominate and they have more often turned to enforced white supremacy. Short-term "success" in muting African protest only makes it more likely that violence will be the only means which Africans can adopt if they are to become free. Voices of moderation are being stilled. In South Africa, Chief Luthuli, the Nobel Peace prize winner who had been the leader of the African people and who advocated peaceful protest, has been increasingly isolated from his people. It is a matter of irony that this man, an advocate of reason and nonviolence, suffers house arrest by the South African regime. Who is to deny the regime the legality of any measure of suppression they wish to undertake? Under the Suppression of Communism Act the decision of the minister is sufficient to inflict penalties upon those seeking to bring about "any political, industrial, social or economic change within the Union." Thus, African opposition is taken over by the clandestine groups preparing more violent steps.

AFRICAN SOCIALISM

"If the measure of socialism is the extent to which the state controls the production and disposition of goods and services, Africa is probably less socialist than the United States...." [52] African states-

[52] Walter H. Drew, "How Socialist *are* African Economies," *Africa Report,* Special Issue on African Socialism, Vol. 8, No. 5, May, 1963.

men claim to be socialists. Concepts of African socialism as expressed by Africans are vague. There is a high degree of consensus that African socialism differs materially from European, Marxist, or other versions of socialist doctrine. A systematic theory of African socialism has not yet been developed.

Certain themes emerge from discussions of African socialism. There is agreement that Africa is in a precapitalist stage of development. Division of the society into social classes is just beginning. Socialism as a historic stage of development emerging from the class struggles of capitalist society cannot yet occur. Socialism is occasionally claimed to be a logical development of the indigenous African communal society. It is felt that the cooperative character of such societies conditions the African to a natural acceptance of collective arrangements and cooperative efforts which are integral to socialist methods. This outlook discounts the impact of modern business enterprise in stimulating acquisitive interests.

African socialism is anti-capitalist. Capitalism, in this connection, remains undefined. It is associated with imperialist exploitation, so that anti-capitalist assertions appear as denunciations of the exploitation of Africa's resources, both material and human, for the good of the European exploiter. Socialism is often the term used for diverse programs of modernization and economic development, and African socialism is evidenced by the distribution of *goods* in a way that will avoid the rise of rich and poor.

African socialism is not meant to discourage the private sector in the economy. All economic activity which adds to the total output of the country is encouraged. As a practical matter private investment from local entrepreneurial groups as well as from abroad is encouraged. Nationalized industry is more likely to result from the absence of private investment and the need for a particular economic activity than from a socialist point of view.

AFRICAN NEUTRALISM

Neutralism, or nonalignment with the United States or the Soviet Union in the conflicts which derive from the "cold war," has been a characteristic of the foreign policy of most underdeveloped states. African neutralism has unique characteristics.

For African states neutralism is considered to be an aspect of independence. Alignment with an alliance—NATO, SEATO, CENTO, or the Warsaw Pact—is tantamount to accepting direction of foreign policy from a colonial master. Neutralism is not intended to avoid decisions on issues in which an "East" and a "West" position has been stated, but is meant to lead to judgments on each issue based upon the merits of the case and, even more, upon the interests of the African state. "In international affairs our position has been that with proper objectivity the policy for each occasion should be selected in Nigeria's national interest and in that of world peace," said Balewa, the former Nigerian Prime Minister.[53]

Neutralism has discouraged foreign military bases on African soil. Its outlook is similar to that of the United States during the early years of its existence. Commerce and friendly relations are sought with all states but entangling alliances with none.

There are few advantages in alignment. Foreign assistance and the weight of African states in the councils of the United Nations would not be enhanced by membership in alliances. The fact that support must be won from unaligned African states gives them a bargaining influence. Neutrality reduces their military commitments and allows them to concentrate with singleminded persistence on internal problems which appear almost overwhelming.

[53] "Nigeria Looks Ahead," *Foreign Affairs*, Vol. 41, No. 1, October, 1962, p. 139.

CHAPTER 11

Asian Nationalism

Asia is the largest continent and it contains the greatest population. It is a continent of great physical multiformity; within it are to be found the highest mountains, great deserts, and mighty rivers, the heat of the tropics, and the frozen wastes of the Arctic. Asia is also a continent of human variety. There are differences of race, nationality, and religion. There are many Moslems and Hindus. In East and Southeast Asia the Buddhist faith has numerous adherents. Most Japanese are Shinto whereas a large proportion of the Chinese population is Confucian. Over the centuries Christianity has gained many converts.[1]

Scholarly investigation of the continent by social scientists has required regional specialization because the continent is too vast, varied, and complex to be studied exhaustively by a single scholar. Subarea specializations exist for Southwest Asia, which covers most of the Middle East (which has been discussed in Chapter 9); South Asia, which includes India, Pakistan, Afghanistan, Ceylon, and Nepal; Southeast Asia, made up of Burma, Thailand, Malaysia, Laos, Cambodia, Vietnam, Indonesia, and the Philippines; and East Asia, consisting of China, Japan, Korea, and the Mongolian Peoples Republic. Such continental subdivisions constitute more manageable areas for intensive study. Soviet Asia is best considered in relation to the Soviet Union. Experts on the single states of China, India, and Japan find plentiful data to occupy their scholarly attention.

---

[1] According to the *World Almanac, 1963,* the leading religious groups, in terms of numbers of adherents, are: Hindu, 334,708,000; Moslem, 331,520,000; Confucian, 300,000,000; Buddhist, 153,000,000; Shinto, 51,000,000; Taoist, 50,000,000; Christian, 49,806,000.

The rich diversity within the continent leads one to wonder whether valid and important generalizations about Asia can be made. But in an introductory study of the continent and its problems, some generalizations must be hazarded. With the exception of Japan the countries of Asia have the following similarities.

1. They have experienced colonial domination by a European power in recent times. In this sense the role of the United States in the Philippines and China led to its inclusion in the list of white European imperialist states. Only the relatively brief experience with Japanese imperialism disturbed the link between imperialism and Europe for Asian peoples.
2. Asian states have experienced an upsurge of nationalism. Nationalism is no longer just a middle-class movement but has attracted the support of the urban masses.
3. Most Asian states are faced with internal instability. Divisive forces, the shortcomings of the ruling groups, and the pressures for change all undermine stability.
4. The states of Asia are underdeveloped. Improvement in the material conditions of the people is the most important problem for Asia as a whole.
5. Contrast between rich and poor and incipient class conflict is a typical situation within Asian states. The degradation of poverty is brought out in stark relief by the visible opulence of a small upper class.
6. Asian states feel a sense of common interest. Their views are given international attention when they are able to speak with one voice as at the Bandung Conference of Asian and African states in 1955.
7. Within Asia the pervasive influence of China and India are deeply felt. The outcome of the rivalry between these two powers will determine the direction, Communist or democratic, which most of the other states of Asia will take. Their success, measured in terms of stability, prosperity, and prestige, influences the choice of a model which other states will adopt in the quest for a better way of life.

Contrary to popular misconception Asian countries are not usually overpopulated. China and India suffer population pressure as

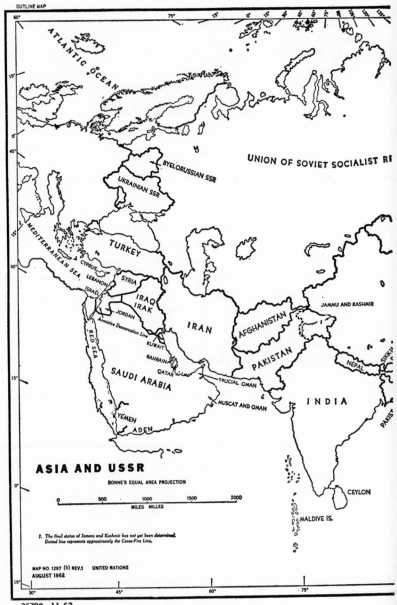

ASIA AND USSR

BONNE'S EQUAL AREA PROJECTION

0   500   1000   1500   2000
MILES MILLES

1. The final status of Jammu and Kashmir has not yet been determined.
Dotted line represents approximately the Cease-Fire Line.

MAP NO. 1297 (b) REV.1   UNITED NATIONS
AUGUST 1962

36788 11-62

314

does East Pakistan and the island of Java in Indonesia. Most other Asian lands can support a larger population.

Our generalizations about the states of Asia excludes Japan. It is not an underdeveloped country but the other states of Asia are. Japan has not been a victim of colonial exploitation but has itself been an imperialist power. Japan seeks to define for itself its role as a leading world power and as a leader of the Asian peoples. Its historic experiences and its international position as an industrial exporting nation make it distinctly different from other Asian countries and beyond the consideration of this chapter.

ANTI-COLONIALISM

Until the end of the Second World War almost all of the states of Asia were under colonial control. Great Britain, France, and the Netherlands were the important imperialist powers. Among them they held most of the territory of South, Southeast, and East Asia. Only Japan was truly independent. Even those states that were nominally independent then, China, Thailand, and Afghanistan, were under semicolonial control. Afghanistan, a dependable British ally, constituted a buffer state between Russia and British India. Thailand similarly served as a buffer state between the British possessions to the West and French Indochina to the East. China itself was prey to the will of the imperialist powers after the eighteenth century. Only after the successful conclusion of Sun Yat Sen's revolution, begun in 1924, did China exert a meaningful sovereignty over her territories. Prior to that time China was carved up by the Japanese, French, Russian, British, and Americans.

South Asia was a British area. In Southeast Asia the British ruled Burma and Malaysia; the French ruled Vietnam, Laos, and Cambodia, territories which they grouped together as French Indochina; the Dutch ruled Indonesia; and the Philippines were an American colony. East Asia was exploited, at various times, by British, French, United States, Russian, Japanese, German, and Italian interests supported by their governments.

The Second World War gave impetus to the nationalist movements of Asia. The early military success of Japan deflated the prestige of white man's rule. Europe's Asian holdings proved vulnerable. The Japanese expulsion of the Dutch from the East Indies, the French from Indochina, and the British from Malaya, Singa-

pore, and Burma inflamed nationalist demands that the imperialists should never return. The voice of the United States during the
war, calling upon the peoples of Asia to help defeat Japanese aggression, put the United States in the anti-imperialist camp. American leaders said that the days of imperialism had come to an end.
The Philippines were promised their independence as soon as was
feasible after the war. The United States put itself on the side of
independence for all of the colonial states of Asia. Its position
heightened the expectation of nationalists that with Japan's defeat
national self-determination would come to each of the Asian states.
When the Dutch and the French proved reluctant to give up their
possessions, nationalist revolutions in Indonesia and Indochina then
broke out.

THE LEGACY OF IMPERIALISM

The influences of imperialism were many. Each imperialist power
left its imprint on the territory that it ruled. The era of imperialism
produced a revolution in the nature of Asian life. The West invaded Asia in the sixteenth century. It caused economic, social, and
political changes in societies that had been static for hundreds of
years. With Western rule came the development of communication
and transportation. The subsistence economy increasingly gave way
to the production of cash crops for export. While many of Asia's
peasants are still engaged in subsistence production the future of
their countries rests largely in the development of commodities for
export. Western concepts of individualism have modified Asian
community-centered values. The development of medical technology
and the promotion of higher standards of sanitation have led to
population increases. It is estimated that in Southeast Asia alone
the population has risen from ten million people in the mid-
nineteenth century to almost twenty times that number in the middle of the twentieth century.[2] Strong local attachments have been
replaced by feelings of nationalism. The ideals and institutions of
democracy have had great influence upon Asian political thought.

Imperialism has had its deleterious influences as well. Foreign
rule robbed the Asian of his sense of dignity. It evoked a natural
desire for independence. Imperialism was condemned for exploit-

[2] Richard Butwell, *Southeast Asia Today—and Tomorrow: A Political
Analysis* (New York: Frederick A. Praeger, 1961), p. 14.

ing man and the natural resources of Asia to enrich the imperialist rulers to the detriment of the Asian people. Even the development of technology was believed to be too limited and too slow because it was tied solely to the profits of Western capitalism rather than the needs of the Asian states. Spokesmen for the Asian peoples won popular support when they preached hostility toward European imperialism and urged that only independence would allow Asians their rightful share in the prosperity that economic development would bring.

NATIONALIST MOVEMENTS IN ASIA

The Second World War heightened the expectation of immediate national independence. For decades Indians had waged a bitter struggle against British rule. The war strained British capacity to reject the demands of Indian nationalism. At the end of the war the Labor government was ready to grant India its freedom. Internal strife between the Hindu and Moslem communities delayed the transfer of power until August 15, 1947. The leadership of Mahatma (Mohandas K.) Gandhi and his political heir Jawaharlal Nehru attracted to the banners of Indian nationalism the widest popular support.

In Indonesia the nationalists, led by Sukarno, Sjahrir, and Hatta, proclaimed their independence on August 17, 1945, even before Japan's defeat became official. For six weeks, until the British landed troops in Java to accept the surrender of Japan, Indonesian nationalists governed the islands. But with the British came the Dutch, and for four years Indonesian nationalists fought Dutch occupation. United States and United Nations pressures helped the Indonesians win the transfer of sovereignty from the Dutch in the Round Table Agreements of the Hague in December, 1949.

Burmese hostility to British rule led Burmese nationalists to welcome Japanese forces during the war. When it became evident that the Japanese had not come as liberators but as colonial exploiters, several Burman leaders organized the Anti-Fascist Peoples Freedom League, an anti-Japanese nationalist movement. At the end of the war the British were prepared to make concessions to Burmese nationalist demands but hoped to stop short of complete independence. When only full independence would satisfy the nationalists, the Labor government concluded a treaty transferring sovereign power to them on October 17, 1947.

The Filipino people caused the Japanese occupation forces the greatest amount of difficulty in all of the territories which they had conquered. Their loyal adherence to alliance with the United States was considered to be a triumph for the benevolent policies of the United States administered by a number of sympathetic High Commissioners. It also demonstrated confidence on the part of the Filipinos in the promise of independence which President Roosevelt had made. Despite internal unrest, wholesale destruction brought on by the war, and serious economic difficulties, the Philippines received their independence on July 4, 1946.

The Japanese held effective control over French Indochina during the war. At the same time a Vietnamese Communist, Ho Chi Minh, organized a coalition of anti-French nationalists named the League for the Independence of Vietnam, commonly called the Vietminh. In its earliest years the Vietminh included nationalists of varying political complexions. In May, 1945, the Vietminh established its own "liberated" area in the north, and after the Japanese surrender it proclaimed a Democratic Republic of Vietnam with Hanoi as its capital. The French, on the one hand, recognized Ho Chi Minh's regime as a free state within Indochina and the French Union but at the same time tried to reestablish their control over the whole of Indochina. By December, 1946, all semblance of agreement between the French and Ho Chi Minh broke down, and for the next eight years the French and the Vietminh fought a bloody war until France finally agreed to the independence of Vietnam, Laos, and Cambodia. The Communist character of the Vietminh did not emerge until 1949. It was then that non-Communist nationalists withdrew their support, albeit they did not support the French. Many sat on a fence between the French and their puppet Emperor Bao Dai and the Communists. In 1954, the French were decisively defeated at Dien Bien Phu and had to come to terms with the demands of Vietnamese nationalism. By agreement reached in Geneva that year French rule in Indochina came to an end. Regardless of the sorry record of the Ngo Dinh Diem regime in its later years, when Diem came to power in July, 1954, this too represented a victory of Vietnamese nationalism (anti-Communist Vietnamese nationalism) over French colonialism.

The presence of Western imperialism made independence the singular concern of Asian leaders. To this end almost all Asian patriots found cause for joining together in their nationalist parties.

The Indian National Congress, the Kuomintang, the Sarekat Islam, and the Anti-Fascist Peoples Freedom League were such nationalist associations in India, China, Indonesia, and Burma and were composed of diverse elements.

During the first six decades of this century, national independence was the overriding issue in Asia. It seldom permitted divisiveness among peoples seeking self-determination to disturb the unity of the nationalist movement. Religious conflict between Muslims and Hindus in India led the Indian Muslim leader Mohammed Ali Jinnah to advocate separate states for Muslims and Hindus. He established the Muslim League to promote this goal. India was to this degree an outstanding exception to the unifying influence of nationalism which discouraged the formation of major competing parties. However, among the Hindu peoples the Indian National Congress enjoyed almost total support.

Even the Communists made little headway against nationalist sentiment. Only where they were able to capture or monopolize the nationalist movement, as in North Vietnam, did Communists emerge as a movement enjoying broad popular support. Where Communists set themselves up in organizations separated from the mainstream of nationalism they remained a relatively small sect. The growth of Communist parties in Asia is largely a development that came after independence.

As the colonial question becomes irrelevant to the issues of the day, and as Asians begin to regard appeals against imperialism as "flogging dead horses," nationalism will prove to become less of a catalyst for uniting the people into a single party. Each succeeding election finds the Indian National Congress more successfully opposed by opposition parties. Indonesia has several major parties. Nationalism has not prevented the formation of competing parties in the Philippines, Ceylon, and Malaysia.

In a word, it was much easier to develop national unity in the context of an anti-imperialist struggle than it has been to maintain this unity during the time of nation-building.

THE PROBLEMS OF INTERNAL STABILITY

The unifying force of nationalism and anti-colonialism is decreasing, and divisive issues are gaining attention in the Asian states. Local and ethnic jealousies, religious differences, linguistic diversity, and conflicts in economic and social interests have increasingly occupied the center stage in Asian politics.

LOCAL DISSIDENCE

The territorial configuration of the Asian state derives largely from the European occupation and administration. History knew no India, Pakistan, Burma, Malaysia, or Indonesia with today's boundaries. The Indian subcontinent was divided among numerous princely states. The islands of Indonesia had always been separate from one another until the Dutch imposed an administrative unity upon them. Hardly more than one hundred years ago Vietnam was divided into three distinct areas: Tonkin, Annam, and Cochinchina. Separatist influence based upon local loyalties still undermines unity in Asian lands. Among the more serious instances of local disaffection are those existing in Indonesia, Burma, India, and China.

Indonesian political authority has been centered on the island of Java. Two-thirds of the country's population lives there and the interests of the island dominate the scene. The outer islands consider themselves disadvantaged by the state although they have great economic importance. Sumatra alone accounts for about 70 percent of Indonesia's exports. Spokesmen for the interests of the outer islands have demanded the allocation of larger resources to their particular island's development and local autonomy. These demands were unfulfilled and as a consequence separatist tendencies gained strength in Sumatra and the Celebes. Uprisings in both islands have been suppressed. The lure of association with Malaysia, a prosperous neighbor, holds a measure of temptation to some Sumatrans which should not be overlooked as a reason for Sukarno's "crush Malaysia" campaign.

Burma has faced rebellion from three different groups, each group seeking local autonomy or self-determination. The Kachins in the north, the Karens in the east, and the Shan people in the hill country of northeastern Burma have supported rebellions against the government in Rangoon.[3]

[3] A recent estimate of forces in revolt lists 3,000 Karen nationalists, 500 in the Kachin's Independence Army, and 1,000 in the Shan Independence Army. These insurgents are still operating on a greatly reduced scale. The earlier Communist rebellions, both White Flag (Stalinist) and Red Flag (Trotskyist), are no longer active. John Scott, *Crisis in Communist China* (New York: Time Inc., 1962), p. 44.

Nationalism has not entirely eliminated strong feelings of local identity. These most often come to the fore when a locality feels that it is denied fair treatment. The success of the Communists in winning control of the local parliament of the state of Kerala in southern India was in part a reaction of the people against the national government, which they felt had not treated their province with equality and justice.

China also contains some diverse populations that have accepted central controls with great reluctance or, as is true in the case of Tibet, only after the use of force. The Mongolian areas in the north of China and the peoples of the province of Sinkiang as well as the Tibetans have proved least amenable to efforts at Sinification.

LINGUISTIC DIFFERENCES

Communication among the people within some of the states of Asia is difficult. Few states have a language common to all of the people. Nationalities have developed without the concomitant development of a national tongue. Often the only language that is spoken in all parts of the land is European—English or French. However, Asians refuse to use English or French as their national tongue because they associate the language with colonial rule and insist on an indigenous language; besides, only a small educated elite speaks these foreign languages.

The choice of a national tongue has been a cause for bloody conflict. The Indian Constitution lists fourteen official state languages. In 1956, Indian states had to be realigned into linguistic units despite Nehru's best efforts to diminish the importance of linguistic identification. Even this did not settle the conflict between the Marathi- and Gujarati-speaking inhabitants over the official language for the state of Bombay. Bloody riots in which several hundred persons lost their lives led to the division of the state, in May, 1960, into the states of Gujarat and Maharashtra.[4] In the view of one authority, "Language is perhaps the most potent divisive force in India...."[5]

Conflict over a national language has been equally divisive in Ceylon. The Tamil-speaking minority, about 20 percent of the population, opposed Sinhalese, spoken by 68 percent of the people,

[4] Paul Grimes, "India: 15 Years of Freedom," *Headline Series*, No. 152, March–April, 1962, pp. 10–11.
[5] *Ibid.*, p. 12.

as the national tongue. Riots in 1958, in which many died, caused the Ceylonese government to temporize on this matter. To date the question of a national language remains unresolved.

RELIGIOUS CONFLICT

Religion may provide both bonds of unity and sources of friction. Buddhism is virtually synonymous with nationalism in Thailand. It also serves to forge links of unity in Cambodia and Burma. The Moslem faith plays a unifying role in Pakistan and Indonesia.

On occasion religious strife has been a disruptive influence. South Vietnam suffered violence because Ngo Dinh Diem, upon becoming Premier, found it necessary to suppress two religious groups, each supported by a private army, the Hoa Hao, a Buddhist sect, and the Cao Dai, an amalgam of many religious beliefs.[6] In 1963, violence broke out anew when Diem's government—he was a Catholic—attacked Buddhists. The UN General Assembly was asked to investigate religious persecution, and an investigating commission was dispatched for an inquiry on the spot. Action by the General Assembly became unnecessary when a military coup overthrew the Diem regime, an action in which Diem and his brother Ngo Dinh Nhu, the reputed "power behind the throne," were killed.

Hindu-Moslem outbreaks have not been eliminated by the two-way population exchange—Moslems moving from India to Pakistan and Hindus leaving Pakistan for India—which took place when India and Pakistan won their independence.

The language conflict between the Sinhalese and Tamils in Ceylon was intensified by religious difference; the Sinhalese are Buddhists, the Tamils, Hindus.

THE PROBLEM OF CHINESE MINORITY GROUPS IN SOUTHEAST ASIA

Southeast Asian states are vitally concerned with the presence of large Chinese minorities within their lands. "All the Southeast Asian countries, probably including even North Viet Nam, feared China. . . . This fear, it should be noted, is not based simply on China's Communist character. Communism only marginally increases the fear."[7] Sheer numbers make the Chinese population an important influence. Never fewer than 2 percent of the popula-

[6] Ellen J. Hammer, *The Struggle for Indochina* (Palo Alto, Calif.: Stanford University Press, 1954), pp. 51–52.
[7] Butwell, *op. cit.*, p. 144.

tion, as in Burma, the Chinese population runs as high as 45 percent of the total population of Malaysia, and an estimated 15 percent of the population of Thailand. Chinese traditions favor group homogeneity. In Moslem states such as Indonesia and Malaysia religious considerations make their integration into the local community difficult. Because a considerable proportion of the Chinese are engaged in commerce and light industry they frequently constitute a homogeneous economic group. In some instances—Thailand and Malaysia—they play a crucial role in the country's business life.

All countries of Southeast Asia consider the assimilation of the Chinese within their lands as vital to their security. Recently some assimilation with the peoples of their host country gives promise that with time the Chinese will lose their sense of Chinese nationhood and their disturbing identification with the China homeland. The fact remains that today the Chinese constitute a group apart from the rest of the population. In a number of instances this is as much a result of the policy of the Southeast Asian states as it is an inclination of the Chinese people themselves.

This situation raises the important question of which China has the loyalty of Chinese minorities. While accurate information is difficult to obtain, there is some evidence that more Chinese identify themselves with Communist China, which they consider permanently entrenched in power, than with Nationalist China. Communist movements in Malaysia and Thailand are almost entirely Chinese in their composition.

ECONOMIC FACTORS IN INTERNAL STABILITY

The degree of governmental participation in the country's economy, an issue that takes the form of socialism versus capitalism in Europe and America, does not as yet appear as a real issue. With the exception of India competition between capitalist and socialist parties has not set in. Socialism as a theoretical concept is widely advocated and engenders little opposition. Capitalism has fewer vocal adherents. Economic policies are rooted in pragmatic considerations, the overriding determinant being that which best ensures economic progress. In the name of socialism many differing economic measures have been tried, for socialism serves more as a slogan and an article of faith than a definition of an operative policy.[8] As

[8] See *New York Times,* Western Edition, October 16, 1963. Article by Thomas F. Brady, "India Looks at Socialism. Political Leaders Pay Respect to It but Each has His Own Interpretation."

in Africa, capitalism has been equated with imperialism. Only Communist states, China, North Korea, and North Vietnam, are trying to establish a socialist and later a Communist state in accordance with a Marxist blueprint. Where anti-imperialist agitation has less popular appeal, socialism has fewer advocates. Thus India, Burma, Ceylon, Cambodia, and Indonesia are avowedly socialist, while states which are not anti-imperialist, Taiwan, Malaysia, South Vietnam, the Philippines, and Thailand, purport to be capitalist. Asian states have a mixed economy. The relative size of the private and the public sector of the economy is unrelated to any assertions of socialism or capitalism.

A more meaningful basis for the application of socialist techniques results from a lack of private capital for projects of industrialization and modernization. Often only the government has been able to provide enough money for economic development. Government-owned industries and regulation of the economy arise out of pragmatic considerations.

Programs of social welfare occasion little opposition within Asian communities whether they are socialist or capitalist. Sometimes social-welfare responsibilities are undertaken beyond a country's means and impose a costly burden for the economy to sustain. As Butwell has observed, "Nations that should be tightening their belts have been seeking to enjoy the benefits of enlightened twentieth-century social legislation . . ." [9]

One might expect that programs of land reform would elicit vigorous opposition from the wealthier classes. In fact they have not. It may be that because, with the exception of Japan and Taiwan,[10] only modest attempts at land reform have taken place, those who might be disadvantaged through redistribution of the land have not fought against land reform.

To a degree, India is concerned with the issue of socialism versus capitalism. The Swatantra Party advocates capitalism. It has as yet presented no serious challenge to the Indian National Congress which is socialist. Nehru, for seventeen years India's Prime Minister, was strongly influenced by the Fabian Socialists during his college years in Great Britain and favored the socialist system. Indian socialism aims more at a mixed economy than total state owner-

[9] Butwell, *op. cit.*, p. 115.
[10] Wolf Ladejinsky, "Agrarian Reform in Asia," *Foreign Affairs*, Vol. 42, No. 3, April, 1964.

ship of all means of production or total regulation of production. There is ample room for a sizable private sector within the Indian economy. Socialism is conceived largely in terms of higher living standards, equal opportunity, better distribution of wealth, and cooperatives in agriculture and rural industry, rather than discouragement of private industry.

A uniquely Indian approach to the problem of land reform, the "land gift" movement of Achari Vinoba Bhave, has secured sizable contributions of land from big landowners for redistribution among the landless. By mid-1960, 4.4 million acres of land had been contributed.[11] Despite all the socialist intentions, and despite the fact that the Indian National Congress has ruled India since its independence in 1947, 90 percent of India's economy is still privately owned.

THE ROLE OF THE MILITARY

Military forces play a large role in the political life of most of the Asian states. The dislocations brought on by the end of the Second World War and the internal instability which appeared with such frequency after independence provided both cause and opportunity for the development of an independent political role for officers. In several states, the Philippines, Cambodia, Japan, Ceylon, and India, the armed forces have refrained from playing a large political role. In the Communist states, North Vietnam, North Korea, and China, party control is paramount. In the other states of Asia officers controlling the main agency of force are political and government leaders as well. The future of Laos will be determined largely by the outcome of the fight between the Communist Pathet Lao regiments, the Kong Le neutralist troops, and the right-wing armies of Phoumi Nosavan. General Ne Win has twice taken control of Burma through a *coup d'état*. Military strong men rule Thailand, Pakistan, South Vietnam, South Korea, and Nationalist China. They provide the locus of power in Indonesia, South Vietnam, and Nepal. When military strong men replace an inefficient, corrupt, and faltering regime they often bring stability. In states where the ideals of democracy have little popular appeal, the military strong man

[11] Paul Grimes, *op. cit.,* pp. 29–30.

may not force popular opposition. Such rule may in fact be more acceptable than inept civilian rule. Stability nevertheless erodes when the military regime itself becomes corrupt, inefficient, and capricious.

RELATIONS AMONG ASIAN STATES

When European states ruled Asia, Asian colonies had international relationships only with European states. After independence foreign relations among Asian states commenced. Conflict of interests and disagreements concerning boundary lines have on occasion disturbed their harmony. Cooperation through the Economic Commission for Asia and the Far East (ECAFE) of ECOSOC, through the Colombo Plan, and in such gatherings as the Bandung Conference and the meetings of the Afro-Asian group at the UN have brought Asian states together. While cooperation among Asian states in a number of delimited areas does take place, Asian states do not present a united front to the world. Some of the clashes between Asian countries have necessitated worldwide involvement.

INDIA AND PAKISTAN

Great Britain's grant of independence to the Indian subcontinent was complicated by divisiveness and hostility between the Hindu majority and Moslem minority. Independence, when it came on August 15, 1947, divided the subcontinent into two sovereign states—India and Pakistan. To reduce bloodshed a large migration was carried out. Hindus and Sikhs left the Pakistani province of Punjab while millions of Moslems departed India to take up residence in Pakistan.

Controversies erupted over the possession of the princely states of Junagadh, Hyderabad, Kashmir, and Jammu. Junagadh and Hyderabad both had populations with a Hindu majority and were surrounded by Indian territory. In each case, however, the ruler was a Moslem who preferred to annex his state to Pakistan. Indian "police action" assured annexation to India in harmony with the popular will. The possession of Kashmir and Jammu is still unsettled.

The provinces of Kashmir and Jammu are located between West Pakistan and India. The possession of these provinces has become the most serious cause for conflict between India and Pakistan.

Kashmir and Jammu were Indian princedoms. Under the Act of Independence of 1947, which provided for the partition of India, Kashmir and Jammu were permitted to accede to either state. The population is predominantly Moslem and is presumed to favor affiliation with Pakistan. However, the Maharajah elected to annex the provinces to India. This decision was touched off by an invasion of the provinces by Pakistani tribesmen. India accepted annexation and said that after Pakistani forces withdrew, the desires of the people would govern the final settlement of this question.[12]

India accused Pakistan of complicity in the invasion. Pakistan contended that it tried to discourage the invasion but held that India's annexations were illegal in any case. During 1948, some fighting between Indian and Pakistani forces took place and war threatened. The issue was therefore brought before the Security Council which appointed a commission to investigate and mediate between the parties. A strategy for settling the conflict was sketched out beginning with a cease-fire and to be followed by the removal of persons and forces from India and Pakistan who were not regular residents of the territory. The Indians would retain responsibility for maintaining internal order, but once order was established, free elections would determine sovereignty.

A cease-fire which went into effect on July 27, 1949, was won, and solution of the substantive issue of possession failed. Some Pakistani forces remain in Kashmir and India insists that they must leave before she reduces her military complement. Pakistan claims that it has removed its forces but that India is not making good on its commitments to leave. It has proposed arbitration of the issue, which India has refused. The Vale of Kashmir, the area that forms the nub of the conflict, is in India's possession, and this may account for her less tractable position in this matter. Later India foreclosed the rights of secession under any circumstance.

While the issue presently appears beyond solution, peripheral questions not without importance have been settled. In 1960, Pakistan and India agreed to the division of the waters of the Indus River system. Part of the headwater lies in Kashmir. With funds from the World Bank, dams, canals, and other devices have been constructed which will enable Pakistan and India to use these waters for irrigation and other purposes. Antagonisms between these

[12] *Everyman's United Nations, op. cit.,* p. 125.

two powers have not prevented them from both participating in the Colombo Plan and the Commonwealth of Nations.

Kashmir is a potentially explosive issue. It defines all relations between India and Pakistan and other states. United States assistance to Pakistan in connection with its membership in SEATO and CENTO was considered a hostile act by India. When the Chinese occupied Indian territory in 1962, Pakistan moved closer to China and agreed to border delimitations unacceptable to India. American assistance to India to defend itself against Peking brought about an anti-American posture by Pakistan. In 1965, Malaysia's friendship with India provoked Pakistan to sever relations with Kuala Lumpur. The danger of this unresolved conflict has been fully underscored by the eruption of fighting in 1965 despite the strongest international pressures against a resort to force. A temporary cease-fire exacted by the Security Council with Washington and Moscow in agreement stopped all but sporadic fighting. Kosygin, the Russian Premier, succeeded in bringing Ayub Khan, the President of Pakistan, and Shastri, the Indian Prime Minister, together for talks in Tashkent. With Kosygin's mediatory assistance, Shastri and Khan agreed to renounce the use of force and troops along the battlefront were withdrawn and thinned out. The possession of Kashmir and Jammu is still at issue. India holds most of the territory and refuses to give it up. Pakistan wants it and insists on self-determination, which would make the area hers.

THE FEDERATION OF MALAYSIA

Among the larger (in area) British colonies of Asia, Malaya was the last to become independent. Only after the Communist rebellion was substantially suppressed,[13] was Malaya given its independence, its defense still guaranteed by Great Britain. At issue in negotiating Malayan independence was the future of Singapore at the southern tip of the country. Singapore provided the most important port facilities for Malaya, and Malaya was the natural hinterland for the port. Malaya and Singapore had been treated as a single entity by the British, and so it seemed that they should become inde-

[13] The Communist rebels were almost entirely drawn from the Chinese population. Remnants of the rebel forces still exist and find refuge in Malayan jungles. They have been of little significance since 1957.

pendent as one. Malayan leaders opposed the inclusion of Singapore in Malaya because of its large Chinese population. 80 percent of its 1,665,000 [14] people were Chinese, and this added to the 37½ percent of Chinese origin in Malaya's population of 7,000,000 would produce a larger Chinese than Malayan population. Singapore remained, therefore, a British colony when Malaya gained its independence.

The People's Action Party, the ruling party of Singapore, led by Lee Kaun Yew, Singapore's Prime Minister, wanted to merge Singapore with Malaya. Tengku Abdul Rahman, the Malayan Prime Minister, suggested an alternative proposal for a Malaysian Federation which would include Malaya, Singapore, and the British possessions on the island of Borneo—Sarawek, Brunei, and British North Borneo.

This proposal had many things to commend it. The addition of Sarawak and Brunei would serve to reduce somewhat the proportion of Chinese in the federation, and make Singapore a more acceptable member of the federation in Malayan eyes. It would also end British rule over four of its Asian possessions. For her part London was more than agreeable to such a solution. There was growing fear that Indonesia had acquisitive interests in this area, and a settlement bringing these colonies into Malaysia would present Indonesia with a final solution which it could not change.

Creation of a Malaysian state had support within the territories.[15] The Sultan of Brunei initially supported the federation but withdrew at the eleventh hour after local disturbances demonstrated opposition. Opposition to the federation came from Indonesia and the Philippines. The Philippines claimed possession of North Borneo and expressed doubt that the federation represented the desires of the peoples of Sabah. Indonesia was even more adamant, insisting that the people of the Bornean territories were against the federation and that the whole federation was no more than an elaborate scheme for retaining British imperialism in the area. It was rumored that the Philippines and Indonesia had an additional objection,

[14] *The World Almanac, 1963* (New York: World-Telegram and Sun, 1963), p. 322.
[15] Robert O. Tilman, "Malaysia: The Problems of Federation," *The Western Political Quarterly*, Vol. XVI, No. 4, December, 1963, pp. 897–898.

which they were loath to state openly, that is, Malaysia would be too weak to prevent Communist China's penetration of Southeast Asia.[16]

A meeting of the heads of state of Malaya, Indonesia, and the Philippines in the summer of 1963 asked U Thant to ascertain the feelings of the peoples of Sarawak and North Borneo on their merger with Malaya. Presumably, favorable opinion would end Philippine and Indonesian objections. U Thant's investigation found general support for the merger of territories, and following the Secretary-General's report, Malaysia was established. The Malaysian Federation, born on September 16, 1963, amalgamated the territory of Malaya, which had been independent since 1957, with the British colonies of Singapore, Sarawak, and North Borneo (Sabah). The Philippines did not press their objections. Sukarno, on the other hand, denounced Malaysia as an outpost of British imperialism, vowed to destroy it, and openly sent armed raiding parties into Malaysian territory. His action, coming hard on the heels of the Indonesian threat to use force to annex West Irian (Dutch New Guinea) without waiting for a plebiscite of the Papuan people concerned, placed Indonesia in the anomalous position of favoring self-determination except when it was disadvantageous to Indonesia. It drew attention to Indonesia's imperialistic ambitions in Southeast Asia. In 1964, Indonesia withdrew from the UN over the election of Malaysia to the Security Council. Together with Communist China, Indonesia rebuked the UN as a tool of American imperialism and called on socialist and neutralist states to secede from the UN and form their own "United Nations." This appeal gained no support. An abortive Communist rebellion in 1965 on the island of Java augured a change in Indonesia's policy. The Communists were suppressed and the army of Indonesia gained effective control of the land. Relations with Peking, implicated in the Communist putsch, cooled considerably. The campaign against the UN came to an end and infiltration of Malaysia by Indonesian forces ended. Singapore, the commercial and industrial center of Malaysia, with its large Chinese population posed a greater threat to Malayan control of the federation, and this led to Singapore's secession in 1965.

[16] Hamilton Fish Armstrong, "The Troubled Birth of Malaysia," *Foreign Affairs,* Vol. 41, No. 4, July, 1963, pp. 673–693.

THE ROLE OF COMMUNIST CHINA IN ASIA

China today may well be the most feared and the most respected state in Asia. Under Communist rule the country has changed from a corrupt, divided, and purposeless land mass to a dynamic, disciplined, big power. Its large population, great area, and incipient atomic arsenal assures its vital influence on the Asian continent. As we have seen, the Chinese communities of Southeast Asia give Peking considerable leverage there. Now it militantly contests the role of the United States, Great Britain, the Soviet Union, and India on the Asian continent.

CHINA AND SOUTHEAST ASIA

A former ambassador to Communist China from a neutral Southeast Asian state is reported to have voiced the sentiment of all Southeast Asian states when he said, "We fear China so much that we must guard our every word lest we reveal how we truly feel." [17] Several countries maintain diplomatic relations with Communist China—Burma, Indonesia, Laos, Cambodia, and North Vietnam. The Philippines, Thailand, and South Vietnam recognize the Nationalist regime. Malaysia has not exchanged ambassadors with either Chinese government.

Of the non-Communist countries of Southeast Asia, Cambodia has moved most completely into Peking's orbit. It has been a spokesman of Communist China in the UN. In 1963, Premier Sihanouk deliberately antagonized the United States and Great Britain, almost severing diplomatic relations, to move more fully into Peking's sphere of influence. Cambodian security was being promoted through the closest association with Communist China.

Indonesia, Burma, and Laos expected to come to terms with Mao's regime through neutralism. For Indonesia this has meant friendly collaboration and virulent anti-Americanism. Sukarno's regime had rested upon a trinity of support, the army, the Moslem organizations, and the Indonesian Communist Party (PKI). After the PKI-supported uprising of 1965, Indonesia moved away from its close collaboration with Peking while reaffirming its intention to sustain harmonious relations.

Burmese neutralism contributed to the climate of opinion needed

[17] Butwell, *op. cit.*, p. 144.

for its border delimitation agreement with China. The presence of Nationalist Chinese military units in northern Burma led to strained relations with Formosa and this in and of itself encouraged closer relations with Peking. Burma, under Ne Win's leadership, conducts a policy of strict neutralism and is neither close to nor hostile to Mao Tse Tung's regime.

Laos has had to contend with fratricidal conflict. Right-wing, neutralist, and Communist forces have all bid for power. Under the Geneva accord of July, 1962, the neutralist Prince Souvanna Phouma became Prime Minister. His regime hoped to win the benevolent interest of Communist China. However, Peking's support was placed behind the Communist-led Pathet Lao headed by Prince Souphanouvong. Laotian security under a non-Communist regime forced Souvanna Phouma to accept American and Russian assistance which helped stabilize his threatened government. A consuming involvement in the Vietnamese fighting has distracted Peking's attention and has given Souvanna Phouma a chance to consolidate his position despite China's distaste for Laotian friendship with the United States and the Soviet Union.

On the other hand, Thailand and the Philippines preferred to deal with the menace of Communist China by membership in the anti-Communist SEATO alliance. South Vietnam, prohibited from participation in SEATO by the Geneva agreements of 1954, has strengthened its hand against Communist China by an alliance with the United States. Escalation of the conflict with the Viet Cong necessitated greater dependence upon Washington. Bombing of North Vietnam and the introduction of large-scale American forces brought forth threats of Chinese intervention on behalf of North Vietnam and the Viet Cong. Such intervention is militarily difficult, probably too difficult to mount in face of United States air power.

COMMUNIST CHINA AND JAPAN

Japan has close historical ties with China. Even at the present time, when Japan has developed political and economic ties with the United States and the countries of Western Europe, its attitudes toward Communist China are influenced by at least a vague understanding of the importance that Chinese culture has played in the molding of Japan's heritage. Despite their differing political attitudes, the Japanese feel that a special relationship exists between China and Japan, and that its historic ties of culture, political destiny, and economic cooperation must eventually lead to closer ties. These factors militate against Japan's pursuit of the same "hard" line toward China as that adopted by the United States.

Trade with China is useful if not essential to the prosperity of Japan. Before the Second World War, China was Japan's most important customer. The Chinese market and the desire for Chinese resources led Japan to exploit the economic opportunities that China offered. Despite the fact that Southeast Asia and the United States have displaced China as a market for Japanese goods, the Japanese are loath to give up the potentialities of the Chinese market. Communist China has not addressed Japan with the same vituperation applied against other Western powers. Over the years the policy toward Japan has shifted between "hard," "soft," and "intermediate" lines.[18] Peking would like to wean Japan away from its close association with the United States and pro-Western policies.

Japan, on the other hand, must be attentive to United States pressures. The United States is a most important ally and provides an essential market for Japanese goods. One authority observed, "In the long run it seems likely that China's total impact on Japan will decrease. Actual Japanese experience in China is now limited almost entirely to the older generations. Culturally and economically, Japan is looking well beyond China and Asia. The growing diversification of Japan's world outlook and its increasing national involvement will tend to reduce China's traditional significance. ... In the over-all picture there would seem to be more opportunities for Sino-Japanese economic and political rivalry than for cooperation." [19]

CHINA AND INDIA

Within the United Nations India has been a spokesman for seating Communist China. It accepted Chinese control of Tibet and said little when Peking's troops suppressed the Tibetan people in 1959. In 1954, it signed an agreement with Communist China based upon the so-called "Five Principles of Peaceful Coexistence," *The Pancha Sheela*. These principles provided for:

[18] Paul F. Langer, "China and Japan," *Current History*, Vol. 45, No. 265, September, 1963, pp. 144–150.
[19] *Ibid.*, p. 181.

1. Mutual respect for each other's territorial integrity and sovereignty;
2. Non-aggression;
3. Non-interference in each other's affairs;
4. Equality and mutual advantage;
5. Peaceful co-existence and cooperation.[20]

Yet, in 1959, the Chinese occupied Indian territory in the northwest. The border areas involved had not been clearly demarked and had not been finally settled. Nevertheless, the manner of Chinese acquisition of the area in question was troubling to the Indians. In the fall of 1954, Nehru had raised the question of Indian-Chinese boundaries. While on a visit to Peking he asked about Chinese maps showing sections of India within China. Chou En-lai assured the Indian Prime Minister that these maps had been produced by Chiang Kai-shek's regime and that corrected versions had not as yet been published. Nehru had every reason to believe that the Chinese Communists did not consider the border issue important and that this could easily be settled through negotiations.[21] Newer maps when they were eventually produced (see map, p. 337) showed that Chinese territorial ambitions involved Indian territory as well as other territories. By 1959, Chou admitted that Peking was ready to press her boundary claims.[22]

In October, 1962, Chinese forces invaded Indian territory. The main attack was in the North East Frontier Agency (NEFA) area but advances were also made in the northwest. This invasion was justified on the grounds that the MacMahon line, which China had crossed, was imposed on China by "imperialist" Britain at a time when China was weak. Peking proposed a revision of the MacMahon-line border under which China would "accept" only territory in the northwestern (Ladakh) area while ceding to India "Chinese" land in the northeast.

China's action was a crudely disguised act of aggression. It undermined the position of those Indian leaders who were most friendly to Peking and strengthened India's dependence on the West. Chinese behavior underlined the futility of treaties of nonaggression with Communist China. Nonaggression pacts were tactical devices

[20] Sripati Chandra-Sekhr, *Red China and Asian View* (New York: Frederick A. Praeger, 1961), p. 202.
[21] Werner Levi, "The Sino-Indian Border War," *Current History,* Vol. 45, No. 265, September, 1963, pp. 136–143.
[22] *Ibid.,* p. 139.

rather than binding commitments and would not be permitted to stand in the way of Peking's ambitions.

Fighting lasted for one month as the Indians were poorly prepared to withstand the Chinese onslaught. Then the Chinese unilaterally declared a cease-fire and on December 1 began a withdrawal of troops from much of the area gained in the fighting. Despite claims by both states that they favored negotiations to settle their dispute, such negotiations have not taken place. The intercession of six "friendly" powers, Burma, Cambodia, Ceylon, Ghana, Indonesia, and the United Arab Republic, yielded no tangible results. The Chinese, basing their claims on their own maps and the "illegality" of the MacMahon line, accused India of intrusion into Chinese territory and justified their action as being merely defensive. The Indians charged that China wanted negotiations on "what part" and "how much" Indian territory it should receive. Nehru proposed settlement by the International Court of Justice or the full acceptance of the proposals of the Afro-Asian "six." These suggestions were rejected by Peking.

The area in dispute was so bleak and sparsely populated that some believed that China was guilty of maladroit as well as aggressive tactics. However, a careful analysis of China's action leads to the conclusion that this aggression was carefully considered and that important national goals were gained thereby.

It is likely that China wishes to establish her primacy among the states of Asia. India is a natural competitor for continental leadership. She is a leading neutralist power and her word enjoys great moral stature. She is a leading force in the United Nations. Her large population and stable regime as well as her talented leadership and friendly associations with the United States and the Soviet Union give her greater weight internationally than Communist China. China used military force to undermine India's role on the continent and in the world at large.

The competing appeals of Chinese and Indian leadership rest in large part upon the success of their efforts in economic development. For China, economic development involves a number of harshly directed forced marches by an unbending dictatorship. The needs of the Chinese people for consumer goods are put aside in the desire to effect rapid industrialization. India's first efforts in economic development have been directed toward the elimination

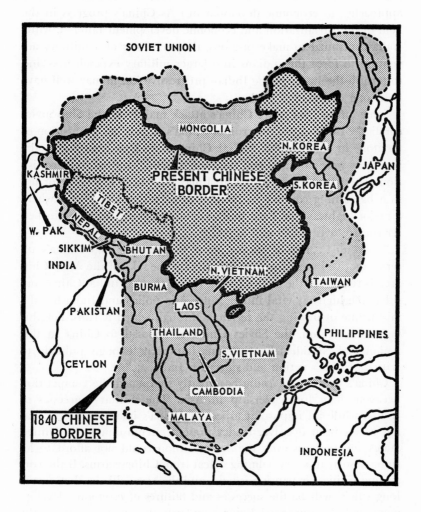

SOVIET UNION

MONGOLIA

N.KOREA

JAPAN

KASHMIR

PRESENT CHINESE
BORDER

S.KOREA

TIBET

NEPAL

W. PAK.

SIKKIM

BHUTAN

INDIA

N.VIETNAM

TAIWAN

BURMA

LAOS

PAKISTAN

THAILAND

PHILIPPINES

S.VIETNAM

CEYLON

CAMBODIA

1840 CHINESE
BORDER

MALAYA

INDONESIA

of starvation. Then, without sacrificing the democratic nature of the Indian state, economic development rests upon planned progress rather than draconian laws. (See Chapter 13 for a discussion of approaches to economic development.) As China's progress in the field of industrialization and economic development faltered, while India continued to make progress, the usefulness of a military adventure to force the Indians into larger military expenditures and to tarnish the luster of the Indian progressive image may well have been one of Peking's goals.

Some authorities relate China's attack mainly to the Sino-Soviet conflict.[23] In this view the crux of China's aims is her acquisition of territory in the Ladakh (Aksai Chin) area. Her interests in the northeast were minimal and clearly negotiable. Indeed, the acquisition of territory in the NEFA area may have been intended for use as a bargaining counter in the aim to gain the Aksai Chin where a major highway had been built, enabling Peking to maintain better control over Tibet and Sinkiang.

"It would ... not be totally amiss to speculate that China's ulterior motive in making war on India for the sake of the Aksai Chin area is related to the Soviet Union rather than to India. China considers the highway vital in her Inner Asia policy and India has the misfortune of owning the territory through which it runs. For this very same reason, the Soviet Union is opposed to China in this region and considers her interests important enough publicly to criticize China's action and side with India. ..."[24]

China's invasion of India has greatly sharpened the competition between them for leadership in Asia. The military successes of China, while an important aspect of China's image of power, has not as yet been decisive. Under present circumstances the United States and perhaps even the Soviet Union could not afford to let India absorb an overwhelming defeat from Chinese arms. If the ring around Chinese expansion is held, and this seems likely, then in the long run it will be the successes and failures of economic development and the improved living standards that will determine the outcome of the conflict over leadership in Asia.

[23] *Ibid.,* pp. 142–143.
[24] *Ibid.,* p. 142.

The Sino-Soviet Conflict

The emergence of a sharp conflict between China and the Soviet Union in the 1960's came as an unexpected development. It seemed no more than logical that with the presence of the United States as a formidable enemy of both China and Russia these Communist states would make common cause in face of a common enemy. Ideologically they were both Communist and presumably at one. Nevertheless, it has become increasingly clear that divisive issues have been too great to maintain unity despite the American enemy.

In 1959, the Soviet Union began to withdraw her economic and technical assistance from China. In 1960, a reduction of trade between them took place. China, with some significant success, appealed for the support of Communist parties in underdeveloped lands against the Soviet leadership. Her success was greatest in Asia where only the Communist parties of India and Ceylon appeared to be in Moscow's camp.[25]

By 1964, the conflict between the Soviet Union and Communist China became an enduring struggle dangerously close to an open break. Leadership of the forces of communism in Asia was at stake, and the expansion of this conflict to Africa and Latin America was visible. While China has met with some success in seeking the leading role among Communists in Asia, as already noted, she has been weakened in having to rely solely on her own resources, human and material, for her economic development. She can no longer rely on assured Soviet assistance should she become involved in war. Only if the Soviet Union's interests are threatened by a defeat of Communist China may China expect military aid. Indeed, as between China and the neutralist leaders in Asian states, Soviet support will go to the latter to build up her own interests in the area and to encourage India and Indonesia to serve as counterweights to China's threatened domination.

COOPERATION AMONG ASIAN STATES

The decade of the 1960's finds the states of Asia absorbed with their internal problems. Tension over Western colonialism is ebbing. The urgent problems of eradicating a legacy of poverty and

[25] Robert A. Scalapino, "Moscow, Peking and the Communist Parties of Asia," *Foreign Affairs*, Vol. 42, No. 2, January, 1963.

stagnation by promoting economic and social development are of overriding concern. Because of its size, its population, and its resources the great powers cannot remain oblivious to the future of Asia and the preoccupation of Asian states with problems of development.

Asia is in the throes of a breakdown in the old social order and a reorganization of social systems. This is an inevitable by-product of urbanization, industrialization, and the spread of literacy and education. Multinational organizations play a needed role in helping countries achieve their economic and social goals. The Afro-Asian group in the United Nations provides coalition strength for winning UN assistance. The Economic Commission for Asia and the Far East (ECAFE) enables its members to cooperate on specific projects. As an institution ECAFE has aided countries in development planning and economic research. It has advised on problems of finance, inland transportation and communication, trade, and resource development. It has undertaken studies on the social consequence of economic development.[26]

The role of the Commonwealth of Nations in Asia has been best exemplified by the Colombo Plan, which it initiated in 1950. Though relatively unpublicized, this may well be the most important agency of cooperation among the non-Communist states of South and Southeast Asia. This plan allows full play for cooperative planning, consultations, and exchanges in technical assistance. In addition to its Asian membership the Colombo Plan associates in its work members of the Commonwealth—Great Britain, Australia, and New Zealand—and also Japan and the United States.

International questions of little concern to Asia elicit no more than passing attention from Asian states. Problems which touch the Asian scene enlist the passionate concern of the whole continent. International peace and security are of overriding importance in Asia. Peace and security are, however, in large part dependent upon stability which in turn rests with the ability of the Asian state to modernize its social system, develop its economy, and distribute widely the benefits gained. The course of history requires that Asia must remain a continent of independent states outside the dominating influence and policy direction of aggressive communism and reactionary imperialism if peace and security are to be preserved.

[26] *Everyman's United Nations, op. cit.,* pp. 245–260.

CHAPTER 12

Latin America in Ferment

LATIN AMERICA today is a continent in ferment. Few of the South and Central American states have been free from the dislocations of social revolution. A revolutionary ideology has taken root, often in the form of *Fidelisma*. What is happening in Latin America to-day is not an outgrowth of nationalist movements as we have seen them arise in the countries of the Middle East, Africa, and Asia. Nationalism as a movement to win freedom from colonial control has no logical place in contemporary Latin America. By 1825, Bolivar led the liberation of the South American states. Still a mystique of anti-imperialism is widespread within Latin American lands. It is not concerned with any identifiable colonial possessions on the continent. However, it is attuned to domination of Latin America by North American businessmen supported by Washington.

Latin American nationalism in a contemporary sense may be more specifically identified as the newly developed political consciousness of the impoverished masses of peasants and working men. These groups are at long last becoming conscious of their existence as part of a nation. Instead of the traditional concept of nationalism which is based on differences between peoples, this nationalism is centered on social revolution. It is more concerned with the social destiny of the people than with national being and national power.

The cold war as a Latin American phenomenon is not a show-down between the United States and the Soviet Union but rather an internal ferment involving indigenous forces and having all of the characteristics of a social revolution. Soviet or Chinese subversion or aggression are of marginal importance here; however, the growth of mass support for communism is a serious concern. Com-

341

LATIN AMERICA

BAHAMA IS

MEXICO

CUBA
JAMAICA HAITI DOMINICAN
REPUBLIC
Puerto Rico

BRITISH
HONDURAS
GUATEMALA
EL SALVADOR
NICARAGUA
COSTA RICA
CANAL
ZONE
PANAMA

Antigua
Guadeloupe
Dominica
Martinique Saint Lucia
Barbados
Aruba Curaçao Grenada TRINIDAD
AND
TOBAGO

VENEZUELA
BRITISH GUIANA
SURINAM
FRENCH GUIANA

COLOMBIA

GALAPAGOS IS.
ECUADOR

PERU

BRAZIL

BOLIVIA

PARAGUAY

JUAN FERNÁNDEZ IS.

CHILE

ARGENTINA

URUGUAY

FALKLAND IS.

:::: Latin American Free Trade Area
▓ Central American Common Market

53058 1-66

342

munists aim to capture control of the forces of revolutionary change. Therefore, Latin America has moved very much to the center of the world's stage and its future is of vital interest to the United States and of more than passing importance to the Soviet Union and Communist China.

Revolutions are not new in Latin America but in the past most were of little lasting importance. They brought to leadership new individuals and groups who ruled in the same way as the old rulers. The masses were unconcerned and largely unaffected by them. The oppression, maladministration, poverty, and corruption did not change.

The revolution of contemporary Latin America is of an entirely different order. Its goals are basic and far-reaching, seeking the fundamental reordering of society. In essence, "the social revolution represents the changeover and restructuring of a whole society, of its institutions and of its relationship to the outside world. Latin America is today going through this revolutionary process, and whether this great transition is accomplished through violent or through peaceful and gradual means, she will fairly soon bear little resemblance to the Latin America we have known until now ..." [1] In other words, the social revolution involves drastic changes in the economic, social, and political life of the Latin American states. It is marked by a growing importance of commerce and industry in the economy of each country. Its motive forces seek the replacement of the traditional leadership of the landowning class by groups concerned with business and industry. The former privileged classes, unable or unwilling to adapt themselves to this change, are eliminated, or, at the very least, their control over the government and politics of the country is brought to an end. They no longer dominate military leadership which now tends to come from other groups within society and therefore is proving ready to disassociate itself from the interests and aspirations of the older privileged classes.

Now labor leaders, businessmen, the younger military officers, and most especially the intellectuals win mass following. They rise in power by promising to bring an end to the extremes of great wealth

[1] Tad Szulc, *The Winds of Revolution, Latin America Today—and Tomorrow* (New York: Frederick A. Praeger, 1963), p. 23.

for the few and grinding poverty for the majority. They proclaim their aim to end all marks of privilege and institute equal treatment for all. In place of ignorance, disease, stagnation, and oppression they promise education, medicine and sanitation, progressive development of the economy, and the rule of law.

Forces advocating social change are the impetus of Latin America's new nationalism and often they are critical of the United States. From 1940 to 1960, during the Second World War and in the postwar era, Latin America was neglected by Washington. The war itself centered in Europe, Africa, Asia, and North Africa and always appeared remote from Latin America. The participation in it by some Latin American states—a Brazilian division fought in Italy and Mexican air units in the Pacific—escaped notice. Although all of the Latin American states except Argentina eventually became allies of the United States, this received little recognition. At the end of the war the United States quickly became preoccupied with the cold war which again focused American attention upon Europe, the Middle East, Asia, and later Africa. From 1945 to 1960, Latin America appeared safely insulated from Communist appeal. The absorbing concern with meeting Communist aggression in other parts of the world resulted in inattention to Latin American developments. Only about 3 percent of United States foreign aid went into the area. Reactionary, corrupt, and self-serving dictators were embraced as partners of the United States, largely because they loudly asserted their anti-communism and maintained order and an outward calm within their countries. American leaders believed that all was well in the hemisphere. Latin American support for United States policies in the UN and in the Organization of American States (OAS) was taken as evidence of friendship for Washington and the people of the United States.

Popular discontent and popular support for social change were already evident during the 1950's. The new trend was clearly recognizable in Bolivia, where in 1952 an uprising did more than replace an oligarchic regime. The tin mines, producing Bolivia's major export commodity, were nationalized. Peasant uprisings drove the owners of large estates off their lands. The new president, Paz Estenssoro, decreed the abolition of large estates—about 70 percent of the land in agriculture was owned by 4.5 percent of the rural landholders [2]—and the redistribution of land among the landless peasantry. The revolution succeeded because the Bolivian army was defeated by armed miners and the revolutionary fervor of the peasantry. It was poorly understood elsewhere that Bolivia's uprising was more than an isolated occurrence. Not until Vice-President Nixon visited South America in May, 1958, and was received in Peru and Colombia with violent attacks, spat upon, and had rocks thrown at his automobile did the realities of the deep unrest and growing hatred for the United States became apparent. The direction of Cuba's government under Castro, which became increasingly clear in 1959 and 1960, served to corroborate the growing suspicions that the cause of democracy and the image of the United States were in deep trouble south of the Rio Grande.

The decade of the 1950's revealed a trend away from the traditional military dictatorships. Such regimes were characterized by their attempts to maintain the old order. All too often rulers amassed great personal fortunes. Governments were corrupt, reactionary, and often led by dissolute and brutal men. Because dictators lacked popular support, an exasperated people was able to overthrow a number of them. A half-dozen of them fell during the decade, in addition to the Bolivian dictator. The dictatorship of Marcos Pérez Jiménez was replaced by the democratic regime of Rómulo Betancourt in Venezuela; Manuel A. Odría was similarly deposed by Pedro G. Beltran in Peru; in Colombia the Pinilla dictatorship was brought to an end by President Alberto Lleras Camargo; Juan B. Peron was driven from power in Argentina by Arturo Frondizi; and in Cuba the dictator Fulgencio Batista fled before the marching armies of Fidel Castro.

THE SOCIAL REVOLUTION

A social revolution expresses itself most visibly in politics, as revolutionary upheaval is always directed against the seat of power, the government. Such rebellion is threatening in most of the countries of Latin America. Social revolutions take place when two sets of conditions are met. First, the life of the people becomes intol-

[2] *The Worldmark Encyclopedia of the Nations* (New York: Worldmark Press, Harper & Brothers, 1960), "Boliva," p. 76.

erable. Their lot is one of misery, injustice, ignorance, and frustration. Recourse to peaceful methods of change is unavailing, and violent overthrow of the group in power is the best solution. This situation making for revolution exists in many Latin American states. Second, forces willing to lead and carry out the revolution must exist. These forces are present. The popular demand for social change cannot be denied. The question is whether Castroite Communist forces will direct the social revolution in the path which they have chosen or whether the anti-Communist progressive forces, using the resources made available through the Alliance for Progress, will guide the revolution along democratic lines putting forward their plans for economic development and instituting social justice.

Conditions Making for a Revolutionary Situation

In Rio de Janeiro they are called *favelas;* in Recife they are known as *mocambos;* in São Paulo, "the garbage room"; in Santiago they are called *callambas;* Lima has its *boradas;* Bogota has its *bohilas;* Caracas calls them *ranchos;* and Buenos Aires refers to them as *villas miserias.* No matter what they are called they are in fact among the world's worst slums. About one-third, perhaps even more, of the people that live in the principal cities of the twenty Latin American states live in these indescribable slums.[3]

These slums are shantytowns made up of tiny wooden or cardboard shacks without light or running water in or near the premises, without facilities for garbage and sewage disposal. They have been considered worse than the worst slum dwellings in Southern Europe or even China. The slums are literally stinking, rat-infested, and disease-ridden. Pure water supplies are exceptional. A great deal of Latin America's health problems can be traced to bad water. Essential knowledge about health and sanitation is unknown and often unavailable to the people living there. Gastrointestinal diseases and communicable and other diseases of childhood, such as dysentery and typhoid fever, are widespread. In Lima half of the children born in the slums die before the age of one.[4] In 1959, infant mortality in Latin America was 9.2 percent. It was highest in

[3] Gerald Clark, *The Coming Explosion in Latin America* (New York: David McKay, 1963), p. 7.
[4] Clark, *op. cit.,* p. 9.

Haiti, 17.1 percent, and only slightly less, 16 percent, in the depressed northeast of Brazil.[5]

The seriousness of this condition is made worse by the lack of doctors, nurses, hospitals, and medicine. Latin America today has about 100,000 physicians, fewer than one doctor per 2,000 inhabitants, where one doctor per 1,000 is considered a necessary minimum, and doctors are unevenly spread throughout the hemisphere. The ratio in Haiti is one doctor for every 10,000 inhabitants, while in the larger cities of Argentina and Uruguay a favorable one to 1,000 relationship exists.[6]

Bad as the urban slums are reputed to be, the situation in the rural areas appears even worse. Almost all of the land, 90 percent, is owned by 10 percent of the people.[7] A large proportion of the peasantry is landless, or almost landless. They live in one-room hovels made of mud with dirt floors together with their few animals. Education is difficult to obtain and among Latin American peasants ignorance and disease are the general rule. Most of the best lands are to be found in the *latifundios,* large landed estates often owned by absentee landlords. Peasants are usually paid in commodities and housing. A large number of peasants earn no money and are, therefore, outside any money economy. *Latifundios* grow cash crops for export. Therefore, despite the general fertility of the soil, Latin American states do not grow enough food to feed their population. This creates a need for large-scale imports of food. It is also a cause of malnutrition and hunger.

During the past decade an enormous number of peasants have moved from their land to the rapidly growing city slums. Peasants have been thronging into the cities because for them the squalor of the city slum seems an improvement over the poverty and hopelessness of life in the village. Some of the peasants bursting the bonds of what is after all essentially a feudal system have invaded estates that were not in production or which were administered for absentee landlords.[8] There has been a growth in squatter occupation

[5] Szulc, *op. cit.,* p. 61.

[6] *Ibid.,* p. 54.

[7] *Ibid.,* p. 62.

[8] John Scott, *How Much Progress?* (New York: A Report to the Publisher of Time, 1963), p. 111. "About 90% of Latin America's farmed land is owned by 10% of the land-owners. For the big owner, land is often a status symbol, rather than a means of production; often he lives in the

of lands. In earlier years squatters were dealt with harshly by local and national police. Recently there has been a tendency by some governments to accommodate this situation and even to legalize the squatters' possessions of land.

The 10 percent of the land existing outside of the *latifundios* provide no useful example for the solution of Latin American land problems. *Minifundios,* dwarf holdings, are uneconomical. They cannot afford the use of modern farm equipment, good seed, and fertilizer. Their landholders lack education to farm effectively.

Little wonder then that the Latin American peasant is among the least productive in the world. As John Scott points out, "While a single U.S. farmer feeds 25 people, and the Soviet farmer 10, the Latino farmer is on the level with the Communist Chinese. His work feeds four." [9] With the growth in population, Latin American agriculture proves less and less able to feed its people. Between 1957 and 1962, the per-capita food production went down by about 3 percent and in some countries—Colombia, Argentina, and Chile— by as much as 14 percent.[10] The United States farmer may be as much as one hundred times more productive than his average Latin American counterpart. Much of the failure in Latin American agriculture may be ascribed to the *latifundios* in which the land is not used to its maximum advantage. Owners are reluctant to make the investments which will increase productivity.

Land reform has, at least until recently, been wholly unacceptable to ruling groups. Landowners who dominated the legislative bodies invariably refused to enact meaningful land reform measures. Even Mexico, which underwent its social revolution thirty or more years ago, has had only limited success with land reform. Bolivia, Venezuela, and, more recently, the Dominican Republic have undertaken programs of land reform. In the latter two states, the lands of the dictators Pérez Jiménez and Trujillo were confiscated for redistribution to the agricultural producer.[11] In several of the other Latin American states—Chile, Panama, Colombia, and Peru—proposals for

---

city, uses the profits of his farm for other ventures. In many cases he does not even farm the land, but allows it to lie fallow until appreciation of values allows him to sell it bit by bit at high prices..."

[9] *op. cit.,* p. 110.
[10] *Ibid.,* p. 110 and table on p. 135.
[11] *Ibid.,* p. 110.

land reform have been under study. The Bolivian experience shows that the division of the large landed estates into *minifundios* are no solution to Latin America's agricultural problems.

The need is for a productive agriculture because small farms that are inherently uneconomic are no solution.[12] Tad Szulc, the *New York Times* correspondent, warned against the "temptation among those inexperienced in land reform . . . to divide the landlord's property like a cake and give each available family a slice, regardless of whether it can cultivate the holding economically. When a nation's agriculture suddenly switches from the *latifundio* to the *minifundio* pattern—primarily to satisfy political urges—an economic catastrophe can easily result." [13] Farms need water, seed, fertilizer, and informed production methods. Only as these elements are made part of the reform programs and only as rural life is made more attractive will Latin America fulfill its capacity for an abundant agricultural sector.

Most of the Latin American states have been going through the throes of a serious inflation. Inflation is worst in Brazil, where it had been running at the rate of more than 5 percent a month; it has also been serious in Argentina, Chile, Colombia, Ecuador, Haiti, Honduras, Nicaragua, Paraguay, and Uruguay. In Cuba the scarcity of commodities had for a time made money almost worthless. Inflation deteriorates the value of wages and savings and it undermines the stability and convertibility of currency.

For the decade 1953–1963 the Brazilian economy had been growing at an exceptional rate of 6 to 7 percent a year. Industry was booming and Brazil was not without rich farms. However, 57.4 percent of her adult population remained illiterate; 8 percent of the landowners held about 75 percent of the land under cultivation; inflation raised prices 75 percent in 1963.[14] Inflation has caused the economy to falter, discouraged the outlook for new economic growth, and brought about a sharp reduction in United States aid after 1962. It sapped the drive for economic development.

Something must be done about housing. It is estimated that

[12] Szulc, *op. cit.*, p. 245. The Alliance for Progress Charter warned against *minifundios* as harmful to the economic and social development of the land.
[13] *Ibid.*, p. 245.
[14] *New York Times*, April 5, 1964, Section 4, p. 1.

Latin America lacks twelve to fourteen million new housing units.[15] Much of the housing is substandard and a large portion of the urban population live in slums. Lima, Peru, one of the worst examples, has more than 50 percent of its population living in the *boradas*. All over the continent dwellings lack piped water, electricity, and sewage disposal. Local governments are doing little to alleviate these shortages and eradicate the slums. Their resources are not equal to the task. Foreign investment from the private sector is an unlikely source of capital. Low-cost housing enjoys at best a low priority to the private investor in comparison with funds that are made available for profit-earning enterprises. Indeed, the construction of a sizable number of luxury apartments and private villas to the neglect of cheap housing only serves to demonstrate where profits can be earned. The social cleavage within the Latin American community is, however, thereby reemphasized. The Latin American slum with its poverty, disease, and with a high percentage of unemployment provides a hospitable host for violence, lawlessness, and revolutionary agitation.

Economic development through the Alliance for Progress has from the beginning emphasized the construction of means of communication and transportation, schools, hospitals, hydroelectric facilities, ports, and land reclamation. These are functions that are ordinarily performed by governments rather than private investors. They should be financed largely through taxation, but Latin American governments have not yet learned to tax people fairly or effectively. Income taxes for the rich are too low, an average 31 percent as a top rate which compared unfavorably with a high rate of 91 percent in the United States prior to 1964.[16] Yet the low rate of taxation has not served to encourage investment in the types of local business and industry which help develop a country's economy. Far too much capital of Latin America's rich is invested in Western Europe and North America. What is worse, tax collections are lax. The penalty for nonpayment is light. It may also be that the complexities of taxing incomes are too difficult an administrative task to be carried out effectively in some of the states.[17]

Latin America has the most rapidly growing population in the world. The estimated average growth rate is about 3 percent. In

[15] Scott, *op. cit.*, p. 118.
[16] Scott, *op. cit.*, p. 113.
[17] *Ibid.*, p. 114.

1950 the population of Latin America was equal to that of the
United States. By 1965 it was 220,000,000. If this rate of population
growth continues, Latin America will have over 600,000,000 people
by the end of the twentieth century. Only two of the twenty Latin
American states are actually too densely populated—Haiti and El
Salvador. However, the rapid growth in population has a negative
influence upon the economic growth. The population explosion
means that the Latin American gross national product must grow
by at least 3 percent to maintain the present low living standards.
The Alliance for Progress seeks an annual net growth of 2.5 percent
over the population increase. Thus an actual growth in the gross
national product of about 5.5 percent becomes mandatory. A growth
rate of such an order has led many to question the realism of the
goals which the Alliance for Progress has set for itself.

The Pan American Health Organization reported that between
1950 and 1960, 25,000,000 additional persons had been supplied with
water. However, the population increase has been in excess of that
figure.[18] In other words, a new deficit in water supply has resulted
from the growth in population. In a word, the all-important quest
for economic growth is seriously handicapped by the rapid growth
in population, and this growth will not be curbed in the near future. While this does not mean that the economic development of
Latin America is beyond achievement, it makes achievement of development goals enormously difficult.

Behind the lag in economic development lies a shortage of development capital, a lack of facilities for educational improvement,
and unrelieved problems of poverty and disease. Shortage of development capital could become ameliorated if it were not sent abroad
"by the nervous rich to Swiss banks, Florida real estate and the New
York stock market..."[19] More recently there has been some reluctance on the part of foreign investors to commit their money to
Latin American industry. Unsettled conditions and the threat of
nationalization of investments are frequently stated reasons for the
lack of desire for Latin America investment. International trade has
been unfavorable to Latin countries. West European and Japanese
exports to the continent have increased markedly during the past
five years, often at the expense of the United States' share; however, Latin American exports to Europe and Japan have not kept

[18] Szulc, *op. cit.*, p. 59.
[19] Scott, *op. cit.*, p. 114.

pace with the growth in imports. The difference has often been underwritten by the extension of credit.

It is estimated that 50 percent of the people in Central and South America are illiterate and lack skills required for the labor market. Adult illiteracy runs as high as 90 percent in Haiti. Argentina has the lowest rate of illiteracy, 12 percent. Probably no more than half of the school-age children ever go to school. Dropouts during the first few years of schooling are heavy. Schools, teachers, and textbooks are in short supply. The Alliance for Progress is therefore financing the construction of schools, the training of teachers, and the production of textbooks and educational materials. A study undertaken by the Organization of American States rated primary education in Latin America at three levels. Group one, the literate states, enjoyed an 88 percent enrollment of its 6,000,000 school-age children. These countries, Argentina, Chile, Uruguay, and Venezuela, hoped to have 100 percent enrollment in children of primary school age in 1965. A second group made up to twelve states, Bolivia, Brazil, Colombia, Costa Rica, the Dominican Republic, Ecuador, El Salvador, Mexico, Nicaragua, Panama, Paraguay, and Peru, enrolled 78 percent of its 24,000,000 children of primary school age, and hoped to achieve 100 percent enrollment by 1970. The third group, with a high rate of illiteracy, Guatemala, Haiti, and Honduras, enrolled only 43 percent of the 2,000,000 children of primary school age, and these countries were not expected to achieve 100 percent literacy for children of primary school age until 1980. Percentage of enrollment in secondary schools and in universities decreases sharply. Planned development in these areas does, however, enjoy a high priority among the aims for educational development.[20]

With the help of CARE and the United States, the free lunches of the Food for Peace Program have been made available to more than one-half million Latin American school children. This has been an important reason for families sending their children to school.

BRAZIL

There is good reason to believe that Castro's activity and Cuba's role in Latin America may be no more than one of instigation. Cuba lacks the intrinsic capacity to dominate the hemisphere. It can

[20] *Ibid.*, p. 116.

provide the Communist world with a base for operations. In the long run, leadership is more likely to come from the large Latin American powers. Brazil with its more than 75,000,000 population, its tremendous size—it is almost as large as the United States today, and actually was larger before the United States included Alaska— its potential wealth, its abundant resources, and its long-term influence might well shape the future of the South American continent.

Brazil has been in deep trouble. The progress that it has made in economic development has taken place almost exclusively around Rio, São Paulo, and in the state of Minas Gerais. But even these centers of prosperity have been threatened by a runaway inflation. The relative prosperity of some urban centers has been entirely absent in the Northeast. Brazil's Northeast is a huge area including nine of Brazil's twenty states and approximately one-third of its population. This is one of the most depressed areas in the world. It is an area of hunger, low life expectancy, and endemic diseases.

> Nearly five hundred of every thousand babies perish in their first year . . . adults must fight tuberculosis and gastric diseases brought about by malnutrition, as well as intestinal hookworms that afflict one out of three, and an ailment called *schistosomiasis* that is spread by snails in polluted waters and causes debilitating belly-swelling in every fifth person.
>
> By the age of thirty-two the average Brazilian in the Northeast is dead, carried to his grave in a paper shroud because a wooden coffin is prohibitively costly. The survivors struggle on as cane-cutters on sugar plantations, for lodgings in mud huts and wages that usually run from sixty-five cents a week but can go as high as 15 cents a day. They do not see actual cash; it is doled out at plantation stores in the form of supplies. . . . The luckier ones toil as sharecroppers for the few feudal landlords who own almost all the land; in lieu of rent, they pay back about 50 percent of their produce, keep a little for family needs, and sell the rest . . . at prices one third to one half below market values.[21]

FIDELISMA

The forces of revolution can be disastrous to the development of free societies. Social change may be modeled upon Castro's revolution and result in a Communist totalitarian dictatorship. For millions of Latin Americans, Castro means desired social change. Many believe that such change can only be carried out through violent revolution. For millions of ignorant, illiterate, poverty-ridden masses

[21] Clark, *op. cit.,* pp. 197–198.

Castro represents a hope for a better life. Few of them know of the failure of Castro's rule in Cuba—the economic deterioration; the fall in the production of sugar, tobacco, and coffee; the estimated decrease of 25 percent in Cuba's gross national product during the first five years of Castro's rule. They know their own misery and that very little is being done to bring about needed change in their own country. There is little interest exhibited in the fact of the suppression of liberty and the filling of prison camps in Cuba. That Cuba is an armed camp has simply been explained away as a condition brought on by a hostile environment. To be sure, the missile crisis of October, 1962, seriously exposed Castro to the accusation that he served the interests of the Soviet Union. While after October, 1962, Castro's image had surely been tarnished, his support was still strong among the most depressed groups in Latin American countries, as well as some intellectuals.

Castro has hemispheric ambitions. For him the revolution that he has enthroned in Cuba is meant for wider dissemination. His former assistant and master planner Ernesto ("Che") Guevara's book on guerrilla warfare is a well-read revolutionary handbook in many parts of Latin America. It is estimated that about one thousand students annually spend six months in Cuba where they undergo indoctrination and training in revolutionary and guerrilla activities.[22]

All of Latin America has been a target of Castro's activity, sometimes supported by the Soviet Union and at other times by Communist China. Certain states which have appeared more vulnerable to the appeals of *fidelisma* have been singled out for greater attention. Thus in Chile, the opportunities provided by the elections of 1964 brought about some concentration of effort by the Communists albeit in a losing cause. In Venezuela *fidelistas* have been working hard to prevent the success of a democratic alternative to Castroism. Brazil and Argentina have been tempting targets for Castroite activity because of the importance of these powers on the South American continent and because improvement of the internal situation seems hopeless and economic problems defy solution.

Outside of Cuba *fidelisma* is probably strongest in Northeast Brazil, where it has a position of leadership among the masses. Francisco Julião, a small-town attorney who leads the disaffected, is an out-

[22] Szulc, *op. cit.,* p. 20.

spoken follower of Fidel Castro. When Castro announced, in December, 1961, that he was a Communist, Julião made an identical declaration several days later.[23] He organized the Peasant Leagues, which by 1962 were reputed to have 80,000 active followers and several times that number of supporters.[24] More than anything else, the Peasant Leagues want land. They fight for the expropriation of large private holdings with redistribution to the peasantry.

Brazilian law denies the vote to illiterates and the high level of illiteracy makes it unlikely that the Peasant Leagues can come to power through the electoral process without a change in the law. When President João Goulart tried to extend suffrage to illiterates this became one of the causes for his overthrow in the spring of 1964. Julião hopes that the impoverished conditions will give the Peasant-Leagues the support of the urban voters in the Northeast. However, he does not foreclose the use of force with Communist arms to attain his objectives.[25]

It should be clear that the conditions in the Northeast cannot long continue without Brazil's government finding a way out of the appalling conditions under which the people live. The forces of *fidelisma* led by Francisco Julião will grow in strength and will attempt a Castroite solution unless the situation is markedly improved.

Fidelistas have been active in other Latin American countries, and not without a modicum of success; in Colombia, Castroites tried to seize control of terrorist bands. For years outlaws have operated in the Colombian mountains. Communists have tried to give a social purpose to their fight against the state. In Chile the Communist Party is a leading party in the *Frenti Acción Popular* (FRAP), which supported the candidacy of Senator Allende for President. Communists infiltrated the Peruvian squatter movements. In the last few years small-scale guerrilla operations, supported by Castro, have been started in Ecuador, Peru, and Guatemala.

It is generally felt that Castro's appeal in the Western Hemisphere reached its zenith and is now declining. Undoubtedly, the missile crisis of 1962 exposed him as an agent of Soviet interests and also as the failures of Cuba become better known his image is

23 Szulc, *op. cit.*, p. 20.
24 Clark, *op. cit.*, p. 206.
25 *Ibid*, p. 210.

tarnished. However, his capacity for mischief in the Western Hemisphere was vigorously underlined, as 1963 drew to a close, in Venezuela and Bolivia. In Venezuela the *Fuerzas Armadas de la Liberación Nacional* (FALN), a terrorist organization of Castroites, attemped to prevent and disrupt the elections of December 1 of that year. This organization tried to enforce a boycott of these elections by threatening to shoot persons attempting to vote. In Bolivia twenty-one persons, including four United States citizens, were kidnapped and held as hostages to secure the release of three Communist labor leaders who had been arrested for terrorism and violence. In both the Venezuelan and Bolivian cases the *fidelistas* failed. Betancourt's candidate, Dr. Raul Leoni, won in Venezuela and about 90 percent of those eligible voted—an impressive rejection of the FALN appeal. In Bolivia the National Miners Federation had to release its hostages without gaining the release of their leaders. In 1964, Edourdo Frei was elected President of Chile defeating Allende, an avowed Castroite.

Alternatives to Castro. The *status quo* can no longer be maintained in Latin America. Social transformation of society is inevitable. It remains to be seen whether the course of social change will be directed by Communist or by anti-Communist forces.

In some countries the alternatives to *fidelisma* appear weak. In Haiti, should President Duvalier be removed from power, the Communists are in a good position to fill a political vacuum which would arise. The situation in Nicaragua may also be similar. Fortunately, in all of the other Latin American countries there are strong and imaginative voices raised on behalf of economic and social development within a democratic system. This has been the path of Mexico's Institutional Revolutionary Party (PRI). Modernization within a democratic context has been tried by Paz Estenssoro in Bolivia, Lleras Camargo in Colombia, Rómulo Betancourt in Venezuela, José Figueres in Costa Rica, Julio Rivera in El Salvador, and their successors. Anti-Communist liberals are fighting for control of labor and student organizations, which in many instances have fallen under Communist leadership.

The Catholic Church, always a great force in Latin American states, had traditionally been allied with the oligarchic governments. The reality of Latin America's stagnation and the need for social change has increasingly forced the Church into the fight for social

justice and economic development, a change strongly influenced by
the Papal Encyclical of 1961, *Mater et Magistra*. *Acción Católica,* an
organization working in a number of countries, has established
schools to eradicate illiteracy, worked for the improvement of conditions in slum areas, and promoted administrative, fiscal, and land-
tenure reforms. In the words of one Venezuelan priest, "We young
priests speak of revolution—a word feared by the rich—because we
realize that revolution will come with or without us. If it comes
without us, it will be against us. We must support the revolution." [26]
The Church is playing a progressive role in promoting higher education through the universities which it operates. It is a vital influence in the trade-union movement through the Latin American
Confederation of Christian Trade Unionists. Christian Democratic
parties have been established in almost every Latin American state.
While their programs range from moderate conservatism to radical
social change, on the whole these parties are a force for the democratic solution of the economic and social problems faced by Latin
American lands.

LATIN AMERICA AND THE UNITED STATES

The United States, the "Colossus of the North," exerts a decisive
influence upon Latin America's future. This has been true from the
early years of the nineteenth century, most pointedly with the enunciation of the Monroe Doctrine in 1823. The Monroe Doctrine
has been a major tenet of American foreign policy. The United
States preoccupation with Latin America was demonstrated by many
events during the nineteenth and twentieth centuries. The Mexican
War, the filibustering expeditions in Central America, and the Os-
tend Manifesto of 1854 proposing that the United States buy Cuba
were a few of the early evidences of such interest. Later came a more
vigorous development of trade and investment in the area. At the
end of the nineteenth century the United States intervened in the
relations between Latin American and European states. President
Cleveland stepped into the boundary dispute between British Guiana
and Venezuela in 1895 and threatened war unless the British accepted arbitration. The McKinley Administration helped free Cuba
through war against Spain. At the turn of the century President

[26] Scott, *op. cit.,* p. 121.

Theodore Roosevelt directed the construction of the Panama Canal and proclaimed his corollary to the Monroe Doctrine, arrogating to the United States the power to intervene in the affairs of other Western Hemisphere states to insure their observation of international obligations and to prevent intervention by European powers. In the twentieth century United States investment in Latin America was greater than in any other area. Under the administrations of Taft and Wilson, Washington established temporary protectorates over Nicaragua, Honduras, Mexico, Haiti, and Santo Domingo.[27] Even during periods of heightened isolationism as during the 1920's and 1930's the United States carried out an active policy *vis-à-vis* Latin America, sending marines into Nicaragua, Haiti, the Dominican Republic, and Cuba. Toward the end of Herbert Hoover's Presidential term, a new policy, that of the "good neighbor," redefined the direction of United States policy. The administrations of Franklin D. Roosevelt took up this policy which he designated the Good Neighbor Policy, and United States policy was recast. Intervention was disavowed and noninterference in the internal affairs of Latin American states and the promotion of cooperation through Pan-American organizations were to characterize Washington's conduct.

As we have seen, during the 1940's and the 1950's, United States attention was focused elsewhere, and the United States gave little leadership in the Western Hemisphere. However, the memory of American intervention in earlier decades failed to disappear. Anti-Yankeeism became an increasingly popular pose. The United States served as a convenient whipping boy for all kinds of Latin American ills, some of which justified United States condemnation. United States support of Latin American dictators was repeatedly called to the attention of the Latin American people as the essence of United States policy. Within Latin America the Organization of American States was smeared as an instrument of United States foreign policy.

American investment in Latin America has often been condemned as exploitive rather than helpful to economic development. Private capital is heavily invested in the extractive fields, petroleum and mining. Little more than a fourth of the $9 billion of private investment is in manufacturing, an area most closely identified with economic development. Exploitation of nonrenewable resources is

[27] Ernest R. May, "The Alliance for Progress in Historical Perspectives," *Foreign Affairs,* Vol. 41, No. 4, July, 1963, pp. 755–774.

resented because it is felt that control over mining should be reserved to the state itself. Exploitation is also charged on the grounds
that inordinate profits are gained by American companies, far too
little of this profit is reinvested, and too much of it is sent home.
U.S. investment is charged further with perpetuating economic control. When investment goes largely into just a few kinds of businesses
it is considered proof that Americans work against diversification
and development. Latin Americans are distressed over unfavorable
trade relations with the United States. Their economies are dependent on Washington's import quotas and price regulations of
commodities such as coffee, sugar, or tin which can change profits
to losses.

This image of American business is not entirely baseless. The
"banana republics" of Central America were dominated by American monopolies, often supported by Washington. It is only recently
that the great U.S. mining, oil, fruit, and shipping companies have
given thought to public relations, worker welfare, and the needs of
the land. In Latin America, as elsewhere, profits were often pursued
unscrupulously and to that end some companies crushed competition, exploited workingmen, corrupted politicians, and engineered
coups.

The U.S. image is grossly over-simplified and considerably out-
of-date. Both American government and U.S. business have adopted
considerably more "enlightened" policies in the past two decades.
American concerns do pay the highest wages, have set up good welfare programs, and offer education and training to recruit local nationals for executive positions. United Fruit has sold its lands to
its employees under advantageous arrangements and contracted to
buy the produce. Creole Petroleum has increased Venezuela's share
of oil profits to about 70 per cent. If in the past Washington's support has gone to dictators like Machado and Batista in Cuba, Trujillo in the Dominican Republic, Jiménez in Venezuela, and Somoza
in Nicaragua, in recent years the U.S. has identified itself with
democracy, social justice, and reform. It withheld recognition of
military seizures of power in Peru and the Dominican Republic and
has supported liberal leaders like Frei in Chile, Betancourt and
Leone in Venezuela, and Belaundi Terry in Peru.

The image of U.S. exploitation doesn't easily give way. Even
today Latin Americans resent having to pay dearly for the tech-

nical know-how of the foreign specialists that they need. They gloss over the risks of foreign investment as a cause for high rates of profit and fail to consider the attractiveness to private capital of investment in the U.S. and Europe as against Latin America. They can be blind to the new jobs, new opportunities, better wages and working conditions which U.S. companies contribute to the nation's economy.

All would agree that Latin America lacks domestic capital to develop its resources. It is dependent on foreign capital both private and governmental. Under the Alliance for Progress, the United States has obligated over $1 billion per year since 1961. These monies have gone into health, education, housing, and other areas vital to development.

With the onset of the 1960's, a reassessment of United States policy in Latin America took place leading to a new emphasis. The central instrument of the new trend in American policy is the Alliance for Progress, introduced by President Kennedy on March 13, 1961. Meeting with the Ambassadors of the Latin American countries, he urged their governments to join with the United States in "a vast effort, unparalleled in magnitude and nobility of purpose..."

At a meeting of the OAS at Punta Del Este, Uruguay, on August 17, 1961, the Alliance for Progress was formally launched. A Charter, signed by the states assembled there, began with a "Declaration to the Peoples of America," pledging "a vast effort to bring a better life to all peoples of the Continent." [28] The OAS states agreed to work for a number of common goals:

1. the improvement and strengthening of democratic institutions;
2. economic and social development to approach a standard of living of industrialized countries;
3. rural and urban housing construction;
4. agrarian reform;
5. assurance of fair wages, satisfactory working conditions and the encouragement of cooperation between organized labor and management groups;
6. the promotion of universal literacy and the development of technical, secondary and higher education;
7. improvement in health and sanitation;

[28] *International Review Service,* "Cuba and the United States," Vol. IX, No. 79, 1963, p. 132.

8. tax reform, the enforcement of tax laws, the fairer redistribution of income and the promotion of savings and investment;
9. policies designed to prevent inflation and deflation and to promote stable prices;
10. policies meant to encourage private enterprise and to eliminate unemployment and promote industrialization;
11. the promotion of price stability in exports;
12. an acceleration of integration of Latin American states to stimulate the economic and social development of the Continent.[29]

The Alliance for Progress was the American initiative for assistance in completing the social revolution that was already in progress. Its aims were economic growth with social reform. The role of the United States was to provide that assistance which would help the states help themselves.

To carry out these aims the Alliance for Progress was to produce one hundred billion dollars in investments over ten years. Eighty billion of this amount was to come from the Latin Americans themselves, the remaining twenty billion from outside sources.

The United States pledged "a major part of the minimum of twenty billion dollars . . . which Latin America will require over the next ten years from all external sources in order to supplement its own efforts." [30] United States lending agencies were to supply 1.1 billion a year over a ten-year period. The remainder was to come in equal amounts of 300 million dollars from international lending agencies, private United States investment, and from private investors and friendly governments in Europe and Japan.

In concrete terms the Alliance for Progress expected to achieve at the end of ten years an average growth in the gross national product per capita of 2.5 percent per year; a more equitable distribution of the national wealth leveling off the extremes between the rich and the poor; diversification in agriculture and extractive industry; increased industrialization; increased agricultural productivity; the eradication of illiteracy and six years of primary education for all school-aged children; a five-year increase in life expectancy; more low-cost housing; and stable currencies and stable prices.

At mid-decade the success of the Alliance for Progress was far from assured. Some achievements should be noted; the declining appeal

[29] *Ibid.*, pp. 132–133.
[30] *Ibid,* p. 133.

of Castroism and communism; increased domestic and foreign investment, largely as planned; increased exports; the beginnings of economic integration through the Central American Common Market and the Latin American Free Trade Area; an International Coffee Agreement signed by fifty-four producing and consuming nations in December, 1963, which may go a long way toward stabilizing world coffee prices; an increase in the output of steel, automobiles, homes, classrooms, hospitals, health centers, and municipal water systems. Several Latin American states have approved detailed economic plans; ten states have enacted tax reforms; and eleven states have enacted land reforms.

For the Alliance for Progress to succeed, many shortcomings will have to be overcome. Inflation is far from controlled. Perhaps as much as 50 percent of the income taxes remain uncollected. Far too much capital leaves the continent with little benefit to the Latin American states. Land reform is talked about and legislated but the level of performance is poor. Diversification of exports has only begun.

Thirteen Latin American states depend primarily on one commodity for their export earnings, while three others depend on two or three products. In 1962, coffee provided Brazil with 58 percent, Colombia with 77 percent, and Costa Rica with 56 percent of their export incomes. Bolivia got 62 percent of its export income from tin, Chile 66 percent from copper, and Venezuela 77 percent from petroleum. The overall growth rate during the first two years of the Alliance has little more than kept up with the population growth, and does not begin to approach the planned 2.5 percent. Food production has increased less than the population growth and there has been relatively little effective planning for economic development. The Alliance often appears as a scattering of unrelated projects.

The Alliance must succeed. Its importance cannot be overrated as upon its success may well hang the future of democracy in Latin America and the prestige of the United States in the Western Hemisphere.

The United States, in a political and military sense, remains the most influential power in the hemisphere. While the policy of non-intervention, dating to Franklin D. Roosevelt's first administration, has become a basic precept of United States policy in the hemisphere, the United States has demonstrated that when its vital interests are at stake it can determine the outcome of events. This truth was dramatically made clear in the Cuban missile crisis, the Dominican rebellion of 1965, and less dramatically but effectively underlined in relation to the Venezuelan election of December, 1963, when the United States said that it would not tolerate a Communist-Castroite take-over in that land.

Nonintervention, as a basic precept of the Good Neighbor Policy, is a self-limiting factor. It derives from a belief that each Latin American state can order its own destiny. It also rests on the assumption that the interventions of the past served United States political and economic interests, not the interests of the hemisphere as a whole. Relations in the hemisphere are currently based on the principles of equality and partnership in political and economic matters. United States diplomacy carries great weight in the formulation of policy by each Latin American state. Increasingly Washington's initiatives have been channeled through the Organization of American States as an agency which can best effect collaboration for mutually agreeable aims.

LATIN AMERICAN INTEGRATION

Integration of Latin American states is only in its early stages of development. Despite the Latin and Indian character of its population, the old Iberian influence, and the similarities of language, there is little common ground for interstate unity. Transportation and communication between Latin American countries is not well developed. A sense of community among the peoples of Latin America is only now beginning to arise. Integrative institutions, with the exception of the OAS, are recent creations. Some cooperation through the OAS and common policy on behalf of interests in the hemisphere within the UN has taken place. But economic competition has stood in the way of unity in most spheres of interest.

Latin American countries compete with one another for export markets. Coffee, bananas, other tropical fruits, cotton, sugar, tropical woods, and cattle are the exports of almost all Central American republics. The situation is similar in South America. There is little intracontinental trade. Cooperative planning in product diversification and a purposive exploitation of a market within the Latin American countries could be a great gain for the economies of all of the states. Institutional arrangements for economic and political co-operation among the Latin American states and with the United States are useful, if not essential, as means for economic improvement and the achievement of Alliance for Progress goals.

THE ORGANIZATION OF AMERICAN STATES (OAS)

The OAS is the oldest of the world's regional organizations. Its importance was recognized both in the Covenant of the League and in the Charter of the UN. Both provide for regional organizations as an approved means for carrying out the purposes of the League and of the UN.

The OAS was established as the International Union of American Republics in 1890. In 1910 it adopted the name Pan American Union, and by the adoption of the Bogota Charter in 1948 it was again renamed as the Organization of American States. Its membership includes the twenty Latin American states and the United States. At the present time Cuba is, in effect, suspended from the organization. Authority in the OAS is vested in the conference of the organization, which meets every five years to establish OAS policy. The foreign ministers meet when necessary to consider urgent matters affecting the peace and security of the hemisphere. A council, made up of ambassadors specially appointed or resident ambassadors in Washington of the Latin American states, makes up an executive body of twenty-one members. The council directs the work of the Pan American Union, which constitutes a secretariat for the OAS. Three suborgans are established by its charter: an Inter-American Cultural Council, an Inter-American Economic and Social Council, and an Inter-American Council of Jurists. These councils are based in the headquarters of the OAS, the Pan American Union Building in Washington, D.C.

The OAS has been instrumental in the pacific settlement of several disputes.[31] The United States had channeled many of its proposals to counteract Castro through the organization. In 1960, the OAS voted diplomatic and economic sanctions against the Domini-

[31] Costa Rica *vs* Nicaragua; Haiti *vs* the Dominican Republic; Haiti *vs* Cuba and Guatemala.

can Republic because of an attempted assassination of Betancourt, the President of Venezuela, by the Dominican dictator Trujillo. In 1963, Venezuela sought action by the OAS to curb the transmission of arms from Cuba to Castroite guerrilla forces operating on the territory of OAS member states.

The OAS has had an official authority for overseeing the Alliance for Progress program. United States participation is channeled through the Agency for International Development (AID), and the OAS has appointed a committee of experts which advises on Alliance project proposals. However, during the first three years of operation of the Alliance, the OAS lacked an administrative organization for supervising its work.

THE INTER-AMERICAN DEVELOPMENT BANK

In 1959, an Inter-American Development Bank was formed. It was provided funds to make investments in development projects, and it was to promote investments of public and private capital that would increase the economic growth of the Latin American states. Its charter was approved in 1960, and its operations began early in 1961. The Bank was capitalized at about one billion dollars. Almost one-half of the funds have been contributed by the United States. The Bank is very much a Latin American operation. The first President was Felipe Herrera, a young Chilean economist-attorney and his country's former finance minister. A seven-man board of directors, with Washington holding one of the seats, supervises the Bank's operations. In less than three years of operation the Bank granted $727 million in loans for 182 projects in 19 countries. Loans were made to public and private borrowers who invested over one billion dollars of their own funds as well. Projects financed were in the areas of agricultural development, water supply, manufacturing, and low-cost housing.[32]

In addition to its own investments, the Bank has administered the Social Progress Fund of $394 million authorized by the United States Congress and devoted to education, public health, and welfare activities. Bank disbursements have been made only where there is high promise for success and where there is assurance that the loans will be repaid.

[32] Scott, *op. cit.*, p. 98.

THE UNITED NATIONS ECONOMIC COMMISSION FOR LATIN AMERICA (ECLA)

Cooperative programs for economic growth were the major purpose of ECLA. Founded in 1948 and with headquarters in Santiago, Chile, the ECLA is a commission of twenty-four members.[33] It undertakes no projects of its own, but engages mainly in studies and surveys. The compilation of factual information has provided much needed data for attacking critical economic and social problems.

ECLA has also worked for the lowering of trade barriers among Latin American states and the reduction of the competitive aspects of their export economy. Its efforts have given birth to a common market and a free trade area approach to inter-American trade and export trade. Given time the efforts could reduce duplication of export commodities and lead to the production of new export crops.[34] (See below, the development of a Central American Common Market and a Latin American Free Trade Area.)

CENTRAL AMERICAN COMMON MARKET (CACM)

A general treaty of Central American Economic Integration was signed in Managua, Nicaragua, in December, 1960. Signatory states were Guatemala, El Salvador, Honduras, and Nicaragua. In 1963, Costa Rica declared her intention to participate. Panama chose not to participate to avoid sharing her income from the Panama Canal and because she preferred a bilateral arrangement with the United States.[35]

The Central American Common Market (CACM) was projected as a twenty-year program of cooperative endeavor. During the first five years a common external tariff was to be instituted. CACM was to oversee the gradual integration of the economies of her member states, developing a single system of taxation, a network of communication and transportation, and a complementary program of economic development, "according to the principles of efficient division of labor." [36]

[33] The twenty-one members of the OAS plus France, the Netherlands, and the United Kingdom, who have interests in the Western Hemisphere.
[34] Tad Szulc, "New Trends in Latin America," *Headline Series,* No. 140, March–April, 1960, pp. 33–34.
[35] Scott, *op. cit.,* p. 21.
[36] *Ibid.,* pp. 16–17.

To administer its activities an Economic Council was formed with headquarters in Guatemala City as well as a Central American Bank, having clearing house functions, in Tegucigalpa. The first years of CACM activity have been responsible for a modest increase in trade among CACM states. From 1958 to 1962, trade within the market area rose from 3 to 11 percent. However, 20 percent of trade still is with the United States and Europe because exports of the CACM are essentially competitive.[37]

Should economic integration succeed and lead to a political union of the CACM states, a new state of twenty million people of significant economic importance would result.

LATIN AMERICAN FREE TRADE AREA (LAFTA)

The Latin American Free Trade Area was established at Montevideo, its present headquarters, in February, 1960. It took more than a year to obtain the necessary ratifications, and the organization began its operations on January 1, 1962, with Argentina, Brazil, Chile, Colombia, Ecuador, Mexico, Paraguay, Peru, and Uruguay as members. Its purpose is the gradual elimination (over a twelve-year period) of duties, tariffs, and other restrictions on commerce among the participant states. Each member retains those customs, tariffs, and other restrictions that it wishes for trade with states outside the LAFTA. In time LAFTA hopes to take on the characteristics of a common market area, that is, with common external trade barriers and with the total elimination of trade barriers within the area.

The weakness of the LAFTA approach lies in the minor role that area trade plays in the economy of the LAFTA states. Trade within the LAFTA amounted to only 7 percent in 1961; [38] nevertheless, Dr. Alberto Sola, Executive Secretary and a former Undersecretary of the Treasury Department in Argentina, believed that LAFTA would be of growing importance to the economies of its member states. In 1962, internal trade increased to 9 percent. Greater increases have been projected for the years to follow.[39]

During the first eighteen months of its existence internal tariffs were down by one-third. On the other hand, no headway was made in organizing the "division of labor" to reduce the competitive

[37] *Ibid.,* p. 17.
[38] *Ibid.,* p. 64.
[39] *Ibid.*

aspects of LAFTA exports. Of greater success has been the 30 percent increase in LAFTA members' imports from one another.[40]

INTERNATIONAL COFFEE AGREEMENT

The Alliance for Progress took a major step in stabilizing world
coffee prices, an all-important commodity for a number of Latin
American states, by organizing the International Coffee Agreement.
Fifty-four producing and consuming states, including fifteen Latin-
American coffee-producing countries, have signed (but not necessarily ratified) this agreement. Through this instrument the International Coffee Board was set up to administer export quotas for
producer states. Consumer countries have been committed to purchase only coffee sold within the quotas assigned to the producing
states.

Latin America is in the throes of a social revolution. The rising
tide of demand for change in the *status quo* can no longer be suppressed. The poverty of the Latin American peasant and the urban
slum dweller existing side by side with the opulence of a small class
of landowners and industrialists cannot continue. The crucial question is whether this revolution will be carried out by governments
seeking the preservation of free societies or by totalitarian Communists following the lead of Fidel Castro. This is a decision likely
to be made within this decade. Freedom for the Latin American
peoples and their security from Communist expansion in the Western Hemisphere depends upon the achievements of those leaders
who strive for progress and democracy. In the outcome of this struggle the United States must play a weighty role. It will take the
greatest exertion by the United States to provide military, political,
economic, and moral support to democratic Latin American states
seeking modernization against the pull of reactionary elements bent
on maintaining the *status quo* as well as against the destructive forces
of Castroite communism.

[40] *Ibid.*

PART IV

Conclusion

CHAPTER 13

The Problems of Economic Development

THE world today is almost obsessed with the need for the economic development of underdeveloped countries. The wealth of industrialized communities has excited the desires of the masses in agrarian societies. A "revolution of rising expectations" is sweeping the Southern Hemisphere and Asia. A share in the benefits of modern civilization has become the focus of hope for peoples long deprived of the essential concomitants of human dignity. In face of such compelling ambitions, the facts show that the greatest increments of economic growth and general affluence are taking place in the industrialized states. Wealth is most broadly shared in the economically developed state. Meanwhile, underdeveloped lands show little increase in their economic output. All too often population growth consumes the gain in gross national product, leaving *per-capita* income as low as before and forestalling investment. To make matters worse, whatever gains occur are narrowly apportioned within the population.

The world is characterized by the existence of rich states, relatively few in number, and a large number of poor lands. While the rich states grow richer, the poor countries seem comparatively poorer. It is increasingly acknowledged that unless this situation soon improves, the affluent way of life will be put in jeopardy. In an economic and political sense this is one world, and the dislocations in the poverty stricken states will undermine the security and well-being of the affluent lands. Simple prudence dictates international attention to economic development and the promotion of programs of assistance by favorably situated countries. A multitude, indeed a proliferation, of economic development agencies and banking institutions established by industrialized states through multilateral agreements exist to facilitate development. In terms of the states involved and the population affected, assistance programs relate a small number of donor states to a large number of poor countries deriving benefits from aid.

No meticulously worked out "score card" is needed to tell the underdeveloped from the developed states. The terms "rich lands" and "poor lands" may be too imprecise for a study of economic development, but the term we use here, "underdeveloped" country, is well understood and enables us to discuss important problems. Occasionally distinctions are made between "undeveloped," "underdeveloped," "developing," and "in position of take off" (where enough capital is generated internally to meet investment needs) to distinguish between different stages of economic development. Such distinctions are useful in evaluating progress toward industrialization. There are some who take exception to the use of the term "underdeveloped," perhaps because they see the word as a more polite reference to the "backwardness" of a country. However, we use this term in its descriptive sense as it relates to economic development. No pejorative connotation is intended. Underdeveloped countries are not backward in their culture and in their ethical or moral values.

The aim of development is to alter the situation existing in most countries where the masses live in poverty their entire life. Such poverty is an outgrowth of "obsolete methods of production and social organization, which means that the poverty is not entirely due to poor natural resources and hence could presumably be lessened by methods already proved in other countries." [1]

At the beginning of the 1960's, two-thirds of the world's three billion people lived in underdeveloped lands. A little more than one-sixth of the world's population lived in states that were developing rapidly but where the average level of consumption remained low. Somewhat less than one-sixth of the people of the world lived in highly developed countries, affluent lands, enjoying what Professor W. W. Rostow denotes as the "age of high mass consumption." For this study precise categories of "developed," "developing," and "underdeveloped" need not be worked out. A typical criterion for establishing levels of development has been the gross national product *per capita*. This method of evaluation does over-

[1] Eugene Staley, *The Future of Underdeveloped Countries,* rev. ed. (New York: Frederick A. Praeger, 1961), p. 13.

look distortions in the division of wealth based on large earnings, such as from oil in Venezuela, Kuwait, Saudi Arabia, and Bahrein. Eugene Staley, using *per-capita* national income, categorizes as "developed" those states enjoying an annual per capita income of $450 or more. On this basis the countries of North America and Western Europe, Australia, and New Zealand qualify. In an intermediate, "developing," group whose *per-capita* income is between $150 and $450 are most of the remaining states of Europe, the Republic of South Africa, Japan, Israel, and a few of the more highly developed states of Latin America. On the basis of an annual *per-capita* income of $150 or less, two-thirds of the world's population lives in underdeveloped lands.

THE NATURE OF UNDERDEVELOPED ECONOMIES

Each underdeveloped country is unique. Each differs from others in countless ways: in climate, size, resources, culture, race, language, and religion. Some are overpopulated. Others could support a much larger population than they have. In many the desire for change has taken hold of the people, while in others the people remain apathetic.

In all of them a majority of the population lives in poverty. People go hungry; they are badly housed or, in extreme instances, not housed at all, living in the streets. They are diseased, die young, and have little medical attention. They are ignorant and illiterate. Paul Hoffman's succinct description of the underdeveloped country is as complete as it is brief:

> An underdeveloped country is not simply a poverty-stricken version of a developed nation. It is a country which lacks the means to eradicate its own poverty. The roads and railroads are insufficient, the communications system is erratic, the factories and the tools for agriculture are mostly lacking. Few people have enough education and training to take part usefully in the development process. . . . Hospitals and other medical services are pitifully inadequate . . .
>
> Whatever wealth underdeveloped countries have is often concentrated in the hands of a few people who live in comparative opulence surrounded by overwhelming poverty. An underdeveloped country's banking system is embryonic; small loans have to be obtained through money lenders who are often little better than extortionists. Not only are there scant savings from which investment could be made, but the people who have wealth usually refuse to invest it productively in their own countries.

The underdeveloped nation's exports typically consist almost entirely of raw materials, ores, fruits, or some other staple product with perhaps a small admixture of handicrafts or luxury goods. Often extraction or production of these export commodities is wholly or partly under foreign control, with little of the profit being reinvested in the country.[2]

The contrast between developed and underdeveloped countries is revealed statistically:

(1) Underdeveloped countries had, in 1965, an average *per-capita* GNP of $155; developed countries, $1,830 (see Table I).

TABLE I

Estimates of Per Capita *Gross National Products* [1]
Calendar Year "1965" in Constant 1962 Market Prices
(Dollar Equivalents)

United States	3,312	Thailand	126
USSR	1,200 [2]	Pakistan	87
Japan	684	India	81
Colombia	286	Indonesia	80 [2]
Iran	216 [2]	Ethiopia	49
Ivory Coast	196 [2]	Somalia	45 [2]
Bolivia	162	Upper Volta	45 [2]

[1] Source: U.S. Agency for International Development, Office of Program Coordination, Statistics and Reports Division, Reports Control-W-138, June 15, 1966.

[2] Source: Civic Education Service, *A World of Facts* (Washington: 1965).

(2) Underdeveloped lands averaged 70 miles of improved roads per 1,000 square miles; developed lands, 550.

(3) Underdeveloped lands averaged an electric power output of 155 kilowatt hours *per capita,* while developed lands averaged 3,340.

(4) The most highly developed lands, with a *per-capita* national income of $1,000 or more, averaged a daily *per-capita* consumption of 3,153 calories. Lands with the lowest *per-capita* national income, less than $100, averaged a *per-capita* consumption of 2,070 calories.

(5) Life expectancy in underdeveloped areas averaged forty years compared with sixty-nine years in developed areas (see Table II).

[2] Paul G. Hoffman, *World Without Want* (New York: Harper & Row, 1962), pp. 33–34.

(6) Despite breakthroughs in the development of medical technology and progress in sanitation and public health, infant mortality remains high in underdeveloped lands (see Table II).

(7) Underdeveloped countries average 3,700 people per physician, while developed lands average 800 (see Table II).

TABLE II

Health Statistics for 1965

Country	Estimated life expectancy, years [1]	Infant mortality per 1,000 live births [2]	Population per physician [3]	Population per hospital beds [4]
United States	70	24.7	730	110
Israel	72	27.3 [a]	400	150
United Arab Republic (Egypt)	50	118.6	12,600	500
India	46	139.	4,500	2,500
Philippines	55	72.8	1,700	1,180 [b]
Japan	69	18.5	920 [d]	100
Italy	68	35.6	610 [d]	110 [b]
Sweden	74	12.4	990 [d]	70
Poland	68	41.7	940 [d]	140
Morocco	50	149.	10,430	620
Dahomey	37	110.5 [b]	26,970	710 [d]
Ethiopia	42	n.a.	76,300	3,000 [b]
Dominican Republic	50 (est.)	102.3 [c]	4,800	440 [d]
Mexico	57	64.5	1,314	590
Chile	52	114.2	1,640	260 [b]

[a] Israel Jewish population—23.9.
[b] 1961.
[c] 1962.
[d] Datum for 1964. United Nations, *Statistical Yearbook, 1965* (New York: 1966).

Sources:

[1] Civic Education Service. *A World of Facts* (Washington: 1965).

[2] Statistics apply for 1964. United Nations, *Demographic Yearbook,* Seventeenth Issue, 1965.

[3] *Proposed Mutual Defense and Development Programs FY 1966,* Superintendent of Documents, United States Govt. Printing Office (Washington: March, 1965), Table No. 7.

[4] World Health Organization, *World Health Statistics Annual,* Vol. III (Geneva: 1965), for 1962, pp. 138–175.

(8)   Hospital beds per population tell the same story (see Table II).

(9)   Literacy averages 35 percent among underdeveloped states as compared with 96 percent for developed countries (see Table III).

TABLE III

Education Statistics for 1964

Country	Literacy, percent [1]	Children in school, percent [2] Age Group 5–14 Primary	Children in school, percent [2] Age Group 15–19 Secondary	Enrollment per 100,000 population higher education [3]	Number of Teachers [4] Primary	Number of Teachers [4] Secondary
U.S.	98	83	76	2,100 c	958,940 d	583,310 d
Japan	98 a	62	95 b	800	350,863	398,030 e
West Germany	99 a	69	78 b	534	176,771	67,562
Bolivia	31	43	15	215	12,007	1,839
Peru	50	50	16	257 c	41,900	11,300
Afghanistan	5–10	5	1	14	5,698 f	— f
India	24	32	22	242 c	731,774	561,512
Indonesia	45	40	13	69	241,574	35,156
Iran	15–20	28	14	111	45,743	12,950
Israel	90	83	45	744	18,880	4,597
Laos	15	20	2	14	3,166	165
Pakistan	20	22	16	154	130,445	63,276
Yemen	25	8	0.4	n.a.	1,332	60
Ethiopia	5	5	0.4	5	6,912	681
Nigeria	20	35	5	9	95,586	8,023
Somalia	5	5	1	4	1,058	30 g

a Civic Education Service, *A World of Facts* (Washington: 1965).
b Figure contains an overlap of primary and secondary schools.
c Based upon 1959 enrollment.
d 1959.
e Includes vocational education.
f Figure combines first- and second-level schools.
g 1955.

Sources:

[1] *Proposed Mutual Defense and Development Programs FY 1966*, Superintendent of Documents, United States Govt. Printing Office (Washington: March, 1965), Table No. 7.

[2] UNESCO, *Statistical Yearbook, 1963* (Paris: 1964).

[3] Calculation based upon statistics contained in the *International Yearbook of Education*, Vol. XXVI, 1964 (Geneva: 1965, International Bureau of Education and UNESCO).

[4] *Ibid.*

(10) UNESCO estimates that in the age groups 5–19, "of every ten children in the world five do not go to school, four are in primary school, one is receiving post-primary education" (see Table III).

(11) Of 109 states containing a population greater than one million twenty-three enrolled 85 percent or more of their children in the 5–14 age bracket in primary school while sixty-one enrolled fewer than 50 percent (see Table III).

(12) Underdeveloped countries suffer from a lack of teachers, especially at the secondary school level (see Table III).

(13) Development problems are intensified by an exploding population. It is estimated that the population of developed countries will increase by 11 percent, 65 million, between 1960 and 1970. During the same decade the population of the underdeveloped lands will grow by 25 percent, or 350 million.

UNFAVORABLE EXPORT POSITION

Other data describe in less human terms the characteristics of underdeveloped economies.

Dependence on one or two exports is a characteristic of a large number of underdeveloped states (see Table IV).

Competition among producers of primary products depresses prices on the world market. A drop of one-half cent a pound in sugar, selling for three cents or four cents a pound, or a few cents a pound less in coffee or rubber, can be ruinous to the economy of the single-export state.[3] Profit margins are erased and the balance of trade between exports and imports upset. Hard currencies, which are scarce, must be used for essential imports. Investment capital intended for economic development and for necessary social services must be diverted to the purchase of food and clothing.

Underdeveloped states left to their own recourses may well get poorer because population growth may exceed economic growth, causing a decrease of *per-capita* income, and because the trend is toward falling prices for primary commodities left to the vicissitudes of the international market and to free exchange with manufactured

[3] "Understanding Foreign Aid," *Headline Series*, No. 160, July–August, 1963, p. 14. A one-cent decline on a pound of green coffee in 1960–61 would have amounted to $41 million; a similar decline in copper in 1960 would have meant $11.7 million less for Chile.

TABLE IV

Countries with One or Two Major Exports, 1964

State	Product	Percent of total exports
Bolivia	Tin	76
Brazil	Coffee	61
Burma	Rice	67
Ceylon	Tea	65 [1]
Chad	Cotton	86
Chile	Copper	63 [1]
Colombia	Coffee	78
Cuba	Sugar	88
Gambia	Peanuts	93
Ghana	Cocoa	65
Guatemala	Coffee	67
Haiti	Coffee	75 [2]
Honduras	Bananas	40 [1]
Iraq	Oil	96
Liberia	Rubber and Iron Ore	90
Malaysia	Rubber and Tin	54
Niger	Peanuts	72
Saudi Arabia	Oil	100
Sudan	Cotton	54
Venezuela	Oil	94

[1] 1963 figures contained in Dan Golenpaul, ed., *Information Please Almanac, Atlas and Yearbook 1966* (New York: Simon and Shuster, 1965).
[2] 1962–63.

Source: Based on export statistics contained in *The Europa Year Book 1966* (London: Europa Publications Limited, 1966).

goods. Already the share of world exports sold by states dealing mainly in raw materials has declined from one-third in 1950–52 to less than one-fourth in 1960–62. An FAO study indicates that the tendency toward declining prices during the 1950's in a number of commodities would most likely continue in any free-market situation.[4] International commodity agreements hold out some hope for the maintenance of stable prices.

[4] Food and Agricultural Organization, *Agricultural Commodities-Projection for 1970*, May, 1962.

CLASS DISTINCTIONS IN UNDERDEVELOPED STATES

Social distinctions intensify instability in underdeveloped lands. The typical Asian and Latin American country—this is not ordinarily the case in sub-Saharan Africa—has sharp class divisions. At one end of the scale is a small ruling class enjoying tremendous wealth, low taxes which they often evade, and favored treatment by law and law enforcement agencies. They control the government and utilize it to protect their privileged position and take advantage of graft and corruption. At the other end of the scale are the exploited masses, poverty-stricken, oppressed, suppressed, frustrated by their evil lot but seeking a way out.

As revolutionary forces of social change mature it is usually the middle class which supplies leadership for this movement. Education endows a person with great prestige in the eyes of the masses. The universities have been incubators for the ideals of nationalism and social justice. The very backwardness of the underdeveloped country brings forward a leadership shamed by the degradation of the people and intent on the most rapid modernization of their land. Generalized grievances are further aggravated by the underemployment of men of training and education. All too often the skills and knowledge gained through higher education have no outlet because the economy is too primitive to find use for the engineer, the economist, or the skilled administrator. Through personal frustration the intellectual is driven to revolutionary activity.

THE REVOLUTION OF RISING EXPECTATIONS

In most respects underdeveloped lands have changed little over the centuries. Poverty, corruption, unequal justice, oppression, extremely rich and extremely poor people always existed. What is new is the desire for change which is directing the thoughts and actions of long-oppressed mankind. The violent rebellions, street demonstrations, riots, and mobs are proof that people are no longer willing to live in the old way. They know that poverty and oppression are not preordained by God. They believe that they can have a better life, and in increasing numbers they are acting to get it. They may well believe that their wants can be satisfied simply by dividing up the wealth of the rich. The more understanding know that a better life can only be won through hard work, and they want leaders who propose to begin with this arduous task.

Reasons for rising expectations of the masses need not detain us. It is now a fact of life that the people "have got their steam up and are ready to roll. We can try to block their advance; we can stand aside; or we can ride with them and help steer. The first course would be foolhardy if not futile; the second, short-sighted; the last is in our national interest." [5]

People seek a better life, and a better life is directly related to the acquisition of possessions. Happiness has been expressed as an equation: [6]

$$\text{Happiness} = \frac{\text{Possessions}}{\text{Desires}}$$

At other times man sought happiness by reducing desires to fit the possessions likely to become available. Such a self-denying attitude has lost ground to the quest for happiness through accumulating possessions.

Conditions of poverty and popular inexperience with self-government provide a suitable milieu for the demagogue. Irresponsible promises of a good life may win a mass following. Juan Perón's social-security system, high wages, and numerous holidays bankrupted Argentina. People must learn that the wealth of the rich divided among the poor will make everyone poor—not rich. Breaking up latifundia into minifundia gives no peasant enough land to earn a decent living, yet it ruins agricultural productivity. Poverty is not simply a result of uneven distribution of available wealth. The better life can only be built through a more abundant economy, and this is difficult to achieve. Many African leaders have acknowledged the truth of this by following their demand for "Uhuru"—independence—with the admonitory slogan "Uhuru na kazi"—independence and work.

THE PROCESS OF ECONOMIC DEVELOPMENT

States cannot simply import economic development. Factories, scientific laboratories, and technical skill cannot be transplanted

[5] Forrest D. Murden, "Underdeveloped Lands: 'Revolution of Rising Expectations,'" Headline Series, No. 119, September–October, 1956, p. 4.
[6] Staley, op. cit., p. 20.

and made to operate efficiently in an underdeveloped country. Economic development entails social, cultural, psychological, and political changes which must take place along with or prior to industrialization. "The process of modernization is a seamless web, and the strands that compose it can be analytically separated only with some loss of realism." [7] It is best begun by a plan for development which takes into consideration the capabilities inherent in the land. Before capital and labor are invested in modernization, preinvestment surveys are needed to determine the most advantageous course for achieving economic growth. A modern economy rests upon an infrastructure without which industry and commerce would be stifled. Bedeviling the whole process of modernization is the problem of financing it, of developing the human skills and resources crucial for its success, of supporting this development by a thorough social transformation of society. States whose economy is based mainly on subsistence agriculture must establish a money economy. There is a need for men willing to accept entrepreneurial risks. Economic development is facilitated if there is some beginning of small-scale manufacturing already taking place. An effective government with fiscal and taxing powers, able to provide competent administration, is vital if development plans are to succeed.

Social Change

The underdeveloped country must adopt a new way of life. In just a brief period of time large numbers of people from farms move into growing cities leaving behind them a smaller rural population to feed the country. The lure of urban life with its excitement, and with its potentials for a fuller and more satisfying existence, is virtually irresistible. Political power must shift from a rural center to an urban arena, from traditional and inherited authority to leadership based on competence and relevant ideals. Development goals of the state must be communicated to its citizens if their energies are to be mobilized.

Social relations must be transformed. Patterns of land ownership which are inefficient and paternalistic must give way to new methods which enhance productivity. Agricultural production must be based

[7] Max F. Millikan and Donald L. M. Blackmer (eds.), *The Emerging Nations, Their Growth and United States Policy* (Boston: Little, Brown, 1961), p. 44.

on farms large enough to utilize efficiently modern techniques. Only those farmers who have self-interest in maximizing their output will provide the energizing force for increased production. Face-to-face relationships between employer and employee and the strong, extended family ties of the old society must be supplanted by more impersonal systems in which productivity is encouraged and rewarded. Wages and status must be based upon performance rather than family ties. The extended family that may require those who work to support uncles, aunts, cousins, nephews, and nieces discourages the individual from hard work because personal gains are minimized.

The individual's future in the industrialized states becomes more precarious. Social mobility in the rural community was virtually unknown. If born a peasant, one would die a peasant. But this creates a society in which one's future was predictable. Modern society offers opportunities for great gain if one will risk doing that which has not been tried and proven. Social mobility makes it unlikely that the individual's destiny is secure.

The ways of old-style religion are undermined. The superstitions of animist belief cannot be sustained against scientific evidence. Medicine men and soothsayers lose their function. It remains to be seen whether Islam will be able to retain the practices of Ramadan, the month when strict fasting is practiced, in an industrial society.

The importance of time as a factor, and adjustment to a much faster tempo of life, becomes an essential prerequisite for man's adaptation to the new society. Often the old generation cannot make the necessary adjustments, and only a new generation can carry out the transformations requisite for building a modernized society.

The demands for modernization may be pressing, but the nature of the transformation is such that it cannot be achieved overnight.

PREINVESTMENT REQUIREMENTS

Modernization is a process. It has been suggested that the process begins with some plan for transforming the economy. In 1957, the General Assembly established the Special Fund to concentrate on preinvestment activity. The Fund was:

(1) to survey the natural resources in underdeveloped lands seeking out those which may be quickly exploited with beneficial effect;

THE PROBLEMS OF ECONOMIC DEVELOPMENT 383

(2) to help develop as rapidly as possible the literacy of children and adults. Economic development requires a literate, educated, and skilled population; therefore educational programs geared to satisfy the most essential manpower needs of national development plans receive high priority;
(3) to utilize the findings and the methods of modern science;
(4) to support research aimed at finding new uses for local materials and products; and
(5) to promote the development of techniques through which the process of development may be accelerated.[8]

Millikan and Blackmer point to three prerequisites for economic development. First, a country must command human resources. In the beginning general literacy, basic administrative skills, and technical knowledge need to be acquired. Later a wider variety of education and skills become necessary. Even a minimal development of such human resources requires a long period of effort before trained persons become available in adequate numbers.[9]

A second prerequisite for economic development is the creation of an infrastructure—means of transportation, communication, sanitation, irrigation, and the construction of power facilities. Modern industry cannot operate profitably until these prerequisites are adequately met. Capital, especially private investment, is unlikely to be drawn to a country lacking the infrastructure for industry. It takes years to build the roads, railways, underground sewage facilities, and to construct dams. The efficient use of railroads, power plants, and telephonic communications requires large-scale enterprise. Unit costs decrease sharply only with large-scale use.

Third, even in the early stages of economic development there is a sizable exodus of people from the agricultural areas to the urban centers. If the people are to be fed without increased imports greater productivity in agriculture is necessary. As Millikan and Blackmer point out, "Peoples who are drawn off the land to build roads and canals and factories, and who are moving to growing towns and cities, must be fed. If they were previously productive on

[8] Francis O. Wilcox and H. Field Haviland, Jr. (eds.), *The United States and the United Nations* (Baltimore: The Johns Hopkins Press, 1961), Paul G. Hoffman, "The Six Imperatives of Economic and Social Progress," Ch. 2.
[9] *Op. cit.*, pp. 46–53.

the land, their departure reduces agricultural production. If they were not—that is if in subsistence agriculture the food supply was divided among an unnecessarily large number of workers—then, as some leave the land, the remaining individuals are likely to eat better. . . ." [10] Shortages of food are aggravated because as economic development takes place the population tends to increase faster and the inadequate production of food will quickly demoralize the most vigorous national effort. In the end even totalitarian dictatorships have been forced to reduce their investments in infrastructure and industry to beef up agricultural production. In 1963, Communist China acknowledged at least a partial failure in her economic development plans by cutting back industrial growth to allow greater investment in the production of food. Both the Soviet Union and Communist China have been forced to purchase wheat abroad to make up for their own shortages in food production. Since 1959, the United States has given surplus agricultural commodities in its "Food for Peace Program" to assist friendly states facing food shortages. The program provides food, paid for in local currencies or on occasion donated outright, so that developing states need not divert capital from other development activities to increase the productivity of their agriculture, at least not immediately.

Fulfilling these preconditions for economic development is made particularly difficult because much of this activity is not attractive to private investors. The construction of roads, sewage systems, schools, bridges, and the draining of unhealthy swamps are not profit-making operations. Loans for funding such projects should be of a low-interest variety and these do not attract private investment. The underdeveloped state can rarely finance these activities locally. This necessitates assistance from other states as well as from international agencies. In addition to the Special Fund, other international assistance agencies have been created with a special concern for preinvestment or infrastructure projects. The Technical Assistance Program of the UN and the specialized agencies has been in this field since 1949. The International Development Association (IDA) undertakes infrastructure projects by providing long-term credit without charging interest. Service charges for loans are low, and the terms of repayment are generous—repayments in some in-

[10] *Op. cit.,* p. 51.

stances may be stretched out over fifty years and may be made in soft currencies. Projects that are not self-liquidating such as the construction of hospitals and schools have been financed through IDA resources. Another assistance program provides operational, executive, and administrative personnel (OPEX). The UN recruits personnel to provide skills that are unavailable or in short supply. In this program the host government must appoint counterpart personnel who are trained by the OPEX officers to take over operation. The program has been small and its drawbacks are less a lack of funds than the unavailability of skilled persons. The 1961 budget allowed for eighty posts but only forty were filled.

A number of states have provided preinvestment and infrastructure assistance on a bilateral basis. Bilateral programs of the United States, France, Great Britain, the Soviet Union, and others carried out through their own agencies have added measurably to the attack on underdevelopment. The United States' "Alliance for Progress" has made sizable contributions to the building of primary schools in Latin American states. The French through their Investment Fund for Economic and Social Development of Overseas Territory (FIDES) have built seaports, railroads, roads, airports, and educational and public facilities in their former African territories. The Soviet Union is helping in the construction of the Aswan Dam in Egypt. Development assistance has also been granted by regional groupings such as the Organization for European Cooperation and Development, the EEC, SEATO, the Colombo Plan, and the Soviet-led Council for Mutual Economic Aid (COMECON).

TRADE

Underdeveloped countries need foreign exchange to carry out programs of modernization, and trade is a major source for accumulating foreign currency. In 1960, trade brought into underdeveloped areas about four times the foreign currency obtained through foreign aid and investment combined.[11] In some countries offering foreign aid, there are those who would eliminate aid and emphasize trade. "Trade not aid" is an attractive slogan but if put into force it would cripple economic development. The need for consumer and for capital imports in underdeveloped areas is so great that

[11] "Understanding Foreign Aid," *op. cit.,* p. 13.

trade, aid, and grants of surplus food are all necessary to cope with problems of development.

CAPITAL FORMATION

Countries in the early stage of economic development are chronically short of capital. Local capital is unavailable in adequate quantity for development purposes. Perhaps as much as a billion dollars a year of "flight capital" has been invested abroad by Latin Americans. Borrowing from banking institutions is difficult because bankers are reluctant to take risks. All too often local investment has gone into business activities that do little or nothing to build the economy of the land. This is often also true of foreign capital. Underdeveloped countries are not markedly developed by investment in the production of soft drinks, real estate in fast-growing cities, usury, gambling casinos, or by permitting illicit sale of narcotics, activities which bring large returns to investors, foreign and domestic. Unfortunately, much wealth is invested, for the purposes of safety, not at home but abroad, where Americans, British, French, and Swiss invest their money, in the stock markets of Wall Street, London, Paris, and Geneva.

If an American wishes to produce a product for which he does not have adequate capital, he will visit his local bank and discuss the project with his local banker. If the banker is convinced that the idea is sound, that the product is marketable and will produce a profit, and that the borrower is accustomed to repaying his debts, loan capital will be forthcoming. The enterprising individual in an underdeveloped country cannot turn to a local bank for the investment capital which he lacks. Towns and villages in underdeveloped countries have no banks. Only large centers are likely to have banks and they will be few in number. There are no local banks outside of major centers because ordinary people do not have money to save. The poor spend their money for the most basic necessities to maintain life. Even with modest annual increases in their income they tend to use their money to eat a little better, dress a little better, and take care of their health a little more adequately. Local sources of investment capital are far too inadequate to fund economic development.

A portion of the capital needed must, nevertheless, be found locally. Some American universities have undertaken projects for the stimulation of small-scale business and industry based upon local resources. The improvement and the enforcement of tax legislation as a source of forced savings would provide capital for government-sponsored development activities. A significant portion of investment capital must necessarily come from abroad.

The Special Fund has surveyed natural resources which could attract foreign investment. About half of its projects have been surveys to determine the prospects in land use, water power, mining, and forest exploitation. At the eleventh session of the Governing Council held in 1964, forty-eight projects were approved: fourteen for surveying natural resources and industrial feasibility; twenty for education and technical training; twelve in applied research; two on economic development planning.[12]

UNITED NATIONS DECADE OF DEVELOPMENT

Left on their own, underdeveloped lands will be unable to develop themselves or they will do it too slowly to maintain stability in face of prevailing aspirations. Rather than fail in their efforts, the underdeveloped countries turn to the more affluent states for assistance. Such assistance is beyond the capacity of any one donor country. Bilateral programs have political implications. It has long been recognized that international programs of assistance are a useful, even an essential, element in the attack on underdevelopment.

President Kennedy proposed a coordinated international effort for economic and social development. Speaking to the Sixteenth General Assembly on September 25, 1961, he proposed that the decade of the 1960's be designated, "as the UN Decade of Development." He believed that such an approach would expand the total effort of assisting development and that development could "become a cooperative, not a competitive enterprise—to enable all nations, however diverse in their systems and beliefs, to become in fact as well as in law free and equal states."

The General Assembly adopted, as a UN program, the Decade of Development,[13] setting a goal of 5 percent annual increase in the income of the developing countries. Despite anticipated popula-

[12] *United Nations Review,* Vol. 11, No. 3, March, 1964, p. 25.
[13] Document A/5058, December 19, 1961.

tion growth this would still allow a net increase of almost 3 percent.[14] Achieving this goal would require organized efforts for maintaining price stability in international trade and sizable injections of foreign aid.

The Decade of Development will concentrate its main efforts in preinvestment and infrastructure projects. For those countries which are beginning to approach a self-generating economy—Colombia, Greece, Israel, Mexico, Taiwan, and Turkey—private investment for industrialization is likely to be found. For the underdeveloped countries, attracting large-scale private investment and achieving industrial development will probably await a future decade.[15]

AGENCIES OF ECONOMIC DEVELOPMENT

International preoccupation with economic growth has brought into being a number of agencies involved with development projects. International, regional, and national organizations have been set up to assist in the development process. Assistance has been provided through advice, consultation, training, donations of surplus food, loans, favorable trade arrangements, and grants of capital.

The United Nations itself is an agency of major importance in helping with economic and social development. Two great operational efforts have been undertaken to this end. The Expanded Program of Technical Assistance (EPTA) has provided services of experts and established training programs from which over one hundred countries have benefited.[16] The Special Fund has steadily increased its resources and has expanded its assistance in preinvestment projects (see pp. 382–383). The Special Fund and the Technical Assistance Program were united as the United Nations Development Program (UNDP) in 1966. On a smaller scale the UN has provided operational and executive services through OPEX. A Commission on International Commodity Trade (CICT) was set up to assist countries in promoting stability for prices on raw materials; an Industrial Development Centre provides consultants on the development of industry. It has been pointed out that "the wrong

[14] Hoffman, *op. cit.*, p. 129.

[15] *Ibid.*, Ch. 14. Hoffman estimates $440 billion in goods and services is necessary for the task; $378 billion must come from earnings of foreign exchange, the remainder in some form of assistance.

[16] Richard N. Swift (ed.), *Annual Review of United Nations Affairs, 1961–1962* (New York: Oceana Publications, 1963), pp. 81–85.

x

factory in the wrong place for the wrong product is the besetting danger of every period of growth."[17]

Specialized agencies have also participated in these activities. Most closely concerned have been the financial institutions, the World Bank, the International Monetary Fund, the International Finance Corporation, and the International Development Association. The Bank has established an advisory service which offers economic and financial advice for the preparation and execution of development programs.

Regional programs of development assistance exist in all continents containing underdeveloped countries. Asia has a Colombo Plan and assistance programs sponsored by SEATO and CENTO. Latin America has its Alliance for Progress and Inter-American Development Bank. Africa has been aided by the European Development Fund of the EEC. NATO countries help in underdeveloped areas through the Organization for Economic Cooperation and Development (OECD). The Warsaw Pact states provide assistance through COMECON.

Most of the great powers have national programs for providing assistance on a bilateral basis. United States assistance is dispensed by the Agency for International Development, the Export-Import Bank, the Food for Peace Program, and the Peace Corps. Great Britain has set up a Colonial Development Corporation for its colonies. France concentrates its assistance in sub-Saharan Africa through its *Fonds d'Investissements pour le Développement Economique et Social*. Bilateral assistance has been given by Communist and Nationalist China, Czechoslovakia, East and West Germany, the Soviet Union, Japan, Belgium, Israel, Egypt, and Italy, among others.

TWO MODELS FOR ECONOMIC DEVELOPMENT

Industrialized states have followed their own path of economic growth. Prior to World War II, development could proceed at a leisurely pace. Popular pressures for improvement were relatively restrained. The population explosion was not yet in full swing. Since the war, popular pressures demand rapid modernization, and

[17] United Nations Press Release SG/1194/Res. 1, 8 May, 1962, pp. 4–5, quoting Acting Secretary-General U Thant.

states are adopting one of two generalized approaches for this end. The contest between communism and democracy in the underdeveloped world may well be determined by their relative success in implementing modernization. At the present time, India and Communist China have been dramatically cast as the protagonists for the "democratic" and "totalitarian" paths.

THE BRITISH-SOVIET-CHINESE APPROACH

Two hundred years ago the British began the process of industrialization. A growing urban population provided an entrepreneur with a large supply of cheap labor. Industry was profitable. The England described in Charles Dickens' novels conveys the degradation caused by harsh exploitation of labor. The twelve- and fourteen-hour day and the exploitation of women and children gained enormous profits for factory owners. The entrepreneur that Marx had in mind in his critique of capitalism was the capitalist of Western Europe and England in the mid-nineteenth century. He reinvested his profits in industry because industrial investment was profitable. He did not use his funds primarily for the satisfaction of creature comforts but essentially to make more money. The process of investment and reinvestment produced a highly industrialized country. In this sense British industrialization was achieved by the sweat, blood, and labor of the exploited British working class. In the nineteenth century the state often assisted capitalism by suppressing labor organization.

The series of five-year plans initiated by the Soviet government beginning in 1928 were essentially similar in approach to the British method of development. Instead of capitalists, the Soviet government became the exploiter of labor. The regime created conditions inducing large-scale peasant migration to cities where the peasants could earn wages. Artificially depressed levels of wages insured that wives as well as husbands would be drawn into the productive process. Nurseries for infants and children made it possible for women to work. The government invested each annual increment of its wealth in industry. Living standards fell below that of 1928 and were not permitted to rise until after Stalin's death. However, through such forced marches the Soviet Union was able to complete its industrialization in the brief period of forty years.

The Chinese sought to do the same things the Russians did, only more quickly. In a very real sense, labor power was substituted for capital which was unavailable. Roads and dams had to be built but modern machinery could not be purchased. Under these circumstances the patriotic Chinese was expected, by the community, to contribute labor, wielding the pick and shovel in construction if necessary, to press forward industrialization very speedily.

Extreme exploitation of labor was utilized, and not without success, to provide infrastructure development which could not be bought or gained through foreign aid. While Peking's statistics may not be reliable, authoritative reports agree that considerable economic development has taken place as a result of the efforts of the Communist government. It may well be that among the underdeveloped countries of Asia, China has won much admiration because it is developing more rapidly than any of the other states. The costs in starvation and misery have been high. Her methods of economic development have been vindicated on the grounds that rapid development has taken place. Despite setbacks and even starvation, food has been exported for political purposes. Production of consumer goods has been both controlled and curtailed for the purpose of maintaining the planned development to an industrial society.

THE UNITED STATES-INDIAN MODEL FOR ECONOMIC DEVELOPMENT

Economic development of the United States in the period after the Civil War rested heavily on foreign investment. While Americans were frugal and tended to save rather than spend, a large share of the capital for industry came from Europe. Investment in the United States was profitable and consequently attracted risk capital. Capital shortages within the United States were made up by foreign investors.

The Indians are trying to achieve a self-generating economy by attracting foreign capital. In this sense they are following the outlines of the United States model. This approach does not require the extreme exploitation of labor. Wages in the United States were always higher than those paid in Great Britain or on the European continent.[18] American labor was never exploited with the severity with which European labor had been. But this circumstance probably placed a high premium on the productivity of American labor.

[18] Earl R. Browder, *Marx and America* (New York: Duell, Sloan and Pearce, 1958).

The fact is that American goods produced at "high" wage rates could hold their own in international competition because of the productivity of American labor. A high standard of living within the United States created a local market that absorbed about 90 percent of American production.

The American-Indian model of capital formation requires no colossal edifice of government. Economic development is promoted rather than forced on the people. Capital can be used for the promotion of consumer industries as well as heavy industry. The social costs of this method of development are thus moderated.

The inherent danger of the United States-Indian model is that the people may be lured into the support of demagogues who promise standards of living which their economy cannot sustain. Perón bankrupted Argentina by making such an appeal. He was popular with the Argentinian workingmen because he gave them high wages, frequent vacations, and a good pension system with a rather early age for retirement even though the wealth of the country could not support such living standards. The large surpluses of the Argentine treasury inherited by Perón were eaten up and eventually Argentina could no longer obtain the money needed to maintain its standard of living. It is reasonable to assume that this situation is not conducive to economic growth but, to the contrary, is likely to lead to a deterioration of the economic strength of the state.

China and India represent two contrasting concepts for economic development. History teaches us that both methods of development can succeed. One may feel confidence that the masses of Asia observing Chinese and Indian development will prefer economic development in the context of a more democratic society which would minimize suffering. There can be no question, however, that the success of the Indian approach is keyed to its ability to meet the goals of economic development that it has set for itself. Because of the "revolution of rising expectations," economic development is a major concern of all the peoples. Democracy without economic development is doomed to failure. Economic development in a totalitarian context will be adopted should other methods fail. If democracy and freedom are to last and if the stability of democratic states is to be assured, democratic states must achieve their development goals and must win the people's confidence that they or their children will share in the affluence that will thereby be attained.

CHAPTER 14

Problems of United States Foreign Policy

THE HISTORIAN of the twenty-first century may point to the Cuban missile crisis as the decisive event in the cold war. Several years after the event is surely too soon to reveal the trend for the remaining part of the century. However, the temptation to make a bold guess cannot be entirely suppressed, and the improvement in relations between the Soviet Union and the United States has been marked. Recent clashes pitting the two powers against one another have been insufficient to deter the general improvements which have pervaded the atmosphere. A long period of peace between the super-powers seems assured.

That fateful confrontation in Cuba illustrated with simplicity the ingredients of a realistic foreign policy. It also made brutally plain how small is the margin for error and how vital it is that foreign policy be guided by an appreciation for what is possible.

For a foreign policy to succeed in serving the national interest several considerations must be kept in mind. First, a state should have a sense of direction, detailed through goals which its foreign policy is designed to achieve. Without goals a foreign policy becomes mere reactions to events of the day. A foreign policy without direction can hardly support a role of leadership.

Second, foreign policy operates in a milieu characteristic of a particular time. Such a milieu influences the nature of the goals which states pursue and the means that are utilized to attain ends. In this decade there must be a sense of proportion with regard to the use of military means. The 1963 dispute between the United States and Panama could have been settled by the United States to its satisfaction through the modest use of military force. However, this would have been intolerable to the American people and to the world at large. In this world where power plays so overriding a role there also exists a sense of morality that powers are loath to ignore. In a vague sense there is some consensus regarding an order of magnitude of means appropriate to a situation. One does not use a pile driver to swat a fly. Among other considerations, for the United States to have solved its differences with Panama with a nuclear bomb would have been unthinkable because as a means of settlement the order of magnitude would be entirely inconsistent with the requirements of the issue in dispute.

Third, this is a world of more than one hundred and twenty-five states, each holding ambitions of its own. The achievement of goals depends greatly upon the manner in which they may impinge upon the goals of other states. Some goals may win the support and cooperation of other states. This is the case where America helps other countries modernize their economies. Other goals are irrelevant to other states. There are goals which run counter to the interests of other states and will therefore fail to gain support. Quarantining China, Cuba, or North Vietnam suits Washington's interests but may militate against advantageous trade relations for the countries of Western Europe or Canada. The juxtaposition of goals must be an essential calculation.

Finally, a state must be cognizant of its capabilities. Capability is predominantly the power to achieve an objective. Calculation of power involves the identification of forces supportive to the achievement of an objective, forces antagonistic to the goal, and the relative power of each force. States should avoid policies designed to achieve goals beyond their power. In October, 1962, Kennedy identified the situation and the needs of the United States. "This ... transformation of Cuba into an important strategic base ... constitutes an explicit threat to the peace and security of all the Americas ..." [1] The threat called for a response in terms of possible nuclear retaliation. There was little opposition from allies and neutrals to the steps the President adopted. The Organization of American States unanimously endorsed the United States' initiative. The goals of all Western hemisphere states except Cuba were in harmony. The confrontation became an equation in power. After the missiles and bombs "were counted," and the capabilities of the

[1] Address of October 22, 1962.

United States and the Soviet Union had been assessed, both sides tacitly agreed that the United States had the capability of quarantining Cuba and forcing the withdrawal of Soviet missiles from the island. Prudence dictated that the Soviet Union draw back.

The Cuban missile crisis also provided a good example of decisive action in the face of great danger and in the absence of assurances as to the manner in which the adversary would react. Acting with such resolution could be reckless unless the concomitants of power are available for support of necessary action.

THE GOALS OF UNITED STATES FOREIGN POLICY

What is it that the United States wants? It aims to help build a world in which it can enjoy peace and prosperity. Secretary of State Rusk described this kind of world as:

A world free of aggression—aggression by whatever means;

A world of independent nations, each with the institutions of its own choice but cooperating with one another to their mutual advantage;

A world which yields continuous progress in economic and social justice for all peoples;

A world which provides sure and equitable means for the peaceful settlement of disputes and moves progressively toward a rule of law which lays down and enforces standards of conduct in relations between nations;

A world in which, in the great tradition shared by peoples in every continent, governments derive "their just powers from the consent of the governed";

A world in which the powers of the state over the individual are limited by law, practice, and custom—in which the personal freedoms essential to the dignity of man are secure.[2]

The cynic will say that such a statement is too idealistic to determine concrete policies. It stands to reason that the United States has some interests which concern it alone, and it would be naive to believe that policy decisions are based on simple justice rather than national advantage. As a *status-quo* power the United States does in fact want to live in the world to which Rusk says it aspires. As long as the United States is not interested in building an empire, does not seek to impose its ways on others, and has confidence in

[2] Department of State, "Five Goals of Our Foreign Policy," *General Foreign Policy Series* 188, Publication 7542, Office of Media Services, Bureau of Public Affairs, Reissued December 1963, p. 1.

the merits of its system, it has everything to gain from an open society of diverse, prospering, and peaceful states. Its aspirations can be shared by others and its aims do not require a solitary effort.

UNITED STATES RESPONSIBILITIES AND CAPABILITIES

International strife has characterized our times. Fear of a nuclear holocaust has in a degree moderated conflicts, but we are living in an era of danger. Peace and security have become United States responsibilities, for only the United States has the power to shoulder the burden of leadership of the non-Communist world. America's leadership is facilitated by its aims which are generally compatible with those of the other states of the free world. As long as the United States remains an affluent flourishing democracy respecting the interests of others its claim to leadership will be accepted.

LEADERSHIP

At the end of the Second World War two circumstances made it necessary for the United States to accept leadership in the free world. First, the rise of the Soviet Union and later China as great revisionist powers threatened the security of Europe and Asia and, therefore, had to be checked. Second, the wartime destruction precluded a leadership role for the powers of Western Europe. Only United States power has stood in the way of the communization of large areas and vast populations. The United States, even largely demobilized as it was in 1946–50, with its great industrial strength, its atomic weapons, and its long-range air power, was able to act forcefully.

The focus of attention of the American people had, until World War II, been directed inward, upon internal development and internal problems. Americans did not naturally accept a role of world leadership. In earlier periods there had been occasions of world leadership by American statesmen. Theodore Roosevelt played a crucial role in the Russo-Japanese War and the Second Hague Conference of 1907. Woodrow Wilson was among the most important international figures at the end of the First World War. Franklin Roosevelt played a prominent role in connection with the crises of the 1930's. Instances of United States leadership tended to be temporary and arose from particular conditions. There was no conception of enduring United States leadership. Even at the end of the Second World War, Americans expected the United Nations to maintain peace and good order. United States abdication of leadership was exemplified by the rapid demobilization of its armed forces and its liquidation of overseas bases.

The situation at the end of the war made it necessary for the United States to accept the mantle of leadership, largely to assure its own security. For most states outside Soviet control United States leadership was quite acceptable. The moral posture of United States policy and the generosity of its behavior during and after the war struck a favorable image for America. Certain moral imperatives were articulated as a basis for United States policy. The United States believed in the central importance of the individual in society and that freedom and independence were birthrights due everyone. Woodrow Wilson and Franklin D. Roosevelt had been acknowledged world figures of the highest moral stature. Their good works made it easier for others to turn to the United States for leadership. The non-Communist lands did not feel threatened by Washington's ambitions.

UNITED STATES CAPABILITIES

In a world in which two opposing ways of life vie for supremacy, leadership is more a function of power than of moral stature. Moral stature is relevant to power. Morally acceptable positions win support, which improves the power position of the moral state over that of the immoral or amoral power. In this sense, the cold-war clash is concerned with moral precepts. However, the question between East and West is not so much "Who is moral?" as, "What is moral?" In this situation other elements of power have greater bearing on the outcome of the struggle. The moral dialogue is, therefore, at best inconclusive. The first-rank power position of the United States is so obviously well established that it has been accepted as a fact. Nevertheless, it is also conceded that there are limits to United States power.

At one extreme are those who believe that United States power is limitless and that the United States can achieve any goal helpful to its position in world affairs. In this view the United States can prevent any territory from falling under Communist leadership; forestall changes in governments that prove hostile to United

States interests; overcome policies to which Washington is opposed; secure passage, in the UN, of such resolutions which it favors and defeat all to which it is opposed. Communist control of Eastern Europe and China was clearly, therefore, a malfunction of United States foreign policy or, perhaps even worse, a result of treason in high places. With the right policies a Communist take-over could have been prevented. The United States should police the globe.

Crises such as the wars in Korea and Vietnam and the threats surrounding West Berlin have made some Americans "gun shy." There is strong sentiment expressed for the contrary view that the United States is trying to do too much. United States involvement in Korea, Formosa, Vietnam, Laos, Malaysia, India, Iran, Israel, Cyprus, Lebanon, Africa, Latin America, Western Europe, and North America are thought beyond the capabilities of even so formidable a power as the United States. The United States should limit its responsibilities to fewer and to the most vital areas.

To know which commitments are within United States power requires much detailed information, a significant portion of which is classified. Guidelines on this subject are in order. The capabilities of the United States should not be evaluated in terms of United States power alone but in terms of the power of the protagonists concerned. For instance, given a desire to assist the Vietnamese government in averting a Communist take-over, the capability of the United States must be assayed in relation to the importance of this commitment as against other obligations of United States power; the forces arrayed against the United States; the forces assisting the United States. It is one thing for the United States to face the Viet Cong; it is a different matter to fight the Viet Cong should they in fact be the peasant masses of Vietnam; it is something else again to fight North Vietnam as well as the Viet Cong; adding Communist China to the enemy forces gives the military confrontation a new dimension; and it would be an entirely altered situation if the Soviet Union were to become militarily involved. Of course equivalent calculations face Communist China and the Soviet Union. The Soviet Union is no more free to act in Asia by depriving herself of strength in Europe than is the United States. With these considerations in view, America's involvement in the war in Vietnam is tenable as being quite within its capabilities.

In sum, in a world in which the United States faces powers, some hostile, others neutral, and still others allied with it, a calculation of power may be made by which the relative power and hence the capability of states may be assessed. An estimate of the gross national products, the military strengths, the populations, the available resources, and the other factors considered in Chapter 2 provide estimates of capability.

INTERNAL BASIS OF UNITED STATES POWER

Prosperity and economic growth are essential aspects of United States influence. Leadership is effected by example. Soviet achievement of a greater rate of economic growth during the 1950's shook international confidence in the future of America. It was felt that perhaps Khrushchev was right when he claimed that the Soviet Union would overtake the United States economy and socialism would provide a greater abundance than capitalism.

Material progress plays a decisive role in proving the durability of a social system. People place great importance upon technological improvements. Economic growth is equated with success. Static economies are taken as proof of failure. Therefore, America's effort to eliminate poverty could have a tremendous favorable international impact. If successful, the United States would become the first country in history to abolish poverty. The appeal of such success would raise the prestige not only of the United States but also of the democratic way of life.

These are times in which the ideal of equality is held in highest esteem. Race relations in the United States blur its image as an equalitarian society and render it vulnerable to attack abroad. Most men are not white and they dislike the United States when they learn of the indignities and second-class treatment accorded nonwhites. Some may know that great improvements in race relations have taken place in the United States. They may know that the government itself has acted to end discrimination against and segregation of Negroes. Many are aware that discriminatory practices have been reduced because of the extraordinary effort that American governments—national, state, and local—have made on this score. The greater access given Negroes to positions of leadership and responsibility have demonstrated the progress which has been made in American race relations. Nevertheless, until equality for all is a reality, hostile interests will be able to capitalize on every instance of racial injustice in the United States.

For a generation or more, United States leaders have been world leaders. Before American statesmen can bestride the world stage and preside over the destiny of mankind they must first achieve the recognition of their own citizenry. The perceptivity of the American people is a precondition for the quality of United States leadership. The wisdom and steadfastness of the American voter is often called into question. Dean Acheson has written: "The United States, which has the material capability, lacks the experience and the discipline needed for responsible management. . . ." [3] Yet the recent record has been that of a strong American guiding hand. In these perilous times security rests upon the resoluteness of leadership while peace depends upon the prudence with which all steps are assayed. In the postwar era, leadership such as that demonstrated by the Truman Doctrine, the Marshall Plan, the defense of Korea, the support of the UN in the Congo, the checkmate of Soviet missiles in Cuba, the Test Ban Agreement, and the tenacious yet limited war in Vietnam under President Johnson are grounds for confidence that United States leadership has come of age. On the other hand, the habits of other peoples and the tendency of Americans to expect others to adopt an American way of life calls into question the relevance of United States leadership to the dilemmas of developing countries.

THE UNITED STATES AND ITS ALLIES

Bilateral and multilateral treaties ally the United States with more than forty other countries. Alliances have been signed to ensure security. "The Parties agree that an armed attack against one . . . shall be considered an attack against them all . . . each of them . . . will assist the Party or Parties so attacked by taking forthwith, individually and in concert with other Parties, such action as it deems necessary . . ." So reads Article 5 of the North Atlantic Treaty.

In the past, American leadership initiated mutual-security treaties, and its influence has been dominant. United States power guaran-

[3] Dean Acheson, *Power and Diplomacy* (New York: Atheneum, 1962), p. 6.

teed the security of its allies and the United States in turn gained protection by forestalling aggression in distant places. In recent years alliances have begun to assume a character of equal partnership. America's leadership has become less dominant. After 1969, the parties to the North Atlantic Pact may leave the organization. A restructuring of the Alliance is in store which could redefine NATO's role in the control of nuclear weapons. The United States provides NATO with a nuclear capability as a part of its own component in NATO forces. Now NATO powers want "their fingers on the trigger." They want to ensure that nuclear weapons will be used when they deem it necessary, and at the same time they seek to preclude their being brought into a nuclear war which they do not wish to fight.

THE USEFULNESS OF ALLIANCES FOR UNITED STATES FOREIGN POLICY GOALS

As tensions waned after 1962, doubt grew about the utility of free-world alliances. Though enmity abated, the quarrels which brought these alliances into being remained. Reduction of tension may itself be no more than a passing phase. As long as none of the large cold-war issues have yet been settled, the cause for alliance still exists. At the same time, alliances do not *ipso facto* stand in the way of efforts for settling unresolved issues.

Alliances such as NATO, SEATO, and CENTO were essential elements in the policy of containment of Soviet expansion. In this respect the alliances have played a useful role and Communist aggression has been contained. The hope that once containment had been effected a roll back of Communist control in Eastern Europe would follow, has not come to pass. Containment has produced a stalemate which is preferable to defeat, and which has deflated the Communist boast of their inevitable victory. However, any sign of weakening in the alliances is likely to be interpreted by the Communists as a reward for their persistence and as evidence of their ultimate success.

Catholics and Protestants fought in bloody war for thirty years in the seventeenth century. Eventually they concluded that both faiths were permanent fixtures in the world and one would not eliminate the other. They were then ready to coexist and they agreed to the Peace of Westphalia (1648). When East and West no longer consider ultimate victory possible then a new "Peace of West-phalia" would be in order and the system of cold-war alliances would become superfluous. For the present the Soviet Union and Communist China still believe in victory over the West. A need for alliances to discourage Communist aggression therefore remains.

The first alliance organized by the United States, NATO, was necessary because the Security Council was unable to function as a guarantor of peace and security since peace was threatened by a member of the Security Council, the Soviet Union (see Chapter 4, p. 117, above). The Security Council is still unable to function as intended and the rationale for the alliances established under Article 51 therefore still exists.

The *raison d'être* of alliances is the maintenance of the *status quo*. However, alliances have also proved effective as a means for cooperation in other fields as well. NATO states have organized the Organization for Economic Cooperation and Development (OECD) to give economic aid. Development activities have been sponsored by SEATO and CENTO. The Alliance for Progress has become a program of the OAS.

An additional benefit of alliance relationships is gained in the interchange which takes place in the establishment of alliance policy. National policies are tempered and made more circumspect as a result of their airing at meetings of the alliance.

FRANCE UNDER DE GAULLE: THE TROUBLESOME ALLY

Since 1963, the United States and France have been at odds on a number of major issues. De Gaulle vetoed British membership in the Common Market, he refused to sign the Test Ban Agreement, he insisted that France develop an independent nuclear deterrent (a move strongly opposed by Washington), he recognized Communist China, and proposed the neutralization of South Vietnam while the United States was trying to fight to achieve victory there.

De Gaulle is attempting to enunciate a French position independent of United States leadership. This is understandable in terms of de Gaulle's well-known desire to reassert the first-rank stature of France. As such his policy might more correctly be seen as an effort to build French leadership rather than a distaste for United States leadership.

De Gaulle has attempted to affirm France's leadership through a number of moves. He has tried to denigrate the supranational characteristics of the Common Market and impose Franco-German leadership upon it. This was one of the reasons for his veto of British membership. When Bonn refused to go along, he tried to frustrate the political development of the EEC. De Gaulle wanted NATO to become a partnership of France, Great Britain, and the United States leading the other powers. Therefore, the overarching leadership of Washington must be challenged. The integrity of Europe as distinct from North America must be brought forward. European leaders must be convinced that over the long term United States defense of Europe is not dependable. All American presidents since the war have pledged that Europe will be defended with nuclear weapons if necessary. The French say that future presidents could bow to Soviet nuclear threats and refuse to defend the European allies. Consequently, France must defend itself by building its own nuclear deterrent.

The French problem poses some real difficulties for the United States alliance policy. France believes that the British enjoy a favored relationship with the United States. She is cautious about a British role on the continent, fearing that Britain would simply be another American voice in Europe. The special relationship between Great Britain and the United States is more apparent than substantive, and other European allies are less concerned with the United States-British relationship. Of greater moment, however, is the question of leadership in NATO. Western Europe today is vastly different from what it was when NATO was formed. European powers expect to play an equal role in the affairs of NATO and be given a greater voice in the nuclear weapons field. The United States has some hard choices to make. On the one hand it favors allowing NATO a larger status in nuclear policy determination. On the other hand, it seeks a nonproliferation agreement with the Soviet Union which insists that the United States commitment to prevent the spread of nuclear capability to additional countries precludes extension of any control over nuclear weapons to NATO.

The United States is ready to concede a larger role in NATO for European states including France. The realities of power permit France no special status over other of the large powers in the alliance. To the contrary, the United States must continue to support the integrative tendencies of European states. NATO states should set limits on de Gaulle's obstruction; if he exceeds these limits they might present a solid front of opposition to his policies. Steps toward the integration of the community, if opposed by De Gaulle, will serve to isolate him and bring into being local forces seeking to make French policy more cooperative.

United States policy has faced the dilemma of choice between supporting its allies and supporting policies which the allies oppose but Washington believes to be correct. During the Suez crisis of 1956, the United States abandoned its allies in favor of efforts to defeat British-French-Israeli "aggression" there. On occasion the United States has supported colonial peoples against the French policy of suppressing colonial revolt. One may suspect that de Gaulle has been "repaying" Washington's reproaches of France with enunciation of his disagreement with United States policy in Asia, Latin America, and Cuba. The closest and most powerful allies of the United States are in Western Europe. While the United States positions adopted on issues derive from a balance of many considerations, unity with and understanding of our West European allies must be the cornerstone of United States foreign policy. Washington cannot permit NATO to falter. Criticism of NATO partners must therefore be friendly and moderate. Their criticism of the United States must be regarded with tolerance.

OTHER ALLIES

The alliance between Japan and the United States was an acknowledgement of postwar harmony. The military aspects of this alliance involve the stationing of United States forces on the islands for the defense of Japanese and United States interests in the Far East. The military arrangements have been satisfactory to both sides. The internal political situation of this populous and prosperous nation is such that the United States must assure Japan the widest degree of independence in the development of her foreign policy. Japan has strong economic incentives to remain very friendly with the United States, and the United States economic policy toward Japan ought to encourage such an attachment.

The United States is allied with over forty states. Relations among our allies may from time to time deteriorate. Turkey and Greece have been in conflict over Cyprus. South Korea and Japan have not outlived their legacy of animus. Latin American states have occasionally engaged in bitter quarrels. On occasion the United States has been able to act as the "good broker" in a dispute. As leader of the alliance it cannot remain oblivious to internecine conflicts. Disinterested suggestions will in the long run make United States leadership least vulnerable to charges of favoritism or of the promotion of its own narrow interest.

Washington's moral stature has too often been blemished by support given brutal and venal dictators ruling allied countries. Walking the tightrope between the expediency of having specific allies regardless of the unsavory character of their leadership and championing the cause of democracy has laid the United States open to charges of unprincipled behavior. Supporting corrupt and unpopular dictators makes little sense when more democratic non-Communist forces exist. When the alternative rests between reactionary and Communist dictatorships—such as Batista and Castro—the "lesser evil" is hard to find. It would be best if United States influence were directed early enough to avoid having to make an impossible choice.

Yet another grievance leveled against American leadership has been the charge that she has been less generous with assistance to her allies than to some nonaligned powers. Foreign aid ought to be channeled to friendly countries who can best accomplish the purposes for which aid is given. States which have the organization to utilize military and economic assistance with effectiveness and which have demonstrated that they use aid to good effect should be the recipients of assistance. States which distribute broadly the benefits of aid ought to be encouraged by generous support from the United States.

THE UNITED STATES AND THE COLD WAR

When Stalin died on March 5, 1953, the United States and the Soviet Union were on a collision course. With his death a thaw in the cold war set in. The Korean War was settled; the Soviet Union affiliated with a number of specialized agencies; in 1955 a treaty was signed terminating the occupation of Austria; agreement had also been reached giving Trieste to Italy; and a package deal admitted sixteen countries to the UN, four of them Communist. The "iron curtain" separation of East and West grew less rigid. Cultural-exchange arrangements allowed Americans and Russians opportunities for contact and dialogue. Despite some sharp clashes, such as those over the Hungarian revolution in 1956, the U-2 overflights of the Soviet Union in 1960, the UN's role in the Congo, the Berlin Wall, the Cuban missile crisis, and United States participation in the war in Vietnam, there was a tacit understanding that a war between Russia and the United States must be averted. Even though the Cuban missile crisis brought the Soviet Union and the United States to the brink of war, once it became clear that Washington was prepared to go to war if necessary to remove the missiles from Cuba, Khrushchev moved toward a détente with Kennedy and tensions were again relaxed.

The reasons for the post-Stalinist change of policy are not yet certain. Perhaps the Kremlin will be some time reveal the grounds for its changed posture. It is clear only that the thaw was initiated by the Kremlin and that it took place after Stalin died. One might surmise that Stalin's rule of terror was inefficient and not productive for achieving the Kremlin's goals. Perhaps the new leaders feared that ultimately the people would rise to end their misery and oppression if Stalin's course were not altered. Khrushchev's secret speech at the 20th Congress of the Communist Party laid bare Stalin's terrorization of party and state officials at all levels, and in all likelihood Stalin's heirs were resolved never again to permit a new Stalin to emerge. Then again, trade with the West was beneficial for Russia's industrial growth. The post-Stalin flexibility also enabled the Soviet Union to pursue friendly relations with Afro-Asian states and enhanced Moscow's influence around the world.

Stalin's policy toward the satellite states was not working well. Yugoslavia made good its defection from the Soviet camp. Some Communist leaders in the satellite states were opposing Russia's plunder of their lands. After 1956 the spirit of polycentrism (see Chapter 6, pp. 170–171) could hardly be contained. Communist parties of Western Europe and America, faced with isolation and falling membership, began to criticize some Kremlin policies and formulate their own course of conduct. The Sino-Soviet dispute deeply undermined the monolithic unity of the Communist camp and Moscow's leadership position.

The ultimate goals of communism remained. There was no need to disavow them. The challenge of United States leadership also continued albeit with care to avert war. Nevertheless, a new policy emerged after Stalin's death which has altered the nature of the cold war. Within Russia some narrowing in scope of totalitarian control occurred; "socialist legality" replaced Stalinist caprice and terror. Gradually the state turned toward improving living standards by allotting a greater portion of production to consumer goods. Externally the Kremlin enunciated the policy of peaceful coexistence, "the repudiation of war as a means of solving controversial issues." [4] War could destroy the Soviet Union as well as the West and as long as this situation existed, "to avert war" became a "prime task."

Peaceful coexistence means an absence of war; it does not portend friendly relations. Class conflict continues unabated. "The policy of peaceful coexistence is thus, so far as its social content is concerned, a form of intense economic, political and ideological struggle between the proletariat and the aggressive imperialist forces in the world arena." [5] The use of force is not entirely abandoned. Proletarian revolutions and wars of national liberation which are unlikely to involve Russia in a major war are encouraged and supported.

> Some people misrepresent our Marxist-Leninist attitude, and allege that by proclaiming the policy of peaceful coexistence we are calling on the revolutionary forces, on the Communist Parties of the capitalist countries, to renounce the class struggle, the struggle to establish the rule of the working class, of the working people, to abandon the national liberation struggle of the peoples. That is not a clever invention; it is slander.... The Soviet Union supports the just wars of peoples....[6]

The policy of peaceful coexistence has facilitated a *de facto* detente in Europe. The dangers of Communist aggression in Europe are minimal. Even Italy and France, the countries with the largest Communist parties, are not threatened by Communist rule. The thrust of Communist policy in these countries has been less concerned with the winning of power and more devoted to winning support for day-to-day policies favorable to the Soviet Union. Similarly North America is a very poor target for the growth of Com-

[4] N. S. Khrushchev, *To Avert War, Our Prime Task* (Moscow: Foreign Languages Publishing House, 1963), p. 61.
[5] *Ibid.*, p. 65.
[6] *Ibid.*, pp. 75–76.

munist strength. In the United States an aging Communist Party is trying to build a youth component because without it the party faces the danger of simply dying out.

It is among the underdeveloped countries that the battle for men's minds is spreading. In its earliest stages Soviet policy has aimed at weaning away the former colonial lands from their European and American ties. To this end the Soviet Union has been quick to side with the Afro-Asian states on the issues which concern them, that is, use of force in Rhodesia, sanctions against South Africa, and removal of British forces from Aden. The Soviet Union has also tried to win the support of these states for its anti-Western stands. Where promising bases of association have been established the Soviet Union has been generous with its aid. Capital has been contributed or loaned by the Soviet Union and the countries of Eastern Europe, and with such assistance have come teams of experts making a considerable impact on policies adopted by recipient states.

THE UNITED STATES AND THE COLD WAR AFTER TWO DECADES

It is in the United States interest that war should be averted. The policy of containment has effectively prevented Russian expansion in Europe and in the process improved the prospects for peace. Arms and alliances discourage the use of force and, in the absence of agreement on cold-war issues, remain a necessary part of the paraphernalia of the attenuated cold war.

Discouraging recourse to force is at best half the answer to East-West relations. The alternative of holding out prospects for advantages to be gained through economic and political cooperation could end the cold war. To borrow a concept from mathematics, if East and West could learn to approach their relations as other than a zero-sum game, where one side's gain is the other side's loss; if democratic and Communist states could view issues as nonzero-sum games in which both sides could win, a brighter future would dawn. The United States holds a key role in relieving tensions by rewarding democratization within Communist lands, the adoption of independent postures by satellite states, and acts of Communist influence in behalf of peaceful settlements and peaceful change. Washington can open up trade and even give loans to Communist lands to encourage them to reconsider their revisionist goals. Collaborative exploration of outer space and the election of an East European as President of the General Assembly might encourage Communist statesmen to assess the gains which would follow from giving up goals of world communization. Perhaps a new generation of leaders is required before a change in the goals of Communist societies will take place. President Lyndon B. Johnson, perceiving opportunities to mitigate the struggle, has pressed forward the effort to end the cold war by eschewing the rhetoric of the cold war and by pressing Congress for legislation liberalizing East-West trade.

Europe remains the area most vital to United States security. The issues of Berlin, a divided Germany, and the Sovietization of Eastern Europe continue to plague East-West relations. American security and the credibility of Washington's guarantees are at stake in the defense of West Berlin and Western Germany. In the foreseeable future the outlook for reunification of Berlin and Germany remains dim. There is just no *quid pro quo* on the horizon which might make a fundamental concession profitable to either side in the cold war. The best which might be gained would be a lessening of tension and a gradual diminution of militancy on this issue leading to accommodation under changed conditions. In the meantime it is in the United States interests that Germany remain a partner in NATO and continue to develop as a bastion of enlightened democracy in Europe. Similarly there is little to be gained by the United States in simply accepting the *status quo* in Eastern Europe beyond the normalization of diplomatic relations which has occurred. Further conciliation with Communist control of Eastern Europe should come in response to growth of independence from Moscow and internal democratization. Should independence and democracy grow, then the communization of Eastern Europe would cease to be a cause for continued cold war. Containment has been necessary in the first two postwar decades, but Washington should be alert to changing conditions which permit agreements that make containment no longer urgent.

In the 1960's Communist China became the more vocal advocate of expansionism. Its attacks on India, its manipulations of aggression by proxy in Vietnam and Laos, and its complicity in the Indonesian coup of 1965 marked it as a revisionist threat. Nevertheless the fundamental weakness of its economy and the limited capability of its military forces in face of American military power forced Peking to act with caution in confronting United States military strength. The extravagance of a Chen Yi's or Lin Piao's words are confuted by care to avoid war with the United States. It may well be that the intent of Peking's policy is to involve the United States and the Soviet Union in war while it itself has no intention of fighting a war on its own. The evidence points to the conclusion that Peking holds aims of continental hegemony; that these can be contained by United States power; and that the United States may well win the backing of other non-Communist countries in Asia in quelling Communist China's aggression.

The mere fact that containment is in great part responsible for the lessening of threatened Russian aggression does not ensure that the same policy would succeed against China. Yet the basic logic of containment, rooted in United States ability to contain and in the belief that, faced by overwhelming countervailing power, revisionist China would also have to gravitate to its version of peaceful coexistence, makes the containment of Peking the starting point of United States policy in Asia. Peace and security could be won if the United States can satisfy Peking that force will fail but that it is prepared to regularize its relations with Peking whenever Peking ends its threats to the security of its neighbors. Peking's *de jure* admission to the family of nations should no longer be withheld if China is ready to cooperate in disarmament and peaceful settlement of conflicts with which it is concerned.

The cold war is now fought in underdeveloped lands. The struggle is ambiguous because presumably the Communist and anti-Communist governments are both seeking to bolster the independence and prosperity of the underdeveloped lands. Yet each accuses the other of base purposes. In the long run actions will prove which side provides disinterested help.

Cuba presents particular difficulties in East-West relations. United States military action to depose Castro would be extremely provocative. The Soviet Union has said that Cuba would be defended although she has not specifically committed herself to use force in Cuba's defense. A new Bay of Pigs invasion by United States forces might bring about a Soviet response at some other place on the globe where the logistic advantages of the Soviet Union would be greater. Aggression against Cuba by the United States could even touch off rebellions in other parts of Latin America. Unless an

unusual opportunity such as an internal uprising presents itself
or unless Castro provokes a dynamic OAS response, United States
policy is likely to be limited to the encouragement of anti-Castro
activity in Cuba and by exile groups, the hampering of Cuba's
potential for economic advancement, the encouragement of OAS solidarity in opposition to Castro's depredations, and assisting Latin
American democracies in their pursuit of economic growth and
social justice.

THE UNITED STATES AND THE NEUTRAL STATES

America's goals are fully compatible with the interests of most
unaligned countries. United States foreign policy no longer discourages neutralist policies by those underdeveloped states that wish
to avoid involvement in the cold war. New alliances are no longer
promoted for the containment of communism. This change of policy reflects an understanding of the minimal contributions which
underdeveloped countries can make to the military edifice of the
West. It also represents an agreement that the threat of communism in most areas of Asia, Africa, and the Middle East does not
come from external aggression but from the appeals of communism
to a downtrodden and oppressed humanity. Conversely, the acceptance of neutralism derives from a general acceptance of economic development as the first priority for underdeveloped lands.

Underdeveloped states which participate in alliances of the free
world, such as the Philippines, Thailand, Pakistan, and Iran, are
not disadvantaged by the alliance. Indeed SEATO and CENTO
have added development programs to their range of effort which
have made these associations more relevant to their purpose of
building security. The need to encourage successful efforts for economic development has put increased importance on assistance programs to lands where it has the greatest chance of being effectively
employed. Political tests of alliances are becoming less important,
and the test of successful operations and wide sharing in the benefits
of "prosperity" are becoming the major criteria for assistance.
This means that assistance grants and loans are evaluated in terms
of an inclination to modernize socio-economic systems.

The United States possesses great wealth and can afford to give
assistance on a massive scale. Two decades of effort have provided

a valuable experience in learning to give assistance effectively. Yet limits upon the amount and character of assistance which the United States can give allows Washington to meet a fractional part of the needs of underdeveloped lands. Priorities should therefore be worked out giving countries whose influence is singularly important and who are striving to form democratic states—India, Brazil, Nigeria, Chile, Costa Rica, Kenya, Philippines, etc.—the most help. The nature of assistance—Peace Corps, loans, food, or capital grants—needs also to be carefully considered to maximize effectiveness.

Colonialism is dying. The remnants of empire nevertheless remain a deeply wounding phenomenon for former colonial states. As a moral issue the United States must condemn imperialism. In the interests of peace, Washington must counsel for peaceful decolonization. As an issue affecting United States security the United States should, as best it can, prevent liberation movements from falling into the hands of irresponsible or Communist leadership. Colonies which continue to command strategic importance should be encouraged to sign defense pacts with free-world powers, such as the arrangements between Singapore and Britain. In special instances, such as Puerto Rico, Hong Kong, the Pacific Islands, or Greenland, the greater advantage for those immediately concerned lies in a loose and benevolent imperial relationship.

Some nonaligned states are caught up in conflicts with their neighbors: India and Pakistan over Kashmir; Kenya, Ethiopia, and Somalia over boundaries; Israel and the Arab states; Cambodia and Thailand. The terms upon which such conflicts are settled are usually of little concern to the United States. Nevertheless, the utilization of pacific procedures and the isolation of these discords from broader involvements is in America's interest and Washington's influence must be exerted accordingly.

Self-serving or even well-meaning totalitarian dictatorship should be discouraged. As long as United States policy is committed to human freedom and dignity, totalitarian dictators deserve no support and benevolent dictators minimal aid. Democracy cannot be and need not be a duplicate of the American or the West European systems. There is a broad range of practices and freedoms which democracies permit. The commitment to human welfare and the opportunity to bring about a measure of change through legal means suffice for new democracies where the people have had little experience with ruling themselves and few opportunities to learn and may, therefore, be unable to practice with responsibility all of the rights available to the people of long-established democratic regimes.

THE UNITED STATES AND THE UNITED NATIONS

Every American president from Truman has said that the United Nations stands at the very center of United States foreign policy. No doubt each president gave a particular content to the role assigned the UN for United States foreign policy purposes. Yet, because each administration was concerned with peace and modernization, the United Nations held a useful and important place in furthering the aims of United States foreign policy. In a fundamental way United Nations and United States purposes have been compatible. American power and wealth have given essential support to UN activities and naturally Washington's influence within the organization has been large. The Kremlin used to speak of the United States' "automatic majority" in the General Assembly and Peking castigates the UN as an arm of American imperialism. Without discounting the great weight accorded Washington's power and wealth, in the long run it is United States peace aims and support for peaceful change which are the greater influence.

In the early years of the United Nations' existence the United States was often able to win support, especially in the General Assembly, for resolutions condemning Communist behavior. With the great increase in membership, with the addition of new states which had been colonies, it has been feared that the character of the organization has changed and that not only will the General Assembly no longer be responsive to United States initiatives but it will often sponsor actions detrimental to the interests of the United States. Therefore some Americans view the organization with a jaundiced eye.

A fuller appreciation of the utility of the UN is necessary. The United Nations is one arena for action and it is suited to certain types of initiatives which the United States may justifiably try. By the same token the UN responds to the desires of other states. Clearly the United Nations is best fitted to carry out decisions reflecting consensus of its members. It lends itself admirably to dealing with efforts where a universal approach is especially useful. Campaigns such as the International Geophysical Year, International Refugee Year, the Development Decade, the campaign to eliminate illiteracy—efforts strongly promoted by the United States —are best undertaken by the UN and the specialized agencies.

Many important issues are best dealt with through multilateral diplomacy. Agreements are hammered out by the UN from which all of humanity gains. America's sense of responsibility for the welfare of man may be demonstrated virtually day by day through furthering this work of the organization. Through the organs of the United Nations the world's attention can be focused upon great problems and the United States stand is given attention. There is no better platform for making manifest American leadership. Washington's disinterested furtherance of pacific settlement is felicitously brought forward through the organization.

Not all disputes need be brought to the UN. When the organization is forced to consider a dispute which it cannot settle, no good purpose is served thereby and the organization acquires a record of failure which weakens its capacity for good work. By and large cold-war issues are not ameliorated through United Nations action and are better handled through negotiations by the parties directly concerned. Only where the dispute threatens to result in war, and no other effective means can be found to deter war, does the United Nations have to enter into the dispute. Western Hemisphere conflicts have, in the main, been referred to the OAS and this reduces the opportunity for mischief by states having few stakes in the outcome of the dispute. By the same token, conflicts between states in other regions ought to be handled by the regional arrangement of the area. There is no good purpose for the United States to involve itself with disputes such as those between Somalia and Ethiopia or Algeria and Morocco when the stakes of the United States in the outcome of these disputes are minimal and where the involvement of the United Nations in the conflict would force the United States to unnecessarily take a stand.

From the point of view of United States interest in building the UN as an effective agency for the peaceful settlement of disputes, American policy ought to give greater attention to opportunities for the fuller utilization of the specialized competence of United Nations organs. While the General Assembly has had its share of disputes, the Security Council should now be ready for fuller exploitation. Its ability to make effective decisions where great power agreement exists could be better exploited. The International Court of Justice renders judgments based on justice and law. The use of the International Court of Justice has been largely unexploited. Advisory opinions have provided useful support for General Assembly efforts in the financing of the Congo operation and in dealing with South West Africa. The Court could be given a more active role in the future by more frequent recourse to advisory opinions.[7]

The use of the Court would be enhanced by the repeal of the Connolly reservations to the Optional Clause by the United States Senate. Such action could be used as an occasion for encouraging other states to adopt the Optional Clause and increase the overall utilization of the processes of the Court and of international law.

The United States has been conscious of the collective-security function which may be promoted through the United Nations. It has strongly supported two types of efforts in this regard, the "Uniting for Peace" resolution and UN forces in the Middle East, the Congo, and Yemen. These efforts, those in the Congo and the Middle East at any rate, have caused a serious financial crisis for the organization because the Soviet Union and several other states have refused to pay their assessments for the Middle East and Congo operations. An attempt to force states in arrears to pay up by denying them a vote in the General Assembly in accordance with Article 19 of the Charter failed. To avoid a showdown and to gain time for agreement, the Nineteenth Session of the General Assembly acted only when unanimous consent was obtained. Eventually the Soviet threat to withdraw from membership influenced most states to oppose application of Article 19. Two issues are involved:

(1) Should the UN be able to act through General Assembly decisions over the objection of a big-five power?

(2) Should all members be required to finance such actions even if opposed to them?

Of these propositions the first is the important one. Even if American pressure could have forced the application of Article 19

---

[7] George Cochran Doub, "The Unused Potential of the World Court," *Foreign Affairs*, Vol. 40, No. 3, April, 1962, pp. 463–470. Contains imaginative proposals for the fuller utilization of the Court.

in 1964–1965, and thus forced Moscow to withdraw from the organization or stand exposed as an inept bluffer, it is questionable whether carrying the point would have been a worthwhile victory. The organization would perforce become another anti-Communist coalition if the Communist states were forced to withdraw. The UN as a stage for international relations between Communist and non-Communist countries should only be surrendered in the most extreme circumstance, perhaps only in face of another world war. An effective UN must enjoy the power gained by the "Uniting for Peace" resolution and UN police forces. The financing of such operations is a matter of secondary importance.

It has been seen that very little has succeeded in the area of disarmament. Agreements such as the Test Ban and "Hot-Line" Treaties have been negotiated outside the organization. On the other hand, the agreement not to use outer space for orbiting nuclear weapons has taken the form of a General Assembly resolution. The organization has acted as an international pressure group on the big powers, demanding persistent efforts to achieve disarmament. It is useful for the United States to have the UN as a sounding board for its disarmament proposals. New states which have not as yet had to consider the intricacies of disarmament agreements could, in the absence of the United Nations discussions, adopt an uninformed or an irresponsible position. A United Nations opinion upon the scope of inspection to safeguard disarmament agreements, the requisites for making effective a treaty to halt the spread of nuclear-weapons capability, could give impetus to concordance in these matters. It is more than likely that the organization will be called upon to play a role in the supervision of disarmament conventions.

Two decades after the end of World War II it seemed that the choice faced by the American people was one between an unpoliced and uninspected agreement which the Kremlin offers or no agreement. Faced with this choice, Washington has accepted the alternative of no agreement while it continues to seek through negotiation more acceptable arrangements. There is as yet no basis for an arrangement based mainly on trust. In a democracy the people will insist that their country live up to its agreement while in a dictatorship public pressures are not allowed to emerge. United States security makes necessary reliance upon power, and in the first place military strength, until a foolproof scheme of arms control will be accepted. The United States is benefited by ability to maintain a goodly measure of safety in an arms race. While the world would be better off were arms reduced and controlled, the second best choice for America is to keep up in the arms race rather than implement an agreement which lacks means of enforcement.

The United States favors the development of international law. If effective international law is ever to evolve, there is a need for an international authority competent to develop it and to harmonize attitudes in this area. No national or regional agency is able to make progress in this matter. The International Law Commission is an agency through which the United States should work to promote universal standards of law.

The *status-quo* character of United States aims is marked by its advocacy of peaceful change. An issue in which peaceful transformation has particular relevance is that of decolonization. Washington's voice in the UN has often been heard in support of removing colonial rule. United States votes have rarely supported the more militant stands on expelling imperialist powers. The counsel of going slow can only be justified when American pressure is effective in causing the imperialist state to accede to greater measures of freedom and benevolence for the colonial peoples. The victims of colonial oppression are never reconciled to a lengthy transition period to independence. Much can be gained during the transitional period by United States influence for training indigenous leaders by allowing them participation in all phases and on many levels of political and governmental activity.

The United States realized that permanent peace and universal prosperity await the economic development of poor states. Since the end of the Second World War the United States has spent over $100 billion dollars and engaged in considerable efforts to assist states in their quest for economic and social development. While much of this effort has taken place because of a selfless interest in the prosperity of others, foreign aid has also been an expression of United States power and an element of pressure to win support for United States policies. With this in mind there have been those who have argued for channeling all United States aid through national agencies and who have therefore opposed the use of the United Nations as an agency for dispensing aid provided by American funds.

Washington has, however, channeled a portion of its assistance through the United Nations. The UN has been an effective agency for providing assistance as it commands a fund of skills often unavailable to the United States. For instance, technical assistance provided by an expert from an underdeveloped land who better understands the thinking and the attitudes of others living in underdeveloped countries may be more effective than the expert whose experience has been entirely in highly developed states. Underdeveloped countries welcome aid from international agencies. Aid given by this source causes no fear of neo-colonialism. In a sense such aid is their own and does not connote an attitude of tutelage. Often international agencies can be much bolder in demanding reforms because they cannot be accused of imperialism. The need for technical assistance and capital goods is so huge that aid from almost any quarter, bilateral, regional, or international, is welcome. A knowledgeable and experienced American businessman, Paul Hoffman, advocates that much more United States aid should be channeled through the United Nations because the UN is capable of doing the most effective job of assistance.[8]

Memories of Nazi and Fascist rule support an urgent concern for human rights. The inhumanity of Communist rule and of religious and racial discrimination, sometimes, as in the case of South Africa, a matter of national policy, have necessitated extensive efforts by the Commission on Human Rights. United States support for the human rights work of the UN was manifested by the appointment of Eleanor Roosevelt to the Commission on Human Rights. Legislation and executive action to end discrimination and segregation of Negroes have strengthened Washington's voice on behalf of human rights. Raising the standards of human rights is uniquely a UN function which America in its national interest must support.

The fact that the United States exists in an interdependent world makes it necessary for the United States to promote international cooperation in a large number of activities. Such cooperation is vital for promoting friendship among nations. International organizations are essential to the transmittal of mail across national boundaries; for uniform standards in civil aviation; for international quarantine to stop the spread of infectious disease; for the

[8] Paul Hoffman, *World Without Want* (New York: Harper & Row, 1962). See Ch. XIII.

promotion of trade and the stabilization of prices in the international market place. Indeed, the United States could not exist as a prosperous democracy without international organizations and especially without the UN.

If the world is to avoid an international holocaust, and if mankind is to survive, men will have to learn to cooperate for their own survival. For this purpose the United Nations has a critical role to play. Its natural instincts lead to the promotion of a better world.

The vision of a future world enjoying the peace, prosperity, and the freedom which marks life in the United States today must come from the United States. The United States is the most powerful and prosperous country in the history of mankind. If it devotes itself solely to the promotion of the creature comforts of its people, an absorbing concern in its own higher levels of consumption, a leaner and more dynamic Communist world will dispose of the future of man. The late President Kennedy initiated a massive effort to get the United States "moving," and to ensure that it understood the challenge of the times and the moral responsibility that it had for meeting this challenge. That the United States has accepted this vocation of leadership will prove to be the greatest monument to his martyrdom.

Item	Unit	Developed Areas [a]	
		Total	United States
POPULATION			
Total (mid-1965)	Millions	628	195
Annual Growth	Percent	1.3	1.5
Persons per Square Mile	Number	50	54
LAND			
Total Area	1,000 Sq. mi.	12,400	3,620
Agricultural Land	% of Area	39	47
Acres per Capita	Number	5	6
GROSS NATIONAL PRODUCT			
Total GNP (1964)	$ Billions	1,200	628
Annual Growth (1957–58 to 1964–65) [b]	Percent	4.7	4.0
GNP per Capita (1964)	Dollars	1,950	3,270
FOOD PRODUCTION			
Production Index (1965)	1957–59 = 100	115	116
Per Capita Production Index (1965) ..	1957–59 = 100	106	104
ELECTRIC POWER PER CAPITA ...	KWH per Year	3,530	5,540
FOREIGN TRADE (*value basis*)			
Total Exports, f.o.b. (1964)	$ Billions	115.4	26.6
Annual Growth, 1959–1964	Percent	9.2	8.5
Total Imports, c.i.f. (1964)	$ Billions	120.0	20.3
Annual Growth, 1959–1964	Percent	9.3	3.6
HEALTH			
Life Expectancy	Years	70	70
Calories per Day	Calories	2,920	3,090
People per Physician	Number	800	730
EDUCATION			
Literacy	Percent	96	98
Pupils as Percent of Population [c]	Percent	18	23

SOURCE: Statistics and Reports Division, Office of Program Coordination, Agency for International Development, June 1966.

[a] Generally the industrial countries of Western Europe, United States, Canada, Australia, New Zealand, Japan, and South Africa.

[b] Based on data in constant 1962 prices.

[c] Primary and Secondary Students only.

Less Developed Non-Communist Areas				
Total	Africa	Far East	Latin America	Near East and South Asia
1,560	250	280	230	760
2.5	2.3	2.7	2.9	2.4
60	20	180	30	180
26,250	10,800	1,560	7,710	4,330
24	26	17	24	30
2.7	7.6	0.6	5.2	1.1
240	27	30	71	86
4.7	3.4	4.4	4.4	4.9
160	115	110	325	115
121	117	128	126	119
102	100	107	103	101
150	80	90	400	80
35.8	6.6	6.0	9.9	9.1
6.3	8.9	3.3	5.1	6.8
38.5	6.4	7.4	8.6	10.1
6.1	4.3	2.5	3.6	7.7
47	40	42	55	47
2,250	2,355	2,160	2,560	2,130
4,300	19,100	5,400	1,600	4,900
37	18	57	67	25
11	8	15	15	10

GENERAL NOTE ON MAIN SOURCES USED:

POPULATION, LAND, FOREIGN TRADE AND EDUCATION—Publications of United Nations and its specialized agencies; AID reports.

GNP—Official government reports and AID estimates.

FOOD—Economic Research Service, USDA.

ELECTRIC POWER—Publications of UN, and US Federal Power Commission.

HEALTH—UN, USDA, and official government publications.

Index

Abako Party, 281, 287
Accion Catolica, 357
Accra, 291, 293
Acheson, D., 400
Action Party, 289
Acts, 88
Aden, 248
Adenauer, K., 52
Addis Ababa, 293, 296
Addis Ababa Conference, 295
Adjudication, 85
Afghanistan, 255, 312, 316
Africa, 10, 11, 12, 13, 16, 30, 53, 69, 97,
    98, 102, 105, 119, 127, 129, 172, 174,
    215, 244, 245, 248ff, 253, 258, 265,
    270–311, 313, 325, 339, 341, 344, 379,
    380, 385, 389, 398, 411
    and the cold war, 231–235
African Miners Union, 302
Afrika Corps, 195
Afrikaaner, 298, 299, 302, 305
Afro-Asian "six", 336, 340
Afro-Asian states, 406, 408
agreements, 87, 88
air power, 31
Aksai Chin, see Ladakh
Ala, H., 196
Alamogordo, 210
Albania, 68, 172, 197
All-African Peoples Conferences (AAPC),
    293, 294
Allende, 355, 356
Algeria, 244, 254, 255, 257, 270, 281, 294,
    295, 296, 414
Alliance for Progress, 241, 351, 352, 360,
    361, 364, 368, 385, 389, 402
alliances, 73–76, 89
Allied and Associated Powers, 134, 135
Allied Control Commission, 188, 189, 204,
    205, 207
Allied Kommandatura, 205, 207
American University, 176
Anders, W., 180
Annam, 321
Anglo-Iranian Oil Co., 268
Angola, 282, 283, 285, 287, 291, 298, 301
Animism, 276, 382

Anopheles mosquito, 297
Anti-Fascist Peoples Freedom League
    (Burma), 318, 320
anti-semitism, 259
Anzus Pact, 117
Apartheid, 70, 302ff
    Table, 306
appeasement, 22–23
Aqaba, 265
Arab, 16, 195, 230, 231, 254, 255–267,
    288, 289, 412
    Christian, 12
    Palestine, 255, 260
Arab Higher Committee, 260
Arab-Israel conflict, 259–267
    cold war, 230, 231
Arab Legion, 256, 258, 259, 266
Arab Refugees, 262–264
Arabian Gulf, 255
Arabian peninsula, 229, 244, 253
Arabian Sea, 255
Arbitration, 85
Archangel, 135
Ardahan, 199, 200
Argentina, 28, 344, 345, 347, 348, 349,
    352, 367, 382
Armenia, 9, 123, 255
Arms Control, see disarmament
Arctic, 46, 312
Arctic Sea, 141
Artvin, 199
Ashanti, 286
Asia, 30, 98, 102, 105, 129, 136, 172, 174,
    209, 215, 218, 221, 243, 245, 248,
    250ff, 262, 264, 265, 272, 305, 312–
    340, 341, 345, 371, 379, 389, 391,
    398, 404, 410, 411
    cold war, 235–238
    religious conflict, 323
    assimilado, 274, 284, 285
Aswan Dam, 385
Atlantic Charter, 90, 92, 144, 186, 193,
    194
Atlantic Community, 296
Atlantic Ocean, 255
Australia, 28, 105, 109, 110, 340, 373
Austria, 11, 137, 177, 208, 209, 405

423